The G...

of

Circle Time and Group Activities

The
GIANT
Encyclopedia of
Circle Time
and
Group Activities
for Children 3 to 6

Over 600 Favorite Circle Time Activities
Created by Teachers for Teachers

Edited by Kathy Charner

gryphon house
Beltsville, Maryland

Published by Gryphon House, Inc.
10726 Tucker Street, Beltsville, MD 20705

World Wide Web: http://www.ghbooks.com

Printed in the United States of America.

Text Illustrations: Rebecca Jones

Library of Congress Cataloging-in-Publication Data
The giant encyclopedia of circle time and group activities for children 3 to 6 :
  over 600 favorite circle time activities created by teachers for teachers /
  edited by Kathy Charner.
    p. cm.
  Includes index.
  ISBN: 978-0-87659-181-9
  1. Early childhood education--Activity programs. 2. Creative activities and seat work. 3. Group work in education. I. Charner, Kathy.

LB1139.35.A37G53 1996
372.21--dc20   96-9098
                                                    CIP

Gryphon House is a member of the Green Press Initiative, a nonprofit program dedicated to supporting publishers in their efforts to reduce their use of fiber-sourced forests. This book is made of 30% post-consumer waste. For further information visit www.greenpressinitiative.org.

Table of Contents

Contents

Contents

Contents

Contents

Introduction

Every day wonderful, dedicated people use their talents and energies to teach young children. To help these teachers share their work with others we conducted a national contest asking teachers to send in their best circle time or group activities. Entries poured in from Seattle to Miami and from San Diego to Bangor. We selected the very best entries to create this book of over 600 circle time or group activities to use with children 3 to 6 years old. This book answers the question, "What shall I do at circle time (or group time) today?". It is packed with days, weeks and months of activities and ideas that teachers around the country have used successfully with the children they teach. We trust that you will benefit from the years of experience reflected in this book.

Keep in mind the following suggestions when involving children in circle time and group activities:

✓ Encourage the children's participation in circle time or group activities, both during the activities and when preparing for them.

✓ Use familiar words or phrases to get the children's attention. Then always use these words or phrases in the same way.

✓ Hold circle time in the same place each day (except for special events). Set up chairs or a rug to mark the space.

✓ While encouraging all children to join the group, offer another choice to children who find it hard to be with the group.

The Giant Encyclopedia of Circle Time and Group Activities for Children 3 to 6 book was created by experienced teachers who contributed their original ideas. publishing this book would not have been possible without the careful, expert mind and eye of Mary Duru and the ever-present genius of Sarabeth Goodwin.

How to Use This Book

Age
The age listed is a suggestion. Each teacher is the best judge of the appropriateness of an activity, based on his or her prior knowledge of the children and the children's responses to the activity.

Materials needed
Each activity includes a list of readily available materials. Investigate all possible sources of free materials in your community, including donations from paper stores, framing shops, woodworking shops, lumber yards and, of course, parents.

What to do
The directions are presented in a step-by-step format. Patterns and illustrations are included where necessary.

More to do
Additional ideas for extending the activity are included in this section. Many activities include suggestions for integrating the circle time or group activity into other areas of the curriculum such as math, dramatic play, art, blocks, language, snack time and cooking.

Related books
Under this heading are titles and authors of popular children's books that can be used to support the circle time or group activity.

Related songs and poems
Familiar songs related to the original circle time or group activity and original songs and poems written by teachers can be found in this section.

Indexes
This book has three indexes. One is an alphabetical index of the activities by the name of the activity. Another is an index of the materials used in the activities, and the last one is an index of children's books with a listing of all the activities that use or mention that children's book.

Guidelines for Circle Time . . . . .3+

Materials needed
None needed

What to do

1. Whenever possible divide a large group (20 children or more) into two smaller groups. This allows for more participation by the children.

2. Schedule circle time for a 15-20 minute period. If an activity is especially lengthy it can be continued later in the day.

3. Use smooth orderly transitions to ease children in and out of group activities.

4. Use the activity itself to gather the children together, like singing a song or making the sound of an animal in the story. A two-minute warning should be given to the children to pick up the toys before circle time. When it is time to come to the circle everyone helps pick up remaining toys and then joins in circle time.

5. Avoid activities where children sit for long periods of time. Alternate listening activities and participation activities so children will be manipulating materials or doing movement activities between listening activities.

6. Give children clear, simple directions about the activity and what they are to do.

7. Be prepared to change, shorten or eliminate an activity that just isn't working.

8. Be prepared to extend an activity that is working.

9. How children behave during and after an activity is a good indication of how successful the activity was.

10. An additional circle time at the end of the day allows for continuity of a morning activity or a time for a closing song or fingerplay.

★ Margaret Connelly, Pocomoke, MD

Best Seat in the House . . . . .3+

Materials needed
Carpet squares

What to do

1. When you are planning a circle time activity that involves a demonstration, book, pictures or any visual material, remember to place the children so that every child has a clear view of you and the materials you are presenting.

2. Instead of using a circle formation, place carpet squares in staggered rows similar to theater seating. This may provide for easier viewing and keeps children from leaning into each other in order to see.

★ Mary Volkman, Ottawa, IL

Circle Time Set Up . . . . .3+

Materials needed
Mats made out of carpet squares or vinyl placemats cut in half

What to do
1. When children have a difficult time staying seated or need to have their space limited, arrange mats in a configuration that suits the needs of circle time.

2. When you take responsibility for the arrangement of the children, you have the opportunity to space children at reasonable distances from each other, and you can choose to keep certain children apart from each other.

★ Mary Volkman, Ottawa, IL

Getting Ready for Circle Time . . . . . . .3+

Materials needed
Rolling cart (several stacking baskets or shelves on wheels)

What to do
1. Gather all the materials necessary for circle time for the entire week (prepare on Friday afternoon or Monday morning).

2. Organize materials on the shelves of the cart; for example, books on one shelf, puppets and flannel board pieces on one shelf and items of special interest (theme, special event) on another shelf.

3. Roll the cart to the circle time area. If you want to have group time outside, the cart rolls with you. The children are fascinated by the teacher materials on the special cart and watch with wide eyes to see what book or special toy rolls out each day. (No more fumbling around while the children wait for you.) In addition, everything is ready when a substitute is needed.

More to do
The cart can also be used to organize art activities or science materials.

★ Tracie O'Hara, Charlotte, NC

The Sun Is Coming Up . . . . .3+

Materials needed
Large drawing of the sun (with words to a song written on it)

What to do
1. Children sit in a circle.

2. Sing the following song every morning, as a way to greet the day and each other. The tune is "The Farmer in the Dell."

> *The sun is coming up*
> *The sun is coming up*
> *We thank you earth for spinning round*
> *And being here for us.*

3. Use motions with hands of the sun slowly coming up and spinning around.

More to do
Art: Ask the children to make pictures of the sun at the art area. At circle time the children can raise their pictures as they sing the song.

Related books
The Way to Start a Day by Byrd Baylor
When the Sun Rose by Barbara Helen Berger

★ Carol Patnaude, Cathy Constantino, Darlene Maloney, Lynn Camara, Warwick, RI

Hear a Pin Drop . . . . .3+

Materials needed
Strait pins or safety pins
Nonbreakable items, such as rubber erasers, feathers, balloons

What to do
1. Getting children to settle down prior to circle time is sometimes difficult. I said repeatedly that it had to be so quiet that "You could hear a pin drop."

2. The children and I decided to find out exactly how much noise a pin makes when it falls to the floor.

3. I found a safety pin, stood in front of the class and dropped the pin on our carpeted floor. It landed with a surprising loud thud.

4. We took that same pin and dropped it on a noncarpeted floor. It made a louder thud.

5. I stood on a chair and dropped it from up high.

6. The results were amazing. Everyone sat quietly at circle, eagerly anticipating the sound of the pin hitting the floor.

More to do

Try dropping feathers, rocks, snow, a snowball, a balloon, an inflated balloon, a helium balloon (works great on backwards day) or have a gravity race with two or more objects. Experiment with dropping things into sand and water tables also.

★ Jane A. Brooks, Chelsea, MI

All the Little Bunnies . . . . .3+

Materials Needed
None needed

What to do

1. Say the following rhyme to quiet the children at the beginning of circle time (or any time).

All the little bunnies hop, hop, hop.
All the little bunnies stop, stop, stop.
Sit around a circle, sit inside your nest
All the little bunnies rest, rest, rest.

★ Ingelore Mix, Massapequa, NY

Itsy Bitsy Spider . . . . .3+

Materials needed
None needed

What to do

1. Use this activity as a transition during circle time to quiet the children before reading a book or storytelling.

2. Lead the group in a familiar fingerplay or song like, "The Itsy Bitsy Spider," using a regular singing voice and actions.

3. Repeat the song in a whispering voice still using the actions.

4. The third repeat of the song is just with actions and no voices.

5. After the last repeat of the song the children are quiet and focused on the teacher for story time.

More to do

Other familiar songs or fingerplays can be used. Also try other voice modalities such as humming.

★ Nancy L. Schwider, Glen Ellyn, IL

Knock, Knock...Nobody's Home . . . . .3+

Materials needed
None needed

What to do
This is a technique I use to get the children's attention (instead of yelling "Quiet!") as they are preparing for circle time, preparing to go to another activity or when there is a spare minute or two.

1. Keep a mental note of clever jokes that would especially appeal to young children. For example, "Why is six afraid of seven? Because seven eight (ate) nine." I like to use jokes that will cause children to think about words or to lighten up a gloomy moment. Be prepared for children to try to make up jokes of their own—often, they make no sense—but they will all laugh, nonetheless.

More to do
Get the children's attention by drawing them into a quick game of "Mississippi says—touch your knees" (use catchy names or have a special word for the day). Begin clapping to various beats, asking the children to copy you.

Related books
Kat Kong by Dav Pilkey
Hattie Baked a Wedding Cake by Toby Speed

★ Cathy Chenoweth, Columbia, MO

Bag of Tricks . . . . .3+

Materials needed
Index cards
Markers
Glitter or sequins

Gift bag (solid color)
Glue

What to do
1. Using the above art materials, decorate the gift bag to look eye-catching and magical.

2. Write the title and words to different fingerplays and songs the children know on the index cards. Add new ones as the children learn them.

3. Place the cards inside the bag.

4. During circle time (or any time) ask a child to reach into the bag and choose a song. Sing the song chosen.

More to do
This activity can be extended into any area of the curriculum by simply changing the cards inside the bag. If the children are learning about animals, place pictures of animals in the bag and ask the children to categorize them. If you need to choose a special helper for something, put the children's names inside the bag and pick one.

★ Donna Austin, Lehighton, PA

Fly Away Dickey Bird . . . . .3+

Materials needed
None needed

What to do
1. As circle time ends and the children are sitting in a circle waiting to go to the next activity, use a fingerplay to help them know when to leave the circle.

2. The teacher holds up the index finger on each hand and begins to sing:

> *Two little dickey birds sitting on a fence, one named (child's name) and the other named (another child's name).*
> *Fly away (child's name), Fly away (another child's name).*

3. As each child's name is called the child goes to the learning center that she has chosen for the next activity.

More to do
This activity can be used to help ease the transition from activities to lunch or snack by adding "Wash your hands, wash your hands" after "Fly away."

★ Deborah J. Pierce, Litchfield, ME

Name Recognition Cards . . . . .3+

Materials needed
Paper
Permanent marker

What to do
1. Design a simple pattern, such as an apple for September.

2. Cut out the pattern to make a name recognition card for each child.

3. Write each child's name on the card.

4. At the end of circle time send each child to the next activity by holding up her name card. It does not take long before each child learns to recognize her name and the other children's names as well.

More to do
Suggested seasonal items for patterns include a pumpkin for October, snowflake for January, umbrella for April.

★ Donna Borges, Crescent City, CA

Goodbye Song . . . . .3+

Materials needed
None needed

What to do
At the end of the day's closing circle, sing "Goodbye Children" to the tune of "Goodnight Ladies."

> *Goodbye, children*
> *Goodbye, children*
> *Goodbye, children, it's time for you to go.*
>
> *We'll see you tomorrow,*
> *We'll see you tomorrow,*
> *We'll see you tomorrow, we'll see you back at school.*

More to do
Sing two verses together, then add a child's name. This activity can be used in helping children recognize their names. Hold up a folder with the child's name printed in large letters and let the children "read" the name of the child. Then sing the song using that child's name. Singing directions and singing the child's name is a great way to get the children's attention. Use simple tunes, such as "Twinkle, Twinkle, Little Star" and add your own words, such as "Time to put your things away, things away, things away. Time to put your things away and hear a story."

★ Beverly Smigielski, DuQuoin, IL

The Curiosity Box . . . . .3+

Materials needed
Large shoebox covered with brightly colored paper
Object that relates to an activity for that day

What to do
1. This activity offers an approach to encouraging children's curiosity and their asking questions during circle time.

2. Prior to the children's arrival, put an object in a box and place it in the circle time area.

3. Ask children if they are curious to find out what is inside the box.

4. Give the children clues that will help them guess the object.

5. Open the box and take out the object and talk about how it will be used during the day.

6. For several days put a different object in the box. The children will look forward to seeing what is inside the box.

More to do

Suggested items for the Curiosity Box:

- ✓ a monkey puppet or stuffed animal to introduce the children to Curious George
- ✓ corks that will be used for a cork painting activity later in the day
- ✓ a ball of kite string on the day you read *Curious George Flies a Kite*

Sometimes children think "curious" means "bad" since George gets into so much trouble. The Curiosity Box reinforces that being curious helps us learn about new things that we didn't know before.

Transition: Use the Curiosity Box during transition time to stimulate curiosity about the next activity.

★ Ann Wenger, Harrisonburg, VA

Circle Time Tips

Air Bags . . . . .3+

Materials needed
Paper lunch bags (1 per child)

What to do
1. At circle time show the children a paper bag and say, "I am going to put something in this bag."

2. Hold the bag up to your mouth and blow air into the bag.

3. Ask the children, "Guess what I have in the bag?" Some children may guess right away; others may need time to think.

4. When the children guess "air" talk about the fact that air is all around us, that it is invisible and that sometimes you can't even feel it. But you can feel it when it is windy and blowing on your face.

5. Ask the children to hold their hands over their ears, then pop the paper bag.

6. Ask the children if they would like to fill a paper bag full of air, then give a paper bag to each child. Younger children may need help inflating their bags.

7. Let the children pop their bags. (Since paper bags can be recycled, keep the bags for recycling.)

More to do
Art: Make boats from styrofoam trays, add a sail and float in the water table. Encourage the children to move the boats by blowing them.

Large motor: Fill a large garbage bag with air by holding the bag open and twirling it around. Seal off the top of the bag by tying it into a knot or using masking tape. (Do not use a twist tie with a wire core.) Roll the bag around the circle or in an open area. After you are finished, deflate, recycle and reuse as a garbage bag. Remember, plastic bags can be dangerous, so always play this game with supervision. It is good to have several garbage bags available because they puncture easily.

Math: As the children pop their bags, count the number of bangs. Who made the biggest noise? Who made the quietest noise?

Related books
Amy Loves the Wind by Julia Hoban
The Four Elements: Air by Maria Rius (one of a series)
It Looked Like Spilt Milk by Charles G. Shaw
Millicent and the Wind by Robert Munsch
The Wind Blew by Pat Hutchins

★ Mark Crouse, Nova Scotia, Canada

Feather Races . . . . .3+

Materials needed

Tissue
Feathers
Masking tape

What to do

1. Show the children that air moves things. Hold a tissue in front of your mouth and blow on it. What happens? Place a feather on the palm of your hand and blow it. What happens?

2. Give each child a feather. Encourage them to experiment with how air moves their feathers.

3. Ask the children to pick a partner and have feather races. Each child tries to blow their feather over a line (marked by masking tape).

More to do

Language: After the races, write a group story about the feather races.

Science: Ask the children to brainstorm about other materials in the room that can be moved by air. Let them experiment with the materials. Show the children a tray of different materials (block, feather, pompom, orange, ping-pong ball, tennis ball) and ask the children to predict if the objects can be moved by air.

Related books

Air Is All Around You by Franklyn M. Branley
The Four Elements Series: Air by Maria Rius
The Tiny Seed by Eric Carle

★ Gina M. Duddy, Arlington, MA

Propulsion . . . . .3+

Materials needed

10 or 15 yards of strong string
Cardboard tube
Several medium round latex balloons
Clothespin
Yardstick

What to do

1. Thread the string through the cardboard tube. Tie one end to a chair or other fairly sturdy object in the classroom. Put this chair in the circle time area. Tie the other end across the room at a slightly higher level (there should be just a small incline in the string).

2. With the children gathered around you, demonstrate how you blow air into a balloon causing its size and shape to change. Tie one balloon off and let the children bounce it around lightly in the air.

3. Toss a deflated balloon in the air and observe how quickly it falls to the floor. Ask the children to begin counting as you toss the balloon up and stop counting when it hits the floor. Toss up an inflated balloon. Have children count again to see how long it takes to settle on the floor.

4. Ask the children to brainstorm: What caused the inflated balloon to float more slowly to the floor? Now ask what would happen to a balloon if you blew it up and suddenly let it go. Demonstrate with a balloon. The children will be amazed as it flies around the room. Tell the children that the trapped air being suddenly released from the balloon caused it to move forward and that this action is called propulsion.

5. Blow the balloon up again and gently tape it to the cardboard tube. Pull the balloon and tube to the low end of the string and let go. The balloon will follow the string until it runs out of air. Mark the spot where it stops with a clothespin and then measure the distance the balloon traveled with a yardstick or ruler.

More to do

Cooking: Pop popcorn using a Hot Air Popper. As the corn is popping, explain how the hot air is forced around the kernels causing them to pop. Hot air then carries the popped kernel up and out of the machine. When the popcorn is cool enjoy eating.

Large motor: Hold relay races using inflated balloons that have been tied off. Divide the group into two groups. Mark a starting line and a turnaround point. Have each child use her hands or breath to keep the balloon up in the air while she walks to the turnaround point and back. She must transfer the balloon to the next player without touching it. Continue until everyone has had a turn.

Sensory table: Add water to the sensory table. Cut a small hole in the bottom of a small milk carton. Make sure the hole is near the edge. Put the balloon inside the milk carton and push the opening of the balloon through the hole. Blow up the balloon. Hold the opening closed while you set the carton down in the water, then let go. The air being released from the balloon will send the little boat in circles. If the boat tips over, use some sand or small rocks to weigh it down.

Related book *Gilberto and the Wind* by Marie Hall Ets

Related song "Popcorn" by Greg and Steve

★ Virginia Jean Herrod, Columbia, SC

Wind Game . . . . .3+

Materials needed

Hair dryer
Assorted objects
Paper and markers

What to do

1. Discuss what wind is and what it does. Talk about how the air coming out of a hair dryer is like wind.

2. Let each child search around the room and bring one object back to circle that they would like to test in the wind.

3. Let each child predict whether her item will be moved by the wind.

4. Turn the hair dryer on and aim it at each object.

5. Record what happens and compare the results to their predictions.

6. Talk about why some things were moved by the wind and others were not.

More to do

Art: Do a group straw painting. Place paint on a large sheet of paper and have each child come up with her own straw and blow on the paint. Make wind socks.

Related book

Amy Loves the Wind by Julia Hoban

★ Suzanne Maxymuk, Cherry Hill, NJ

Did You Get Wind of That? . . . . .4+

Materials needed

None needed

What to do

1. At circle time tell the children that they will pretend to be the wind.

2. Ask the children to blow into their hands softly, creating a gentle breeze. Ask them to blow a stronger wind into their hands. Then ask them to blow harder, creating a blustery wind. Now ask them to blow even harder, creating a hurricane wind.

3. Tell the children to decide what kind of wind they wish to be. Ask them to think about what their wind could blow away.

4. The teacher begins the game by blowing a wind.

5. The children ask, "Who is that?"

6. The teacher answers, "It's the wind."

7. The children ask, "What are you blowing?"

8. The teacher responds, "I'm blowing a leaf."

9. Continue the game until everyone has had a turn pretending to be the wind and saying what their wind is blowing.

More to do

Stop the game after the third child has had a turn. Ask the children if they can remember what the other children blew away. Repeat after a few more children. This is a wonderful way to build listening skills by remembering the sequence.

★ Dalia Behr, Ozone Park, NY

Hot Air Balloon . . . . .4+

Materials needed

Pictures of hot air balloons
Large box
4 small paper sacks
Yarn
Newspapers

What to do

1. Look at the pictures of hot air balloons with the children. Explain the use of the sand bags.

2. Put the box in the middle of the circle. This activity can be done inside or outside on the playground.

3. Stuff the sacks with newspaper and tie it closed.

4. Tie the sacks to the corners of the box with yarn.

5. Ask two or three children to climb into the box (the number of children depends on the size of box).

6. Children pull the sacks (sand bags) inside the box and "fly away" into the sky.

7. To "land" children put the sacks (sand bags) outside the box and "down they come" to earth.

More to do

Art: Make a hot air balloon at art time using wallpaper samples for the balloon, construction paper for the basket, yarn for the ropes. It can be glued on blue paper with cotton ball clouds in the sky. Draw people in the basket.

Science: Blow up a large balloon, let the air out and show children how air pushed the balloon high into the air. Explain that real hot air balloons use gas to keep the balloon inflated.

Related book *Hot Air Henry* by Mary Calhoun

Related song "Up, Up and Away" by the Fifth Dimension

★ Denise Covert, Perris, CA

Our Class Alphabet . . . . .4+

Materials needed

Photograph of each child
Construction paper (various colors)
Magazines or toy catalogs

What to do

1. Cut construction paper in half.

2. Use one half page for each child.

3. On each page glue the photograph of an individual child.

4. Under the picture print the first letter of the child's name.

5. Under the first letter print the child's first name.

6. Repeat for each child in the class.

7. Arrange the pages in alphabetical order. It is all right to have a number of children with the same first letter in their names.

8. Determine which letters are missing, for example you probably won't have any children whose name starts with Q, X or Z.

9. Use the magazine or toy catalog to find colored pictures of objects that start with the missing letters and make a page for each letter, so that each letter of the alphabet has at least one page with either a photograph of a child or a picture of an object that starts with that letter.

10. Read the children their "Class Alphabet Book" during circle time. Encourage the children to "read" the book aloud: "A for Allison, B for Bill, etc." Make the book available for them to look at during playtime.

More to do

Language: Let the children take turns bringing the "Class Alphabet Book" home to read with their families. When a new child or parent volunteer joins the class, ask that person to take the book home. It is a great way to learn the names of the children in the class. Have double prints made of the photographs and use the second set in the same way for a bulletin board.

Related books

Anno's Alphabet by Anno Mitsmasa
Dr. Seuss ABC's by Dr. Seuss
On Market Street by Arnold Lobel

★ Barbara Saul, Eureka, CA

Different Alphabets . . . . .5+

Materials needed

Copies of Braille pages (available from the Braille Institute, libraries, Federation for the Blind)
Books on American Sign Language for children
Pictures or charts of other alphabets (Hebrew, Egyptian hieroglyphics)

What to do

1. At circle time show the children a few alphabet cards or a child's name card to illustrate the letters of the alphabet.

2. Ask the children what they would do if they could not see letters. Pass the Braille pages around the circle for children to feel and talk about.

3. After discussing the Braille alphabet, ask the children what they would do if they could not hear words that were spoken. Demonstrate the fingerspelling alphabet and talk about sign language.

4. Show other alphabet or language charts and talk about their use. Discuss their similarities and differences.

More to do

Cooking: Cook alphabet soup for snack.

Fine motor: Children learn to sign their names in fingerspelling.

Language: Create pictographs. The children write their names using symbols from another language chart (hieroglyphics is a fun one to explore). Read books about children who are hearing or visually impaired.

★ Gail Dezube, Vienna, VA

Everyday Alphabet . . . . .5+

Materials needed

Felt board
Felt alphabet letters
Objects that begin with a specific letter (for example, A for apple, airplane)

What to do

1. Read an alphabet book at circle time.

2. Talk about the alphabet and place one alphabet letter on the felt board.

3. The children name objects (that start with the letter on the felt board) and then place the objects in the middle of the circle. The children can bring objects from home (send a note to parents beforehand) or choose something from the classroom.

More to do

Art: Decorate letters cut from cardboard with things that begin with that letter. For example, decorate the letter B with buttons.

Music: Sing a variety of alphabet songs.

Snack: Eat a snack that begins with a specific letter for example, eat apples the day the letter A is discussed.

Related books

Aaron and Gayla's Alphabet Book by Eloise Greenfield
Eating the Alphabet by Lois Ehlert

★ Victoria D. Cetrone, Matteson, IL

Rope Tricks . . . . .5+

Materials needed

Lengths of rope (each 24" long)

What to do

1. At circle time give each child a piece of rope.

2. Tell the children that they are going to form letter shapes by laying their pieces of rope on the floor. Demonstrate a letter (V is an easy one to make). Ask the children to make the same letter.

3. Start with other letters that are easy to make : C, D, I, J, L, N, O, S, U, Z.

4. For a challenge try other letters. Demonstrate how to overlap the rope in order to make them.

5. Use the rope to form numbers and shapes also.

More to do

Fine motor: Make available several pieces of rope so the children can spell out their names with the pieces of rope.

★ Valerie Chellew, Marshfield, WI

What Animal Is This? . . . . .3+

Materials needed
None needed

What to do
1. Ask the children to identify an animal. Look at pictures of the animal and talk about the animal's characteristics.

2. Pretend to be the animal, making movements and sounds that the animal makes.

Suggested animals:

> ✓ Birds--waddle, fly, swim, run, chirp, peep, quack, hoot
> ✓ Amphibians (frogs)--hop, jump, croak
> ✓ Fish--make swimming movements, blow into the air
> ✓ Insects--crawl, fly, hop, buzz, hum
> ✓ Reptiles--crawl like a snake, move like a turtle

3. Sing songs about the animal. Some choices include: "Five Little Ducks," "Hello, Mr. Robin," "Five Green and Spectacled Frogs" and "Baby Bumble Bee."

4. Encourage children to make up rhyming lyrics, such as catching a shark and putting it in a park, catching a fish and putting it in a dish, catching a perch and taking it to church. The children can sing their original song, "A-Fishing We Will Go," to the tune of "A-Hunting We Will Go."

> *Oh a-fishing we will go,*
> *A-fishing we will go,*
> *We'll catch a little shark,*
> *And put him in a park,*
> *And then we'll let him go.*

More to do
Large motor: Ask each child to pretend to be an animal by moving and making sounds like that animal. The other children try to guess the name of the animal.

★ Rayne P. Reese, Glendale, MO

Animal Backs . . . . .3+

Materials needed
None needed

What to do
This is an excellent ice breaker for communication with children at circle time, or it may be used as a tension reliever prior to rest time. If the activity is used during rest time, you may want to follow up with a back rub for each child.

1. Choose a child and ask her to sit in front of you on the rug.

2. Ask the child to choose a favorite animal.

3. If the child chose an elephant, say in a sing-song voice, "Here tromps an elephant up your back." While singing, firmly walk your fingers up her back.

4. The next child chooses another animal, use your finger or hand movements to imitate the way it moves. For example: snake, gliding or slithering; mouse, skittering lightly; spider, crawling slowly, stopping in the middle and crawling quickly; crocodile, gently snapping or pinching; horse, galloping quickly.

★ Jan Dusoleil, Tacoma, WA

Guessing Game . . . . .3+

Materials needed
Small bag with drawstring
Small pictures of animals (pictures of animals can be cut from magazines and laminated for durability)

What to do
1. Put the pictures of animals in the bag.

2. Shake the bag and say the following chant.

> *Bag, oh bag*
> *Shake, shake, shake.*
> *Bag, oh bag,*
> *What shall I take?*

3. Take one animal out of the bag and hide it in your hand.

4. Describe the animal until a child guesses what animal it is.

5. Give the picture of the animal to the child to hold.

6. Continue until all children have a chance to play.

Note: Use pictures of familiar animals, but if the child cannot guess the animal ask other children to help.

More to do
Language: Use pictures relating to a theme (trees, plants, flowers, insects). When children understand how to describe the pictures, let them have a turn to shake and choose a child to guess the animal.

★ Denise Covert, Perris, CA

In the Sea, In a Tree

Materials needed
Pictures of animals

What to do
1. Explain to the children that animals live in different places (habitats), such as in the sea, on the farm, in the ground or in a tree. Display the pictures of animals for children to see.

2. Name an animal habitat and talk about the habitat.

3. Ask each child to select a picture of an animal that lives in that habitat.

4. Name another habitat category and ask the children to select pictures of animals that live in that habitat.

★ Lisa Sunbury, Cambridge, MA

Turtles . . . . .4+

Materials needed
Pictures of turtles

What to do
1. Look at the pictures of turtles and discuss how a turtle looks, how it has a hard shell, a snake-like head, is part of the reptile family and moves slowly.

2. Ask the children if they have ever seen a turtle. How did it move? What did it eat?

3. Sing the following original song "Turtle," extremely slowly to the tune of "Mary Had a Little Lamb."

> The turtle goes across the road
> Across the road
> Across the road
> The turtle goes across the road
> It takes him all day long.

4. Children can change the destination to give variety to the activity.

Paint box with glue mixture: 2/3 school glue + 1/3 water.

Before glue dries ~ apply scraps of colored tissue.

Cut semicircles from each side.

More to do

Art: Get three boxes from the supermarket, small, medium and large. Cut large semicircles on the bottom of each side. Ask the children to paint the boxes with tempera paint or to paint them with a glue and water mixture (2/3 cup of white glue and 1/3 cup of water). While the glue and water mixture is still wet, place scraps of colored tissue on the boxes. When dry the boxes will have a shiny shell-like appearance.

Dramatic play: Children can use the supermarket boxes as props in the dramatic play area.

Large motor: Children take turns wearing the box shells and role playing life as a turtle. Play music having a slow, relaxing pace or a tape with nature and pond sounds.

Math: The boxes can also be used to help teach the children the concept of big, bigger, biggest, sequencing and one to one correspondence.

Related Books

I Can't Get My Turtle to Move by Elizabeth L. O'Donnell

★ Marie Wimmer, Holbrook, NY

What Will My Pet Eat? . . . . .4+

Materials needed

Pictures of pets and samples of pet food in sealed clear plastic bags or containers (Parents are a good source of food samples. Find pictures of pet food on bags or in magazines. Stores that sell bulk food may donate food and pictures).

What to do

1. Give the pictures and food samples to the children.

2. Ask one child to show a pet food and to describe its appearance and texture. Ask the other children to guess which animal will eat the pet food. The child (or children since more than one child could have a picture of the same animal or more than one animal could eat the food) with the correct animal picture shows it to the other children.

3. If children have pets at home encourage them to talk about how their pets are fed, who feeds them, when they are fed and the kinds of feeding dish used.

More to do

Language: The children discuss why people eat different foods than animals eat.

Math: Make a graph of the different pets the children have and the amount of food the animals eat each day.

★ Brenda Miller, Olean, NY

Animal Antics . . . . .5+

Materials needed
Pictures of animals

What to do

1. Look at pictures of animals with the children during circle time.

2. Talk about what the animals look like, how they move and what sounds they make.

3. One child stands in the middle of the circle and decides on a specific animal to role play.

4. He makes the noise that animal makes and moves like that animal moves.

5. The other children guess which animal he is pretending to be.

More to do

Play Animal Antics after learning about a specific group of animals and limit the type of animal the children can role play, such as farm animals, meadow and forest animals, pond and stream animals, zoo animals or marine animals.

Art: Make an animal paper bag puppet.

Math: Count animal crackers, felt cutouts of animals or plastic animals.

Original Poem

"Ten Little Beavers"

> One little beaver swam near his home
> He dived in the water and called his brother to come.
> Two little beavers swam around and around
> They went inside their house and another beaver found.
>
> Three little beavers were swimming near the shore
> Another one joined them and that made four.
> Four little beavers jumped in the water for a dive.
> Another beaver came along and that made five.
>
> Five little beavers chewed on some tender sticks
> Another was behind a tree and that made six.
> Six little beavers went swimming once again
> One was behind a rock and that made seven.
>
> Seven little beavers were feeling just great
> Another one peeked at them and that made eight.
> Eight little beavers were swimming in a line
> A little baby beaver came and that made nine.

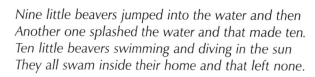

Nine little beavers jumped into the water and then
Another one splashed the water and that made ten.
Ten little beavers swimming and diving in the sun
They all swam inside their home and that left none.

Related books

Animals Do the Strangest Things by Leonora and Arthur Hornblow
Black Bear Cub by Alan Lind
Percy and the Five Houses by Else Minarik
Polar Bear, Polar Bear, What Do You Hear? by Bill Martin, Jr.
Walpole by Syd Hoff

★ Mary Brehm, Aurora, OH

Animals

Sprinkle Art . . . . .3+

Materials needed
Blue and green powder tempera in salt shakers
Spray water bottle
Sheets of 9" x 12" white construction paper (thinner paper will not hold up in the water)
Scraps of other colored paper

What to do
1. Read *Teddy Bears at the Seaside*. While reading, draw attention to the pictures, descriptive words and colors of the water.

2. After the story, let children shake paint on the sheets of paper. Take turns spraying with water to blend the paint and make the shades of ocean water.

3. While the pictures dry, ask the children to cut and create ocean creatures to glue on their ocean water.

More to do
Change the color of powdered paint to create different backgrounds (white and black for clouds during a weather unit, shades of green for treetops).

Related book
Teddy Bears at the Seaside by Susanna Gretz and Alison Sage

★ Diane Shatto, Kansas City, MO

Sticky Paper Art . . . . .3+

Materials needed
Self-adhesive paper, clear or colored
Collage materials, sequins
Basket

What to do
1. Cut self-adhesive paper in desired shapes, relating to the season or a theme. Be sure to cut one shape large enough to use for a class mural.

2. Place the large shape (sticky side up) in the middle of the circle and put the collage materials in a basket near the shape.

3. Each child selects one collage material and places it on the shape. If desired, create designs with the collage materials on the shape.

4. Display the class mural on the wall, either sticky side up or down.

Art

More to do

Art: Cut a piece of self-adhesive paper for individual placemats or cubby tags. Place a second sheet of clear self-adhesive paper over individual designs to enclose them.

Transition: Ask each child to point to the part of the class mural collage she contributed before leaving the table or after the collage is completed.

★ Rinnie Wells, Shawnee, OK

My First Quilt .3+

Materials needed

Pieces of cardboard or construction paper (1 per child)
Pieces of fabric (2" x 2" square)
Glue or paste
Handmade quilt

What to do

1. Each child decorates an 8" x 10" piece of cardboard or construction paper with fabric squares, filling the cardboard.

2. At circle time place the children's quilts on the floor in the middle of the circle. Talk about the designs and colors. If possible look at a handmade quilt with the children. Talk about how their quilts are different or similar to the large quilt.

3. Display the children's quilts on the wall.

★ Nancy Tucker, Emporia, KS

Starburst Painting . . . . .4+

Materials needed

Clear corn syrup, such as Karo®
Sponge paint brushes
Food coloring
Eyedroppers
Construction paper or tagboard

What to do

1. At circle time place a large piece of paper in the middle of the circle. Use a sponge paintbrush to cover the paper with a layer of corn syrup, such as Karo®.

2. Each child can take a turn dripping food coloring with an eyedropper on the wet corn syrup.

3. When the colors hit the wet syrup they will make a sunburst design.

4. Allow their creations to dry as flat as possible in a warm room.

5. Encourage the children to make their own starburst designs in the art center.

Note: Prior to circle time set up the art center with the necessary materials for children to do this activity independently following circle time.

More to do

Science: Offer the children red, yellow and blue food coloring. Give each child a plastic ice cube tray (preferably white) filled with water. Put one drop of red in one compartment, one of blue in another and one of yellow in another. Using an eyedropper, encourage the children to move drops of color to the empty compartments. Ask questions such as, "What do you think will happen when you put one drop of yellow with three drops of red?"

Related books

Little Blue and Little Yellow by Leo Lionni
The Great Blueness by Arnold Lobel
Harold and the Purple Crayon by Crockett Johnson

★ Donna Rehder, Sonora, CA

Rolling Pin Painting . . . . .4+

Materials needed

Rolling pin
Rubber puzzle pieces or foam shoe insoles and rubber cement
Tempera paint
Tray
Butcher paper or large construction paper
Newspaper

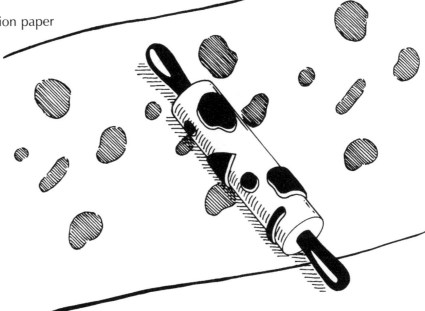

What to do

1. If you have rubber puzzles that are missing pieces, this is a good way to recycle the remaining pieces. If not, cut various shapes out of foam insoles.

2. Using rubber cement, glue the insole shapes or puzzle pieces onto the rolling pin.

3. Spread tempera paint in a tray that is long enough to hold the rolling pin. Gently roll the rolling pin in the paint.

4. Place the large piece of paper in the middle of the circle. Lay newspaper under each edge of the paper. Ask the children to roll the rolling pin across the large piece of paper.

5. This makes great murals and wrapping paper.

More to do

Art: Ask the children if they can find other objects that they would like to paint with in the classroom. Cubes, bristle blocks and cookie cutters make interesting designs.

★ Donna Rehder, Sonora, CA

The Artist . . . . .5+

Materials needed
Monet by Mike Venezia
Brushes
Palette knife (that is not sharp)
Palette
Prestretched canvas
Picture books of Van Gogh, Monet, Degas, Renoir
What to do

1. Read *Monet* by Mike Venezia. Talk about artists, the materials they use and how they use these materials.

2. Pass the following materials around for the children to see: brushes, a palette, a palette knife and a piece of canvas.

3. Demonstrate the technique of applying paint by using both a palette knife and a brush. Tell the children that different artists use different techniques to apply paint on the canvas.

4. Sing the following song, "The Artist," to the tune of "The Farmer in the Dell."

> *The artist paints a picture (the children act out painting)*
> *The artist paints a picture.*
> *He uses brushes, paint and canvas.*
> *The artist paints a picture.*
>
> *He hangs it in his gallery (pretend to hammer a nail)*
> *He hangs it in his gallery.*
> *He uses hammer, nails and wire.*
> *He hangs it in his gallery.*
>
> *The patron buys the art (pretend to take the work of art)*
> *The patron buys the art.*
> *He puts it in his living room.*
> *The patron buys the art.*

Related books
Mary Cassatt by Mike Venezia
Van Gogh by Mike Venezia

★ Martha E. Chew, Dayton, OH

The Great Artists . . . . .5+

Materials needed

Paper
Masking tape
Markers, pencils and crayons
Tables or chairs
Paint
Books about great artists and their paintings (Picasso, Michelangelo, DaVinci)
Classical music
Carpet squares

What to do

1. Talk about great artists and how they expressed their feelings through art. For example, talk (and show) about how Picasso had a "Blue Period" when he was sad and painted with blue paint. He then met a friend who he felt happy with and he painted with lots of pinks and reds and called that his "Rose Period."

2. Talk about different art media—paint, clay, crayons, pencil, charcoal, ink.

3. Talk about different ways people paint—using models, imagination, sitting down, standing up and lying down.

4. After circle time ask the children to take a piece of paper and masking tape, and tape the paper to the "ceiling" of a table or chair. Each child chooses markers, pencils or crayons to use. She also takes a carpet square and lies down underneath her paper taped under the table or chair. Now she too can paint like Michelangelo, drawing in her own "Sistine Chapel."

5. Play classical music to provide background music for the children to listen to as they paint.

6. When the children have finished hang their drawings with a brief description of how they were made (where else?) on the ceiling.

More to do

Michelangelo was just one of the great artists. Feature a different artist each week: first week, role play Michelangelo and draw on the ceiling of a table or chair; second week, role play Picasso and draw in either blues or reds depending on the mood that the child chooses; third week, role play DaVinci and draw a girl with a smile like the Mona Lisa.

Related book

The Art Lesson by Tomie dePaola

★ Ann Wolff, Exton, PA

Art

Does It Sink or Float? . . . . .3+

Materials needed

A Beach Day by Douglas Florian
Beach umbrella and other beach props
Seashells
Basket filled with a variety of objects
Clear container filled with water
Paper and markers

What to do

1. Read *A Beach Day* and talk about the story.

2. Set the ambiance in the room. Bring in a beach umbrella, put seashells in the sandbox. Bring in a raft, set up a pond for fishing with magnets.

3. Ask children to wear summer clothes and beach hats. I like to plan this activity during the winter to show the contrast with warm weather.

4. Bring a basket filled with a variety of objects, such as a sponge, rock, pine cone, cup and feather to the circle.

5. Place a clear container filled with water in the middle of the circle.

6. Ask the children to predict whether an object will sink or float.

7. Graph the predictions and the results.

More to do

Art: Create sand terrariums by adding dry tempera to sand. Let the children put layers of different colored sand in a baby food jar. Make beach collages using sand, shells, paper fish and seaweed. After gluing the items on the paper cover the collage with blue plastic wrap, if desired.

Snack: Eat snack on blankets picnic style.

★ Cindy Winther, Oxford, *MI*

Discovering the Beach . . . . .3+

Materials needed

Chart paper and markers
Tray
Cloth
Beach objects (shells, pebbles, pail, shovel, starfish, plastic fish, container with sand)

What to do

1. Talk with the children about things that can be found at the beach and make a list on chart paper.

2. Show the children the beach objects displayed on the tray and ask the children to name the objects.

3. Play the game, "What's Missing?" Place a cloth over the tray of beach objects. Ask one child to take an object and hide it (other children close their eyes). Take the cloth off the tray and ask the children to identify what is missing. Continue the game until each child has had a turn.

More to do

Art: Make a beach scene with shells, sand and pebbles.

Large motor: Have a treasure hunt in the sandbox. Hide beach objects in the sandbox for the children to find.

Water table: Set up a beach in the water table. Color the water blue with food coloring.

Related books

A Day at the Beach by Mircea Vasiliu
Homer the Beachcomber by Janet Craig

★ Gina M. Duddy, Arlington, MA

Homemade Beach . . . . .3+

Materials needed

Towel
Paper and markers or chalk and chalkboard
Water table
Beach sand or gravel (purchased at hardware stores, garden supply stores, pet stores)
Seashells, rocks, seaweed, driftwood
Water

What to do

1. Place the items from the beach in the middle of the circle and ask, "Where do you think I found these items?"

2. After talking about the beach ask the children if they have visited a beach at the ocean, a lake or a river. Ask the children to tell you what they enjoy doing at the beach.

3. List the children's favorite beach activities on chart paper or on the chalkboard.

4. Ask the children to help you add the beach items to the water table, adding the sand first. Explain that the beach items will be available at the water table for them to explore and to feel the different textures—the slimy seaweed, smooth shells, slippery driftwood and rough rocks.

More to do

Dramatic play: Have a Beach Day Celebration. Dress up in summer clothes, sun glasses, straw hats, sandals. Play with sand toys, drink lemonade, have a picnic. Listen to music by the Beach Boys.

Field trip: Travel to the local aquarium or nature center to observe fish, or travel to a local beach to collect shells, stones and other beach treasures.

Math: Count and sort the shells.

Science: Set up an aquarium in the classroom.

Related books
The Beach Day by Douglas Florian
Just Grandma and Me by Mercer Mayer

Related songs
"Down by the Bay" and "Baby Beluga" by Raffi

★ Mark Crouse, Nova Scotia, Canada

I'm Going to the Beach . . . . .3+

Materials needed
Beach bag
Items or pictures of items you would take to the beach (beach towel, sunscreen, sunglasses, bathing suit, book, pail, shovel, beach chair, beach umbrella, cooler)
Paper and markers

What to do
1. Before circle time, pack the beach items into the beach bag.

2. Explain to the children that you will be taking a trip to the beach and that your beach bag is packed.

3. Give the children clues about what is in your bag without actually showing them the objects. When they guess the item, pull that item out of your bag. For example, "I have something in my bag that I can wear into the water when I get to the beach" (a bathing suit) or "I'm going to put this all over my body so that the sun doesn't burn my skin" (sunscreen).

4. When your bag is empty, ask the children if they can think of anything you have forgotten. You may want to omit one obvious item from your bag and see what good beach detectives the children are.

5. As a follow-up activity, have the children help you make a list of everything you would need to bring to the beach. List their ideas on large chart paper. To assist the children in "reading" the list, draw a picture of the item next to the word and hang the list in the classroom.

More to do
Dramatic play: Place the beach props in the block area or dramatic play area for the children to pretend they are at the beach. Enjoy a beach day when all of the children wear their bathing suits to school, fill pools with water and let the children play with beach balls. Serve hotdogs, chips and lemonade for lunch one day during the beach unit.

Sensory table: Fill the water table with plastic animals that you could find at the beach or in the ocean. Put seashells in the sand table to bury and dig up.

★ Michelle A. Gajda, Cheshire, MA

Making a Seashell Paper Weight ......3+

Materials needed

Small seashells
Sand
Large tray
Baby food jars with lids
Colored adhesive tape
Containers with beach sand

What to do

1. Prior to circle time spread the sand on a tray to make sure that it is thoroughly dry.

2. At circle time show the childre a container of sand from the beach.

3. Divide the children into groups and ask them to put their hands in the container and describe what they see and feel, such as small shells, pebbles and sand. They will discover that as the sand is moved around new shells and pebbles are found.

4. Discuss the type and size of the shells discovered.

5. To make a seashell paper weight give each child a baby food jar. Scoop dry sand into the jar until approximately 3/4 full.

6. Each child then selects small shells to put into the jar.

7. Ask each child to select a color of decorative tape and tape the lid to the jar.

8. Invert the jar and as the child shakes the container different shells can be seen.

More to do

Math: Count shells found in the beach sand. Categorize shells by size, color, shape. Compare the sand to sand found at the beach.

Related books

Discovering Seashells by Douglas Florian
Sea Animals by Dorling Kindersley

★ Sandi Fisher, Kutztown, PA

Ocean Mural ....3+

Materials needed

Blue and green art chalk
Large piece of newsprint (mural size)
Tissues
Scraps of colored construction paper
Glue

What to do

1. Place the large piece of newsprint in the middle of the circle.

2. Ask the children to shade blue and green chalk on newsprint.

3. Rub the chalk with tissues to blend the colors.

4. Children can create ocean creatures from construction paper to glue on the mural.

5. Hang the ocean mural on the wall.

More to do

Art: Older children may be able to use ocean stencils. They can trace the stencil on paper and cut it out to glue on the mural. Change the color of chalk to make murals for other themes. Shades of green will make tree tops and bird stencils can be used. Dark blue shades can be blended for space and add planets and stars.

★ Diane Shatto, Kansas City, MO

Sort the Shells . . . . .3+

Materials needed

Assortment of shells
Beach bag or bucket

What to do

1. Conceal the shells in a beach bag or bucket. Bring them to circle time.

2. Let each child take a turn pulling a shell out. Let the children decide how they want to sort them. You may want to suggest that they sort them by shape, size or color.

3. Talk about the different shapes, colors and textures of the shells. The children will want to talk about shells and the beach. This is a good way to start a discussion about the beach, the ocean or summer vacations.

More to do

Dramatic play: Add beach props to housekeeping and put the shells in the dramatic play center on that day.

Math: Put the shells in the math center and ask the children as they work in pairs to sort the shells into the groups of their choice.

Related books

The Fish Who Could Wish by John Bush
A House for a Hermit Crab by Eric Carle
Ocean Alphabet Book by Jerry Pallotta
When the Tide is Low by Sheila Cole

★ Julie W. Lawhorn, Gaithersburg, MD

Story Shell . . . . .3+

Materials needed
Large seashell (preferably a conch shell)

What to do
1. Teach the children the following chant: "Story shell, story shell, What is the story you have to tell?"

2. Children and teacher chant together as the shell is presented at circle time.

3. A collective story is told as the shell is passed from child to child. The teacher starts by holding the shell to her ear, as if listening to the story idea from the shell. The teacher says, "Once upon a time there was a _____."

4. The shell is passed to a child. The child "listens" to the shell and fills in the blank (for example, "crab"). The shell is passed to the next child to add to the story. "The crab went for a walk."

5. The activity continues around the circle until all who wish to contribute have a turn.

More to do
Language: The activity could be recorded or written on chart paper for shared reading. A book of the story could also be written with the children drawing the illustrations.

Related book
A House for Hermit Crab by Eric Carle

★ Sarah Dill, Madison, WI

By the Sea . . . . .4+

Materials needed
Seashells (at least 1 per child)
Pictures of shellfish
Sand shovels

What to do
1. Before circle time bury all of the seashells except one in the outdoor sand area.

2. At circle time, go outdoors and sit in a circle near the area where you buried the shells.

3. Show the pictures of shellfish. Help the children name each one. Tell the children a few details about where and how each one lives.

4. Hold up the seashell you did not bury. Talk with the children about the shell.

5. Tell the children that you buried seashells in the sand and ask the children to find the shells. Pass out the sand shovels and start exploring.

6. Have the children put the shells they find in a common pile. After the last shell has been found, gather the shovels and direct the children back to their chair or towel.

7. Pass the shells out, one per child. In turn have each child holds up her shell and describes it.

8. If the children can keep their shells, have them put them in their cubbies before you move on to another activity.

More to do

Language: Ask the children to draw a picture of the type of shellfish they think might have lived in their seashell. Write what the child says about the shellfish on a sentence strip and attach it to the bottom of the picture. Ask the children to think of a title and design for the cover. Bind the pictures together and add the cover the children have made for the class book.

Science: Use a magnifying glass and microscope to study the seashells. What colors and designs can you see with magnification that you missed when looking at the shells without a magnifying glass or microscope?

Related books

A House for Hermit Crab by Eric Carle
Swimmy by Leo Lionni

★ Virginia Jean Herrod, Columbia, SC

The Silly Seal Song . . . . .4+

Materials needed

None needed

What to do

1. Sing the following song to the tune of "I'm a Little Teapot."

> *I'm a silly seal, on the go,*
> *I swim fast, and I swim slow,*
> *When the day is over and it's time to sleep,*
> *I leap up high, then dive down deep.*

More to do

Art: Paint a group mural of the ocean on a large sheet of butcher paper. Add pictures of seals, swimming and leaping in the waves.

Related books

Greyling by Jane Yolen
Sammy the Seal by Syd Hoff

★ Donna Borges, Crescent City, CA

Beach Day ....4+

Materials needed
Items from the beach

What to do
1. Encourage the children to bring an item from the ocean or beach.

Note: Have extra beach items for children who forget or who do not have something from the beach.

2. Each child tells something about his beach item or makes up a story about it.

3. Sing the following song, "Have You Ever Seen a Mermaid or a Merman?" to the tune of "Have You Ever Seen a Lassie?"

> *Have you ever seen a mermaid, a mermaid, a mermaid?*
> *Have you ever seen a mermaid, swim this way and that?*
> *Swim this way and that way, swim this way and that way.*
> *Have you ever seen a mermaid swim this way and that?*
>
> *Have you ever seen a merman, a merman, a merman,*
> *Have you ever seen a merman, flip his tail like that?*
> *Flip it this way and that way, flip it this way and that way.*
> *Have you ever seen a merman flip his tail like that?*
>
> *Have you ever seen a mermaid, or a merman, or a mermaid*
> *Have you ever seen a merman, blow a big kiss to you?*

More to do
Art: Provide materials for the children to paint a picture of the ocean using butcher paper and blue paint. Make pieces of seaweed from crepe paper, yarn or construction paper and glue it on the paper. Ask the children to create their own sea life and draw it on the mural. Mix sand and water and use brushes or hands to paint with. Use small seashells to glue on paper to create pictures.

Fine motor: Make a necklace with seashells and beads. Let children string beads and shells with teacher supervision.

Language: Make an Ocean Book. Precut pages shaped like whales, fish, shells. Ask children to create pictures and describe them to the other children. The teacher writes what each child says on each page. Put the pictures together as a class book or as individual books.

Science: Make an ocean bottle with a clear plastic soda bottle. Fill the bottle with 1/2 mineral oil (or clearest oil you can find) and 1/2 water. Add a few drops of blue food coloring. Let children add small shells and glitter to make an ocean effect. Be sure the cap is on tight or hot glue the cap on the bottle to seal it securely.

Original song

"Mermaids and Mermen" (Tune: "I'm a Little Teapot")

I'm a little mermaid
See my tail
My friends are the dolphins
And so are the whales.

I live in the ocean
So big and blue
I love to swim
With the little fishes too.

I'm a little merman
Strong and brave
See my big ol' tail
I can make it wave.

I live in the ocean
So big and blue
I love to play
With the little fishes too.

"Mermen and Mermaids" (fingerplay)

We live in the ocean
With the whales
You may not believe us
But it's no tale.

With the crabs and fish
We love to play
But from the sharks
We stay away.

I love the land
It's really neat
But it's better underwater
'Cuz we have no feet.

"Five Little Seahorses" (fingerplay)

Five little seahorses
Play on the ocean floor
One went to swim
And that left four.

Four little seahorses
Live in the sea
One went to bed
And that left three.

Three little seahorses
In the ocean blue
One went to play
And that left two.

Two little seahorses
Having some fun
One went home
And that left one.

One little seahorse
Yes, just one,
He swam away
And that left none!

Related books

Baby Beluga by Raffi
Going on a Whale Watch by Bruce McMillan
One Sun by Bruce McMillan
The Several Tricks of Edgar Dolphin by Nathaniel Benchley
Swimmy by Leo Lionni
Whale and Dolphin by Vincent Serventy

★ Sheryl A. Smith, Jonesborough, TN

Measuring Up to a Baby Whale . . . . . .4+

Materials needed

Whales, Dolphins and Porpoises by Mark Cowadine
Yarn
Tape measure
Colored rolls of masking or electrical tape
Masking tape
Scissors
Paper and markers
Large open floor space

What to do

1. At circle time read the paragraph labeled "Baby" on page 17 in the book listed above. Show the children the photo on page 16 that compares the baby killer whale's length to a human's length.

2. Ask the children to use the tape measure to determine the killer whale baby's length on the floor (approximately 6′ 10″).

3. Leave the tape measure on the floor.

4. Cut a piece of yarn, measuring enough yarn to equal the whale's length and cut the yarn.

5. Let the children use plain masking tape to hold the yarn in place on the floor.

6. Using a different colored tape for each child, let each child lay next to the yarn taped to the floor to compare their own lengths in relation to the whole after measuring the child. Write the child's name on the piece of tape.

7. With older children place the tape measure beside the yarn (whale) and allow the children to measure the whale's length and their height.

8. After measuring ask the children, "Who is bigger, the child or the whale? Who is tallest, smallest? How many are the same? Where could the baby whale live if it were to come to our school? Playground? Sidewalk? Sensory table? Block area? Art area?" Display the children's answers for parents and children to see.

More to do
Dramatic Play: Using a pair of binoculars and predrawn whale pictures, mount photos around the room and let the children use the binoculars to locate whales like on a real whale watch.

Field trip: Visit an aquarium or ocean aquatic center to learn more about whales and sea life.

Language: Locate a whale puppet and use during storytime or allow children to play with it in all areas of the room.

Sensory table: Using a water or sensory table, color the water with blue food coloring and add sand and plastic sea animals or whales and fish to resemble the ocean.

Related books
Whales by Laura Bour
Going on a Whale Watch by Bruce McMillan
The Whales' Song by Dyan Sheldon
Move Over, Mother Goose! by Ruth Dowell

Related song
"Baby Beluga" by Raffi

★ Tina Woehler, Nashville, TN

Under the Sea . . . . .4+

Materials needed
1 twin size sheet, preferably blue
Precut pictures of animals and mammals that live in the ocean, at least 1 per child.

What to do
1. Place the pictures on the floor in the circle area. Lay the sheet on the floor over the pictures.

2. Ask each child to stand around the edge of the sheet. Help place the children on all sides of the sheet.

3. Ask the children to pick up their edge of the sheet. Help the children to move the sheet up and down to create waves.

4. While you are making waves talk about what they may find in an ocean.

5. Call one or two children at a time to "swim" under the sheet and pick up a picture.

6. When the children surface they should tell the group what they found. If they cannot tell what it is they can put it back for another child to find or the group can help identify it.

7. As the pictures are identified toss them on top of the sheet and let them bounce in the waves. It makes holding the sheet more exciting while they are waiting their turn.

8. Continue until all the pictures have been identified. Ask the children if they can think of anything else that lives in the sea.

More to do
Dramatic play: Provide goggles and fins for the children when they "swim."

Music: Play ocean music or songs about the ocean with fast and slow rhythms as you make the waves with the sheet. Move the waves to the rhythm.

Science: Provide starfish, sea horses and seashells for the children to touch. Put them in a feely box or use them at the water table. Match the objects with their pictures.

★ Julia A. Masury, Raymond, NH

Making an Octopus . . . . .5+

Materials needed
Brown trash bags
Glue
Scraps of construction paper
Picture of an octopus

Newspapers
Styrofoam packing half circles
Tape

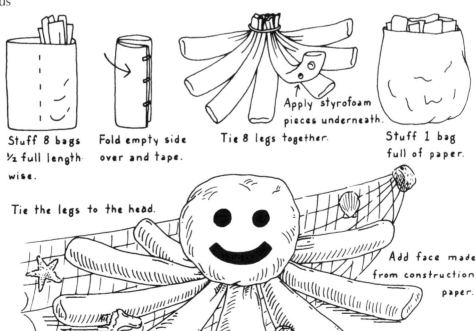

Stuff 8 bags ½ full lengthwise.

Fold empty side over and tape.

Tie 8 legs together.

Apply styrofoam pieces underneath.

Stuff 1 bag full of paper.

Tie the legs to the head.

Add face made from construction paper.

What to do

1. As the children are seated for circle time show them a picture of an octopus.

2. Discuss the characteristics of the octopus—color, size, how many arms, how it moves.

3. Have the children work cooperatively in nine groups giving each group a trash bag and newspapers. (Eight groups will each make an arm and one group will make the head.)

4. Each group making an arm stuffs a trash bag with newspapers filling only half of the bag lengthwise. Tie the bags.

5. Fold the other side of the trash bag over the stuffed side and tape it, making a large narrow arm.

6. Using the stryrofoam packing half circles, have the children glue them to the bottom of each arm representing the octopus' suction cups.

7. The group making the head will stuff the entire bag with newspaper and use construction paper scraps to make the facial features of the octopus.

8. When the eight arms are finished, tie them together and then tie them to the stuffed head.

9. Display the octopus on the floor for an ocean scene.

More to do

Math: Count eight objects—octopus' arms, seashells, fish.

Science: Compare the octopus to other ocean life such as fish, squid, dolphin, whale and shark.

Related book

I Was All Thumbs by Bernard Waber

★ Sandi Fisher, Kutztown, PA

Let's Be Bears . . . . .3+

Materials needed
None needed

What to do

1. Children sit on the floor at circle time.

2. Teacher chants the first verse of the following song as children pretend to be bears asleep in a cave lying down.

Verse 1:

> *The little bears are sleeping, sleeping, sleeping*
> *The little bears are sleeping in their caves.*

3. Repeat the first verse until all children are lying down.

4. Children follow the directions of each verse as it changes their activity.

5. Teacher chants next verses in order.

> *The little bears all open their eyes, open their eyes, open their eyes.*
> *The little bears all open their eyes and look around.*

> *The little bears all sit up, sit up, sit up.*
> *The little bears all sit up and stretch out their arms.*

> *The little bears all stand up, stand up, stand up.*
> *The little bears all stand up and peek out of their cave.*

> *The little bears all creep out, creep out, creep out.*
> *The little bears all creep out and look for something to eat.*

> *The little bears all pick up berries, pick up berries, pick up berries.*
> *The little bears all pick up berries and put them in their mouths.*

More to do

Art: Each child paints a cave with brown paint on newsprint, leaving a circle in the middle for the cave entrance. Add a bear sticker either inside or outside the cave. For polar bears, use light blue paper and paint a white bear, adding grits to the paint to give it texture. Children tear 1" strips of white paper into several pieces and paste them onto a large upside down U-like shape that has been drawn by the teacher to make an igloo next to the bear. Talk about panda bears and give children precut black and white sections of paper that when pasted together make a bear. Talk about pandas that live at the zoo and why they do not sleep all winter.

Dramatic play: Have a Teddy Bear Day. Each child is invited to bring a bear to school. Include the bears in all activities. Each bear is given a tag with the owner's name on it to wear. Finish the day with a teddy bear parade.

Science: Talk about how bears sleep all winter and come out in the spring. Talk about what it would be like to sleep all winter. What would we miss? Where would we sleep? Could we go this long without food? Talk about different types of bears and where they might live. Is it cold where they live and do they need to go into a cave for the winter?

Related books

Beady Bear by Don Freeman
Bear Child's Book of Hours by Anne Rockwell
Blueberries for Sal by Robert McCloskey
Brown Bear, Brown Bear, What Do You See by Bill Martin, Jr.
Corduroy by Don Freeman
Goldilocks and the Three Bears retold by Shari Lewis
Jesse Bear, What Will You Wear? by Nancy White Carlstrom
Little Bear by Else Holmelund Minarik
The Little Mouse, the Red Ripe Strawberry and the Big Hungry Bear by Don and Audrey Wood
One Teddy Bear Is Enough by Ginnie Hofmann
The Runaway Teddy Bear by Ginnie Hofmann
Sleepy Bear by Lydia Dabcovich
What Next, Baby Bear? by Jill Murphy
Where Does the Brown Bear Go? by Nicki Weiss
Who Lives Here? by Rozanne Lanczak Williams
Who Wants an Old Teddy Bear? by Ginnie Hofmann

★ Diaine K. Weiss, Fairfax, VA

Teddy Bear Circle . . . . .3+

Materials needed

3 paper plates
Black and brown construction paper
Several 4" x 4" squares of construction paper (various colors)
Pictures of items related to songs (animals for "Old McDonald Had a Farm," spider for
   "The Itsy, Bitsy Spider," bear for "The Bear Went Over the Mountain)"
Glue
Clear self-adhesive paper (optional)

What to do

1. Construct the bear from paper plates, one for the head, two for the body with concave sides of the plates facing each other and one of the two plates cut in half. Staple the plate and one-half plate together for the body of the bear. Staple one plate to the top of body for the head. Cut the paws out and glue them to the body of the bear and attach the ears to head. Draw in the eyes and mouth.

2. Collect pictures related to circle time songs and attach these to the 4" x 4" construction paper pieces (or cover with self-adhesive paper) and place the pictures in the pocket made from the half paper plate.

3. During circle time show the chidren the teddy bear made from paper plates.

4. Allow the children to choose from the back pocket of the bear a card with a picture. Ask them to guess the song related to the picture.

5. Continue until every child has a turn to choose a picture.

More to do

Cooking: Make bear cookies for snack.

Dramatic play: Place teddy bears in the dramatic play area of the room.

Related books

Amy the Dancing Bear by Carly Simon
Bear's Bargain by Frank Asch
Better Not Get Wet, Jessie Bear by Nancy White Carlstrom
Happy Birthday Moon by Frank Asch
The Happy Day by Ruth Krauss
Little Mouse, the Red Ripe Strawberry and the Big Hungry Bear by Don and Audrey Wood

★ Tina M. Taylor, Johnson City, TN

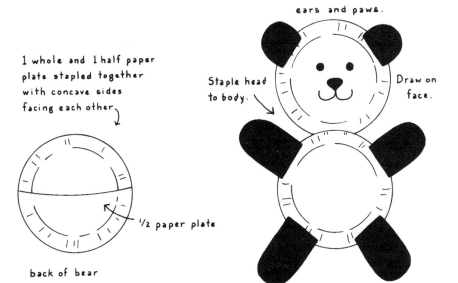

Add construction paper ears and paws.

1 whole and 1 half paper plate stapled together with concave sides facing each other

Staple head to body.

Draw on face.

½ paper plate

back of bear

Teddy Bear Picnic . . . . .3+

Materials needed

Teddy bears
Large picnic tablecloth
Napkins and paper cups

Gummy bears (different colors)
Graham bears
Punch or milk

What to do

1. Send a note home announcing Teddy Bear Picnic Day.

> Dear Parents,
>   Tomorrow is Teddy Bear Picnic Day. The children may bring their favorite bears to school with them.
>
>   Sincerely,
>   Teacher's Name

2. Tell the children that the bears may participate in all the activities of the day.

3. Bring a bear yourself and model how to introduce your bear to the class during circle time. Describe the bear and tell where you got the bear.

4. Allow each child to introduce his bear to the other children and talk about the bear.

5. Set a large picnic tablecloth outside or on the floor and have a picnic, serving the graham bears and punch.

Bears

More to do

Language: Take a photo of each child with his bear. Have the children dictate a story about their bears and draw a picture of their bears. Make a book with each child having a page with his picture and story. Read the book aloud to the class and let the children take turns bringing the book home to share. At the end of the year, give each child his page to keep.

Math: Make a floor graph with the children's bears, using three or four headings to categorize the bears, such as: bears with clothes, bears with hats, brown bears, white bears. Place the headings on the floor and have the children put their bears under the appropriate heading. Talk about which group has the most and the least in it and count the number in each group. Use the gummy bears for a math sorting activity. Ask the children to estimate how many gummy bears are in a clear plastic cup and which color is predominate. Sort the gummy bears by color. Make a graph using one color for each line of the graph. Count the bears into groups of ten and count by tens to find out how many bears there are. At the end of the activity let the children decide how to divide the gummy bears fairly and let them eat them or take them home for a snack later.

Related books

A Button for Corduroy by Don Freeman
Corduroy by Don Freeman

★ Barbara Saul, Eureka, CA

Teddy Was His Name-O . . . . .4+

Materials needed

None needed

What to do

1. Sing the following song, "TEDDY" to the tune of "BINGO" with the children.

> *There was a boy who had a bear*
> *And TEDDY WAS HIS NAME-O.*
> *T E D D Y, T E D D Y, T E D D Y*
> *And TEDDY WAS HIS NAME-O.*

More to do

Art: Children trace one large and one small circle using a paper plate onto brown construction paper. Children trace their feet, once with their shoes on and then with their shoes off, for the bear legs. Cut out these tracings. Attach the small brown circle to the large circle (body and head) using a paper fastener. Attach the shoe tracings with fasteners for the legs. Attach the foot tracings at the sides of the body for the bear arms. Attach two eyes. The other circles are used on the paws and for the mouth. Punch a hole and attach the string at the top of bear's head and the tips of the feet. Attach a string to the paper towel holder and have the bear dance as you play music.

Cooking: Bake a bear using refrigerated biscuits flattened for the head and let children roll extra dough into little balls and stick on for ears and raisins for eyes.

Large motor: Play "Teddy Says" instead of "Simon Says."

Math: Children each bring teddy bears to school and measure them with yarn to discover which bear is the fattest or the tallest.

Punch hole and attach string.

Shapes cut from brown construction paper and joined together with paper fasteners

Original song

"Brown Bear, Brown Bear" (Tune: "Baa, Baa, Black Sheep")

> *Brown bear, brown bear, turn around*
> *Brown bear, brown bear, touch the ground*
> *Brown bear, brown bear, tie your shoe,*
> *Brown bear, brown bear, I love you.*

Related books

Alphabears by Kathleen Hague
Brown Bear, Brown Bear, What Do You See? by Bill Martin, Jr.
Corduroy by Don Freeman
Jamberry by Bruce Degan
Jesse Bear, What Will You Wear? by Nancy White Carlstrom
Somebody and the Three Blairs by Marilyn Tolhurst
Teddy Bears' Picnic by Renate Kozikowski

★ Holly Ciepluch, Whitefish Bay, WI

Shadow Lesson . . . . .4+

Materials needed

Bear Shadow by Frank Asch
Bear silhouette (enlarge bear shape to about 3' tall, trace on cardbord and cut out, make a stand for silhouette)
Butcher paper (large enough to place under the bear silhouette to trace the shadow)
Marker
Sunny day

What to do

1. Read the book *Bear Shadow*.

2. Introduce the big bear and ask the children if they think it has a shadow.

3. Take the children outside and lay butcher paper on a flat, hard surface that is in an area that gets direct sunlight all day.

4. Place the bear in the center of the paper and have the children look for its shadow.

5. Trace the bear's shadow with a marker. Look at where the sun is in the sky. Write down the time of day near the tracing.

6. Ideally, leave the bear and paper outside all day and return to it at lunch time and again in the afternoon. Repeat Step 5 at each of these times.

7. Bring the tracing inside and discuss what happened to the bear's shadow and why.

More to do

Art: Have children draw an animal and then cut it out. Trace it onto black paper and cut it out. Glue the shapes end to end, like a shadow would look. Take sidewalk chalk outside and ask the children to work in pairs to trace each other's shadow.

Language: Ask the children to use their own shadow to follow directions, such as stand with your shadow behind you or stand with your shadow beside you. Ask the children to talk about and write or draw pictures about other ways to get rid of their shadows.

Math: Ask the children to measure the bear's shadow with unifix cubes. Trace the bear's shadow each hour at school, then measure the shadow and graph the results.

Movement: Play shadow tag outside.

Related books

Footprints and Shadows by Anne Dodd
Henry and the Dragon by Eileen Christelow
Me and My Shadow by Christina Krayer
My Shadow by Robert Louis Stevenson
Shadows Are About by Ann W. Paul

★ Nancy Tatum, Williamsburg, VA

The Three Bears . . . . .4+

Materials needed
Pictures or book about real bears
Flannel story of *The Three Bears* with flannel board
Bear song, such as "The Bear Went Over the Mountain" or "Smoky the Bear"

What to do
1. Read and share the story of *The Three Bears*.

2. Give the children the flannel pieces of the story.

3. Tell the story of *The Three Bears* as the children place flannel pieces on the flannel board.

4. Ask the children if real bears live in houses, wear clothes, sit in chairs.

5. Share the book or pictures of bears, discussing how real bears live.

6. Sing your favorite bear song.

More to do
Blocks: Put small bears and a doll in the block area.

Cooking: Prepare and serve hot cereal for a snack. Involve the children in measuring the uncooked cereal, adding the ingredients and stirring the cereal.

Dramatic play: Put out three different sized bowls, chairs and beds.

Related book
The Three Bears by Paul Galdone

★ Ann Chandler, Felton, CA

Bears

Birds ....3+

Materials needed

Pictures of birds from magazines, especially nature magazines

What to do

1. Collect pictures from magazines of many types of birds.

2. At circle time show the pictures and talk about the birds with the children. Compare the colors and shapes of the birds.

3. Sort the birds by beak shape or foot type. This characteristic also indicates habitat and type of food.

4. With the children investigate what materials birds use to make nests and where they build their nests.

More to do

Language: Construct a story tree about birds with the children. Label branches on a tree drawing: birds eat, birds do, bird babies and birds look like. Ask the children what they know about birds. Draw limbs extending from the branches and label them with the children's ideas.

Science: Put nests, egg shells, seeds on the science table for children to explore and discuss. Collect dryer lint, string, yarn scraps and hair to put outside for birds to use in nests in the spring.

★ Sandra W. Gratias, Perkasie, PA

Penguins ....3+

Materials needed

2 bowls
Bottle of oil
Container of water
Paint brushes
Feathers
Pictures of penguins

What to do

1. Discuss how birds stay warm in very cold temperatures of air and water.

2. Show samples of various feathers and discuss how feathers overlap to create a dense layer of protection.

3. Dip a feather in water and notice what happens. Take another feather and coat it with oil discussing how birds do this. Immerse the feather in the bowl of water and ask the children to look at it and talk about what they see.

More to do

Science: If you have several feathers, encourage the children to experiment with the feathers. Use a paper towel to coat the feather with oil, then put it in the water and see if it gets wet. Gather a variety of materials that have a waterproof coating, that are plastic coated or that have a resistant finish and compare differences in absorbency.

★ Barbara M. Bergstrom, Spokane, WA

Feather Bookmarks . . . . .3+

Materials needed

Feathers
Dish pan
Dish soap
Absorbent paper
Clear self-adhesive paper

What to do

1. Take the children on a nature hike or on a trip to an aviary.

2. Collect the feathers that have been dropped by the birds.

3. Wash the feathers by soaking them in dish soap and water in a dish pan.

4. Rinse and lay the feathers on absorbent paper to dry.

5. The next day press each feather between two pieces of clear self-adhesive paper that has been precut to bookmark size.

More to do

This activity can be done with flowers or leaves but be sure they are dry before sealing between self-adhesive paper to prevent mildew from forming. Follow up this activity with a study of different types of feathers and coloration of different birds.

Related books

Birds We Know by Margaret Friskey
Feathers by Dorothy H. Patent

Related poem

> *Two little dickey birds sitting on a hill.*
> *One named Jack and the other named Jill (hold up index finger of each hand)*
> *Fly away Jack. Fly away Jill. (move fingers behind back)*
> *Come back Jack. Come back Jill. (bring fingers back)*

Substitute dickey birds with other birds.

★ Wanda K. Pelton, Lafayette, IN

Little Baby Robin Eggs · · · · · · · · · · · .3+

Materials needed

Copy of fingerplay "Little Baby Robin Eggs"
Oversized white T-shirt per child (have each child bring an old one from home)

What to do

1. Sing "Little Baby Robin Eggs" to the tune of "Puff, the Magic Dragon."

> *Little baby robin eggs (cup palm of hands together)*
> *Amidst the leaves so still (raise hands up high)*
> *Never will I touch your nest (shake pointer finger)*
> *For it would surely spill. (drop hands to the floor)*
>
> *I'll listen for your little chirps (point to ear)*
> *As you begin to hatch (close palm, then open)*
> *And watch when you try hard to fly (point to eye)*
> *Above the garden patch. (wiggle fingers as if to fly)*
>
> *Little baby robin eggs (cup palm of hands together)*
> *I'll wait to hear you sing (touch lips)*
> *For then I'll know without a doubt (go down low)*
> *The season must be Spring. (jump up high)*

2. Explain that everyone will have a chance to pretend to be inside of an egg (inside the T-shirt).

3. Teacher demonstrates by putting on a T-shirt and tucking her body inside the shirt. (Head inside head hole, arms inside arm holes and knees bent toward stomach so the entire body is encased inside of the shirt.) Slowly poke out head, then arms and legs. Pretend to hatch and fly.

4. Ask each child to put on a T-shirt and to act out motions of pretending to hatch and fly.

5. After the children have emerged from their T-shirts, they slowly fly back to their place in the circle.

More to do

Art: Provide colorful modeling dough to make eggs, nests and worms. Make a plaster of Paris egg mold. Before it hardens, put a small plastic chicken inside the plaster of Paris. Let the children chip away the plaster of Paris with simple and safe tools until it breaks apart.

Dramatic play: Play Birds in a Nest. Make the nest by taping to the floor a large cardboard enclosure that is about 8" high and wide enough for several children to step into pretending to be chicks. Make chick headbands and paper wings as props for the play. Fill the nest with straw if none of the children are allergic to straw.

Math: Make matching paper eggshells and matching mother bird and baby bird sets. Seriate bird nests. Make an inchworm number line. Make bird footprints out of masking tape and tape to the floor. Count how many bird steps it takes to get to a certain mark.

Science: Obtain an incubator and several fertilized eggs. Watch as baby chicks hatch. After the chicks hatch, put them in a large aquarium or box with a heat lamp. Make arrangements with someone who is willing to adopt the chicks about three weeks after they hatch. As a class project make a bird nest. This is a messy but excellent group activity. To make a supply of mud, mix lots of dirt with water and add straw, scraps and twigs. Take a bird walk. Watch birds flying and look for old and new nests. Listen for bird calls.

★ Patricia Moeser, McFarland, WI

Milk Carton Bird Feeder . . . . .4+

Materials needed

Empty half-gallon milk carton (1 per child)
Pieces of string (18" long)
Thin sticks or twigs
Bird seed and spoon
Thin wood chips, leaves, straw, moss, short pieces of string (for decoration)
Glue

string through hole for hanging

Milk carton decorated with wood chips, leaves, straw

What to do

1. Bring the materials needed to make a bird feeder to circle time. Talk about and show pictures of different kinds of bird feeders.

2. Demonstrate how to make the milk carton bird feeder. On one side of the carton, about 2/3 of the way down, cut a square hole for the door.

hole

3. Poke a hole about 1/2" below the door on each side of the door.

birdseed

stick poked into hole

4. Decorate the bird feeder by gluing the wood chips on the roof for shingles and the straw, sting and moss on the sides of the carton.

5. Put the sticks or twigs through the holes under the door and fasten securely.

6. Tie the string through the hole on the top for the hanger.

7. Spoon bird seed into the carton. Hang it outside a window and ask the children to check during the day for birds at the feeder. Remember that once you start feeding the birds you need to keep feeding them because they will come back throughout the winter.

8. Provide additional materials for children to make bird feeders. Encourage them to take the feeders home to hang in their neighborhoods.

Related book

Birds Eat and Eat and Eat by Roma Gans

★ Kathy Boeche, Livermore, CA

Edible Bird Nests . . . . .4+

Materials needed

Pictures of birds and their nests
Hot plate set up in a separate area
Mixing spoon
6-ounce package of chocolate chips
3-ounce can of chow mein noodles

Paper plates
Double boiler
Oven mitt
6-ounce package of butterscotch pieces
1 bag of miniature marshmallows

What to do

1. At circle time talk with the children about birds and their nests.

2. Explain that you and the children will make pretend bird nests that can be eaten. Prepare the above recipe with the children.

3. In a double boiler over low heat, melt the chocolate and butterscotch pieces. Stir in noodles and mix well.

4. When warm but not hot, drop three tablespoon portions onto each child's plate.

5. Show the children how to mold the mixture into nest shapes, making a hollow in the center of each nest.

6. When cool the children can then drop three or four miniature marshmallows into the hollow to represent eggs.

7. Allow the nests to become firm before eating the nest for snack.

Note: This recipe makes eight 3" nests.

Related song

"Birds" from *Learning Basic Skills Through Music* by Hap Palmer

Related book

Horton Hatches the Egg by Dr. Seuss

★ Carol Taylor, Alexandria, LA

Bird Watching . . . . .5+

Materials needed

2 identical sets of 6 or more colored pictures of birds

What to do

1. Place one set of colored pictures of birds around the classroom in out-of-the-way areas. (This is done while the children are not in the classroom.)

2. Talk with the children about bird watching.

3. Show the children the other set of bird pictures. See if the children can see any of the matching pictures while they are sitting in the circle.

4. Ask the children to quietly move around the room looking for the matching bird pictures.

5. When the children have located all the birds (they leave the pictures in their places), the children return to the circle.

★ Edith Kuhlmann, London, England

Bird Words . . . . .5+

Materials needed
Chart size drawing of a familiar bird (cardinal, blue jay, sparrow)
Precut paper feathers
Glue stick
Marker
Area to display the class bird
Lined chart paper

What to do
1. At circle time introduce the concept of ornithology (the study of birds).

2. Ask the children what words do they think of when they think about birds and list the words on lined chart paper.

3. Ask the children questions about birds, such as what is the name of a bird that says its name (chickadee dee dee).

4. As children respond record their answers on the precut feathers.

5. Ask the children to glue the feather with their response on the bird.

6. Display the bird that the children worked together to create.

7. As children learn new words about birds add additional feathers to the class bird.

More to do
Art: Ask children to paint pictures of birds and display them in the classroom.

Field trip: Visit a bird sanctuary or take a walk in the neighborhood.

Language: Use the children's vocabulary words about birds for poetry writing, a class dictionary or bird observation journals.

Math: Graph the number of birds that children observe outdoors.

Science: Invite an ornithologist or bird watcher in the community to visit.

Related books
Feathers for Lunch by Lois Ehlert
What Makes a Bird a Bird? by May Garelick

★ Carol Patnaude, Cathy Constantino, Darlene Maloney, Lynn Camara, Warwick, RI

Body Sounds .3+

Materials needed
None needed

What to do
1. Ask the children, "Can you make a sound with your hands?" (Encourage children to clap hands together, tap hand to wrist, snap fingers.)

2. "Can you make a sound with your mouth?" (Encourage children to tap teeth, pop lips, tap cheeks, click tongue.)

3. "Can you make sounds with your feet?" (Encourage children to tap feet together, stamp on floor.)

4. Ask children if they can make sounds with other parts of their bodies.

More to do
Have children choose a partner and discover ways they can make body sounds together.

★ Margery A. Kranyik, Hyde Park, MA

Body Tracing . . . . .3+

Materials needed
Roll of newsprint
Marker
Scissors
Multicultural crayons or paint
Pencil

What to do
1. During circle time demonstrate tracing around an object to show its shape and size. Tell the children that you will trace around them to show their shape and size. Talk about the children's similarities and differences. Approach children individually throughout the day to trace their bodies.

2. Ask a child if he is ready to be traced. Let him watch someone else if he is not ready.

3. Ask a child who is ready to lie down on the newsprint. Trace the outline of his whole body. Allow children to put arms any way they like on the paper.

4. After tracing, ask the children to color or paint their body shapes with multicultural paint or crayons. Cut out the body shapes and display in the room.

More to do
Math: After several months draw body tracings again and display each child's two tracings, side by side. Ask the children to compare the tracings.

★ Terri B. Garrou, Lenoir, NC

Follow the Footprints . . . . .3+

Materials needed

Footprint pattern
Scissors

Black construction paper
Clear self-adhesive paper

What to do

1. Cut out footprints from black construction paper.

2. Cover with self-adhesive paper if desired.

3. During circle time show the footprints to the children.

4. Arrange footprints on the floor in various patterns.

5. Have the children follow the patterns.

More to do

Large motor: Ask the children to walk on only the right footprints or the left footprints. Ask the children to walk on the footprints pretending to be various animals. Change the footprints to look like those of various animals and proceed as above. Play different types of music as the children move.

★ Cindy Maloof, South Easton, MA

The Handprints Are on the Wall . . . . . .3+

Materials needed

Poster board
Paper plates
Tempera paint in 3 colors

What to do

1. Mount poster board vertically on the wall. Draw a line down the middle. Write the date and year at the top.

2. Put small amounts of three colors of paint into separate paper plates.

3. At circle time help each child carefully press her hands into one color of paint.

4. Guide her hands to the left side of the poster board and press firmly. Save the right side of the poster board to repeat the activity at the end of the year to see how hands have changed. Write child's name by the handprints.

5. If possible, put a group picture of the children somewhere on the poster board.

6. Collect handprints of each class over the years. Children may have the opportunity to compare their hand sizes several years later.

Related book

The Little Painter of Sabana Grande by Patricia Maloney Markun

★ Cathy Chenoweth, Columbia, MO

Cleversticks  .4+

Materials needed
Cleversticks by Bernard Ashley
Chopsticks
Classroom items

What to do
1. Read *Cleversticks* during circle time.

2. Divide the group of children in half and challenge the children to try and pick up different items with chopsticks.

3. Encourage the children to work together in pairs to try and pick up blocks with each child holding one of the chopsticks.

Note: Give Cleverstick Awards to each child for something she does well.

More to do
Art: Paint on paper at the easel with chopsticks.

Language: Read *How My Parents Learned To Eat* by Ina R. Friedman.

Snack: Try eating food with chopsticks. Talk about different ways to eat food.

★ Ann Scalley, Wellfleet, MA

The BIGGEST Paperdoll ....4+

Materials needed
Roll of newsprint, cut into 4' lengths, 2 per child
Crayons
Scissors
Tape or stapler
Lots of old newspapers

What to do
1. Children take turns lying on the pieces of newsprint to have their bodies traced (if you trace children with their legs together and their arms by their sides, Step 6 will be much easier). Talk to the children about paperdolls. "Do any of you have paperdolls? How big are they? What kind of clothes do they wear?"

2. Ask the children to draw clothes on their body tracings. Tell them to use the same colors as the clothes they are wearing and also draw in their facial features.

3. Lay each child's tracing on the second sheet of paper that is the same size.

4. Staple the sheets together in several places inside the line of the body tracing to hold the sheets together.

5. Help each child to carefully cut out his paperdoll, cutting through both papers.

6. Tape the sheets together along the edge, leaving a large opening at the torso.

7. Wad up newspaper and stuff into the body shape giving the paperdoll dimension.

8. Tape the torso shut.

9. Bring the paperdolls to circle time to dance the "Hokey Pokey."

★ Cathy Chenoweth, Columbia, MO

The Heart Machine . . . . .5+

Materials needed
None needed

What to do
1. Tell the children about Dr. Daniel Hale Williams who was the first doctor to perform heart surgery and save a man's life. Read the poem and book listed.

> Dr. Dan, Dr. Dan, a famous black man,
> Dr. Dan, Dr. Dan, he once was a barber who cut people's hair.
> He did it with ease and care.
> Dr. Dan, Dr. Dan, a famous black man,
> Dr. Dan, Dr. Dan traded in his barber tools to work his way through medical school.
> Dr. Dan, Dr. Dan, a famous black man,
> In 1891 a hospital he helped start.
> Dr. Dan, Dr. Dan operated first in 1893.
> Thank you, Dr. Dan, for helping you and me.
> Dr. Daniel Hale Williams is his name.
> A successful heart operation is his fame.
>
>
> Dr. Dan, Dr. Dan, an African American,
> Born in 1856 one of seven children.
> Dr. Dan, Dr. Dan was a barber man.
> And worked his way through medical school
> To become a black surgeon.
>
>
> Dr. Dan, Dr. Dan, the man loved medicine.
> In 1891 he help start the Provident Hospital.
> That's where he operated on the man's heart.
> Dr. Dan, Dr. Dan did the first successful heart operation in 1893.
> Thanks to Dr. Dan for helping you and me.

2. Talk about the function of the heart. Ask each child to put her hand over her heart and feel it beating. To speed up the heart, run in place or do jumping jacks. Feel how fast the heart is beating now. Do a cool down activity. Discuss the difference in the heart beat.

Related book
Daniel Hale Williams: Surgeon by Flossie E. Thompson-Peters

★ Patricia Murchison, Chesapeake, VA

Mobility Impaired . . . . .5+

Materials needed

Magazine and catalog pictures of various mobility aids
Magazine pictures of activities children like to do
Large chart paper
Marker

What to do

1. Introduce the words "mobility impaired." Explain to the class that some people's bodies and body parts need help to stand, walk or move from one place to another, or just to move parts of their bodies.

2. Show the children pictures of various mobility aids (crutches, braces, walkers, canes, wheel chairs) and discuss how these mobility aids help people move.

3. Emphasize that differently-abled people do many of the same things the children do, for example, eat, sleep, play basketball, ride a bus.

More to do

Art: Paint a picture without using hands. Encourage the children to think of ways to hold a paintbrush using other body parts such as teeth, elbows or toes.

Large motor: Ask the children which part of their body they would like to pretend is mobility impaired. To restrict the child's movement, place splints on either side of the body part and secure with athletic tape.

Related books

Friends in the Park by Rochelle Bunnett
We Can Do It! by Laura Dwight
Why Am I Different? by Norma Simon

★ Debi Behr, Diana Reed, New Castle, PA

Footwear Rubbings . . . . .3+

Materials needed
Blank paper
Crayons

What to do
1. At circle time ask the children to look at the soles of their shoes and talk about the variety of sole designs.

2. Explain that you will do a rubbing of the sole of each child's shoe to see what design will appear.

3. The first child holds one foot so that you can place a sheet of paper over the sole of his shoe. Rub with a crayon that the child chooses. Older children can do their own rubbings.

4. Show the children the resulting design, soliciting their comments about shapes, numbers or textures they see and recognize.

5. Label the rubbing with the child's name and information such as left or right shoe, boot or tennis shoe.

6. Continue until all the children have had a turn.

7. Rubbings may be assembled in a book, sent home or posted on a bulletin board at the children's eye level.

More to do
Art: Make prints by pressing the shoe onto an ink pad and then onto blank paper. Discuss with the children how these prints differ from the crayon rubbings.

Math: Mount the rubbings on heavy paper. Allow children to arrange them according to increasing or decreasing sizes or sort them into piles of same sizes.

Outdoors: Take rubbings outdoors and see if children can match them to impressions made by their shoes in the sand.

Science: Compare treads on boots versus shoes or slippers. Ask why boots might have more pronounced treads. Compare treads on old versus new shoes. Ask why old soles are often smoother. Check auto tires for treads and try to include snow tires. Examine footwear suited to varying weather conditions. Note similarities and differences and discuss reasons for these.

★ E. L. Nadler, Jerusalem, Israel

The Dressing Song ....3+

Materials needed
None needed

What to do
1. Chant "The Dressing Song" and act out pantomime as suggested by the words.

"The Dressing Song"

*My snowpants on my legs I put
Then one boot upon each foot.
Then my arms go in my sleeves
Zip me up, would you please?*

*My hat upon my head I"ll place
Then my scarf around my face.
My mittens on my hands will go
Now I can play in the snow.*

More to do
Art: Let children find pictures of snow activities and people dressed for outdoors.

Dramatic play: Place snowsuits and outdoor clothing in dress-up area. Add dress-up outdoor clothes for dolls.

Language: Make a dressing puppet in which clothes are added as the song is sung. Write a story about the puppet and the clothing.

Large motor: Take the children outside and let them play in the snow, observe snow under a magnifying glass, paint on snow.

Math: Make a flannel graph boy and girl. Allow each child to place an article of clothing on the flannel child as that article appears in the song.

Water table: Bring in snow from outside. Along with a discussion about snow, talk about why we don't need boots and snow pants to play with snow inside. Be sure children wear mittens.

Writing: Give each child a "blank book," several pieces of white paper stapled together. Let them draw pictures of things they like to do in the snow and ask them to dictate stories about their pictures to you.

Related books
The Big Snow by Elmer and Berta Hader
Look! Snow! by Kathryn O. Galbraith
The Snowman by Raymond Briggs
The Snowy Day by Ezra Jack Keats
White Snow, Bright Snow by Alvin Tresselt

★ Helen Buemi, Binghamton, NY

What Should We Wear? ....3+

Materials needed
4 boxes or crates
Various clothing for different seasons
Colored construction paper

What to do
1. Decorate each crate seasonally—a beach scene for summer, leaves or pumpkin for fall, snowflakes for winter and flowers for spring.

2. Discuss the proper clothing for different weather situations. Ask the children if they would wear a bathing suit to go sleigh riding or a jacket to the beach.

3. Distribute the clothing—have enough for each child to take a turn.

4. Take turns placing the clothing in the appropriate season's crate.

5. Ask the rest of the children if they agree.

6. Ask if there could be another answer and discuss all answers given.

Related books
First Comes Spring by Anne Rockwell
The Jacket I Wear in the Snow by Shirley Neitzel

★ Teresa J. Nos, Baltimore, MD

Bibs and Bonnets ....4+

Materials needed
Bibs and bonnets (baby hats) in a variety of sizes

What to do
1. Arrange a number of bibs or bonnets in the middle of the circle.

2. Ask the children to help you seriate the bibs or bonnets according to their size.

3. Add an additional bib or bonnet when the children are ready for working with a larger number of items.

4. Seriate other baby items that you have collected.

More to do
Dramatic play: Use the bibs or bonnets as props with the dolls. Other baby clothes and blankets can be added.

Language: Ask each child to dictate a baby story to you. The stories can be bound in a book and read to the class.

Math: Children can experiment with rattles. Ask the children to seriate the rattles by size.

Visitor: Ask a parent or grandparent to bring a baby dressed in a bonnet and bib to class. Discuss the reasons for wearing these items.

★ Jean Lortz, Seattle, WA

What Did You Wear Today? ....4+

Materials needed

Set of blocks (all the same size and shape)
Marker

2 sheets of chart paper or tagboard
Basket or bucket

What to do

1. Ahead of time, gather enough blocks so that each child in the group may have four or five blocks. Place blocks in the basket or bucket. Have chart paper and marker available.

2. Introduce the activity by asking the children to name different kinds of clothing. Record their responses by making a list on the first sheet of paper. Position the paper so that the children can watch as you write each word. Occasionally reread the list and encourage further responses.

3. Focus the children's attention on the items from the list that they actually wore today. "Did you wear a hat today?" "Who wore a sweatshirt today?"

4. Use the second piece of paper to create a chart: select five or six items from the children's list and write the names of those items as titles across the top of the chart. Put the chart on an easel ledge or against a cupboard so that blocks my be stacked in front of the chart to form columns under the titles.

5. Reading one title (item) at a time, invite the children who are wearing that item to take one block from the basket and place it under the word, forming a stack. Continue until there are stacks of blocks under each of the titles, although the stacks will be of varying heights.

6. Comment on the number of blocks in each stack. Which stack is the highest? What does that mean? Help the children understand that the stacks show which items of clothing are being worn by the most children. Which stack is the shortest? Are any stacks the same?

7. Count the number of blocks in each stack and record that number under the appropriate title.

8. Leave the chart and blocks in an area that is available to the children during play time, so that they can repeat the activity, independently stacking and counting the blocks to match the numbers written in each category.

9. If desired, repeat this activity daily as a check on which items of clothing are worn by the most people. The charted items may be changed daily, if desired.

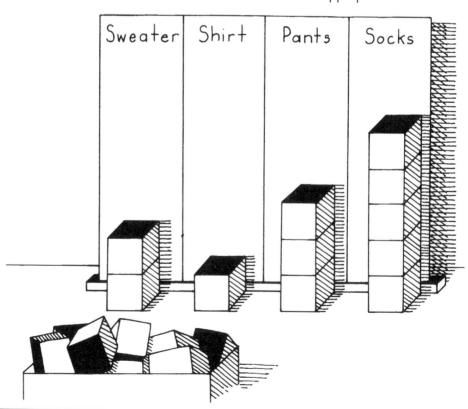

Sweater | Shirt | Pants | Socks

More to do

This math activity introduces children to the concept of graphing and reinforces their understanding of one-to-one representation. Many adaptations are possible. This activity may be used at the end of play time to survey the children's choices of activities that day. How many children painted at the easel today? Who worked at the puzzle table this morning? Who used the slide? Enhance nutrition lessons by using this activity to survey children's breakfast menus, favorite snack or meal choices. Favorite colors may be graphed in the same way. Pictures or simple drawings may be used as titles for each category to reinforce the written words.

Related books

Bear Gets Dressed by Harriet Ziefert
Charlie Needs a Cloak by Tomie dePaola
Jesse Bear, What Will Your Wear? by Nancy White Carlstrom
Max's New Suit by Rosemary Wells
You'll Soon Grow Into Them, Titch by Pat Hutchins

★ Karen Wojahn, Windom, MN

Grab Your Hat . . . . .4+

Materials needed

Hats, all varieties, all sizes—chef's hat, ski hat, baseball cap, infant bonnet, football helmet, swimming cap, police officer's hat
Covered box or basket
Hand-held mirrors

What to do

1. Place a variety of hats in a covered box or basket, in the center of the circle.

2. Invite children to predict what's inside the box by guessing the answers to riddles.

   ✓ It's something you can wear.
   ✓ You wear it on one part of your body—not your hands, not your feet, not your chest.
   ✓ Sometimes people wear one that's part of the uniform they wear for their job (for sports).

3. Confirm the children's predictions and introduce the activity.

   ✓ Here's a hat someone might wear as part of the uniform they wear for their job.
   (Take an appropriate hat from the box.) Repeat with various types of hats.

4. Encourage each child to think of a hat she has worn. Invite children to describe their hats.

5. Explain that we will be hat detectives (talk about what a detective does) by investigating hats. Invite each child to select a hat from the box, try it on, look at it in the mirror and think about all the things she can tell about the hat (color, size, association with sports or occupation).

More to do

Art: Create hats by decorating a paper plate with a wide variety of objects (feathers, ribbon, seashells, leaves, colored paper). Use string to tie hats on and have a hat parade. Repeat the writing extension with hats the children have created. Repeat various sorting activities with hats the children have created. (You may want to share the book *Jennie's Hat* when you make hats.)

Dramatic play: Read *Caps for Sale* and invite children to play the parts of the peddler and monkeys.

Math: Sorting—use yarn to divide the circle into two parts. Explain that one half of the circle is for hats that are "job" hats and the other for hats that are not for "jobs." After hats are sorted ask children to name the job associated with the hats. Seriation—arrange hats from smallest to largest. Counting—after counting the number of hats, invite the children to study their hats and see if there is anything on the hat they can count.

Music: Sing the song, "My Hat It Has Three Corners." Adapt the song "Mary Wore Her Red Dress" to "Mary Is Wearing a _____ Hat" and sing the song about hats the children have selected from the collection or brought from home.

Writing: Display three hats. Place a strip of two-sided masking tape vertically under each hat. Identify words describing each hat. Print each word on a card and attach each card to the strip below the appropriate hat.

Related books

A Three Hat Day by Laura Geringer
Hats, Hats, Hats by Ann Morris
Ho for a Hat by William J. Smith
Martin's Hats by Joan W. Blos

★ Sue Jorgensen, Casper, WY

Build a Rainbow . . . . .3+

Materials needed
Sheets of construction paper (various colors)

What to do
1. Ask the children to sit in a circle and give each child a sheet of construction paper.

2. Select one child to be the Rainbow Builder.

3. As children hold up their colored sheets of paper everyone sings "The Rainbow Needs a Red" to the tune of "The Farmer in the Dell."

4. The Rainbow Builder taps the child (or children) who holds a red paper on the shoulder. This child (children) now goes to the inside of the circle.

More to do
Use this activity with shapes, numbers and letters.

★ Ingelore Mix, Massapequa, NY

Color Caterpillar . . . . .3+

Materials needed
Cardboard egg carton (cut in half lengthwise making a strip of 6 cups)
Construction paper scraps of 6 different colors (red, yellow, blue, green, purple and black)
1 pipe cleaner
Black marker or crayon
Glue
Piece of yarn (12"-16" long)

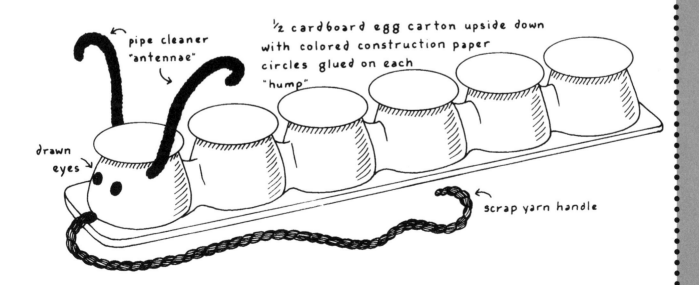

pipe cleaner "antennae"

½ cardboard egg carton upside down with colored construction paper circles glued on each "hump"

drawn eyes

scrap yarn handle

What to do

1. Children cut out one circle from each colored sheet of the construction paper. The circles can be drawn on the paper to make it easier for younger children.

2. Children glue one circle on each hump of the upside-down egg carton strip.

3. Children bend the pipe cleaner in half and insert it to make the antennae in the first egg cup.

4. Children draw eyes on the first egg cup.

5. Children push a piece of yarn through the hole (made by the teacher) in the front of the first egg cup. The yarn is knotted and it makes a pulling handle.

More to do

Language: Talk about the different colors used.

Large motor: Take your caterpillar for a walk. The caterpillars are also fun to run with outside.

Science: Use the different circles of color to match colors of things in your room. For example, "The first color on Ben's caterpillar is yellow. Who sees something yellow?"

★ Margaret Howard, Northglenn, CO

White Bunny, White Bunny . . . . .3+

Materials needed
Felt board
Felt silhouettes of items (bunny, carrot, sun, cloud, raindrop and flower, cut from the specific color of felt noted in the poem—white, orange, yellow, gray, blue, pink)

What to do

1. The children sit in a semicircle around the felt board.

2. Say the poem, "White Bunny, White Bunny" placing objects on the felt board.

> White bunny, white bunny,
> What do you see?
> I see an orange carrot
> Waiting for me.
>
> Orange carrot, orange carrot
> What do you see?
> I see yellow sun
> Shining on me.
>
> Yellow sun, yellow sun,
> What do you see?
> I see a gray cloud
> Moving toward me.

Gray cloud, gray cloud,
What do you see?
I see a little blue raindrop
Falling from me.

Blue raindrop, blue raindrop,
What do you see?
I see pink flowers
Growing, because of me.

Pink flower, pink flower,
What do you see?
I see lots of white bunnies
Hopping around me.

More to do

The poem could be used as an action rhyme—hopping for the rabbit, standing straight and tall for the carrot, arms raised above head for the sun, arms lowered and child bent over for the cloud, fingers trickling down for the rain, squatting and opening up arms for the flower, hopping around for the bunnies.

★ Sara J. Hittle, Wichita, KS

Color Dance . . . . .3+

Materials needed

Music of all types
Squares of colored construction paper (cover with clear self-adhesive paper)

What to do

1. Lay squares on the floor in any order.

2. Each child stands on a square.

3. Play music.

4. Children move from square to square as the music plays.

5. Stop music.

6. Children say the color of the square on which they are standing.

7. Repeat.

More to do

Large motor: The children decide how they will move from square to square (backwards, sideways, hopping, crawling, holding hands, slow, fast).

Music: The children will sing songs instead of listening to music as they move.

★ Cynthia A. Maloof, South Easton, MA

Color Magic ....3+

Materials needed

Plastic or glass cups
Food coloring (red, yellow, blue, green)
Water
Spoons to mix colors

What to do

1. Read a book about colors.

2. Say, "Let's see what colors you are wearing today."

3. Sing, "Red stand up, red stand up, red sit down, blue stand up..." Give all children a chance to participate.

4. Say, "We're going to see what happens when we mix colors."

5. Let children take turns mixing the food coloring in the water.

6. Ask children what they think will happen if you mix red and yellow, yellow and blue (or any two colors).

7. Mix the two colors that you ask the children about immediately after discussing their predictions, such as mixing red and yellow, blue and yellow.

More to do

Art: Fingerpaint with primary colors. Make colored playdough. What happens when you mix red and yellow or yellow and blue playdough? Celebrate a specific color by asking the children to wear clothes of a specific color during that week. Friday can be Multicolored Day.

Related books

Growing Colors by Bruce McMillan
Is It Red? Is It Yellow? Is It Blue? by Tana Hoban
Red, Yellow, Blue Shoe by Tana Hoban

★ Sharon Milner, Carrollton, GA

Color Our World ....3+

Materials needed

Pieces of cardboard
Stapler
Colored cellophane

What to do

1. Make cellophane viewers.

2. Cut two rings of cardboard (about 6" in diameter).

3. Put cellophane between the cardboard rings and staple.

4. At circle time give the viewers to the children. Ask them to describe one thing in the room that looks different when they look at it through the viewer.

More to do

Science: Combine two viewers to get a third color.

Related books

Blue Bug's Book of Colors by Virginia Poulet
Green Bear by Alan Rogers
Harold and the Purple Crayon by Crockett Johnson
Is It Red? Is It Yellow? Is It Blue? by Tana Hoban
Red Rhino by Alan Rogers

★ Sandy Scott, Vancouver, WA

Color Shade Match . . . . .3+

Materials needed

Paint strip samples, 2 of each color from paint stores (with older children use subtle shade differences to make the game more challenging)
Clothespins (wooden spring type)
Poster board
White glue
Scissors

What to do

1. Glue one paint strip onto a poster board. Let dry and trim around the strip. With the matching strip, cut each individual shade piece apart. Glue the individual shades on the flat, closed end of the clothespins. Dry thoroughly. Repeat for each set of color strips used.

2. At circle time discuss cooperation and working with a partner.

3. Children choose partners. Give each pair a full paint strip and a set of matching clothespins.

4. Children work together to clip the color pieces glued to the clothespins to the matching color on the paint strip.

More to do

Fine motor: Give each of the children a spring clothespin. Let them experiment by trying to pick up toys and other materials in the room. They will try to pick up chairs, dolls. Discuss why some objects cannot be picked up by the clothespins, (too heavy, no edge). Hand a clothesline inside or outside and hang children's clothes and doll clothes, using different types and sizes of clothespins.

Original song

"Clothespin Song" (Tune: "Sailing, Sailing")

Pinching, pinching
We're pinching our clothespins it's true.
Pinching, pinching,
Why don't you do it too?

★ Yvonne Thompson, Ashtabula, OH

Discovering Green . . . . .3+

Materials needed

Yellow and blue tempera paint
Clear plastic container with lid
Yellow and blue cellophane (or colored plastic wrap) shapes
9" x 12" white construction paper
Glue
Green construction paper
Markers

What to do

1. As the children are seated for circle time, pour some yellow and then blue tempera paint into a clear plastic container. Secure the container with a lid.

2. Pass the container around the group and have each child shake it, observing what happens to the color.

3. Discuss what happened to the yellow and blue paint.

4. Give each child a piece of white construction paper and ask them to glue yellow and blue cellophane shapes to the paper, making sure they overlap some of the shapes.

5. Mount the cellophane pictures on green construction paper and display.

6. Using the appropriate colored markers, label the display Yellow + Blue = Green.

More to do

Art: Place yellow and blue tempera paint at the easel for painting. Using small plastic containers, have the children mix yellow and blue paint to achieve different shades of green. Collect green items found in the classroom.

Related books

Colors by Tana Hoban
Little Blue and Little Yellow by Leo Lionni
Red Day, Green Day by Edith Kunhardt

★ Sandi Fisher, Kutztown, PA

Experimenting With Color . . . . .3+

Materials needed

Little Blue and Little Yellow by Leo Lionni
Glass bowl
Water
Blue and yellow food coloring
Transparent blue and yellow precut circles

What to do

1. Read *Little Blue and Little Yellow*.

2. Tell the children they are going to help you create a little magic. Fill a glass bowl with water.

3. Let a child squirt yellow food coloring in the bowl.

4. Let another child squirt blue food coloring in the bowl.

5. The colors will combine and make green.

6. Give the children blue and yellow transparent circles cut from report covers (found at office supply stores). Let the children experiment creating new colors.

More to do

Art: Put out bowls of yellow and blue fingerpaint and let the children explore.

Music: Place a variety of colored circles on the carpet. Put on lively music. Let the children march around the circles. When the music stops they can pick up a circle and name the color.

★ Cindy Winther, Oxford, MI

My Favorite Color Chart . . . . .3+

Materials needed

Poster board
Markers in basic colors

What to do

1. Talk to children about having a favorite color. Explain that favorite means the one you like best and that you like it because you think it is pretty or it makes you feel good.

2. One at a time, write each child's name on the poster board and have them indicate their favorite color. For children who know the names of colors, encourage them to say it. For younger children, ask them to point to the marker of the color they like. Next to each child's name, color a circle or happy face in the color they chose.

3. Display the chart in the classroom.

More to do

Art: Children make a favorite color collage, using crayons, markers, paint, pipe cleaners and other materials that are the color they chose.

Home connection: Send a note home to parents asking them to dress their child the next day in his favorite color.

Math: Make available different colored objects so that children can categorize favorite color and nonfavorite color items. Provide several objects that are a child's favorite color. Ask the child to close his eyes. Remove one of the objects and ask the child which object is missing.

Related book

The Blue Balloon by Mike Inkpen

★ Suzanne Pearson, Winchester, VA

Our Class and Crayons ....3+

Materials needed
Harold and the Purple Crayon by Crockett Johnson
Large pieces of white construction paper, 18" x 24" (1 per child)
Crayons
Hole punch
3 small pieces of yarn
Clear self-adhesive paper or laminating film
Background music, classical

What to do
1. Read *Harold and the Purple Crayon*.

2. Children select one crayon from a wide selection of crayons.

3. Give each child one piece of white paper.

4. Write the child's name and the crayon color name on top of the white paper.

5. Children find a quiet place to draw just like Harold did.

6. Put on classical music for the children to listen to while drawing.

7. Collect completed works to make a class book.

8. Write "Our Class and Crayons" on a large piece of paper to make a book cover.

9. Cover the pages with clear self-adhesive paper or laminate.

10. Punch three holes on the left margin of each page.

11. Tie the pages together at the holes with yarn.

12. Bring the book to story time and read it to the class.

13. Each night allow one child to take the book home to share with her family. Attach a letter describing how this book was created and encourage parents to enjoy the book with their child, remembering to return it the next day.

More to do
Make this book accessible to the children in a quiet area throughout the day.

★ Anne Lippincott, New Hartford, CT

Paint in a Bag ....3+

Materials needed
Quart-size resealable plastic bags (1 per child)
Permanent marker
Nontoxic liquid tempera paint (various colors)
Flat, clean surface

What to do

1. Write each child's name on a bag with a permanent marker.

2. Ask a child to choose the colors to put into her bag.

3. Allow the child to zip the bag closed (check that the seal is good).

4. Place the bags on a flat, clean surface where the children can squeeze, squish, squash and mix the paint by manipulating the bags.

5. At circle time ask each child to describe the colors in her bag.

More to do

Art: Mix liquid tempera with liquid dish detergent. You'll extend the paint and it will wash out of clothes more easily.

★ Dani B. Rosensteel, Payson, AZ

Pick Up the Garbage . . . . .3+

Materials needed

6 small plastic garbage pails with lids (red, yellow, blue, white, green and orange—6-inch plastic pails are usually found in the houseware area of stores)
Small toys, paper, yarn, matching the colors of the garbage cans. (at least 10 items for each can)

What to do

1. At circle time the teacher presents each can and asks, "What color is this garbage can?"

2. The teacher then dumps the garbage (items) in the middle of the circle and asks, "What color is the garbage?"

3. Repeat until all of the garbage cans are emptied.

4. Choose one child to stir the garbage until it is well mixed.

5. The teacher exclaims, "What a mess. Somebody call the garbage collector." Sing the following song, "The Garbage Collector," to the tune of "Brother John."

> *Where is the garbage collector?*
> *Where is the garbage collector?*
> *We need you.*
> *We need you.*
> *There is a big mess here,*
> *What are we to do, dear?*
> *Please come soon.*
> *Please come soon.*

6. The teacher then chooses a garbage collector. The garbage collector goes to the pile, picks up some garbage and puts it in the matching color garbage can.

7. Repeat until each child gets a turn to be the garbage collector and all the garbage is picked up.

More to do

Use the garbage cans for sorting a variety of manipulatives according to color. Old crayons may also be used for sorting by color.

★ Deborah A. Cole, Madison, OH

Rainbows . . . . .3+

Materials needed

Record or tape cassette, "Color Me a Rainbow" by Melody House (play the "Come and Make a Rainbow" song)
Strips of crepe paper in different colors
Toilet paper rolls
Colored markers
Tape

What to do

1. Decorate toilet paper rolls with colored markers.

2. Cut strips of colored crepe paper. Attach to the toilet paper rolls.

3. Teach the children the song: "Come and Make a Rainbow."

4. Move the rainbows to the actions in the song.

More to do

Art: Make rainbows using paint or colored glue on construction paper.

Cooking: Make rainbow gelatin.

Science: Make rainbow playdough. Observe rainbows outside. Look at prisms.

Related book

Planting a Rainbow by Lois Ehlert

Related song

"The World Is a Rainbow" on *We All Live Together, Volume 2* by Greg and Steve

★ Laethe J. Lewandowski, Centreville, VA

The Color Game . . . . .3+

Materials needed

Flannel board (or a large piece of cardboard, poster board or construction paper for background)
Felt in a variety of colors (red, yellow, blue, green, orange, purple)

What to do

1. Ahead of time, cut one large (2" x 2") square and four small (1" x 1") squares out of each color of felt.

2. At circle time tell the children you need their help to find all the red squares.

3. Place the large red square on the background board for all to see, explaining that it is red and ask if the small red squares will match. (If you use something other than a flannel board for a background you will need to stick the felt pieces on with tape.)

4. One by one, place a small square on the background. Ask the children, "What color is this?"

5. Continue the game finding all the red squares. Depending on the interest level of the children find all the yellow squares, blue squares, etc.

More to do

Search for toys of a certain color in the room. When cleaning up toys, separate them by color. Have a color basket and change the color each week. During red week encourage the children to find something red to put in the basket, either in the classroom or from home.

Art: Cut squares from construction paper and let the children create collages or pictures by gluing them to another paper.

Related book

Red, Blue, Yellow Shoe by Tana Hoban

Related poems

"Baa, Baa, Black Sheep"
"Little Boy Blue"
"Little White Duck"
"Mary Wore Her Red Dress"

★ Susan Rinas, Parma, OH

Who Is Wearing Red Today? . . . . .3+

Materials needed

None needed

What to do

1. While children are sitting at circle time, sing the following song to the tune of "Mary Had a Little Lamb."

> *Who is wearing red today,*
> *Red today, red today?*
> *Who is wearing red today?*
> *Please stand up.*

2. Ask the children (one child at a time) to show you where they are wearing the color you asked for.

3. Change the color each time you sing the song, making sure each child gets a turn.

More to do

Game: Play "I Spy" and have the children look around the room for specific colors.

Music: During music time, play Hap Palmer's recording of "What Are You Wearing?" and "Colors."

Related books

Red Bear by Bodel Rikys
Tana Hoban's Red, Blue, Yellow Shoe by Tana Hoban

★ Denise Covert, Perris, CA

Yellow, Blue and Green . . . . .4+

Materials needed

Hula hoop or string
Items or pictures that are yellow, blue and green
Blue, yellow, green and white construction paper
Scissors
3 popsicle sticks
Glue or tape

What to do

1. Encourage children to join the circle by singing each child's name as they sit down quietly. ("Tarik is sitting down, Bethany is sitting down, Jose and Adam are all sitting down." The tune is "The Farmer in the Dell.")

2. Using a hula hoop or string, place various things inside the circle that are yellow, blue or green. Be sure to have one item for each child plus one item for you. Now ask the children to select one item from the circle. The children can say the name and color of their item. Use an item as an example. "I have a blue horse, what do you have?" You may need to repeat the above statement for each child if the group is very young. With older children you might extend the game by asking them to repeat what each person ahead of them said and then state what they selected.

3. Using construction paper circles glued to popsicle sticks, tell the children that when you hold up the yellow circle they are to clap their hands. When you hold up the blue circle they are to stand up and when you hold up the green circle they are to sit down. Start out slowly and gradually increase the speed. To calm the children, reduce the speed and end the game hold up the green circle (they are to sit down).

More to do

Art: Put a small amount of blue paint in one hand and a small amount of yellow paint in the other hand. Children rub their hands together and make the color green. Provide white construction paper to make handprints on the paper. Take a Colors Walk around the school. Ask the children to point out things that are yellow, blue or green. From your scrap paper box, take yellow, blue and green paper. Children can cut (if age appropriate), tear and paste scraps onto a paper plate.

Related book

Little Blue and Little Yellow by Leo Lionni

★ Diana Thomas, West Hills, CA

Let's Make Colors . . . . .4+

Materials needed
Little Blue and Little Yellow by Leo Lionni
White paper (1 sheet per child)
Plastic wrap or cellophane cut into 3" squares (various colors)
White glue

What to do
1. Read *Little Blue and Little Yellow* by Leo Lionni.

2. Place a piece of blue cellophane on top of a piece of yellow cellophane. Ask the children what color they see. Discuss that blue and yellow make the color green.

3. Give each child a sheet of white paper and ask him to glue the blue and yellow cellophane on the paper overlapping the pieces. The cellophane tends to stick together but this just intensifies the colors.

More to do
Art: By using different colors of cellophane the children will discover what different colors they can make by gluing the cellophane on their paper.

Related books
Colors Everywhere by Tana Hoban
Mouse Paint by Ellen Stoll Walsh

★ Diane Angus, Kittery Point, ME

Color Recognition . . . . .4+

Materials needed
Construction paper squares (various colors)

What to do
1. At circle time give each child one square of construction paper.

2. Ask the children to stand and take two steps backwards to provide them with extra space.

3. Explain to the children that they will be playing a game about colors. They will need to listen carefully. Tell the children that you will call out a color and then give directions for them to follow. The children should only follow the directions if they are holding the color you called.

4. Begin each direction with "If you are holding the color _____" (and tell them to do a specific movement) for example, run in place, jump up and down, touch your toes, spin around, walk to the door, touch it and walk back, touch your paper to your nose, walk around the circle and return to your place. Continue until every color has been called at least once.

5. Conclude by asking children to look around the classroom and find an object that is the same color as their square. Then ask them to put their square on the object and then return to the circle.

6. At another time play this game and conclude by letting the children find a partner who has a matching color (if there is an odd number of children, have three of the same color). Tell the children that they are now a detective team and can move about the classroom finding objects that are the same color as their square. They do not have to move the objects, but they can point and name the objects or count them.

★ Connie Heagerty, Trumbull, CT

Marble Paint . . . . .4+

Materials needed
Red and yellow tempera paint
White construction paper (9″ x 12″)
Bottom part of cardboard box that holds a case of soda (1 per child)
Marbles

What to do
1. Discuss the procedure for marble painting. The marble remains in the box. Move the box back and forth very slowly. Leave the paper in the box.

2. Give each child one box.

3. Give each child one piece of paper.

4. Put one tablespoon of paint of each color in each child's box.

5. Give each child a marble.

6. Let the children roll their marbles back and forth.

7. Ask the children to describe the color they are making.

8. Leave the paper in the box to dry.

9. Write each child's name on the paper.

10. Clean up the project with the children's help.

More to do
Talk about the colors the children made. Recall that they started out with red and yellow paint. Ask them what they observed about the two colors.

★ Cindy L. Knutson, Vermillion, SD

Pompom Pickup . . . . .4+

Materials needed
Assorted sizes and colors of craft pompoms
Assorted tongs (meatball tongs, metal spring tongs, canning tongs, strawberry huller, tweezers)
Berry baskets (1 per child)
Plastic shoebox (to store tongs)
Coffee can with lid (to store pompoms)

What to do

1. Children choose the type of tong they want to use.

2. Give each child a berry basket.

3. Put pompoms on the floor or on a table.

4. Have children pick up some of the pompoms with tongs (singing "Pompom Song" to the tune of "Paw Paw Patch") and put them in their basket.

> *Picking up pompoms put them in my basket.*
> *PIcking up pompoms put them in my basket.*
> *Picking up pompoms put them in my basket.*
> *This is a lot of fun.*

5. When children have picked up all the pompoms, have them count how many they have and separate the pompoms by colors.

6. Ask the children to trade tongs and repeat the game to experience using different types of tongs.

7. Discuss which tongs were the easiest to use and which were the most difficult.

More to do

Fine motor: Place different colored construction paper on the table or floor. Ask children to carry their pompoms to the matching colored paper.

Science: Try picking up other toys and materials using tongs. Children will learn that some items such as a chair are too heavy to pick up. This can lead to discussion about heavy and light.

★ Yvonne Thompson, Ashtabula, OH

Color Rhymes . . . . .4+

Materials needed

Collection of poems about cats
Color chart

What to do

1. At circle time read one of the poems listed below to the children.

2. Talk about making up poems about cats with the children. Help the children think of rhymes to connect a cat with a color. For example:

> *My cat is black. His name is Jack.*
> *My cat is yellow. He's a friendly fellow.*

More to do

Art: Collect cat pictures and talk about the different colors of cats.

Home connection: Have a Pet Day when children bring photos of pets for circle time sharing.

Language: Make a language experience chart of the rhymes the children create.

Storytelling: Use the rhymes to encourage storytelling about each special cat.

Poems to use with the activity

"Cat" by Dorothy Baruch
"A Kitten" by Eleanor Farjeon
"The Owl and the Pussy Cat" by Edward Lear
"The Mysterious Cat" by Vachel Lindsay
"Cat" by Mary Britton Miller
"In Honour of Taffy Lopez" by Christopher Morley
"Tiger-Cat Tim" by Edith Newlin
"I Love a Little Pussy" by Jane Taylor

★ Barbara Hershberger, Watertown, WI

Flying Beach Umbrellas . . . . .5+

Materials needed

Small white paper plates
Large plastic drinking straws
Scissors
Markers (red, yellow and blue)
Tape

What to do

1. In advance, section the bottom-side of each plate into eight equal wedges. Mark each wedge with a color, alternating between two primary colors to help children keep their place when coloring the wedges.

2. Give each child a marked plate and two different primary color markers. Explain how they are to use one color on the marked sections and the other on the unmarked sections.

3. Cut downward on one end of a straw 1 1/2". Give the straw a half turn and make a similar cut, now separating the two parts into four. When fanned out, the cut end should resemble an X.

4. Center and tape the straw X to the uncolored side of the plate.

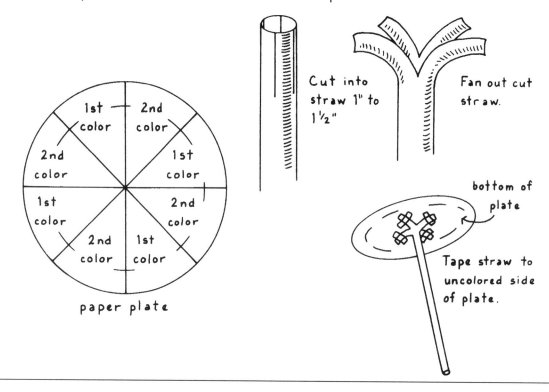

paper plate

Cut into straw 1" to 1½"

Fan out cut straw.

bottom of plate

Tape straw to uncolored side of plate.

5. Ask each child to bring his colored plate (umbrella top) to circle time. Ask each child to roll the straw between their palms. Depending on the primary colors on their plates, the children should see orange, green or purple. Ask the children to describe the new colors.

6. Show the children how to roll the straw quickly and let go as it is moving away from them. The beach umbrella should "fly" as it spins and displays its color blend.

More to do

Science: Color similar but smaller circles and slide them over the posts of plastic or wooden tops. Secondary colors are formed as they spin. Using colored transparency sheets or cellophane, have children look through one color first then two colors together.

★ Theresa Usilton, Easton, MD

Slide Field Trip . . . . .5+

Materials needed

Slides of different scenes in the neighborhood
Slide projector
Screen or blank wall

What to do

1. It is not always practical or convenient to take the class on a field trip. You can solve that problem by bringing the field trip to the classroom with slide pictures. Go around the community taking slide pictures of items of different colors (red flowers, green leaves, orange pumpkins, yellow school bus, black cat, white car).

2. Talk with the children about all the colors that are around us. Ask them to imagine the classroom if everything in it were the same color?

3. Show the slide field trip and ask the children to identify the colors they see.

More to do

Take slide pictures when you visit the doctor's or dentist's office, the grocery store, go on vacation, get your hair cut. Instead of looking for colors, as the children to look for numbers, shapes or modes of transportation.

Large motor: Go for a color-search walk in the neighborhood.

Related book

Little Blue and Little Yellow by Leo Lionni

★ Valerie Chellew, Marshfield, WI

Cooking Bread and Butter Song . . . . . .3+

Materials needed
None needed

What to do
This song is to be sung when making bread. I'm not sure which is more fun, making the bread or singing the song.

1. Sing the following song, "Bread and Butter Song," to the tune of "Frere Jacques" with the appropriate motions.

> *Mix the flour, mix the flour, in the bowl, in the bowl.*
> *Mix it all together, mix it all together in the bowl, in the bowl. (pretend to mix flour in a bowl)*
>
> *Knead the bread, knead the bread, on the table, on the table.*
> *Knead it all together, knead it all together, on the table, on the table. (pretend to knead bread)*
>
> *Bake the bread, bake the bread, in the pan, in the pan. (hold pretend pan in*
> *   your hand)*
> *Put it in the oven, put it in the oven 'til it's done, 'til it's done. (pretend to put pan in the oven)*
>
> *Shake the butter, shake the butter, in the jar, in the jar.*
> *Shake it all together, shake it all together in the jar, in the jar. (pretend to shake jar)*
>
> *Bread and butter, bread and butter, here at school, here at school.*
> *Eat it all together, eat it all together, yum, yum, yum. (rub your tummy)*

★ Diann Spalding, Santa Rosa, CA

Ladybugs . . . . .3+

Materials needed
Individual plastic circular-shaped salad molds
Red gelatin, such as Jell-O® (2 or 3 packages)
Raisins
Licorice sticks
Large mixing bowl
Large spoon for mixing

What to do
1. Ask the children to stand around a table to make ladybug gelatin.

2. Mix the gelatin according to the directions on the package.

3. Pass the bowl around the table so each child participates in mixing.

4. Pour into individual plastic salad molds.

5. Each child adds raisins for ladybug spots to his mold.

6. Each child adds two pieces of a licorice stick for antennae or the licorice may be added later after the gelatin sets firmly.

More to do
Language: Correlate the activity with reading children's literature, such as *The Grouchy Ladybug* by Eric Carle.

★ Cindy Hewitt, Houston, TX

The Little Red Hen . . . . .3+

Materials needed
The Little Red Hen by Paul Galdone

What to do
1. Read *The Little Red Hen* at circle time.

2. Dramatize the story. Choose several children to be the main characters, hen, pig, duck. The remaining children will be the audience until it is their turn to be the actors.

3. Children love pretending to be the different animal characters repeating "Not I," or "I won't" to the little red hen and then having her answer, "Then I will."

More to do
Art: Cut out pictures of bread and make a bread collage. Make a pictograph. Each time a child eats a slice of bread, she pastes or draws a picture of bread on a graph next to her name. After a week see who ate the most bread, the least bread. Provide each child with a copy of the recipe in the book and ask them to draw pictures of the steps involved . The children can take their copy of the illustrated recipe home.

Cooking: Make mini loaves of bread with the children. Read the recipe for making bread with the children. To reduce the time required in mixing the dough, you may use frozen bread dough, bread mix. To make individual loaves use refrigerated rolls (using muffin tins is convenient). After the loaves are baked, serve with jam.

Related books
Bread and Jam for Frances by Russell Hoban
The Giant Jam Sandwich by John Vernon Lord
In the Night Kitchen by Maurice Sendak

★ Wendy Pfeffer, Pennington, NJ

Cooking

Making Butter . . . . .3+

Materials needed

1 cup whipping cream
Several ice cubes
Water
Salt
Quart jar with rubber gasket canning lid
Mixing bowl
Wooden spoon
Crackers

What to do

1. At circle time pour cream into a jar and screw the lid on tightly.

2. Demonstrate how to shake the jar with an up and down movement, holding it firmly with both hands while saying the following chant.

> *Come, butter, come. Churn, butter, churn.*
> *Shake it up and shake it up.*
> *And now it's (child's name) turn.*

Note: This chant ensures that each child has equal time in shaking the jar.

3. Ask each child to pass the jar to the child on her right and invite that child to shake it. The entire group chants as each child has a turn. Usually the butter will break—begin to separate into lumps—by the time each child has had a turn (if it is a large group).

4. Occasionally you may need to loosen the lid to let air escape, then screw it on again.

5. When the butter has formed, carefully pour off the buttermilk and partially fill the jar with water and a few ice cubes.

6. Shake the jar vigorously to wash the butter, then pour off the water and shake the butter into the mixing bowl.

7. Use the spoon to pat the butter into one ball. Drain off excess water.

8. Let the children take turns spreading butter on crackers with a plastic knife.

More to do

Cooking: Make bread and soup and invite parents to come and share lunch.

Science: With older children, this activity can be used to show that solid fat can be separated from the liquid cream. Note that the butter floats on top of the buttermilk and water because the fat is lighter than water. Experiment to see if whole milk or light cream will make butter.

Social studies: Use the activity as part of a study to show how foods were prepared long ago. Make butter when you study farm animals and talk about the other foods made from cream and milk.

★ Mary Jo Shannon, Roanoke, VA

Making Soft Pretzels . . . . .3+

Materials needed

Large bowl
Cookie sheet
Yeast
Water
Salt
Wax paper
Kosher salt

Measuring cups and spoons
Aluminum foil
Twisted pretzel (sample to show)
Sugar
Flour
Beaten egg

What to do

1. Prior to circle time, line the cookie sheet with foil and preheat the oven to 425º F.

2. As the children sit in a circle, show them a twisted pretzel. Discuss how the pretzel could be made.

3. Have the children wash their hands and prepare the pretzel dough.

> *1 packet yeast*
> *1 1/2 cup warm water*
> *1 tablespoon sugar*
> *1 teaspoon salt*
> *Stir in 4 cups flour*
> *Knead the dough until smooth.*

4. Give each child a piece of wax paper for their workspace.

5. Pull off pieces of dough for each child to roll into a long rope that she can shape into a pretzel.

6. Place pretzels on a cookie sheet, coat with beaten egg and sprinkle with salt.

7. Bake at 425º F for 12-15 minutes until golden brown. Cool and serve.

More to do

Art: Make pretzels from playdough.

Math: Categorize pretzels by sizes and shapes. Sequence the steps for making pretzels.

Sensory: Compare the taste of various pretzels—soft, hard, twists, sticks and nuggets.

Related books

The Magic Pretzel by James Magorian
Walter the Baker by Eric Carle

★ Sandi Fisher, Kutztown, PA

Cooking

Morning Snack and Lunch ....3+

Materials needed

5 medium-size potatoes
1 onion
2 sweet green peppers
4 large carrots
Salt to taste
1 teaspoon sweet basil
Vegetable juice, such as V-8®
Bowls and spoons

2 turnips
4 or 5 celery stalks
2 sweet red peppers
Cutting boards
Sharp knife for teacher and table knives for children
Water
Large kettle
Crackers

What to do

At circle time pass around a potato, a turnip, an onion, a celery stalk, a green pepper, a red pepper and a carrot. Talk about how these vegetables look, smell and feel. Talk about how they might taste.

Potatoes: Ask about different ways potatoes are fixed. Most children are familiar with french fries but may not realize they start as raw potatoes. Discuss how potatoes grow underground and that the little spots on the potatoes are called eyes. The eyes are like the seeds from which new potatoes sprout.

Carrots: Most children like to eat raw carrots. It is best to cut carrots in strips to prevent children from choking on round pieces. Explain that animals eat carrots, not just rabbits but also horses, cows and some zoo animals.

Turnips: Children may not have been introduced to turnips before. Talk about how turnips grow underground. Most children like to eat them raw.

Peppers: The green and red peppers are called sweet peppers but belong to a large family of peppers. Different types of peppers may taste very spicy or hot and make your mouth feel hot when eaten.

Onions: Used for seasoning, they have a strong flavor and may make your mouth feel hot. Onions lose this strong flavor when cooked. The children may be familiar with onion rings.

1. Tell the children that they will find out how these vegetable taste by cooking them together in a delicious soup.

2. Wash hands.

3. Provide pans of water and allow the children to scrub the vegetables.

4. Seat children around a table. Sit at the table and show them how you prepare the vegetables for cooking.

5. Prepare vegetables one at a time, by peeling and cutting them into chunks for soup.

6. Give each child a piece to taste as you talk about each vegetable.

7. Cover the vegetables with water in a pan to cook. When the vegetables are tender flavor with salt, basil and vegetable juice.

8. Serve the soup with crackers for lunch.

Cooking

More to do

Dramatic play: Introduce pretend vegetables to the housekeeping corner.

Games: Play "Hot Potato" with a beanbag.

Language: Tell the flannel board story of "The Big Turnip."

Math: Make a graph of different colored vegetables or children's favorite vegetables.

Science: Cut 1/2" off the top of the carrots and place upright in a tray with water just covering the surface of the tray. If you keep the tray moist, the carrot rounds will sprout green tops.

Related books

Eating the Alphabet by Lois Ehlert
Growing Vegetable Soup by Lois Ehlert
The Victory Garden Vegetable Alphabet Book by Jerry Pallotta and Bob Thomson

★ Helen DeWitt, Carol Stream, IL

Mystery Cookies . . . . .3+

Materials needed

Resealable plastic bags
Mixing bowl
Cookie sheet
Marker

Ingredients for a cookie recipe
Spoon
Large sheet of paper

What to do

1. Tell the children that you received a cookie recipe in the mail, but without the name of the cookies listed so you do not know what kind of cookies the recipe will make. All we know are the ingredients listed on the recipe.

2. Put each of the dry ingredients in a bag. Pass each bag for each child to look at and smell the ingredient and to guess the name of the ingredient in the bag.

3. As the children guess the names of the ingredients, list the ingredients on the sheet of paper.

4. Ask the children to pour each ingredient into a bowl and mix well. (The teacher may want to add the ingredients in the order that the recipe recommends or as the children suggest.)

5. Ask the children to smell the dough and guess what kind of cookie they think the dough will make.

6. Place the dough on the cookie sheet and bake.

7. Gather children at snack time to taste the cookie and make a final decision about the type of cookie.

More to do

Language: Bring in other items, such as odd tools, fancy dresses or costumes, parts of broken toys, and ask the children to tell a story about what they think the item is or who they think wore the item.

★ Melissa Browning, West Allis, WI

Popcorn . . . . .3+

Materials needed

Popcorn popper (not an air popper)
Oil and popcorn
Large bed sheet
Small cups to hold popcorn

What to do

1. Hide the popcorn popper, ready for popping corn in the room.

2. Ask the children to guess the name of a food you are thinking of. Give them clues, such as: it is white and puffed, you put salt and butter on it, you might eat it for a snack or when you go to a movie.

3. At this point another adult should secretly plug in the popper.

4. Continue the discussion, asking if they know how to make popcorn, what makes the little kernels pop.

5. As the sizzling begins, stop and listen—what do you hear?

6. Begin a search for the source of the sound that they will have already guessed is popcorn.

7. When the popcorn is ready, serve it in a cup to each child.

More to do

Spread a sheet on the floor and place the popper in the middle (an extension cord may be needed). Ask the children to sit around the sheet (far enough from where the popcorn might pop or the oil might splatter). Make popcorn again but this time do not put the top on the popper. Ask the children how high they think they can count while waiting for the kernels to pop, then begin counting. Talk about what the popcorn looks like while it is popping. Are they surprised when it looks like fireworks? Make sure the children do not move closer because the kernels are very hot. Gather up the sheet and shake it outside so the birds can have a treat.

Large motor: Tell the children that now they are going to pretend to be popcorn. Ask them to make their body as small as they can crouching down on the floor. Tell them they are popcorn kernels, pour pretend oil over them and pretend to plug in the popcorn popper. Rattle a tambourine gently and they begin to sizzle, a little louder as they get hotter and hotter. Bang the tambourine slowly at first and a few kernels should pop up, then faster as they all begin to pop. Repeat a few times. Make popcorn another way. The children gather around a parachute or large sheet. If children aren't familiar with the parachute, review guidelines for using a parachute first. Hold the parachute down low and very still with ping-pong balls in the center. Pretend to pour in the oil and plug in the popper (children love to do this). Move the parachute slowly as the pretend popcorn starts to sizzle, then make the movements more active and then up and down as all the kernels pop. When all the balls have bounced off, have the children find them and put them back on the parachute and make another batch. Repeat as many times as the children want.

Related books

Popcorn by Frank Asch
Popcorn Dragon by Jane Thayer

★ Linda Westman, Rockford, IL

Popping Popcorn .3+

Materials needed

Cob of popcorn and cob of regular corn
Popcorn popper
Large bowl

Popcorn kernels
Paper cups

What to do

1. As children sit at circle time, pass around a cob of popcorn and a cob of regular corn. Discuss the characteristics of each: size, texture, color, shape, smell.

2. Discuss what happens when popcorn is heated.

3. Pour popcorn into the popper and count how long it takes for the first kernel to pop. Discuss the smell of popcorn popping. Keep children away from the hot popcorn popper.

4. Fill paper cups with popcorn and give to the children.

5. Discuss what happened to the popcorn and how it tastes. Compared the characteristics of the popped corn to the unpopped kernels.

More to do

Language: As the children describe the characteristics of the popcorn, write a list of descriptive words.

Math: Using a clock, time how long it takes the first kernel to pop.

Music: Play music and ask the children to dance to the music pretending that they are kernels popping.

Science: Plant kernels of popcorn and chart the growth once the kernels sprout. Compare and contrast regular corn, Indian corn and popcorn.

Related book

The Popcorn Book by Tomie dePaola

★ Sandi Fisher, Kutztown, PA

Quick Ice Cream . . . . .3+

Materials needed

4 cups of milk
4 bananas
Blender
Bowls and spoons

2 trays of ice
1 can of frozen orange juice concentrate
Freezer

What to do

1. Set up a table in the middle of the circle.

2. Children can help peel the bananas and place them in the blender.

3. Add milk.

4. Add the orange concentrate and blend for a few minutes.

5. Children can help put in the ices cubes.

6. Place in the freezer for 15 minutes and serve. Yum!

More to do

This is a great activity for hot days. It helps children cool off and have fun preparing the ice cream.

★ Elmida Baghdaserians, Glendale, CA

Stone Soup .3+

Materials needed

Crock pot
2 cans stewed tomatoes
Bowls
Napkins
Crackers

1 lb. ground beef
Stew seasonings
Spoons
Canned vegetables
Stone Soup by Marcia Brown

What to do

1. Assign children to bring a small can of vegetables, crackers, bowls, spoons or napkins to class.

2. Sauté ground beef in the crock pot.

3. Read *Stone Soup* during circle time.

4. After reading the book, ask each child to contribute to the stew by pouring the vegetables into the stew pot. Let each child stir the stew.

5. The children who bring, bowls, spoons napkins or crackers contribute to the meal by setting the table and passing out the crackers. This is a good activity during fall, particularly during the Thanksgiving season.

More to do

Language: Talk about how to plant and harvest the vegetables in the stew.

Large motor: Provide materials for the children to create a scarecrow.

★ Lisa Eason, Grapevine, TX

Pizza Time .4+

Materials needed

Pizza ingredient for each child (request donations from parents) including dough or English muffins, tomato sauce, cheese, toppings
Chart showing food groups (see illustration on page 175)

What to do

1. Children sit in a circle each holding the pizza ingredient brought from home.

2. Give clues describing an ingredient. Ask the children to guess the name of the ingredient based on the clues about the ingredient and about the children holding that ingredient.

3. Ask the children holding that ingredient to come forward and identify on the chart whether it belongs in the vegetable, bread, dairy or meat category.

4. Continue with clues and categorizing until all ingredients are identified.

5. Mix, measure and sprinkle the ingredients to make a delicious pizza.

More to do

Dramatic play: Set up a pizza shop in the house area. Ask local pizza shops to donate boxes and other items.

Writing: Encourage children to create menus and make their own money while playing in the pizza shop.

★ Laleña L. Williams, Beacon, NY

Dragon Chili . . . . .4+

Materials needed

Note to parents requesting an ingredient
Paring knife (for teacher only)
Measuring cups
Hot plate or stove
Bowls and spoons

Can opener
Measuring spoons
Large pot
Large spoon

What to do

1. Send note to parents requesting that they send in one of the following ingredients:

   ✓ 4 children, each brings 1/4 lb. ground beef browned (dragon meat)
   ✓ 6 children, each brings 1 can vegetable juice (8-ounce size), such as V-8® (dragon blood)
   ✓ 4 children, each brings 1 can (8-ounce size) chili beans (dragon fire)
   ✓ 4 children, each brings 1/4 diced onion, cut in triangles if possible (dragon teeth)
   ✓ 2 children, each brings 1 can (1-ounce size) green chilies (dragon scales)
   ✓ 2 children, each brings 1 teaspoon chili powder

Note: I ask parents to refer to the ingredients as dragon meat, dragon blood, dragon fire, dragon teeth and dragon scales.

2. Write the recipe on chart paper.

3. With the help of the children combine all the ingredients. Simmer 45 minutes.

4. Serve and enjoy.

Related song

"Puff the Magic Dragon"

Related books
The Knight and the Dragon by Tomie dePaola
Popcorn Dragon by Jane Thayer
Saint George and the Dragon by Margaret Hodges

★ Kimberle S. Byrd, Wyoming, MI

Wolf's Stew . . . . .4+

Materials needed

Note to parents requesting an ingredient
Paring knife (for teacher only)
Measuring cups
Hot plate or stove
Paper and markers

Can opener
Measuring spoons
Large pot
Large spoon
Bowls and spoons

What to do

1. Send note to parents requesting that they send in one of the following ingredients:

✓ 1 child brings 1 large wolf bone (any beef bone)
✓ 7 children, each brings 1 can of pond water (broth)
✓ 3 children, each brings a tree (1 stalk of celery)
✓ 2 children, each brings 10 wolf teeth (potato cut in diamond shapes)
✓ 1 child brings 20 wolf claws (elbow macaroni)
✓ 2 children, each brings a wolf eye (1 small onion)
✓ 1 child brings a wolf heart (1 can of whole tomatoes)
✓ 2 children, each brings wolf ears (1 carrot)
✓ 2 children, each brings 1 Tablespoon leaves (parsley)
✓ 1 child brings 1 teaspoon dirt (pepper)
✓ 2 children, each brings 1 teaspoon wolf dandruff (salt)

Note: I ask parents to refer to the ingredients as wolf bone, pond water, wolf heart, etc.

2. Write the recipe on the chart paper.

3. Let each child place an ingredient in the large pot. Simmer until done (approximately 1 to 1 1/2 hours).

4. Serve and enjoy.

Related books

Little Red Riding Hood by David McPhail
Three Little Pigs by David McPhail
The True Story of the Three Little Pigs by Jon Sczieska

★ Kimberle S. Byrd, Wyoming, *MI*

Octopus on a Rock . . . . .5+

Materials needed

Old sheet or tablecloth
Large cooking pot
Hot plate
Oven mitts
Potato chips (optional)

Pictures of an octopus
Water
Colander
Squeeze containers of mayonnaise and mustard

1 per child—paper plate; hot dog; half of a bun, English muffin or flat roll; plastic knife

What to do

1. In a separate area, begin heating the large pot of water on the hot plate. Ask the children to wash their hands and sit in a circle on an old sheet or tablecloth.

2. Talk about the octopus—how it looks, where it lives, what it eats, how it moves.

3. Tell the children, "Now we will make a snack that is called an octopus on a rock."

4. Give each child a paper plate, plastic knife and hot dog. Show the children how to hold the hot dog upright and cut or saw it in half, beginning at the top end and stopping an inch or so from the bottom end. Next the children hold those two parts of the hot dogs together and slowly repeat the procedure, making this cut perpendicular to the first cut. (The two cuts will make a X shape.) Place the hot dogs in the boiling water and the ends will curl to represent the tentacles of an octopus. When heated, remove and drain.

5. Give each child a "rock" (bun, muffin or roll) and have her spread it with mayonnaise and mustard. Top with the cooled "octopus." Chips can be placed around it as seashells. Then the children can eat and enjoy their creations.

Note: If the children are not able to cut the hotdog the teacher can cut them in advance, but one hot-dog can be cut to show the children how it was done.

Related book *I Was All Thumbs* by Bernard Waber

Related song "Octopus' Garden" sung by Raffi, originally written by the Beatles

★ Carol Taylor, Alexandria, LA

Cut wiener in half, stopping 1" from the end.

Make a perpendicular cut.

Place cut wiener in boiling water.

cooked "octopus"

mustard or mayonnaise

bun "rock"

potato chip "shells"

Cooking

Egg Carton Recycling . . . . .3+

Materials needed
Cardboard egg cartons
Water
Large buckets

What to do
1. Allow egg cartons to stand in water for several days. When the cardboard is soft remove from the water and drain.

2. Ask the children to tear the egg cartons apart and squeeze the water out of the pieces.

3. Layer the material over inverted plastic bowls.

4. Let dry on newspapers.

5. Add powdered paint to the mixture or paint the material after it has dried.

6. Remove the recycled cardboard from the plastic bowls and use as plant pots or for decorations.

More to do
Water table: Place the cardboard egg cartons in the water table to soak. Allow the children to squeeze and squish the material. Remove from the water table when the cardboard is soft and drain. Place the material over inflated dinosaurs or other inflated shapes. After drying deflate the shapes to make piñata-type animals.

★ Barbara M. Bergstrom, Spokane, WA

Unbirthday Party With Party Hat . . . . .3+

Materials needed
Paper plates, cut in half and with a hole punched at each point (see illustration), 1 per child
Yarn or ribbon, 2 pieces per child (16" in length)
Colorful, fluffy feathers (optional)
Crayons
Scotch tape
Cupcakes or cookies and fruit punch
Paper cups and napkins

What to do
1. Explain that today we will celebrate everyone's "unbirthday." (This can also be used to celebrate children who have summer birthdays.)

yarn or ribbon ties

feathers

Happy Unbirthday

1/2 paper plate

2. Using crayons, the children may color and decorate their paper plates that have been cut in half.

3. Feathers can be taped to the top of the plate (see illustration).

4. One end of the yarn or ribbon is tied through each hole in the plate.

5. As each child holds her plate with the cut side against her forehead, an adult ties the yarn behind the child's head.

6. Cupcakes and a beverage can be served as the class sings "Happy Unbirthday to Us."

> *Happy unbirthday to us,*
> *Happy unbirthday to us,*
> *Happy unbirthday to everyone,*
> *Happy unbirthday to us!*

More to do
A summer bulletin board featuring the months of June, July and August can show favorite summertime activities and highlight the summer birthdays of children in the class.

Related books
Annie Flies the Birthday Bike by Crescent Dragonwagon
Nellie's Knot by Ken Brown
Little Mouse's Birthday by Thacher Hurd

★ Christina Chilcote, New Freedom, PA

Fairy Tale Hats . . . . .4+

Materials needed
Several double sheets of newspaper
Large assorted colored feathers
Poster paint or broad-tip markers
Paintbrush, if poster paint is used
Hole punch
Stapler

What to do
1. Over a period of several days read and tell a variety of fairy tales, using the flannel board, finger puppets and big books. Point out the Robin Hood-type hats many characters in the stories wear. Talk with the children about making fairy tale hats.

2. Gather the children around a table and demonstrate step by step how the hat is made. Each child has a double sheet of newspaper on the table before him.

3. Fold a double sheet of newspaper twice (see illustration on the next page).

4. Fold the top two corners down to make the pointed top of the hat.

5. Fold up the bottom sides of the newspaper to finish the hat.

6. Staple the ends of the hat to make it hold together better.

7. Pinch together one side of the hat and punch two holes in it to stick a feather through.

8. If painting the hat, do so before inserting the feather.

More to do

Art: The children can select a variety of colors with which to decorate the hats, drawing or painting designs on the hats to make them more colorful. Texture can be added if desired, by gluing buttons and other collage materials around the hat brim.

Math: Look for shapes in the hats. (Fold the top part of the newspaper into a triangle and the bottom part into rectangles.) Making the hat is a simple form of origami, the Japanese art of folding paper into shapes.

★ Lesley S. Potts, Franklin, TN

Fold double sheet of newspaper twice.

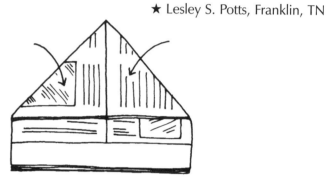

Fold top two corners down.

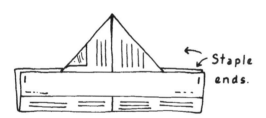

Fold bottom of newspaper up along each side to make hat brim.

Paint hat and apply a feather after paint has dried.

Dried Flower Boxes . . . . .5+

Materials needed

Box pattern (see illustration)
Pencil
Ruler
Playdough
Aquarium gravel

Construction paper
Scissors
Stapler
Dried flowers

What to do

1. Hand out predrawn and precut box shapes.

2. Show the children how to fold the box shapes on the pencil lines.

3. Ask them to staple the top and bottom flaps to make a stand-up box.

4. Give each child a small piece of playdough.

5. Ask the children to knead the playdough and press it on the inside bottom of the box.

6. Provide assorted dried flowers.

7. Show the children how to break off the long stems and stick a variety of dried flowers into the playdough.

8. Provide aquarium gravel.

9. Ask the children to press several pieces of gravel into the playdough to compete decorating the flower box.

More to do

Dried flower boxes are a simple activity for young children. They love to make boxes, work with playdough and arrange dried flowers in designs of their own choosing. By drawing and cutting the box shapes in various colors of construction paper in advance minimizes the amount of adult help the children will need to complete the project. Flower boxes also make good gifts for Mom or Dad. Children especially like the three-dimensional nature of the project and the many colors used—the flowers, construction paper boxes, playdough and colored aquarium gravel.

Language: Do this activity after reading stories, such as *Planting a Rainbow* by Lois Ehlert and *The Tiny Seed* by Eric Carle.

Science: Plant flower seeds and dried seeds from various weeds. Observe and record their growth after they sprout. Children learn that even weeds can be both decorative and useful in nature.

★ Lesley S. Potts, Franklin, TN

·BOX PATTERN·

Staple to side	TOP	Staple to side
CUT	FOLD	CUT
FOLD	FOLD	
CUT	FOLD	CUT
Staple to side	BOTTOM	Staple to side

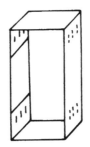

Fold flaps inside box and staple.

Finished box decorated with dried flowers, playdough and gravel.

Fat Frog Visor . . . . .5+

Materials needed

Sturdy paper or oak tag for head band
Black marker
Glue

Green construction paper
1" wiggle eyes or cut out paper eyes
Stapler

What to do

1. Draw a pattern of a frog face about 7" high and 10" wide.

2. Trace on green paper.

3. Mark along the bottom edge with a black marker.

4. Cut out the frog face.

5. Cut one slit in each eye the shape of eyebrows.

6. Fold a flap about 2 1/2" up from the chin.

7. Fold down the flap 2" from the edge of the chin to form the visor.

8. Staple along the fold line to secure it.

9. Glue the eyes in front of the slit openings and slide the eye upward through the slit so the slit resembles an eye lid.

10. Add two black dots for the nose.

11. Staple the visor to the precut headband strip.

12. Measure the strip to fit the child's head and staple.

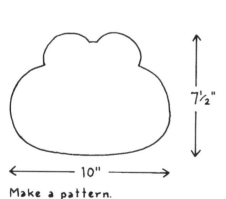

7½"

← 10" →

Make a pattern.

Trace on green paper, mark along bottom edge with black marker and cut out.

Cut slits for eyebrows.

staple

Glue on eyes.
Draw two black dots for nose.

Fold up flap 2½" from chin.
Fold down to create 2" visor.

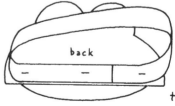

back

Staple headband to visor.

More to do

Music: Sing songs and act out fingerplays about frogs.

Science: Study the frog life cycle. Keep tadpoles in an aquarium and observe the changes as they grow legs and develop into frogs. Expand the study of the frog to include other animals living in the pond, stream and meadow.

Original poem

"Be a Patient Little Tadpole"

> *"How come I can't jump?" said little tadpole one day.*
> *"All I can do is swim and I'm so ugly and gray.*
> *"Be patient," said Mr. Bullfrog, "You will change as you grow."*
> *And before very long two back legs did show.*
> *"You're right, Mr. Bullfrog," said little tadpole with glee.*
> *"I did need to learn patience," as he swam very happily.*
> *And the next time he looked, tadpole had green legs four.*
> *He was very surprised and now he could jump to shore.*

Related books

From Tadpole to Frog by Wendy Pfeffer
Hop Jump by Ellen Stoll Walsh
In the Small, Small Pond by Denise Fleming
Jump, Frog, Jump! by Robert Kalan

★ Mary Brehm, Aurora, OH

Hobby Horse . . . . .5+

Materials needed

Brown lunch bags
16" tree branch with fork-shape on one end
Tan construction paper
1" wiggle eyes
Newspaper
Red and black markers
Yarn
Thin wire or twisty

What to do

1. Read *Fritz and the Beautiful Horses* by Jan Brett to the children at circle time. Explain that they will each make a hobby horse.

2. Cut construction paper 4" x 12" for horse mane (see illustration).

3. Fold strip in half to measure 2" x 12".

4. Draw line 1/2 up from the open edge. Fringe cut folded edge to line.

5. Fold uncut edges out, creating and gluing the strips.

6. Wrap two full newspaper sheets around forked end of the branch.

7. Stuff into brown bag, squeeze the paper at the neck to form the head.

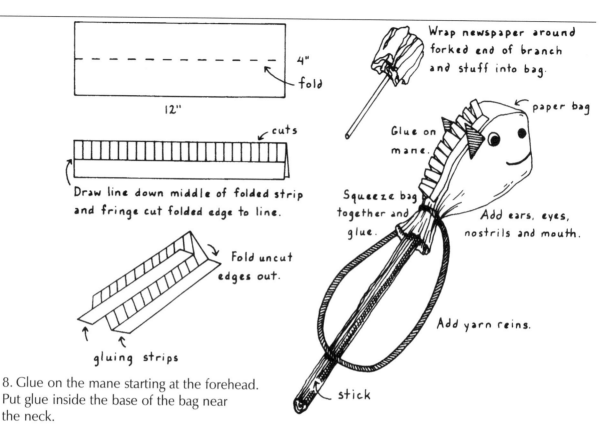

8. Glue on the mane starting at the forehead. Put glue inside the base of the bag near the neck.

9. Secure at the neck with a thin wire or twisty.

10. Add facial features: two triangle shaped ears, two nostrils, two wiggle eyes and a mouth.

11. Add yarn for the reins.

More to do

Large motor: Children use hobby horses to practice galloping while other children make galloping noises with their hands, slapping their legs just above the knee. Discuss various uses of horses: circus horses perform with bareback riders; farm horses pull a plow; race horses are trained to run very fast and jumping horses learn to jump over fences. Visit a horse stable or farm. Discuss the care of horses: brushing, exercising, feeding.

Original poem
"Ride 'm Cowboy"

> I'm a rough and tumble cowboy
> Riding on my horse.
> I can make him trot real slow
> Or gallop of course.
> Then I swing my lariat
> Round and round and round.
> And sometimes my bronco
> Throws me to the ground.
> Whenever I'm a cowboy
> I'm brave as can be.
> Even wild animals
> Don't frighten me.

★ Mary Brehm, Aurora, OH

Dinosaur Song: Triceratops . . . . .3+

Materials needed
None needed

What to do
1. Add this song to your collection of songs about dinosaurs and sing with the children during circle time.

"Triceratops" (Tune: "Yankee Doodle Dandy")

> *Triceratops, Triceratops,*
> *He's such a fearsome sight.*
> *All the other dinosaurs*
> *Will think before they fight.*
> *He has one horn above each eye*
> *And one upon his nose.*
> *He's got his weapons on his head*
> *Everywhere he goes.*

★ Christine Maiorano, Duxbury, MA

Dinosaur Friends . . . . .3+

Materials needed
Cardboard from refrigerator boxes
Markers
Pictures of plants and animals

What to do
1. Draw a dinosaur on each large piece of cardboard and cut them out. Color the dinosaurs with markers and make a stand for each dinosaur.

2. Introduce the dinosaurs to the children. (To add an element of suspense, hide the dinosaurs and have the children follow cardboard footprints on the floor to find each dinosaur.)

3. At circle time discuss which dinosaurs were meat eaters and which were plant eaters. Have several pictures of plants and animals that children can choose from to pretend to feed the dinosaurs. Introduce the words "carnivores" and "herbivores" and talk about which types of dinosaurs were carnivores and which were herbivores.

★ Trixie Andrews, Holland, MI

Five Little Dinosaurs . . . . .3+

Materials needed

None needed
Puppet mitt with 5 little dinosaur fingers (optional)

What to do

1. During circle time the children sing the following song with accompanying motions to the tune of "Five Little Elephants Went Out to Play."

> Five little dinosaurs went out to play (walk across the classroom)
> Out in the land of the lost one day.
> Tyrannasaurus Rex ate one for a snack
> And four little dinosaurs came running back (one child stays and the others walk back)
>
> Four little dinosaurs....(continue singing using the words above)
>
> Three little dinosaurs....
>
> Two little dinosaurs....
>
> One little dinosaur went out to play
> Out in the land of the lost one day.
> Tyrannosaurus Rex ate him for a snack
> And no little dinosaurs came running back.
>
> No little dinosaurs went out to play
> Out in the land of the lost one day.
> Tyrannosaurus Rex couldn't find anything to eat
> So off she went to go to sleep.

More to do

This activity can be adapted for other units of study by using different animals and changing a few words. For example, the song "Six Little Ducks Went Out to Play" could be sung and acted out when learning about farm animals.

Related books

The Biggest Dinosaurs by Michael Berenstain
Count-a-Saurus by Nancy Blumenthal
Danny and the Dinosaur by Syd Hoff
Digging Up Dinosaurs by Aliki
Dinosaurs by Gail Gibbons
Dinosaur Bob and His Adventures With the Family Lazardo by William Joyce
Dinosaur Day by Liza Donnelly
How I Captured a Dinosaur by Henry Schwartz
I'm Tyrannosaurus! A Book of Dinosaur Rhymes by Jean Marzollo
Mrs. Tuggle and the Dinosaur by Robin Pulver

★ Margaret P. Comes, Memphis, TN

Papier-Mâché Dinosaurs ....3+

Materials needed
2 plastic inflatable dinosaurs
Paint and brushes
Masking tape

Liquid starch in a bowl
Newspapers
Pictures of dinosaurs

What to do
1. Discuss the activity at circle time. The children who want to participate should wear smocks.

2. Inflate the dinosaurs and cover with about six layers of dry newspapers, taping the newspapers together. Make sure that the masking tape does not touch the inflatable plastic.

3. The children tear strips of newspapers and dip them in a large bowl of starch. As the children remove a strip from the bowl, they drag the strip along the edge of the bowl to remove excess starch from the strip. Place the strips on the dinosaurs.

4. Let dry. Deflate the plastic dinosaurs. After looking at pictures of dinosaurs discuss the type of skin the dinosaurs might have had and the colors of the skin. Paint the dinosaurs using the colors suggested. The paint tends to flake off and look old and wrinkled providing a rough texture.

More to do
Blocks: Make a dinosaur cave out of papier-mâché for the block area by covering a wastebasket with newspaper, then following the steps listed above.

Language: The children dictate a story about how they made the papier-mâché dinosaurs.

Science: Make paper dinosaur eggs using rolled up paper towels covered with liquid starch and then place tissue paper on the top.

★ Barbara Bergstrom, Spokane, WA

Dino-Classification ....4+

Materials needed
Dinosaur counters or dinosaurs of different colors, kinds, sizes

What to do
1. Hand each child a dinosaur and talk about how the dinosaurs are different. Name each type of dinosaur.

2. The children take their dinosaurs to the different areas of the room based on certain characteristics: "All meat eaters go to the house area. All plant eaters go to the block area."

3. Follow with additional classification, such as: colors of dinosaurs, kinds of dinosaurs, flying or walking dinosaurs, small or large dinosaurs.

More to do
Language: Ask the children to suggest why the dinosaurs disappeared. List all responses on chart paper.

Math: Use the dinosaurs in counting and spatial relationship activities.

★ Laleña L. Williams, Beacon, NY

Find Those Bones So Old . . . . .4+

Materials needed
5 large dinosaur patterns (Stegosaurus, Triceratops, Pterodactyl, Diplodocus, Tyrannosaurus Rex)

What to do
1. The children are standing in a circle.

2. Teacher places the five dinosaur patterns in the center.

3. The children join hands and move clockwise singing the first verse of the following original song to the tune of "Kookaburra."

> *Dinosaurs lived so long ago,*
> *Their skeletons are buried in the earth below.*
> *Chorus: Dig paleontologist! Dig paleontologist! Find those bones so old!*
>
> *Stegosaurs lived so long ago,*
> *Protective armored plates down his spine would grow. (Chorus)*
>
> *Triceratops lived so long ago,*
> *Three pointed horns on his face would show. (Chorus)*
>
> *Pteradactyl lived so long ago*
> *Flying over swampland down below. (Chorus)*
>
> *Diplodocus lived so long ago,*
> *Measuring ninety feet long or so. (Chorus)*
>
> *Tyrannosaurus Rex lived long ago,*
> *King of the dinosaurs—this we know! (Chorus)*

4. After the children move counter clockwise singing the second verse, a child is chosen to hold up the dinosaur pattern described.

5. The song continues until all dinosaur patterns have been identified.

More to do
Art: Create skeletons by gluing popsicle sticks and toothpicks on black construction paper dinosaur patterns.

Large motor: Follow the rules for playing Duck, Duck Goose! saying Herbivore, Herbivore, Carnivore!

Math: Make a paper footprint three feet long and three feet wide. Ask children to trace and cut out their own footprints to see how many fit into one Tyrannosaurus Rex footprint.

Science: Categorize dinosaurs as plant eaters (herbivores) or meat eaters (carnivores) and as having walked on two legs or four legs.

Related books
Magic School Bus in the Time of the Dinosaurs by Joanna Cole
You Can Name 100 Dinosaurs and Other Prehistoric Animals by Randy Chewning

★ Debbie A. Eikland, Palmdale, CA

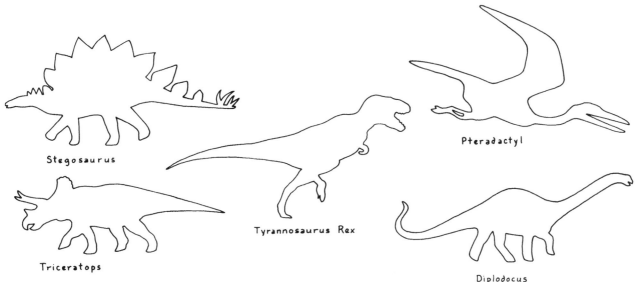

Stegosaurus

Pteradactyl

Triceratops

Tyrannosaurus Rex

Diplodocus

Many, Many Years Ago . . . . .4+

Materials needed

Pictures of dinosaurs

What to do

This is a great activity to do while introducing dinosaurs. After looking at pictures or reading a story about dinosaurs discuss the following concepts.

1. Some dinosaurs ate meat. They had sharp teeth.

2. Some dinosaurs ate plants. They had longer necks and usually flat teeth.

3. Dinosaurs moved about in different ways. Some flew in the air, others walked on land.

4. Dinosaurs do not live today. There are many theories (reasons people believe) that the dinosaurs died. One is that the temperature of where they lived, changed. That it became too cold for the dinosaurs. Ask the children what they think might have happened.

5. After looking at models and pictures and talking about dinosaurs sing the following song using the motions listed below. Repeat the song a few times to allow children time to learn the words and the motions.

"Many, Many Years Ago" (Tune: "Twinkle, Twinkle, Little Star")

> *Many, many years ago,*
> *Lived the great big dinosaurs.*
> *Some ate plants,*
> *Some ate meat,*
> *Traveled by air or on their feet.*
> *Then the earth turned very cold,*
> *The dinosaurs died, so I've been told.*

More to do

Art: Draw large outlines of different types of dinosaurs. Provide the children with brown, black and green crayons to color the dinosaurs. Ask the children to decide what kind of teeth each dinosaur probably would have had and ask them to draw that type of teeth on the dinosaur.

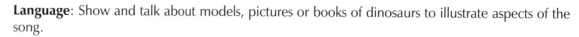

Language: Show and talk about models, pictures or books of dinosaurs to illustrate aspects of the song.

Large motor: Use body motions as the song is sung: spreading arms to indicate great big, moving fingers toward the mouth to indicate eating, spreading the arms like wings to indicate traveled by air and stomping the feet to indicate on their feet.

Sand table: Provide small models of various dinosaurs in the sandbox area. Put twigs and leafy branch clippings in the area. The children can pretend that the dinosaurs are eating plants, walking, stomping.

★　Sandra Nagel, White Lake, MI

Why Were the Dinosaurs So BIG? . . . .4+

Materials needed
The Dinosaur Who Lived in My Backyard by B.G. Hennessy
Ruler
Yarn or heavy string

What to do
1. Introduce the lesson by reading *The Dinosaur Who Lived in My Backyard*.

2. Ask the children why they think the dinosaurs were so big. They may answer that the dinosaurs ate a lot or that they lived for a long time, accept all the children's answers as possibilities.

3. Ask one child who is about 4 feet tall to stand up. Measure the child using a ruler, explaining that the ruler measures 1 foot. Explain that many dinosaur eggs were as big as the child.

4. Show the children the approximate size of a Pterodactyl by involving the children in representing the measurements. Ask one child to represent the body by lying in the middle of the circle. The wings of the Pterodactyl were about 10 feet so ask three children to represent each wing. Ask the children to lie down head-to-toe spreading out on each side of the child in the middle. Measure 10 ruler lengths for the class to see how big it was.

5. The Apatosaurus was one of the largest dinosaurs and measured about 80 feet long. Ask the children to help you count as you measure 80 feet of yarn. (This is a good activity to do outside if weather permits.) Unroll the yarn and measure how many children have to lie down to make the length of an Apatosaurus. If you need more children ask the ones at the beginning to lie down at the end. This is lots of fun, and it also gives the children some idea of how big some of the dinosaurs were.

More to do
Enhance this activity about BIG by celebrating BIG DAY. Prior to the day notify the children's parents that the children should wear clothing that is too big for them on the day. Talk with the children about BIG DAY and explain that they should wear clothes that belong to a parent or big brother or sister so that the clothes will be too big for them. The teachers should also wear clothing that is very large.

★ Linda Westman, Rockford, IL

Dinosaur Bone Hunt . . . . .5+

Materials needed
Large leg bones of a cow from a grocery store or butcher shop
Several shovels
Magnifying glass

What to do
1. For the outdoor dinosaur hunt the teacher should obtain large cow bones that are then boiled, bleached and dried. This process takes approximately a week.

2. When the bones have thoroughly dried, bury the bones outside in sand.

3. At circle time explain to the children that they are going on a dinosaur bone hunt.

4. Make maps that will lead the children to where the bones are buried. Before the hunt, sing the following song.

"Little Stegosaurus" (Tune: "Little Bunny Foo Foo")

> *Little Stegosaurus*
> *Tromping through the forest*
> *With his Mama Doris*
> *And his sister Chloris*
> *And his brother Horace*
> *And his Uncle Boris.*
> *Singing the chorus to his favorite song.*

(The chorus is sung to the tune of "London Bridge")

> *I'm a little dinosaur*
> *Won't you teach me how to snore?*
> *All I know is roar, roar, roar*
> *'Cause I'm a little dinosaur.*

5. Allow children to explore the bones up close with a magnifying glass. (Explain that these bones are from a cow and that you are pretending that they are from a dinosaur.) This is a perfect time to talk about the role of a paleontologist who digs up dinosaur bones and other fossils that are displayed in museums.

More to do
Art: Make dinosaur collages. Tear small pieces of colored tissue paper (brown, black, green, yellow). Glue the paper to meat trays. Glue small plastic dinosaurs to the tissue paper, fastening securely.

Language: Discuss the job of a paleontologist, where the bones of dinosaurs are displayed, the different types of dinosaurs and the various theories about what happened to the dinosaurs.

★ Penni Smith and Donna Karnes, Riverside, CA

Emotions We Feel . . . . .3+

Materials needed
Pictures of people's expressions
Mirror

What to do
1. Talk with the children about the emotions we all feel: happy, sad, angry, scared. Explain that these emotions or expressions are natural and all right to feel and express.

2. Show a variety of pictures of people and talk about the emotions the people in the pictures might be feeling. Discuss the pictures and encourage the children to express how they feel about the pictures.

3. Use a mirror to show facial expressions, what your face looks like when you are happy, sad, angry or scared. Ask each child to make a facial expression in the mirror.

More to do
Art: Draw a picture of a child who feels happy, sad, angry or scared. Ask the children to tell you about their pictures and write what they say in their own words.

Language: Ask the children to dictate a story about a certain emotion.

Related books
Faces by Barbara Brenner
I Feel Like a Mouse by Jeanne Modesitt

Related song
"If You're Happy and You Know It, Clap Your Hands"

★ Kathleen Steenhusen, Kansas City, MO

Feelings . . . . .3+

Materials needed
None needed

What to do
1. Adapt the song "If You're Happy and You Know It" to reflect feelings.

For example:

> *If you're sad and you know it, cry boo hoo....*
> *If you're loving and you know it, give a hug....*
> *If you're angry and you know it, stamp your feet....*
> *If you're sleepy and you know it, give a stretch....*

★ Lisa Sunbury, Cambridge, MA

Friends . . . . .3+

Materials needed
Charlie the Caterpillar by Dom DeLuise

What to do
1. Ask the children, "Have you ever asked someone if you could play with her and she told you 'No'?" (Wait for responses.) "How did it make you feel?" (Wait for responses.) "Today's story is about a caterpillar named Charlie who had that very thing happen to him, not just once, but three times. Let's see what happened to him." Read *Charlie the Caterpillar*.

2. Talk about what it means to be friends. Friends are special. Friends share with each other; do things together; play together; care about each other; help each other; talk and listen to each other; don't call each other names, tease or make fun of each other. Sometimes friends get mad at each other and fight, but friends make up and forgive each other. Friends can be at home, in the neighborhood or at school.

3. Sing the following song, "Friends," to the tune of "Jingle Bells."

> *Friends are here, friends are there*
> *Friends are everywhere.*
> *Lots of laughter, come and play*
> *All throughout the day.*
> *Friends have fun in the sun.*
> *And even in the rain.*
> *Friends love to play and share*
> *To show how much they care.*

More to do
Art: Friendship picture—two children color at the easel together or on a shared paper at a table.

Language: Make an audio tape of children's voices; children try to identify their voices and their classmates' voices.

Science: Make fingerprints with washable ink and use a magnifying glass to compare the prints of all the children.

Related books
Don't Call Me Names by Joanna Cole
Grover and the New Kid by Jennifer Smith
Teach Me About Friends by Joy Berry
This Is My Friend by Mercer Mayer
Will I Have a Friend? by Miriam Cohen

★ Deborah R. Gallagher, Bridgeport, CT

Emotions

Mr. Happy and Mr. Sad Clown . . . . . . .3+

Materials needed

2 sturdy paper plates
1 soft ball
Index card
Glue stick or glue
Stapler
Construction paper

Yarn
Colored markers
Magazine pictures of happy or sad situations
Scissors
Velcro
Self-adhesive paper or laminating film

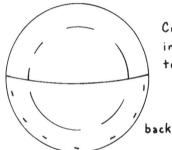

Cut one paper plate in half and staple it to another.

back of clown face

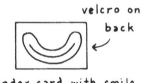

velcro on back

index card with smile or frown, laminated

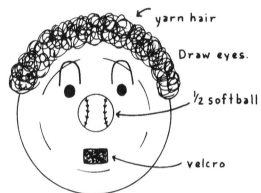

yarn hair
Draw eyes.
½ softball
velcro

magazine pictures in back pocket

What to do

1. Prior to the activity, create a clown puppet by cutting one paper plate in half and stapling one half to a whole paper plate with the curved sides facing each other. On the back side of the whole paper plate create a clown face using yarn for hair, half of the soft ball for a nose and markers to create other facial features, except for the mouth. On an index card draw a sausage-type mouth that can look like a smile or a frown. Color the mouth red and cover with clear self-adhesive paper or laminating film. Attach velcro to the mouth and on the lower half of the paper plate face where the mouth will go. Mount magazine pictures on construction paper and cover with clear self-adhesive paper or laminating film. Place the pictures in the pocket made by the half of the paper plate.

2. Introduce the clown to the children; discuss that some clowns make their faces happy while other clowns make their faces look sad. Talk about why a clown might choose a happy face or a sad face. Show the children how this clown can be either happy or sad just by moving the mouth.

3. Ask the children to name things that might make them happy or sad.

4. Show one picture at a time and let children decide if the clown would have a happy face or a sad face about the situation. You or a child can place the clown's mouth in the position that best matches the feeling depicted.

More to do

Art: Pass out paper plates and crayons. Let the children create their own happy or sad clown faces.

Music: Play Hap Palmer's album "Getting to Know Myself" and sing the song, "Feelings" with the children. Stress that people have a wide variety of emotions.

★ Marzee Woodward, Murfreesboro, TN

Posters of Feelings . . . . .3+

Materials needed
Photographs of the children   White paper
Crayons, markers

What to do
1. Look at the photographs with the children (make sure there are two or three photos of each child) and discuss who is in the photos, what they are doing and how they felt when the photos were taken.

2. Tape the photograph of each child on a separate piece of paper.

3. Ask the children to draw a picture of what they remember doing when the photo was taken. Ask the children to tell you about their picture as you write their comments on their paper.

More to do
Display papers with the children's comments on tagboard. Save the tagboard posters and periodically display them throughout the year to help the children remember and talk about past happenings. Ask the children to bring photos of their parents and discuss what their parents are doing in the photos.

★ Billiana Miteva, Pomona, NJ

Feelings Cube . . . . .4+

Materials needed
6-sided cube with a different face expressing a feeling on each side   Chart paper and markers

What to do
1. Prepare the Feelings Cube before circle time. (Cubes can be made by cutting in half a half-gallon paper milk carton. Put one half of the carton inside the other to form a cube. Cover the cube with white paper and draw faces or glue magazine pictures of facial expressions on the sides of the cube. Cover the cube with clear self-adhesive paper. Facial expressions to draw include happy, sad, angry, scared, silly and tired.)

2. Discuss each feeling expressed on the cube. Ask the children to talk about a time when they had one of those feelings.

3. Record the children's responses on the chart paper.

4. Children take turns rolling the cube. Everyone makes a face to express the feeling shown on the cube.

5. Sing the following song, "Feelings Song," to the tune of Hap Palmer's "Colors Song."

> *This is the song about feelings,*
> *You have them every day.*
> *This is the song about feelings,*
> *The way you feel is okay.*

*If you're happy give a smile
If you're sad give a frown.
If you're scared give a shiver,
If you're angry stomp the ground.*

*This is the song about feelings,
You have them every day.
This is the song about feelings,
The way you feel is okay.*

*If you're grumpy give a growl,
If you're proud pat your back.
If you're silly go like this. (make a funny face)
If you're tired hit the sack. (pretend to go to sleep)*

*This is the song about feelings
You have them every day
This is the song about feelings,
The way you feel is okay.*

More to do

Art: Provide paper plates and scraps of construction paper to make feelings face puppets. Encourage the children to add features to express the feelings discussed at circle time. (For younger children precut the facial expressions and let them choose one to glue on a paper plate.)

Table games: Make a feelings face lotto game. Make four boards with six squares each. Draw in a different face in each square. Make call cards with the same facial expressions. The children use checkers to cover the boards as the call cards are drawn.

Writing: Describe an emotion and ask the children to draw pictures and dictate stories about different times when they had that feeling. Staple the papers together to make books about feelings. Have the children take turns "reading" their books at circle time.

Related books

Feelings by Aliki
I Was So Mad by Mercer Mayer
There's a Nightmare in My Closet by Mercer Mayer

★ Frances Youngblood, Reeds Spring, MO

Friendships .4+

Materials needed

Large sheet of paper
That's What a Friend Is by P.K. Hallinan
Record or cassette tape player
"Free to Be You and Me" music and book by Marlo Thomas and Friends

What to do

1. On a sheet of paper write the title, "Friendship Is..."

2. Play "Glad to Have a Friend Like You." Read the lyrics from the book. Encourage children to sing along.

3. Ask each child to contribute his own definition of what a friend is.

4. Review the definitions and talk about why each is important.

5. Read *That's What a Friend Is* and discuss the story.

More to do

Art: Children can draw or paint a picture entitled, "This Is What I Like to Do With My Friend."

★ Debbie Bokor, Richmond Hill, Ontario, Canada

Peaceful and Quiet . . . . .4+

Materials needed

Large sheets of paper
Marker
Tape player
Tape cassette with familiar sounds recorded

What to do

1. Draw a vertical line to divide the paper in half.

2. Children sit in a circle where they can see the paper.

3. Ask each child to think of a sound that is peaceful and quiet.

4. List the children's responses on one side of the sheet of paper.

5. After the list is completed have children name things that are loud and not peaceful.

6. List these things on the other side of the paper.

7. Ask the children to listen to the tape of familiar sounds.

8. On another sheet of paper list the sounds as the children identify them.

9. Ask the children to sort the recorded sounds into the two categories of peaceful and not peaceful.

More to do

Encourage the children to become aware of peaceful sounds they hear during the day and how they feel when they hear these sounds.

★ Melissa Browning, West Allis, WI

Composting . . . . .3+

Materials needed

Yard waste (grass clippings, leaves)
Kitchen scraps
Plastic container

What to do

1. On a continuing basis collect kitchen scraps and yard waste. A 1-quart plastic container is convenient to hold the kitchen scraps.

2. Sort out any of the following items: plastic, metal, bones or meat. Everything else can be used including the leftover sandwiches and fruit from the children's meals.

3. Make a pile in a sunny corner outdoors. It should be about three feet square. Make it larger if you have more compost materials, but don't let it get higher than about three feet or it will be hard to care for. The pile can be freestanding or enclosed inexpensively with a piece of chicken wire rolled into a three-foot diameter circle.

4. Add items as you accumulate them, making the trip to the compost pile an exciting time (make it a weekly activity). Check on the height and width of the growing pile. Check the temperature—just pull away materials from the center and reach in to feel the heat. Check to see how the materials are becoming less recognizable as they rot.

5. Read books about composting and talk about how you're making something valuable—good garden compost—out of trash that was headed for the landfill. At the end of the season send everyone home with a bag of "Black Gold."

★ Margaret Howard, Northglenn, CO

Earth Day Song . . . . .3+

Materials needed

None needed

What to do

1. At circle time sing the following "Earth Day Song" to the tune of "Mary Had a Little Lamb."

Plant a seed and you will see, you will see, you will see, you will see.
Plant a seed and you will see
What a beautiful world it can be.

Help us to recycle things, recycle things, recycle things, recycle things.
Help us to recycle things
What a beautiful world it brings.

Put your trash where it belongs, where it belongs, where it belongs, where it belongs.
Put your trash where it belongs
And the world stays beautiful for long.

More to do

Art: Decorate a lunch bag. Add a yarn handle to hang it in an automobile to collect car litter and trash.

Recycling: Keep a Recycle Box for families to bring items from home for the children to recycle at school for projects, such as egg cartons and milk jugs.

★ Christine Maiorano, Duxbury, MA

Earth Day .3+

Materials needed
Flannel board pieces to accompany song (optional)

What to do
1. Prepare flannel board, if desired.

2. Discuss with the children various earth awareness topics, such as recycling, conservation, rainforests.

3. Have the children draft a letter to an organization that works with Earth preservation or awareness, such as:

> Earth Island Institute
> 300 Broadway, Suite 28
> San Francisco, CA 94133

4. Sing one of the following songs.

"Earth Day Song" (Tune: "Twinkle, Twinkle, Little Star")

> *Earth Day, Earth Day,*
> *Comes once a year.*
> *But we should make our message clear.*
> *Love and clean our Earth each day.*
> *Make that plan a plan to stay.*
> *Earth Day, Earth Day,*
> *Comes once a year,*
> *Love and care for our Earth so dear.*

"Pick Up Trash" (Tune: "Mulberry Bush")

> *This is the way we pick up trash, pick up trash, pick up trash.*
> *This is the way we pick up trash to help our Mother Earth.*

"Recycling" (Tune: "Mulberry Bush")

> *Recycling is the smart thing to do, smart thing to do, smart thing to do.*
> *Recycling is the smart thing to do, separating things we can use.*

"Clean Up the Earth" (Tune: "Who Built the Ark")

Let's clean up the Earth,
Clean up the Earth,
Clean up the Earth.
Saving and recycling will clean up the Earth,
Clean up the Earth today.

More to do

Dramatic play: Make a recycling center. Use milk crates for the recycling bins. Supply plenty of paper and pencils for writing receipts and notes. Don't forget the recyclable trash for the children to sort.

Field trip: Visit a recycling center or host a local trash pick-up outside and around the school.

Game: Make an Earth Awareness Lotto Game. Cut poster board into 6" x 8" pieces and divide those cards into six squares. Make four cards. After dividing the cards into six spaces put a different recycling sticker in each space. After completing the lotto cards be sure to cover with clear self-adhesive paper for durability. Make a caller's set of cards using all of the stickers that you put on your different lotto cards.

★ Debora L. Stuck, Reeds Spring, MO

Recycled Castle . . . . .3+

Materials needed

Recycled items and clean trash (plastic bottles, cans)

Large piece of cardboard	Masking tape
Newspaper	Flour and water paste
Paint and brushes	Toothpicks and paper

What to do

1. Make sure the recyled items are clean and washed. Put a large table in the middle of the circle. This will be the building site. Build the castle on a large piece of cardboard since you may want to move the castle later.

2. Start taping trash to the large piece of cardboard using masking tape. Tape bottle on bottle; tub on box, toilet paper roll on butter lid, etc. Just start building the castle.

3. After the castle is completed apply a coating of papier-mâché to the castle. Cover every piece of trash with newspaper strips and flour and water paste.

4. When the castle is dry involve the children in painting the castle. Paint windows, doors, people; make flags made with toothpicks and paper. (One child made a drawbridge with string and cardboard.)

5. When finished you may want to call the local bank or local supermarket and ask if they would put the creation on display. What a compliment for the children to see their castle displayed in a public place.

★ Kim Jeanette-Sheffield, Atlanta, GA

Save the Earth ....3+

Materials needed
Contents from children's lunch boxes or trays (paper plates, cups, straws, plastic items, aluminum cans)
Large cardboard boxes for recycling containers
Pictures of recyclable items
Masking tape

What to do
1. Each child puts items in appropriately marked recycling bins

2. Pictures of recyclable items are taped to the floor in a circle.

3. Stand in front of a picture and identify it.

4. Then the children sing the following song and move to the next item after each verse. The tune is "Row, Row, Row Your Boat."

> *Save, save, save the cans throw them in the bin,*
> *We can help to save the earth if we all pitch in.*
>
> *Save, save, save the paper....*
> *Save, save, save the bottles....*
> *Save, save, save the plastics....*

More to do
Math: Graph the types and number of recyclable items.

★ Wilma Kaplan, Medford, NY

Rock Around the Earth ....4+

Materials needed
Small covered container (margarine tub) filled 1/4 full of sand
Sheets or blankets   Glass jar or bottle
Rocks (1 per child)   Large sheet of paper
Marker   Outside area where rocks can be found
Everybody Needs a Rock by Byrd Baylor

What to do
1. To introduce this topic, take the children outside and lie on blankets or sheets in the grass. Have the children rest quietly and encourage them to think about how it feels lying on the ground.

2. Explain that Earth is the name we call the ground, soil and the world around us.

3. As the children are lying or sitting on the blankets or sheets, have them look around for something they see that is beautiful. Ask the children to share their discovery.

4. Talk about the beautiful Earth and how we need to help take care of it because it is really our home.

5. Show the children a glass jar or bottle. Explain that glass is made from something that comes from the Earth. Ask the children if anyone knows what glass is made from.

6. Show the covered container of sand and shake it. Explain that glass is made for the item inside the container. Shake it again and see if the children can guess what is inside.

7. Open the container and show the sand. Explain that sand can be heated and melted and made into glass. Glass can also be recycled; old jars and bottles can be made into new ones. This is done by special machines that can break up the glass in very small pieces, melt it and make it into new items.

8. Pour a small amount of sand into the hand of each child. Explain that sand comes from the Earth. Encourage the children to look closely at the sand.

9. Give each child a rock to hold in her other (empty) hand. Explain that the sand is very small pieces of rock. Have the children hold their two hands close together and compare the rock and sand. Discuss the similarities and differences. Collect the rocks from the children. Depending on the age and attention span of the children, the following activity can be continued or done the next day as a circle time activity.

10. Explain that you will read a story called *Everybody Needs a Rock*. The person who wrote the book thinks that rocks are very special and that there are special rules about choosing a rock. Encourage the children to listen carefully and see if they can remember some of the rules. To add novelty and a relaxing atmosphere for story time ask the children to lie on their backs, close their eyes and listen to the story. Read the story.

11. After reading the story ask the children to describe the rules about collecting rocks that they remember. Using a large sheet of paper and marker, record their answers. Also record any of the rules that are not mentioned. Review all the rules.

12. Send the children off to find their perfect rock.

13. Ask the children to return to the blanket when they find their perfect rock. Give the children an opportunity to show their rock—but remember what the book said: "Nobody is to know what is special about another person's rock!"

More to do

Outdoors: Enjoy the outdoors. Almost any activity that can be done inside can be brought outside. For example, eat lunch or snacks outside under the shade of a tree. Spread out a blanket and provide books for the children. Bring out a box of old dramatic play clothes and hang them on the fence for children to wear. Bring music outside including cassette tapes or musical instruments.

Science: Place trays of sand and different sizes and shapes of rocks on the science table. Have magnifying glasses available for the children to observe and explore.

Related books

Come to the Meadow by Anna Grossnickle Hines
Hello, Tree! by Joanne Ryder
The Sun's Asleep Behind the Hill by Mirra Ginsburg

★ Kathy Lone, Sioux Falls, SD

The Earth-Friendly Game . . . . .4+

Materials needed
Large trash bag of assorted recyclable materials
3 cardboard boxes or 3 paper grocery bags
Marker

What to do
1. Fill a large trash can with an assortment of different recyclable materials (at least one item per child and items from three categories). Examples include: paper—newspaper, paper bag, magazine, cereal box, junk mail, worksheet, toilet paper roll, milk carton; plastic—soda bottle, margarine tub, plastic bag, six-pack holder, dishwashing liquid bottle, medicine or vitamin bottle, milk jug, film container; metal—aluminum and tin cans, sheet or ball of foil, jar lids, pie tins, bottle caps.

2. Label the three boxes or bags: paper, plastic, metal.

3. Ask the children to sit in a circle. Place the materials beside you and describe the activity. Explain that there is a big bag of trash that you brought from home filled with things that you don't want to throw away but that you want to recycle. One earth-friendly way to reduce the amount of trash is to recycle it. Recycling means to sort and send things to a place where they can be used again. Ask the children how many of them recycle things at home. Ask them if they would like to help sort the trash for recycling? Show the children the trash bag and the three recycling bins (labeled boxes or bags: one for paper, one for plastic and one for metal). Ask the children to take turns picking something out of the trash bag and placing it in the correct recycling bin.

4. Continue until the trash bag is empty. Thank the children for their help in recycling the trash.

More to do
Large Motor: Use soda bottles and a ball for bowling, bottle caps and a pie tin for target-tossing and plastic lids to make frisbees.

Music: Make and play rhythm instruments, such as pie tin tambourines, shakers made from dishwashing liquid bottles or cardboard tubes filled with beans or popcorn.

Science: Plant seeds in pots cut from milk cartons or soda bottles.

Related books
Beautiful Junk by Karen Brackett and Rosie Manley
Beautiful Junk II by Karen Brackett and Rosie Manley
EcoArt! Earth-Friendly Arts and Craft Experiences for 3 to 9 Year Olds by Laurie Carlson
Good Earth Art by MaryAnn F. Kohl and Cindy Gainer
Teachables From Trashables by Rhoda Redleaf
Teachables II by Rhoda Redleaf

★ Susan Sharkey, La Mesa, CA

The Environment

It's Cool to Car Pool . . . . .5+

Materials needed

1 chair for each child
Tongue depressors or straws
Gray or black construction paper
Scissors
Tape
Music

What to do

1. Ahead of time, construct smoke or exhaust props by cutting out cloud shapes from black or gray construction paper. Tape the cloud shape to the top of the tongue depressor or straw, leaving enough room at the bottom for a handle. Each child participating in the activity will need a prop.

2. As the activity begins arrange the chairs as they would be on a bus. Start with one chair for the bus driver and one chair behind the driver. Add more chairs as the game continues.

3. With the children discuss that cars, trucks and other vehicles need gasoline to run. Ask the children if they know what it smells like behind a car that is running. The smoke or odor they see and smell is called exhaust. Discuss that being close to the back of a car and smelling the exhaust can make people very sick. Point out that the more cars there are, the more exhaust there is in the air. Explain that a car pool is a group of people who ride together to work or other places so only one vehicle is needed for everyone. One vehicle that has seats for many people is called a bus.

4. Give each child an exhaust prop to hold. Choose one child to be the bus driver and have her sit in the front chair, holding the prop. At this time the other chair is empty.

5. As a group count the number of exhaust clouds that are in the room.

6. Turn on the music. Have the remaining children walk around the chairs (like in Musical Chairs) pretending to drive a car or truck. Explain that when the music stops, someone needs to car pool and sit in the empty chair.

7. Stop the music and shout "Car pool!"

8. When the empty chair has been filled, take the prop from the child. Count the remaining exhaust clouds and point out the decrease in number.

9. Add another chair to the bus.

10. Continue Steps 5-7 until all the children are seated in the bus. The only remaining exhaust cloud should be held by the bus driver.

11. Discuss the decrease in cars, air pollution and gasoline usage. Also discuss how riding bicycles and walking are good ways to help the environment.

More to do

Art: Provide materials for the children to make their own exhaust props for circle time by cutting out the cloud shape and decorating it with cotton balls. The cotton balls can be tinted with black powdered tempera paint and glued to the shape. Let the cloud shape dry and tape it to a straw or tongue depressor.

Dramatic play: Set up the area for bus play: arrange chairs in rows, make bus stop signs and have (or make) play money and tickets available to the children. Set up an area of the playground as a gas station or mechanic shop. Encourage the children using riding toys to stop to have a tune-up or to check under the hood. Explain that a car that is running in good condition uses less gas and makes less pollution in the air.

Original song

"Care About Our Air" (Tune: "The Wheels on the Bus")

> *Dirty air can make us sick,*
> *Make us sick, make us sick.*
> *Dirty air can make up sick,*
> *Here's what you can do.*
>
> *Walk, bike, skate; it's good for you,*
> *Good for you, good for you.*
> *Walk, bike, skate; it's good for you,*
> *And great for the air we breathe.*
>
> *The people on a bus are helping our air,*
> *Helping our air, helping our air.*
> *The people on the bus are helping our air,*
> *By not driving their cars.*
>
> *Car pool, car pool, it's cool to do,*
> *Cool to do, cool to do.*
> *Car pool, car pool, it's cool to do,*
> *And thanks for helping, too!*

Related book

For the Love of Our Earth by P. K. Hallinan

★ Kathy A. Lone, Sioux Falls, SD

To the Dump .5+

Materials needed

Clean recycled trash
Small trash can
Index cards
White paper and colored paper
Stapler

What to do

1. At circle time place a small trash can with the lid on in the center of the circle. (Inside the trash can place trashables—cereal boxes, juice boxes, plastic food bags—all with labels intact.)

2. With the children list on index cards the items that are thrown away at their home. Tape their ideas to the outside of the trash can.

3. Ask the children how these items could be recycled. Acknowledge all suggestions given.

4. Open the trash can while talking about recycling and reusing trash to protect our environment. Pull trash out of the can and have the children help read the labels and identify the colors and shapes.

5. Depending on the children's age level, there are many opportunities for teaching about recycling.

6. Place items in the can. Allow each child to pull out an item and describe the item.

7. Children are encouraged to identify words from the labels of the recycled items. The children can make a trash can book by cutting the front of boxes, samples of colors and letters and gluing or taping them into their book. Include a title page with the author's name. Encourage each child to write a story for the trash can book.

8. In a bookmaking center place directions and materials for making a class trash can book, involving children in a group project.

Related book

Gregory the Terrible Eater by Mitchell Sharmat

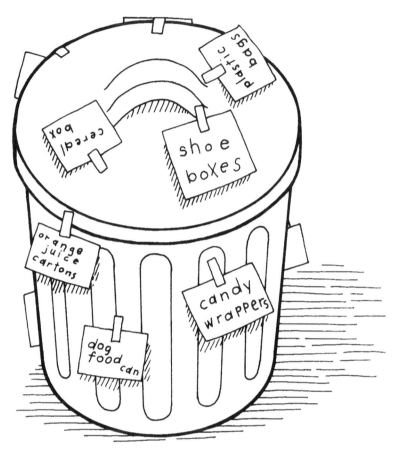

★ Vera M. Peters, Johnson City, TN

Leaf Match . . . . .3+

Materials needed
Variety of leaves
Large poster board
Clear self-adhesive paper

What to do
1. Glue one of each different kind of leaf onto the poster board and cover with self-adhesive paper.

2. Cover the remaining leaves with self-adhesive paper and cut them apart.

3. Let the children explore the individual leaves. Talk about their color, size and shape.

4. Point to a leaf on the poster board and tell the children the name of the tree it came from. Ask the children to bring up the leaves that look like the one you pointed to (name the leaf, example—maple leaf) and place their leaves next to the maple leaf on the poster board.

5. Continue asking the children to bring up leaves until all the leaves are placed on the poster board.

More to do
Math: Sort the leaves by size or by color. Count the total number of leaves.

Related book
A Busy Year by Leo Lionni

★ Ann Gudowski, Lake Forest, CA

Acorns . . . . .3+

Materials needed
Variety of nuts, including acorns

What to do
1. Talk about the seeds that grow on plants in the Fall. Tell them that nuts are the seeds of trees. Compare different kinds of nuts. Talk about how animals depend on nuts for food.

2. Use a squirrel puppet, if you have one, while saying the following fingerplay with the children.

> *With a little round face and a little brown cap,*
> *He fell from the tree to the ground.*
> *On a bed of leaves he was taking a nap,*
> *Just look! It's an acorn I've found.*

More to do
Dramatic play: Use an acorn cap on a thumb to make a finger puppet. Draw a face on the finger or use a small tissue for the body.

Game: Drop acorns into a container.

Math: Weigh acorns on a balance scale. Sort them into egg cartons or berry baskets. Ask each child to grab a handful of acorns and together count how many each child can hold. Graph the number of acorns that each child can hold.

Science: Plant an acorn and see if it grows. Examine acorns and caps and other nuts under a magnifying glass. Break open an acorn and see what is inside.

★ Sandra Gratias, Perkasie, PA

Apples, Apples, Apples . . . . .3+

Materials needed

Variety of apples (Ask each child to bring an apple.)
Container to hold the apples
Small terrycloth towels

What to do

1. Show the container of apples and discuss the different kinds of apples with the children. Make note of the different colors, shapes and sizes. Talk about whether they think that the apples would taste the same.

2. Ask the children to help you count the apples as you take them out of the container.

3. Sort the apples according to color or size and count each pile of apples.

4. Let each child choose one apple to wash and then shine with the terrycloth towel and put back in the container.

More to do

Snack: Cut some of the apples in pieces to taste. Bake apple pie or cook applesauce.

Related book

The Seasons of Arnold's Apple Tree by Gail Gibbons

★ Susan Rinas, Parma, OH

Create a Class Tree . . . . .3+

Materials needed

Brown lunch bags
Crayons
Tape

White paper
Large sheet of brown paper

What to do

1. Gather the children at the circle time area. Introduce the season of Autumn. Talk about the changes that Autumn brings (cool weather, leaves changing colors and falling, school starting).

2. Take the children for a nature walk. Supply a small brown lunch bag for each child. Have the children collect leaves of various kinds, colors and sizes. Point out textures, colors, sights and sounds of the season.

3. Back in the classroom, ask children to sort the leaves by color.

4. Ask each child to select two or three leaves to use in making rubbings. The child places the leaf under a piece of white paper and rubs the paper with a crayon.

5. The leaves are cut out and taped to a paper outline of a tree to create a class tree.

More to do

Creative Movement: Play flowing music and have children move like leaves blowing in the wind.

Math: Graph the leaves by color.

Science: Examine leaves with a magnifying glass.

Related books

Autumn by Gerda Muller
Why Do Leaves Change Color by Betsy Maestro

★ Amy Lieberman, Worcester, MA

Fall Leaves . . . . .3+

Materials needed

Different leaf patterns in different leaf colors (scattered around the room)

What to do

1. Ask each child to find a leaf in the room and bring it to circle time.

2. After the children are sitting in the circle ask them about their leaf. Ask who found leaves that look the same.

3. Sort out the leaves first by size.

4. Count and see which group has the most and which group has the least.

5. Then sort the leaves by colors.

6. Count the leaves again and see which group has more and which has less or the same number.

7. The children each hold a leaf, stand up pretending to be a tree and let the leaves fall to the ground. After the children pick up their leaves ask the children to drop only the yellow leaves, then the red leaves, then the green leaves, then the brown leaves.

More to do

Outdoors: Have circle time outside and watch the leaves falling. Go leaf hunting. Collect the leaves to sort or make collages with the leaves. Rake the leaves on the playground and jump in them.

Sensory: Put a collection of leaves into a tub with magnifying glasses and let children explore them.

Related books

A Busy Year by Leo Lionni
Caps, Hats, Socks and Mittens by Louise Borden

★ Holly Dzierzanowski, Austin, TX

Fall Is Here! .3+

Materials needed

Leaves

Scissors

Stapler

Colored construction paper (orange, tan, gold and red)

Yarn

What to do

1. Send the following note to parents:

> Dear Parents,
>
> On (day of the week), (date) we are going on a fall walk around the neighborhood. We are going to look for signs of fall, such as colored leaves, squirrels, nuts and seed pods. We will also learn about safely crossing streets and how to read street signs. We would love to have you come with us, please contact me if you can join us.
>
> Sincerely,
>
> Teacher's Name

2. Map out the walk beforehand so the route will include some colorful fall trees.

3. Ask the children to walk in pairs. On the walk look at all points of interest and ask the children to tell you if you pass their house. (If any parents live on the walking route, ask if they would provide a snack at their home.)

4. Ask the children to collect fall leaves on the walk.

More to do

Art: Leaf mobiles—enlarge leaf patterns and reproduce them on colored construction paper. Ask the children to cut the leaves out (precut for younger children). Cut a length of yarn and staple three or four leaves on it to make fall leaf mobiles. Use collected leaves to make a window hanging: Place two or three leaves on a sheet of wax paper. Paint over the leaves with liquid starch. Place a second sheet of wax paper on top of the first. Iron the two sheets of wax paper together. Staple strips of colored paper around the wax paper for a frame and hang in a window.

★ Barbara Saul, Eureka, CA

Leaf Dancing . . . . .3+

Materials needed

Ribbon (14"-16" per child)

Leaves cut out of construction paper or tagboard (1 per child)

Classical music

Large open area

What to do

1. Staple a leaf to the end of each ribbon length.

2. Gather the children for circle time and give each child a leaf ribbon.

3. Show the children how to move their leaf ribbons, up high, down low, in a circle, fast, slow, behind their back.

4. Start the music.

5. Ask the children to move their leaf ribbons with the music.

6. Ask a child to tell the other children how to move the leaf ribbons. Make sure there is time for everyone to have a turn being the leader.

7. When the children have finished collect the leaf ribbons for future use.

More to do
For a winter activity, substitute snowflakes for leaves.

Original song
(Tune: "Mary Wore Her Red Dress")

> *Mary had a red leaf, red leaf, red leaf.*
> *Mary had a red leaf and danced all day.*

Related book
Red Leaf, Yellow Leaf by Lois Ehlert

★ Glenda Manchanda, Huber Heights, OH

Walking Through the Forest With Our Fingers . . . . .3+

Materials needed
Red Leaf, Yellow Leaf by Lois Ehlert
Large piece of white butcher paper to cover a long table
Chart paper   Green fingerpaint
Sponge to add water to the paper   Yellow, red, orange tempera paint in shakers

What to do
1. Read *Red Leaf, Yellow Leaf* (or any book about the forest and leaves). Talk about walking in the forest and the things you would see. List responses on chart paper.

2. The children put on aprons and gather around the table. Explain that we will use our fingers to walk through the forest.

3. Put a large tablespoon of green fingerpaint in front of each child. Squeeze water from a sponge to thin the paint.

4. After awhile shake the different colors of tempera paint to make fall leaves on the paper.

★ Marilyn E. Ewing, Richmond, TX

Leaf People . . . . .3+

Materials needed
Paper bag
Colored leaves
Scarves

What to do

1. At circle time the children try to guess what is in the bag.

2. Pull out different color leaves from the bag and ask the children to name the colors.

3. Ask the children if they were a leaf what color would they like to be. Children discuss their choices.

4. Let's pretend we are leaves in a bag. When I count to three let's turn ourselves into leaves (1-2-3).

5. When I count to three again, let's jump out of the bag (1-2-3).

6. Now, let's pretend we are each a big tree (extend arms). Let's grow leaves on the tree (shake hands).

7. The teacher pretends to be the wind. The wind blows the leaves to the ground. (Children pretend to be leaves gently falling to the ground).

8. Now, the children stand up and raise their hands above their heads. Then they make their hands fall touching the ground. The teacher asks the children to copy her motions of raising and lowering her arms as she walks around the room. The teacher leads the children in the following chant.

> *Yellow leaves falling down*
> *Orange leaves falling down*
> *Green leaves falling down*
> *Brown leaves falling down*
> *Red leaves falling down*
> *Falling to the ground, falling to the ground. (children gently fall to the ground)*

★ Diann Spalding, Santa Rosa, CA

Autumn Leaves Are Falling Down . . . . .3+

Materials needed
Sheets of colored construction paper cut into leaf shapes (fall colors)

What to do

1. Give each child one or two leaves of different colors. Ask the children to stand in a circle.

2. Sing the song "Autumn Leaves Are Falling Down" to the children one or two times so they become familiar with the words and melody. The tune is "London Bridge."

> *Autumn leaves are falling down, falling down, falling down.*
> *Autumn leaves are falling down.*
> *Yellow, orange, red and brown.*
>
> *Rake them up and make a pile, make a pile, make a pile.*
> *Rake them up and make a pile.*
> *Ready! Jump and smile.*

3. Children raise their arms high, holding the colored leaves in their hands.

4. As the colors of the leaves are mentioned in the song, children should drop that colored leaf on the floor. By the end of the first verse, all leaves are on the floor. As the second verse is sung, children mimic raking leaves into a pile. On the word "jump" all children jump in place in the circle as if jumping into a pile of leaves.

More to do

Language: Read a story about autumn.

Outdoors: Take a nature walk to collect colorful leaves.

Related books

Red Leaf, Yellow Leaf by Lois Ehlert
Autumn Harvest by Alvin Tresselt

★ Joan Bowman, Bensalem, PA

Autumn Under Glass . . . . .4+

Materials needed

Sheets of black construction paper (1 per child)
Rectangles of clear self-adhesive paper, 2″ wider and 2″ longer than black construction paper (1 per child)
Glue sticks
Scissors
Assortment of colorful autumn leaves

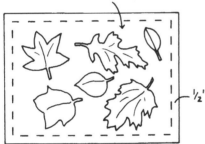

leaves glued on, leaving
½″ border clear

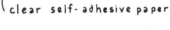
clear self-adhesive paper

Cut corners of self-adhesive paper
and fold edges onto back of black paper.

What to do

1. Ask each child to choose four or five leaves and arrange them on the black construction paper.

2. Leaving an uncovered 1/2″ border around the edge of the black construction paper, ask the child to glue each leaf on the paper using the glue stick.

3. Leaving a 1" border of self-adhesive paper beyond the edges of the black construction paper, place the self-adhesive paper over the leaf collage. Hint: Removing the backing slowly and applying pressure from the center of the collage outward will help the self-adhesive paper to unroll evenly.

4. Carefully turn the collage face down. Cut the corners from the self-adhesive paper (see illustration). Fold down the self-adhesive paper border onto the back of the black construction paper.

5. Turn the collage over and admire the leaves.

More to do
Math: Match leaves by shape, size or color before beginning to make the collage.

Original song
"Hello, Fall" (Tune: "Frère Jacques")

> *Red leaves, yellow leaves,*
> *Brown leaves, orange leaves,*
> *See them fall,*
> *One and all.*
> *Bare trees gently swaying,*
> *Everybody's saying,*
> *Hello, Fall! Hello, Fall!*

Related books
Why Do Leaves Change Color? by Betsy Maestro
Ska-tat! by Kimberley Knutson

★ Christina Chilcote, New Freedom, PA

Falling Leaves . . . . .4+

Materials needed
Leaves cut from construction paper (fall colors)
Circles (9" in diameter) cut from 9" x 12" brown construction paper
Scissors
Tape or glue for each child

What to do
1. Draw a spiral as shown on the next page on the brown circles.

2. Ask the children to cut along the spiral line on the circle.

3. When children finish cutting the spirals ask them to lift the cut circle and see their results.

4. Provide precut leaves (or materials for children to cut leaves). The children glue or tape the leaves along the spiral.

5. Hang the spirals with the leaves from the ceiling of the classroom.

More to do
Art: Brush the leaves on each side with vegetable oil. Place leaves that have been oiled between layers of newspaper. Place a heavy object on the newspaper for about three days. You will have beautifully preserved leaves. Make leaf rubbings by placing the leaves under paper. The children will rub their crayons over the top of the paper in a back and forth motion until the leaf impression appears.

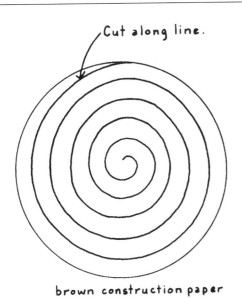

Cut along line.

brown construction paper

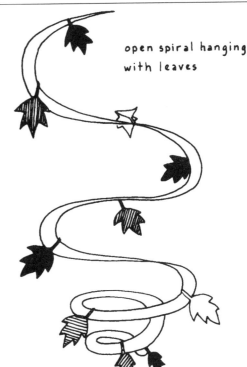

open spiral hanging with leaves

Outdoors: Rake a pile of leaves and let children jump in the pile.

Science: Discuss why leaves change colors. Go for a walk and collect colorful leaves.

"Falling Leaves" (Tune: "London Bridge")

> *See the leaves come falling down,*
> *Falling down,*
> *Falling down,*
> *See the leaves come falling down,*
> *Can you catch them?*

★ Linda Andrews, Sonora, CA

Great Gourds . . . . .4+

Materials needed

3 or 4 gourds
Wooden cubes
Paper and markers

Balance scale
Feely box

What to do

1. Before circle time place a gourd in the feely box.

2. Pass the feely box around the circle and have the children guess the contents.

3. Show the gourd to the class and pass it around the circle so each child can examine it briefly.

4. Explain to the children that they will be weighing the gourd. Place the gourd on one side of a balance scale. Ask the children to guess how many wooden cubes it will take to balance the scale. Write down their predictions. Place a cube, one at a time, on the other side of the scale until it balances. Record the number of cubes. Repeat this procedure with at least two other gourds. Discuss which was the heaviest and which was the lightest.

5. Place the scale and the gourds at a center for the children to explore on their own.

More to do

Science: Examine the gourds with magnifying glasses. Cut open a gourd and examine its contents.

Math: Balance the gourds with other manipulatives such as unifix cubes or multilinks.

★ Amy Lieberman, Worcester, MA

Pick a Pumpkin . . . . .4+

Materials needed
Pumpkin-shaped poster
Markers
Smaller pumpkin shapes (each with a child's name)

What to do

1. Teach the children the "I Saw a Pumpkin" song to the tune of "Clementine"

> *I saw a pumpkin,*
> *A big fat pumpkin*
> *It was hanging on a vine.*
> *_____ came along and picked it,*
> *Took it home and said,*
> *"It's mine!"*

2. At the point in the song where the words are "_____ came along and picked it," the child whose name is on the first small pumpkin comes forward and picks his name off the poster, revealing another small pumpkin with another child's name. The song is repeated until all children have picked their names from the poster. This is a good name recognition song. The children enjoy watching for their names to appear.

★ Ann Wenger, Harrisonburg, VA

Pounding Leaves . . . . .4+

Materials needed
Blocks of wood
Goggles
Leaves (colored if possible)

Hammers
Squares of white muslin (1 per child)

What to do

1. During circle time talk about fall leaves.

2. Show the children a variety of leaves.

3. Place a leaf or leaves on a block of wood.

4. Cover with muslin and tape it down to hold it in place.

5. Let children hammer on the wood. Liquid from the leaves will come through the cloth and leave color on the muslin.

More to do

Art: Cut coffee filters into leaf shapes and tint with food coloring mixed with water.

Large motor: Rake leaves into piles outdoors and jump in them.

Related books

Autumn by Gerda Muller
Why Do Leaves Change Color by Betsy Maestro

★ Carol L. Carpenter, New Port Richey, FL

Sorting Gourds . . . . .4+

Materials needed

Assortment of gourds in a basket (1 gourd per child)
Large grid and name tags for graphing (optional)

What to do

1. At circle time show and talk about gourds that people use as a decoration in their homes in the fall.

2. Look at the gourds and ask the children in what ways are the gourds similar and in what ways are they different (consider size, color, texture).

3. Let each child select one gourd from the basket. Ask each child to tell something about her gourd.

4. Ask the children to get in groups according to one characteristic of the gourds (consider size, color, texture). Designate areas around the circle where each group should line up.

5. Count the number of children in each line. Which group is the largest? Which is the smallest?

More to do

Science: Ask the children to predict what may be inside each gourd, then cut them open to find out. Are there seeds? What are seeds for? What do the seeds look like? How many seeds are there? What else is inside?

Related book

Pumpkin, Pumpkin by Jeanne Titherington

★ Kim Arnold, Kent, OH

Five Little Leaves . . . . .4+

Materials needed

None needed

What to do

1. Sing the following song, "Five Little Leaves" with the children. The tune is "Six Little Ducks."

> *Five little leaves were hanging on a tree (hold up five fingers, then put arms out and*
>   *hands down as if you were a tree)*
> *Red, orange, yellow, green, pretty as can be. (clasp hands as if delighted)*
> *"Whoosh!" came a breeze of cold fall air (throw out arms as if scattering)*
> *And four little leaves were hanging there.*

2. Repeat verses for 4, 3 and 2 leaves.

3. Sing the last verse:

> One little lonely leaf hanging on a tree. (repeat gestures as above)
> "Whoosh!" came a breeze of cold fall air. (repeat gestures)
> And left the tree and branches bare!

More to do

Art: Leaf prints—use red and yellow paint to make leaf prints.

Related book   *Red Leaf, Yellow Leaf* by Lois Ehlert

★ Lori Schaffer Zellers, Danville, IL

Tie Dye Leaves . . . . .4+

Materials needed

Leaf patterns   Pencils
Scissors   White paper towels
Food coloring—mix each color with a little water and place in a shallow container

What to do

1. Bring the materials to circle time and demonstrate how tie dye leaves are made. Tell the children that following circle time the materials for making tie dye leaves will be available so they can make their own leaves.

2. Ask each child to trace one leaf shape on a paper towel and to cut out the shape.

3. Fold the leaf shape several times.

4. Dip the corners of each leaf quickly into different food coloring solutions to create a tie dye effect (be sure not to hold the leaf in the solution since the paper towel is so absorbent).

5. Unfold the leaf carefully and let it dry.

More to do

Attach the leaves to crepe paper streamers and move to different kinds of music.

Original song

"Leaves Are Falling" (Tune: "Row, Row, Row Your Boat")

> Leaves, leaves falling down
> Falling to the ground.
> Red, yellow, orange and brown
> Leaves are falling down.

★ Joyce Montag, Slippery Rock, PA

Building a Scarecrow . . . . .5+

Materials needed

Sweatshirt
Socks
Pair of shoes
Plastic pumpkin head
Safety pins

Pants
Mittens
Chair for scarecrow to sit in
Straw hat (to fit pumpkin head)
Lots of fiberfill, rags or crumpled newspaper

Note: Clothes should be adult size without any holes.

What to do

1. Talk to the children about scarecrows. Explain that farmers sometimes put scarecrows in fields to keep the crows and other birds from eating corn that had not yet been harvested.

2. At circle time the children work together to build a scarecrow for the classroom. It will be built by stuffing old clothes and fitting them together to look like a person.

3. Show the children how to stuff the clothes with fiberfill, rags or newspaper, then ask pairs of children to stuff assigned pieces of clothing. (Two children could work together to stuff the pants, shirt, socks and mittens.)

4. When all of the clothes are stuffed, assemble the scarecrow in its assigned chair. Begin with the pants. The children who stuffed the pants bring them forward and place them in the chair in a sitting position. Next attach the sweatshirt with the help of the children who stuffed it. (The children hold it in place while the teacher pins it to the pants. Attach remaining body parts the same way.)

5. As body parts are added, ask the children to name the part of the scarecrow that should be added next.

6. Ask the children to choose a name for the scarecrow.

More to do

Language: Use the scarecrow as a model for discussions about color. Ask the children to name the colors of the scarecrow's clothing. Invite the children to make up stories about the scarecrow. Write the stories as the children tell them. Ask the children to draw pictures to help tell their stories.

Math: Ask children to stand up if they are wearing the same color shirt (or pants, socks) that the scarecrow is wearing. Count the number of children who are standing. Review the concept of two using the scarecrow as a model—ask what the scarecrow has two of (arms, legs, eyes). As Halloween approaches, walk around the neighborhood and count how many people used scarecrows to decorate for the holiday. (While you're walking, talk about other decorations like jack-o-lanterns and corn stalks.)

Science: Take a trip to a nearby farm to look for a real scarecrow. What did the farmer plant in the field? What animals might try to eat his crops? Children could look at the crops growing in the field, describe what they see, talk about what animals might try to eat those crops and think about ways a scarecrow might help the farmer.

Related books

Autumn by Gerda Muller
Fall Is Here! I Love It! by Elaine W. Good
The Little Old Woman Who Was Not Afraid of Anything by Linda Williams

★ Kim Arnold, Kent, OH

Fall

Family Hats .... .3+

Materials needed
Variety of hats

What to do
1. Pile the hats in the middle of the circle. Teach the children the following song to the tune of "Pop Goes the Weasel."

> *Marching around the family hats*
> *So early in the morning.*
> *I'll pick one up and put it on*
> *Now I'm my (family member).*

2. Ask one child to march around the circle while the group sings the song. The child picks out one hat, puts it on and says which member of his family might wear a hat like that.

3. The child says something about the family member he has chosen or the child pretends to be that family member.

4. The child puts the hat back in the middle of the circle. Continue until everyone has had a turn. Make sure you take a turn yourself.

More to do
Art: Make paper plate portraits using 9" round plates. Provide a variety of yarn, fabric scraps, wiggly eyes and other materials. Display the creations on a bulletin board titled "Our Families."

Dramatic play: Add the collection of hats to the dramatic play area. Encourage the children to use the props to role play the people in their families.

Language: Ask the children to draw and color a portrait of the family member they chose to role play. Write what the child says about that person on the drawing and bind all of the pictures together into a class book.

Original poem
> *These are Grandfather's glasses (circle fingers around eyes)*
> *And this is Grandfather's hat (place hands on head)*
> *And this is the way he folds his arms (fold arms across chest)*
> *Just like that!*
> *These are Grandmother's glasses....*

Related books
Away Went the Farmer's Hat by Jane B. Moncure
Grandpa's Great City Tour by James Stevenson
Mufaro's Beautiful Daughters by John Steptoe
Song and Dance Man by Karen Ackerman

Hats, Hats, Hats by Ann Morris
Lyle Finds His Mother by Bernard Waber
The Napping House by Don and Audrey Wood
Uncle Elephant by Arnold Lobel

★ Virginia Jean Herrod, Columbia, SC

Families

Getting to Know Families ....3+

Materials needed
None needed

What to do
1. Familiarize yourself with the names of each of the children's parents and siblings.

2. When dismissing the children from circle time use their names. For example, "If your mother's name is Kathy you may wash your hands for snack. If your big brother's name is Jeremy you may go to an activity center."

3. This is an excellent activity for teachers as well as the children. It helps children know that they are each important. It helps teachers become involved with the children at a more personal level.

More to do
As you get to know more about each family you can use this information. For example, "If you have a big brown dog named Spot you may wait to go outside. If you had spaghetti last night for dinner you may sit down for lunch." Have children bring in photos of their families. Make a large tree on the wall using crumpled brown paper bags as the trunk. Mount family photos on construction paper leaves. Ask the children to hang the leaves on the "Family Tree."

Related books
Is Your Mama a Llama? by Deborah Guarino
The Tub People by Pam Conrad

The Quilt Story by Tomie dePaola
Whose Mouse Are You? by Robert Kraus

★ Donna Rehder, Sonora, CA

Child of the Week ....3+

Materials needed
8 x 10 inch frame
Magazine pictures of children

What to do
1. Place a picture in the frame.

2. Include with the picture a fictional biography of the child including a name, age, ethnic background, who the child lives with, special abilities or needs, favorite foods, favorite activities.

3. Introduce the child to the class during circle time.

4. Explain any special abilities or needs.

5. Discuss the things that we have in common with each other.

6. Leave the picture out where all can see. On another day, share a snack or activity that the fictional child likes. Sing a song that is a favorite of the fictional child.

7. One by one, highlight each child in the group following the format used in highlighting the fictional child.

★ Cathy Badorek, Bozrah, CT

A Family for All Seasons ....4+

Materials needed
Outlines of 4 trees depicting spring, summer, autumn and winter
Leaf shapes
Glue or tape
Yonder by Tony Johnston

What to do
1. Invite the children to circle time and discuss the dynamics of a family and the people who make a family. Be sure to include all types of families.

2. Read *Yonder* to the children.

3. Discuss with the children the various activities families do together. Discuss if the activity is seasonal or year long. Have the children place a leaf on the tree that is appropriate to the activity. Older children may write the activity on the leaf prior to placing it on the tree.

More to do
Ask the children to make their own family trees, designating a leaf for each family member.

★ Cathlene M. Hedden, Livonia, MI

Cinnamon, Mint and Mothballs ......4+

Materials needed
Cinnamon, Mint and Mothballs by Ruth Tiller

What to do
1. Read *Cinnamon, Mint and Mothballs* during circle time.

2. Ask the children about their grandmother's house or the house of an older family friend.

3. Suggest that the children ask their mom or dad (or grandparent) to tell them a story about when they were a child and visited their grandparent's house. Tell the children to be prepared to share their parent's story at circle time if they would like to.

4. Send a note home explaining this project to parents and ask them to send an old photograph of their family.

More to do
Invite the children's mother or father to circle time. Have a Grandparent's Day and invite grandparents for a tea party. Ask if any grandparents would share memories of a visit with their grandparents.

★ Cathy Chenoweth, Columbia, MO

Sibling Shower .... .4+

Materials Needed

Large carpeted or grassy area
Crepe paper
Paper and marker
Variety of baby items (baby clothing, teething biscuits, jars of baby food)
Tape cassette of baby crying and tape player

Pictures of babies
Balloons
Tray

What to do

1. Involve the children in this activity before or shortly after the birth of a child's sibling.

2. The children can help decorate the classroom with pictures of babies, crepe paper, balloons.

3. Ask the children if they have baby brothers or sisters at home. Talk about the child (or children) who will soon become a big brother or sister. Discuss things that four year olds can do that babies cannot do.

4. Play "Where's the Baby?" Hide pictures of babies in the room. The children try to find all the pictures. Tape record a baby crying and hide the tape player. The Children try to find the crying baby.

5. Place a collection of six or seven baby related items on a tray. Cover the objects with a cloth and remove one or more of the objects. Hide the object you removed by wrapping it in a cloth. Ask the children to guess which object you removed.

More to do

If several of the children will become siblings this year spend a whole week or longer on this topic.

Art: Make rattles or shakers for an art project.

Dramatic play: Set up a pediatrician's office next to the housekeeping area. Provide rattles and diapers for baby dolls in the housekeeping area.

Field trip: Visit the infant room at a child care center or visit the nursery of a nearby hospital.

Home connection: Ask a parent and baby to spend a day in the classroom.

Science: Match baby rattles by the sound the rattles make.

Water table: Wash baby dolls in the water table.

Related books

Arthur's Baby by Marc Brown
A Baby Sister for Frances by Russell Hoban
The New Baby by Mercer Mayer
More More More Said the Baby by Vera Williams
That New Baby! by Patricia Relf

★ Linda N. Ford, Sacramento, CA

My Family Tree . . . . .5+

Materials needed

Love You Forever by Robert Munsch
Large sheets of white construction paper
Crayons
Scissors

Sheets of construction paper (various colors)
Glue
Markers

What to do

1. At circle time talk about families. What things do we do with our families? How do we help each other? What responsibilities do we each have?

2. Read *Love You Forever* and talk about the story.

3. Take the children outside to look for leaves. Ask each child to gather four or five leaves.

4. Let children choose different colors of construction paper to trace their leaves onto (one leaf per family member). Cut out the shapes of the leaves.

5. Distribute large sheets of white construction paper. Ask the children to draw a large tree and at the top or bottom of the sheet write "My Family Tree." Down the trunk of the tree ask the children to write their family's last name. (The teacher may help the children write, if needed.)

6. Then the children write (or teacher writes) the names of their family members on the leaves they have cut out. Glue the leaves onto the tree to make a family tree.

More to do

Math: Graph the number of family members each child has. Which family has the most family members? Which family has the least? Then, individually, ask each child to graph the number of family members in their own family who have certain specified characteristics (color of hair or eyes).

Science: Choose one recipe from family favorites to prepare with the class. Involve the children measuring the ingredients. Notice the differences in the food before and after baking or freezing. Taste the food after it has been prepared. How does it taste? Salty? Sweet? Bitter?

Writing: As a class, construct a cookbook. Ask each child to think of his favorite family recipe (it need not be a secret family recipe—it can be anything they like to eat). Ask each child to write his version of the recipe, the ingredients and measurements that he thinks are in the recipe. Combine all the recipes into a cookbook. Duplicate copies so that each child has one to give as a gift to family members. Keep the original copy of the cookbook to be added to the reading center.

Related books

The Terrible Thing That Happened at Our House by Marge Blaine
Nana Upstairs, Nana Downstairs by Tomie dePaola
A House Is a House for Me by Mary Ann Hoberman
I Go With My Family to Grandma's by Rikki Levinson
All Kinds of Families by Norma Simon

★ Lori Dunlap, Royersford, PA

Where Do You Live? . . . . .5+

Materials needed
Construction paper houses (with name, address and photo of each child)

What to do
1. Place the paper houses on a wall in the circle time area.

2. At circle time show the children the paper houses and explain that each house has a child's address written on it. Tell the children that you will say each of their addresses and ask them to stand when they hear their address.

3. Repeat each child's address. Discuss with the children that only one child lives at a specific address (or apartment number at the same address).

4. Ask the children who live on a certain street to stand and note the number.

5. Ask the children who live in a specific town to stand. Discuss that the town and nearby towns are located in the same state.

6. Talk about the names of nearby states.

7. Show the location of the states on a map and discuss that the states are located in the United States of America.

8. Vary the activity by letting a child ask the questions.

More to do
Art: Ask children to draw pictures of their homes and copy their address at the bottom of the paper. On the back of the paper, ask the children to draw the people in their family. Visit the neighborhood post office, or ask a mail carrier to visit the class and explain why each house has a different number.

★ Mary Jo Shannon, Roanoke, VA

Families

Old MacDonald Loves Fruits and Vegetables . . . . .3+

Materials needed

White paper plates   Glue
Markers   Craft sticks
Pictures of fruits and vegetables from seed catalogs or magazines (glue 1 picture on each paper plate
    and tape a craft stick to the back of each plate to make a fruit or vegetable puppet)

What to do

1. As you give each child a fruit or vegetable puppet ask the children to name the fruit or vegetable.

2. Talk about garden farms where fruits and vegetables are raised, rather than animals. Sing "Old MacDonald Had a Farm" but sing about the fruits and vegetables that grow on the farm (name the vegetables on the paper plates).

> *Old MacDonald had a farm, E I E I O*
> *And on his farm he had some veggies, E I E I O*
> *(Sing the name of one of the vegetable puppets, such as carrot.)*
> *And on his farm he had a carrot, E I E I O.*
> *With a carrot here and a carrot there, here a carrot, there a carrot, everywhere a carrot.*
> *Old MacDonald had a farm, E I E I O.*

3. Continue until all the children have a turn saying the name of their fruit or vegetable puppet. As the children become more familiar with the names of other fruits and vegetables add them to the lyrics of the song.

Related books

The Carrot Seed by Ruth Krauss   *Planting a Rainbow* by Lois Ehlert
The Tale of Peter Rabbit by Beatrix Potter   *This Year's Garden* by Cynthia Rylant
Titch by Pat Hutchins   *Vegetable Soup* by Jeanne Modesett

★ Anne Kuhlman, Woodville, OH

The Animals on the Farm . . . . .3+

Materials needed

Small plastic and wooden farm animals or pictures of farm animals

What to do

1. Ask each child to select an animal (or picture) from the collection and then sit in a circle.

2. Start with one child. Ask her (or the group) to identify her animal and make the sound that the animal makes.

3. Sing the following song to the tune of "The Wheels on the Bus."

> *The (cow) on the farm says (moo moo moo)*
> *(moo moo moo), (moo moo moo).*
> *The (cow) on the farm says (moo moo moo)*
> *All through the day!*

Other farm animals:

Dog   bow wow wow
Pig   oink oink oink
Rooster   cock-a-doodle-doo
Sheep   baa baa baa
Cat   meow meow meow
Horse   neigh neigh neigh
Chicken   cluck cluck cluck
Duck   quack quack quack

4. Repeat with the next child and her farm animal.

More to do
Art: Use animals created during an art activity as props for the song. Repeat the activity using pictures of zoo animals.

★ Leslie Kuehn Meyer, Austin, MN

Be a Seed! . . . . .3+

Materials needed
Carpet barrel or other large cylinder (or box) to use as a flower pot (large enough for a child to climb into)
Large square piece of brown felt (2' x 2')
Large flower watering can

What to do
1. Ask one child to be the "seed" and another child to hold the watering can.

2. The "seed" steps into the flower pot and hides inside. Place the brown felt on his head as soil.

3. Teach the children the following song to the tune of "Pop Goes the Weasel."

> *The seed goes down inside of the ground, (sing slowly)*
> *Waiting for some water. (child tips watering can)*
> *The sun shines brightly on the seed. (child stretches arms above head)*
> *Pop! Goes the flower! ("seed" jumps up)*

4. Act out the process of planting while singing the song. Encourage every child to help the "seed" by using hand motions for pouring and sunshine.

More to do
Dramatic play: Make the planting song props available for the children to act out the planting sequence.

Science: Observe seed growth by using small seedling pots or plastic cups to plant marigolds or other flowers.

★ Laleña L. Williams, Beacon, NY

Seed Development . . . . .3+

Materials needed

The Tiny Seed by Eric Carle
Large picture of the sun (cardboard)
Watering can

What to do

1. Read *The Tiny Seed* to the children at circle time.

2. Explain to the children that they are going to pretend they are seeds trying to grow.

3. Ask the children to crouch low to the floor.

4. As the children are crouched down, wave the sun (made from cardboard) over them (talking about how seeds need the warmth of the sun to grow).

5. Pretend to pour water on the children with an empty watering can (talking about how seeds need water to grow).

6. Exclaim "The seeds are sprouting!" and encourage the children to slowly stand up until they are fully extended. Talk about how beautiful the flower garden is.

★ Cindy Winther, Oxford, MI

Seed to Flower Rhyme Play . . . . .4+

Materials needed

None needed

What to do

1. The children change from seeds to flowers as they say the following poem.

> *In spring there was a little seed, sleeping in the ground, (children pretend to be asleep)*
> *In the sky there were gray clouds and rain was coming down. (tap floor for raindrop sound)*
> *Water made the seed wake up, before it could get dry, (children pretend to wake up)*
> *Pushing up to see the sun, so big up in the sky. (turn the head upward while standing up)*
> *First a little shoot popped out, (jump up)*
> *Then one by one leaves grew. (lift one arm, then the other, as leaves)*
> *And last, a bud became a flower, (move hands with fingers fanned out to frame face)*
> *And Nature smiles at me and you. (children "draw" a smile on their faces, point to*
> *   themselves and then to others)*

More to do

Art: Make tissue paper flowers.

Related book

The Story of the Root Children by Helen D. Fish

★ Theresa Usilton, Easton, MD

Peekaboo Farm . . . . .4+

Materials needed
Magnetic board or metal cookie sheet
Animal cutouts with magnetic tape on back

What to do
1. The teacher sings "Old MacDonald's Farm" while holding the magnetic board. The animal cutouts are attached to the back of the board.

2. During the part of the song, "...and on his farm, he had a _____," the teacher very slowly exposes part of the animal picture or cutout from behind the board.

3. The children are encouraged to identify the animal as soon as they can and to sing about that animal in the song. Place the animal on the front of the board once it is identified.

4. At the same part in the next verse of the song, the process repeats until all animals are on the front of the magnetic board.

Note: The slow process of exposing the animals should take place at different points on the board (side, top, corner, bottom). Show different parts of the animals (tail of the pig, wing of the bird, foot of the cat).

More to do
After all animals are on the front of the board, the teacher points to one animal and the children respond with the appropriate sound the animal makes. Ask the children, "Do we know a song about a _____?" and point to one of the animals on the board. Sing that song. This game could be played with cutouts of other items such as transportation vehicles, zoo animals, community helpers.

Math: Sort or classify the animals into various groups, such as animals that have fur, animals that have feathers, animals that eat hay.

Related books
Barn Dance! by Bill Martin, Jr.   *The Big Red Barn* by Margaret Wise Brown
Early Morning in the Barn by Nancy Tafuri   *Good Morning, Chick* by Mirra Ginsburg
I Went Walking by Sue Williams   *Old MacDonald Had a Farm* by Tracey C. Pearson
Sheep in a Jeep by Nancy Shaw   *Who Took Farmer's Hat?* by Joan L. Nodset

Related songs
"Three Little Ducks"   "Mary Had a Little Lamb"
"Boogie Woogie Piggie"   "Old Lady Leary's Cow"

★ Beverly C. Dugger, Johnson City, TN

Old MacDonald Had a Garden . . . . . . .5+

Materials needed
Cut-out pictures of several garden vegetables, carrots, potatoes, broccoli, beans, squash, onions
  (glue pictures to poster board and back them with flannel)

Flannel board with string dividing it horizontally (label top half "Above the ground" and bottom half
  "Below the ground")

What to do

1. The children sit in a circle and the vegetable cutouts are in the middle of the floor. Set the flannel board up on one edge of the circle so all the children can see it.

2. Teach the children the following version of "Old MacDonald."

"Old MacDonald Had a Garden"

Old MacDonald had a garden, E I E I O
And in his garden he grew some (vegetable name), E I E I O
Dig up the dirt and put the plant down.
(Vegetable name) grow (above or below) the ground.
Old MacDonald had a garden, E I E I O

3. Each child names a vegetable, finds it among those on the floor, takes it to the flannel board and attaches it above or below the ground. During each child's turn, use her name in the song, for example, MacDenise, MacShatara, MacJoel, MacDarrell.

4. Continue until each child has had a turn and all of the vegetables are placed on the flannel board. Review the garden, first name the vegetables that grow above the ground, then those that grow below the ground. Count the number in both groups, compare the two and ask the children, "Which has more? Which has less?"

More to do

Language: Make an alphabet book using the names of vegetables. A is for Asparagus, B is for Beans, C is for Carrots. Ask the children to give the book a title and design the cover. Let each child draw one or more illustrations. Bind the pages together.

Math: Using plastic food or pictures of food, sort the vegetables into two groups using this criteria: those that grow above the ground and those that grow below the ground. Graph the results. Ask the children if they can tell by the graph which group has more.

Outdoors: If possible, designate a small area on the playground as a class garden. Cultivate the ground and plant the seeds or seedlings. Ask the children to water, weed and tend the garden. If you cannot dig up a portion of the playground, you can plant a container garden using planters, tubs or just about anything that holds dirt.

Science: Grow vegetables in the science area. Cut a one-inch round from the top of carrots that have green tops attached and place the rounds in a shallow dish of water. Suspend a sweet potato or avocado seed (using toothpicks over the opening of a jar filled with water). Fill a small aquarium with potting soil. Plant beans or other fast growing seeds. Make sure the seeds are planted close to the aquarium glass so the children can observe the seeds as they develop. Buy a sprout starter kit from you local grocery or health food store. Follow directions included in the kit. Ask the children to make daily observations and record the development of the sprouts.

Related book

Eating the Alphabet by Lois Ehlert

★ Virginia Jean Herrod, Columbia, SC

Food Song . . . . .3+

Materials needed
White paper
Notebook or book cover
Markers

What to do
1. Sing the following song and encourage the children to think of the names of foods to fill in the blanks.

> *There was a man lived in the moon, in the moon, in the moon.*
> *There was a man lived in the moon and his name was Aiken Drum.*
> *And he played upon a ladle, ladle, ladle.*
> *And he played upon a ladle and his name was Aiken Drum.*
> *And his hair was made of ____, ____, ____.*
> *And his hair was made of _____ and his name was Aiken Drum.*
> *And his eyes...nose...mouth...ears.... (additional verses)*

2. Draw a circle for a face and then draw the food items as the children suggest them. Next to the face write the names of the foods.

3. When the face is finished, put it in the notebook. Repeat the song during the next few days (each time making a new face) until each child has had a chance to suggest a food for the drawing.

4. Sing the lyrics of the book together at circle time, and later you may wish to put it in the listening center with a tape of the class singing the song.

5. If you prefer, you can use cutout pictures of food instead of drawing the foods.

More to do
Art: Make collages on paper plates with food pictures cut from magazines or food labels.

Home connection: Put the book and tape in a bag and encourage children to take it home to share with their families and to add a food feature to a new face (provide blank pages in the book).

Snack: Spread peanut butter on rice cakes and add raisins or banana slices for facial features.

Related books
Eating the Alphabet: Fruits and Vegetables from A-Z by Lois Ehlert
Mooncake by Frank Asch
Vegetable in the Garden: A First Discovery Book by Pascale De Bourgoing

★ Laura Egge Durbrow, Lake Oswego, OR

All About Corn .3+

Materials needed

Different types of corn
Paste
Corn flakes
Popcorn

Stapler
Construction paper (blue, brown, yellow, green)
Corn meal

What to do

1. At circle time show samples of different types of corn and discuss the use of each; sweet corn for people to eat, feed corn for animals to eat, Indian corn for decorative use and popcorn for popping. Talk about the similarities and differences of the four types of corn.

2. Tell the children that Native Americans taught the Pilgrims to plant corn. It was a very important food to the first settlers of our country.

3. Make a picture of a corn seed growing. Use one piece of blue paper (sky), 1/2 piece of brown paper (earth), a small piece of yellow paper (corn seed) and a long piece of green paper (stalk and leaves). Cut the shape of a corn kernel from yellow paper and leaves from green paper. Paste these together on the blue paper to form a plant. Place the top edge of the brown paper on top of the corn seed. Staple the side and bottom edges of the brown paper onto the bottom half of the blue paper so that the leaves of the corn plant are above the brown paper (earth).

More to do

Art: String popcorn to make necklaces and bracelets.

Cooking: Grind corn kernels with a mortar and pestle or between rocks to show the children how the Native Americans ground corn into meal. Encourage the children to grind the corn. Compare the ground meal to purchased corn meal. Mix and bake corn muffins to serve for snack.

Science: Show the children one cup of popcorn kernels and ask children how many cups the popped corn will fill. Pop one cup of kernels and see if it will fill the number of cups the children predict (30 cups is the approximate number of cups). Eat the popcorn or fill bags to give as a gift for each family.

Snack: Eat corn flakes, with or without milk, for snack.

Related books

The Popcorn Book by Tomie dePaola
Popcorn by Frank Asch

★ Wendy Pfeffer, Pennington, NJ

Berry Delightful . . . . .3+

Materials needed

Jamberry by Bruce Degan
Paper

Variety of berries (thawed frozen berries may be used)
Crayons

What to do

1. Read *Jamberry* at circle time.

2. Talk about berries and ask children what they know about berries. Some facts are that they grow in the summer; birds like to eat them; they grow on trees, large bushes, small bushes, prickly bushes.

Note: Tell children never to eat a wild berry without asking an adult since some berries are not safe to eat.

3. On a low table in the center of the circle, place several berry samples for the children to smell and taste as you talk about each.

More to do

Art: Encourage the children to draw pictures of one or all of the different types of berries.

Snack: Bring in several types of berry preserves and spread on crackers or bread cut into small pieces.

Related book

Blueberries for Sal by Robert McCloskey

★ Cathy Chenoweth, Columbia, MO

Exploring Vegetables . . . . .3+

Materials needed

Vegetables
Cutting board
Sharp knife (for teacher only)

What to do

1. At circle time talk about and show the children the vegetables.

2. Pass the vegetables around the circle so the children can feel the vegetables with their hands and smell the vegetables.

3. Tap the vegetables on a cutting board and ask the children to listen to the noise the vegetables make.

4. Wash the vegetables and cut them into pieces for tasting.

5. Ask questions about each vegetable as the children eat it. "How does it feel? Does it have a smell? Does it make a noise as it is chewed? How does it taste?"

★ Renee L. Parker, Fort Washington, MD

Where Does It Come From? . . . . .3+

Materials needed

1 bowl of each (ketchup, orange juice, peanut butter, applesauce)
Spoons
1 of each, in a covered box (tomato, orange, peanut, apple)

What to do

1. At circle time talk about and show the children what is in each bowl. Using spoons, let the children taste each food.

2. Talk about the taste and smell of each food.

3. Ask if anyone knows where ketchup comes from. After the children make several guesses, show them the tomato and talk about how the tomato is made into tomato ketchup.

4. Continue tasting and talking about the item in each bowl and compare it to its food source.

More to do

Art: Use peanut shells to make a peanut shell collage.

Snack: Provide oranges that are cut in half and a manual juicer and help the children make orange juice.

★ Holly Dzierzanowlski, Austin, TX

Is It Food? .3+

Materials needed

2 paper grocery bags
Glue

Newspapers and magazines
Coupons (food and nonfood items)

What to do

1. Cut out pictures of food and non-food items from the newspaper or magazine ads.

2. Glue pictures of food on the front of one grocery bag.

3. Glue pictures of nonfood items on the front of the other grocery bag.

4. Draw a red "no" symbol (see illustration) around the nonfood pictures on the bag.

5. Pass out one coupon to each child in the circle.

6. The children take turns putting their coupons in the correct bag (in the food bag if it is a food item and in the nonfood bag if it is not a food item).

More to do

Empty packages and boxes could be used instead of coupons.

Dramatic play: Put empty packages and boxes in the dramatic play center for the children to use in playing grocery store.

Math: Sort packages and boxes.

★ Yvonne Anderson, Oakdale, MN

In the Veggie Patch ....3+

Materials needed
Vegetables (1 for each child to hold)

What to do
1. Review names of the vegetables with the children.

2. Place the vegetables in the center of the circle.

3. Sing the following song to the tune of "Paw Paw Patch." Insert child's name into the blank; depending on the group size, you may wish to repeat one name three times or use three different names.

> *Where oh where is our friend _____?*
> *Where oh where is our friend _____?*
> *Where oh where is our friend _____?*
> *Way down yonder in the veggie patch.*
> *Pick yourself a (name of veggie) and put it in your basket.*
> *Pick yourself a (name of veggie) and put it in your basket.*
> *Pick yourself a (name of veggie) and put it in your basket.*
> *Way down yonder in the veggie patch.*

4. Repeat song until all children have had a turn to pick a vegetable.

More to do
Science: Plant vegetable seeds.

Snack: Eat the vegetables that the children explored in the activity.

Related books
Growing Vegetable Soup by Lois Ehlert
Victory Garden Kid's Book by Marjorie Waters

★ Linda N. Ford, Sacramento, CA

Sandwiches ....3+

Materials needed
Bread cards with pictures of sandwich items (the cards are cut from poster board in the shape of bread slices and glue magazine pictures onto the bread shapes)

What to do
1. At circle time each child receives a card. Each child takes a turn showing the other children what is on her card.

2. Children who are holding a card with a matching picture of the sandwich item hold their pictures up too. For example, one child holds up a card with cheese on it and other children with pictures of cheese would also hold up their cards.

More to do

Art: The children find pictures in magazines to cut out and glue on bread cards. In addition to cutting out food items they like on sandwiches, the children could cut out pictures of items they think would make a silly sandwich.

Games: Play the memory game with twelve cards (six matched sets) at a time.

Home connection: Each child signs up to bring a sandwich item and the children make sandwiches for snack.

Language: Talk about different kinds of sandwiches: Tacos, Pita bread pockets, rolled sandwiches, open-faced sandwiches.

Related books

Bread, Bread, Bread by Ann Morris
Jamberry by Bruce Degan
Sam's Sandwich by David Pelham

Gregory the Terrible Eater by Mitchell Sharmat
Potluck by Anne Shelby

★ Sandra Nagel, White Lake, MI

Peanuts . . . . .3+

Materials needed

Large sheets of paper
Peanuts
Bowl

Marker
Butter or margarine
Rolling pin or blender (for crushing peanuts)

What to do

1. Talk about George Washington Carver, the botanist who discovered many different ways to use peanuts.

2. Ask the children to describe the things they can do with peanuts and list them on a sheet of paper.

3. Ask the children the different ways they can use peanut butter and list them on a sheet of paper.

4. Explain that George Washington Carver listed 300 different things to do with peanuts. He wrote a book about all the ways to use peanuts.

5. Encourage each child to open a peanut and taste it. Together open the remaining peanut shells and help the children crush the peanuts using a rolling pin or a blender.

6. Add a small amount of butter or margarine and mix well.

7. Spread the peanut butter on crackers for the children to taste.

More to do

Art: Provide empty peanut shells for the children to use in different art projects.

Cooking: Make peanut butter cookies or peanut bread.

Home connection: Ask the children to look for pictures and labels that have peanuts or peanut butter on them. The items can be shared with the other children and used in the dramatic play area or art area.

★ Melissa Browning, West Allis, WI

Vegetables ....3+

Materials needed

Pieces of flannel (orange, green, white, red, yellow, tan, brown)
Scissors
Fabric paints
Patterns of a pumpkin, onion, carrot, cabbage, ear of sweet corn and green beans
Vegetables (corresponding to the vegetable patterns)

What to do

1. Cut the vegetable pictures from pieces of flannel using the patterns and decorate using fabric paints. Let dry at least four hours.

2. During circle time show and talk about the fresh vegetables and the vegetable pictures made of flannel with the children.

3. Use the flannel board while singing the following song, "Vegetables," to the tune of "Mary Had a Little Lamb."

> *We are pumpkins, big and round,*
> *Big and round, big and round.*
> *We are pumpkins, big and round,*
> *Seated on the ground.*
>
> *We are string beans, green and fine....*
> *Growing on a vine.*
>
> *We are onions, round and white....*
> *We make soup taste just right.*
>
> *We are carrots, orange and long....*
> *Help us sing this song.*
>
> *We are cabbage, green or red....*
> *See our funny head.*
>
> *We are ears of corn, tall and straight....*
> *Don't we taste just great!*

4. Repeat the song and encourage the children to sing along. Make the flannel board and vegetable pictures available during play time.

More to do

Field trip: Visit a farm or grocery store.

Math: Make a matching game using identical pictures from two copies of a seed catalog.

Snack: Have a tasting party. Cut vegetables into pieces and serve with salad dressing.

Related books

Jack and the Beanstalk by Paul Galdone
Growing Vegetable Soup by Lois Ehlert

★ Cory McIntyre, Crystal Lake, IL

What Did You Eat for Breakfast . . . . . .3+

Materials needed
None needed

What to do
1. Talk about different kinds of breakfast foods and what the children ate for breakfast.

2. Sing the following song to the tune of "Johnny Pounds with One Hammer."

"The Breakfast Song"

What did you eat for breakfast, for breakfast, for breakfast?
What did you eat for breakfast (child's name) today?
Allow them time to tell you, then sing:

(Child's name) ate (child's answer), (child's answer), (child's answer)
(Child's name) ate (child's answer) for breakfast today.
3. Continue until each child has had an opportunity to participate.

More to do
Art: Collect pictures of foods to create a mural or book of the children's favorite foods.

Cooking: Prepare breakfast foods for snack or as a cooking activity. Extend the cooking experiences to include other foods the children eat at home.

Related books
Growing Vegetable Soup by Lois Ehlert   *Lunch* by Denise Fleming
Pancakes, Pancakes by Eric Carle   *Today Is Monday* by Eric Carle

★ Tina M. Taylor, Johnson City, TN

What shall We Buy at the Market? . . .3+

Materials needed
Pictures of food from magazines (laminate for durability)
Resonator bells

What to do
1. Place the pictures of food on the floor, naming each as you set it down in front of the children,

2. Chant the following song.

What shall we buy at the market?
What shall we buy at the market?
What shall we buy at the market?
Yo-ho-ho-yo-ho

Play resonator bells to accompany last sentence. Let the children take turns using the bells.

3. Each child will choose one picture and tell the other children what food he has chosen.

More to do

Art: Make a class mural by gluing pictures of food onto a picture of a table that is drawn on a large sheet of paper.

Cooking: Introduce children to different foods and prepare a variety of ethnic foods.

Science: Provide fruits and vegetables for children to handle. Discuss the colors and textures of the various foods.

Related book

Eating the Alphabet by Lois Ehlert

★ Denise Covert, Perris, CA

Corn Weaving . . . . .4+

Materials needed

1 sheet of yellow construction paper per child (12" x 18")
Strips of paper in shades of gold, yellow, brown, tan, blue, red (12" x 1")
1 sheet of green construction paper per child (9" x 12")
Glue

What to do

1. Cut the yellow sheet of paper into the shape of an ear of corn (straight across the top and curved to a point at the bottom). Cut slits 1" apart down the length of the paper.

2. Using the ear shape as the base, the children weave the assorted strips in and out of the yellow paper to fill all the slits.

3. Trim excess strips that stick over the edge of the paper.

4. Glue down the ends.

5. Trace and cut long green leaves to glue across the top edge of the ear of corn.

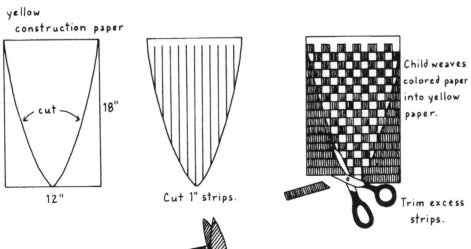

yellow construction paper

cut · 18"

12"

Cut 1" strips.

Child weaves colored paper into yellow paper.

Trim excess strips.

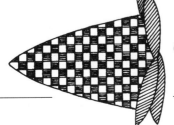

Cut out green leaves and glue across straight edge.

More to do

Manipulatives: Cover the bottom of a 9" x 13" pan with cornmeal. Use fingers to write or draw in it. Tap or shake gently to erase.

Science: Mix cornstarch and water until it feels stiff but still runs off the spoon. Pour into a jelly roll pan. Push it and try to pick it up. It seems to be solid, then turns to liquid. Sprout different types of corn—popcorn, feed corn, Indian corn, decorative miniature corn—and observe changes in growth. Leave an ear of fresh corn out and watch it dry over the span of a week. Use a balance scale to weigh kernels of unpopped corn and popped corn.

Snack: Bake cornbread or corn muffins. Sample blue corn chips. Try popcorn dipped in honey or maple syrup.

★ Sandra W. Gratias, Perkasie, PA

It's A Carrot Seed! . . . . .4+

Materials needed

Variety of vegetable seed packets (carrots, beans, radishes, pumpkins)
Vegetables that correspond to the seed packets
Chart paper and marker or chalk board and chalk
Paper plates
Magnifying glass

What to do

1. Place the vegetables on a low table in the middle of the circle for the children to examine. Involve the children in discussing the name of each vegetable and if they have eaten it. Encourage them to describe each vegetable. Is it smooth? Rough? Bumpy? The children can categorize the vegetables according to size, color, shape, texture.

2. Place the vegetable seed packets on the table with the vegetables. Encourage the children to match the seed packets with the vegetables. Ask the children to predict what the seeds in each packet look like. The children can feel the seeds through the packets as they think about the seed's size and shape. As the children make their predictions, help them record their ideas on chart paper or the chalk board.

3. While the children watch, open each packet of seeds and encourage the children to talk about the seeds. Place each seed packet on a paper plate and tape the packet wrapper onto the plate by the seeds. Involve the children in examining the different seeds with a magnifying glass, comparing and contrasting the seed's color, size, shape. Encourage the children to talk about the size of the seeds and the size of the vegetables produced.

More to do

Art: Using paints, markers or crayons, ask the children to draw pictures of the vegetables on large white sheets of paper. Encourage the children to carefully observe, hold and feel the vegetables as they work on their pictures.

Cooking: Take the vegetables and include the children in making a simple vegetable soup using the recipe in *Growing Vegetable Soup* or the favorite soup recipe of one of the children.

Game: Play the game "Vegetable Soup." Children stand in a circle and choose a vegetable they want to be. Place a large, empty soup pot and a wooden spoon in the middle of the circle as props. One child is the cook and pretends to stir the soup. He says, "I need more (name of vegetable)." Children who have chosen to be that vegetable go to the center of the circle, touch the soup pot and then go back to their places in the circle. The child stirring the soup tries to run to one of the places left by the children. The child left standing without a place in the circle then becomes the cook and the game continues.

Language: After making vegetable soup, ask the children to describe the steps they followed to make the soup. Record the steps on a chart. Ask the children to bring a favorite vegetable soup recipe from home that can be compiled into a recipe book for each child.

Science: Decide as a group which seeds to plant. The seeds can be planted in soil inside of empty milk cartons. Together read on the back of the seed packets how to plant the seeds. Select ones that will grow in the area where you live.

Snack: Involve the children in cleaning the vegetables using a small brush and lots of water. After they are clean, encourage the children to taste the different vegetables and describe the texture and taste.

★ Susan Thompson, Casper, WY

Jug Garden .4+

Materials needed
Plastic gallon milk jugs (washed)
Wooden dowels, 15" to 18" tall (3/8" or 1/4" in diameter)
Velcro strips
Glue
Tagboard (various colors)

What to do
1. Draw and cut out pictures of familiar fruits and vegetables from tagboard or cut out magazine pictures and glue onto tagboard.

2. Glue velcro strips to the dowels that have been cut to various lengths.

3. Glue the other half of the velcro strip to the back of the pictures of food.

4. Place wooden dowels in empty milk jugs and space the jugs in rows like a garden.

5. Introduce the activity to the children at circle time by reading a story or showing and discussing a picture of a garden.

6. Each child chooses a fruit or vegetable to attach to a dowel in a milk jug and talks about the fruit or vegetable she has planted in the class garden.

More to do
Dramatic play: Children love to plant and harvest the fruits and vegetables from the milk jug garden.

Snack: Involve the children in preparing the fruits and vegetables.

Original song

"This is the Way We Plant a Garden" (Tune: "Early in the Morning")

This is the way we plant a garden,
This is the way we plant a garden,
This is the way we plant a garden,
Early in the morning.

Related books

Growing Colors by Bruce McMillan
Growing Vegetable Soup by Lois Ehlert

★ Linda Yuska, Buckingham, IA

Junk Food or Healthy Food . . . . .4+

Materials needed

Small plastic garbage can
Basket
Pictures of foods cut from magazines and food labels (include both healthy and junk food)

What to do

1. Discuss the difference between foods that taste good and foods that are good for you. Talk about food that tastes good and also help your body grow.

2. Show pictures of food to the children and identify each.

3. Ask children to categorize foods by placing junk food in the garbage can and healthy food in the basket.

4. Discuss what should be considered as the children are sorting the foods.

More to do

Art: Cut pictures out of magazines and make two class collages, one of healthy food and one of junk food.

Related books

Bread and Jam for Frances by Russell Hoban
Gregory the Terrible Eater by Garret Christopher

★ Linda Ford, Sacramento, CA

Perky Peanut . . . . .4+

Materials needed

Peanuts in the shell (1 lb.)
Box
Sheets of newspaper
Wooden mallets or blocks of wood

What to do

1. Put peanuts in a box and pass it around the circle for each child to take one peanut.

2. Discuss how the peanut looks, how it feels and its shape.

3. Using a wooden block or mallet on a sheet of newspaper, ask the children to crack open their peanuts.

4. Discuss what is inside the shell, how many coverings the seed has, what part of the peanut is eaten.

5. Invite the children to help make peanut butter and discuss the steps in the recipe.

Peanut Butter Recipe

Roasted peanuts, blender, 2 tablespoons oil, 1/4 teaspoon salt
✓ Put the roasted peanuts in the blender.
✓ Add oil and salt
✓ Grind.
✓ Eat on crackers or with apple wedges.

More to do

Math: A Handful of peanuts—Put peanuts in a box and ask each child to take a handful of peanuts. Count the number of peanuts in each handful and record the number on a graph. Also make a concrete graph by laying each child's peanuts in a row on a table. Compare the number of peanuts in each row with the number on the graph.

Puppetry: Make Perky Peanut Puppet. A nylon stocking, cotton stuffing and two circles for eyes are needed for each puppet. Use two handfuls of cotton stuffing to create two balls. Stuff the cotton balls into the nylon stocking, one on top of the other. Squeeze the middle space between them to get a figure eight or peanut shape. Tie the stocking in a knot at the end of the cotton ball. Pull the rest of the stocking over the cotton ball again, then tie another knot. Cut off the excess stocking. Glue on the circles for eyes making a face on one of the cotton balls.

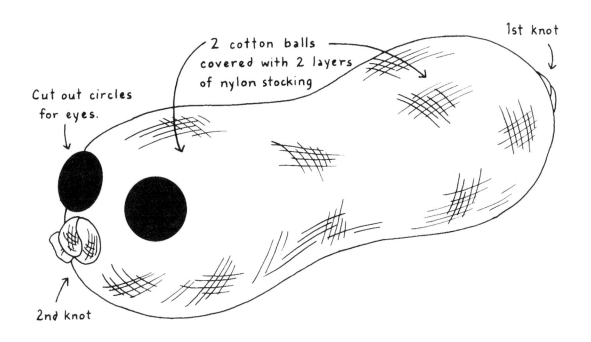

Cut out circles for eyes.

2 cotton balls covered with 2 layers of nylon stocking

1st knot

2nd knot

Original poem

"The Perky Peanut Poem"

My name is Perky Peanut
I grow underground.
When the farmer digs me out
I'm always upside down.
Crunchy little seedlings
Grow inside my shell.
They'll change into peanut butter
If ground up very well.

"What's Under the Ground"

What's in my garden, under the ground,
Wiggling and jiggling and crawling around.
Could it be ants, earthworms or slugs?
Are there creatures bigger than bugs?
Do they make holes and burrow trails?
What's under the ground—do you want to see?
Then come to my garden and dig with me!

★ Beverly Cornish, Philadelphia, PA

Using the Food Pyramid . . . . .5+

Materials needed

Chart paper
Marker
Scissors
Pictures of food (from magazines or the newspaper food section)

What to do

1. Cut out many pictures of food and draw a large food pyramid on chart paper with each of the six sections labeled with the name of a food group (see illustration on page 175).

2. Talk about and show the food pyramid with the children and identify the foods that are in each of the food groups.

3. Show the children one food picture at a time, ask them to identify the food and name its food group.

4. Each child takes a turn taping the picture of the food in the appropriate space on the food pyramid.

★ Elaine C. Commins, Atlanta, GA

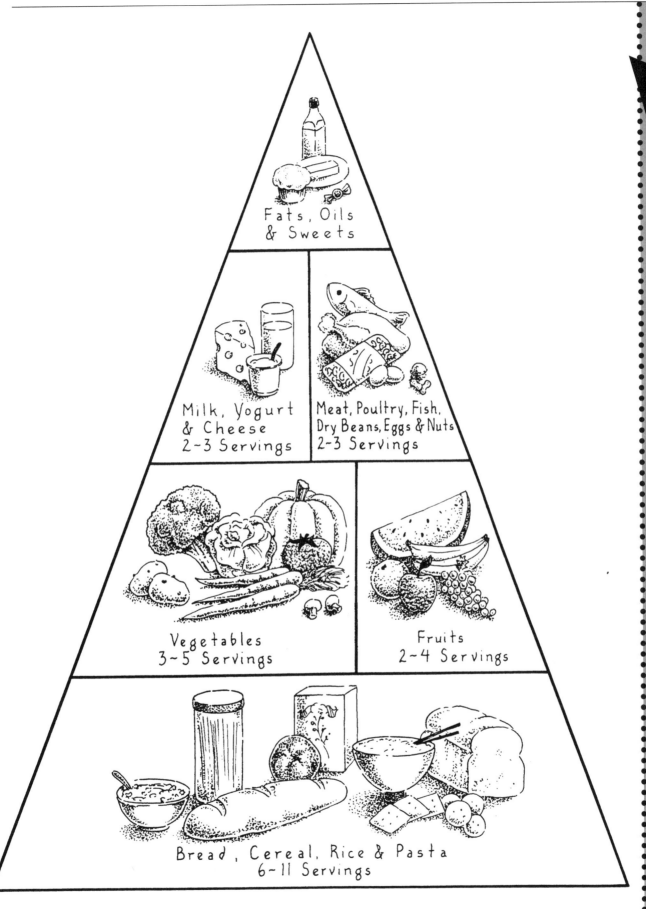

Fats, Oils
& Sweets

Milk, Yogurt
& Cheese
2-3 Servings

Meat, Poultry, Fish,
Dry Beans, Eggs & Nuts
2-3 Servings

Vegetables
3~5 Servings

Fruits
2~4 Servings

Bread, Cereal, Rice & Pasta
6-11 Servings

Stand On . . . . .5+

Materials needed

Masking tape
Pictures of food from the food groups (see illustration on page 175)

What to do

1. Cut out several pictures of food from each food group. Laminate pictures if desired.

2. Tape the pictures to the floor in the middle of the circle and discuss the different foods and their respective food groups.

3. The teacher calls the name of one of the food groups. The children move to stand on a picture of a food in that food group. More than one child can have her foot on a picture. (If there are several children divide the class into groups to limit the number of children moving at a time.)

4. After naming a food group talk about the number of servings children should eat each day from that group.

More to do

Snack: Have a tasting party with foods the children may not be familiar with, such as raw parsnips, kiwi.

Original song

(Tune: "Mulberry Bush")

> *I like food from the (vegetable) group,*
> *The (vegetable) group,*
> *The (vegetable) group,*
> *I like to eat....(pause and point to one child who is to name an appropriate food).*

Incorporate child's answer into the next verse;

> *I like to eat lots of (zucchini),*
> *Eat (zucchini),*
> *Eat (zucchini),*
> *It's in the vegetable group.*

Related books

The Very Hungry Caterpillar by Eric Carle
The Milk Makers by Gail Gibbons
Strega Nona by Tomie dePaola

★ Cathy Allen Falk, Fort Wayne, IN

What Should I Eat? . . . . .5+

Materials needed

6 boxes of graduated sizes, each representing 1 of the 6 food groups (The largest box represents the bread group and serves as the base for building the food pyramid.)

Pictures of foods (number of pictures in each food group corresponds to the number of recommended daily servings in that food group)

Spring clothespins (attach a picture of a food item to each)

What to do

1. Arrange the boxes according to size and label each with the name of a food group (see Illustration on page 175).

2. Ask the children to choose a picture of a food.

3. The children take turns identifying the food in their pictures and clipping the pictures to the box that is labeled with the food group that the food belongs in.

4. After all the pictures are clipped to the labeled boxes, talk about the number of food items that are recommended from each food group daily.

5. Build a food pyramid using the six boxes to emphasize the recommended number of servings in each food group.

More to do

Children sort the food pictures into three meals that they would eat during a day and clip the pictures onto three paper plates.

Related books

Bread and Jam for Frances by Russell Hoban
Gregory the Terrible Eater by Mitchell Sharmat
The Very Hungry Caterpillar by Eric Carle

★ Brenda Miller, Oleon, NY

Healthy Plates . . . . .5+

Materials needed

Paper plates
Scissors

Magazines (with pictures of a variety of foods)
Glue

What to do

1. Talk about healthy foods and the food groups (see illustration on page 175). Show the children pictures of food that make a well balanced meal.

2. Provide the children with magazines to use in cutting pictures of foods that represent a healthy meal and glue the pictures onto a paper plate.

3. Ask the children to describe the foods that they have glued on their paper plates.

More to do

After lunch each day for a week ask the children to evaluate their lunch using the food groups to determine if it is a well balanced meal.

★ Angela Williamson, Greensboro, NC

Nutrition . . . . .5+

Materials needed

6 posters, 1 for each food group (with pictures of food cut from magazines)
Plastic food items
Ingredients for cooking and snack preparation

What to do

1. To provide an extended discussion of nutrition (see illustration on page 175) activities are planned over a five day period:

Day 1: milk and dairy food group

Day 2: fruit food group

Day 3: vegetable food group

Day 4: meat and protein food group

Day 5: bread and grains food group; fats, oils and sweets food group

2. Talk about what nutrition means and that it describes the process by which our bodies are nourished by the foods we eat and how they use the food for growth and energy.

3. Introduce one of the food groups on its respective day (listed in step 1). Talk about and show the poster containing pictures of food items that are familiar to the children.

4. Provide a variety of plastic food items (or real foods) that the children can identify. Ask the children to select the foods that are in the food group being discussed that day. Encourage children to look at the food group poster as they select the foods.

5. Read a story about foods that are in the food group (see related books on the next page).

6. Involve the children in preparing foods from the food group for snack.

7. Explain that foods containing fats, oils and sweets should be used sparingly since these foods have few nutrients and should not be eaten in large quantities.

More to do

Cooking: On **Dairy Day**, make butter. Give each child a clean baby food jar with a small amount of heavy cream. Ask the children to shake the jars vigorously until the cream turns into butter. Spread the butter sparingly on crackers and explain that it is healthy to use only a small amount of oils and fats. On **Fruit Day** make a fresh fruit salad. (The week before the nutrition activity, send a note to parents telling them about the nutrition week and ask them to give their child a fruit and vegetable to contribute to the class cooking projects.) On **Vegetable Day** make vegetable soup using the vegetables that children had brought from home. On **Meat and Protein Day**, make peanut butter. Ask the children to shell peanuts. Put the peanuts in a blender and blend until the peanut butter is smooth (or chunky). On **Bread and Grains Day**, make muffins or bread (choose from the children's favorite recipes). Spread a small amount of butter or margarine on the muffins or bread and talk about why these foods are used sparingly.

Original songs

"Bread Song" (Tune: "Ten Little Indians")

Plant the wheat seeds in the ground,
Plant the wheat seeds in the ground,
Plant the wheat seeds in the ground,
We want to make some bread.

Water the seeds everyday....
Watch the wheat grow taller, taller....
Gather up the wheat now, it is ready....
Grind the wheat into flour....
Mix the flour into bread dough....
Put the bread dough in the oven....
Smell it baking, yummy, yummy....
It is ready, time to eat it....
Yum-m-m-m-m-m, oh so good!

"Butter Song" (Tune: ("Hi Ho the Derry-O")

We're going to make some butter
We're going to make some butter
Hi ho the derry-o
We're going to make some butter.

Pour cream in the jar
Pour cream in the jar
Hi ho the derry-o
We're going to make some butter.

Shake it up and down
Shake it up and down
Hi ho the derry-o
We have made some butter.

Related books

Milk by Dorothy Turner
The Milk Makers by Gail Gibbons
Blueberries for Sal by Robert McClosky
Growing Vegetable Soup by Lois Ehlert
Jamie O'Rourke and the Big Potato by Tomie dePaola
Cloudy With a Chance of Meatballs by Judi Barrett
Green Eggs and Ham by Dr.Seuss
Peanut Butter and Jelly by Nadine Bernard Westcott
Bread, Bread, Bread by Ann Morris
Bread and Jam for Frances by Russel Hoban
Pancakes, Pancakes by Eric Carle
Gregory the Terrible Eater by Mitchell Sharmat

★ Deborah Gallagher, Bridgeport, CT

Food

Cooperation Spider Web . . . . .3+

Materials needed
Ball of yarn

What to do
1. Ask the children to sit on the floor in a circle.

2. Hold the end of the yarn from a ball of yarn and gently toss or roll the ball of yarn to a child sitting across the circle.

3. The child who catches the ball holds the section of the yarn that has unrolled in her hands and tosses the ball to a child sitting across the circle.

4. This continues until every child is holding a section of yarn.

5. Once the web is woven, ask the children to place the yarn they are holding on the floor in front of them.

6. Ask the children to stand and look at the web that they created by working together.

7. Talk about other things the children can do by cooperating and working together.

More to do
Art: Create webs using yarn glued on construction paper. Create a web on a large plastic lid. Sprinkle glitter over the glue and allow it to dry. After the web is dry lift the web from the lid and hang it in the classroom.

Related book
Anansi the Spider: A Tale From the Ashanti by Gerald McDermott

★ Carol Patnaude, Cathy Costantino, Darlene Maloney, Lynn Camara, Warwick, RI

Making a Friendship Quilt . . . . .3+

Materials needed
Items significant to each child (ask parents to send items, such as pictures of the child and family members, pictures of favorite foods)

Variety of quilts (ask parents to loan quilts for display)
Squares of muslin
Glue

What to do
1. At circle time show the children a variety of quilts. Talk about the art of quilting and explain how quilting is a group effort.

2. Give each child a square of muslin and ask them to glue the items that they brought from home on their square.

3. Help the children assemble the quilt by placing the squares next to each other. To add contrasting colors to the quilt cut out solid colored squares and intersperse with the children's squares.

4. Use colored tape to attach the squares to each other (or ask a parent to sew the blocks together).

5. Display the quilt on a wall to share the children's cooperative work of art.

★ Cindy Winther, Oxford, MI

Encouragement Circle . . . . .4+

Materials needed
Ball of yarn

What to do
1. Ask the children to sit on the floor in a circle.

2. Explain that each child will choose a child to roll the ball of yarn to and will give that child a compliment. For example, "I choose Bobby. I like Bobby's smile." Then the child rolls the ball of yarn to Bobby. The activity continues until all the children are included in the encouragement circle.

3. Remind the children to think of a compliment they would like to say to another child when it is their turn.

4. As the ball of yarn is passed a web is formed, connecting everyone to each other. Explain that when we say encouraging words to each other we also become closer to one another.

More to do
At the beginning of the school year use this idea as a getting to know you activity. Ask the children to say their names and something about themselves to the class before rolling the ball of yarn to another child in the circle.

★ Stephanie Person, Kingsburg, CA

Friendship Fruit Salad . . . . .4+

Materials needed
Variety of fruit (ask each child to bring a piece of fruit, use a sign up sheet to ensure a variety)
Tablecloth

What to do
1. Ask the children to bring their piece of fruit to circle time.

2. Each child holds her fruit, describes it and places it on a tablecloth in the middle of the circle so that the children can look at the fruit and make comparisons.

3. Discuss the similarities and differences of the fruit. For example, all apples are not red.

4. With adult supervision, each child prepares her fruit for the salad.

5. Enjoy the fruit salad for snack and talk about how all the children worked together to make the salad.

★ Rayne P. Reese, Glendale, MO

Draw Me a Quilt . . . . .5+

Materials needed

Paper
Paints, pastels, markers, crayons
Tissue paper (optional)
Draw Me a Star by Eric Carle

What to do

1. Read *Draw Me a Star* to the children as they sit in a circle.

2. Distribute the papers that have one line drawn on each paper. The line may be any shape or length. Explain to the children that they will create a picture from the single line in groups of two or three. The papers may also be passed around the circle for children to add to each picture. The results are interesting.

3. Ask the children to collaborate and develop a picture from the single line. Utilize the techniques in the book.

4. Tape the backs of the papers together to form a quilt that shows the results of the children's group effort.

More to do

Language: Ask the children to write or dictate a story about their pictures.

★ Cathlene M. Hedden, Livonia, MI

Passing the Torch . . . . .5+

Materials needed

Empty paper towel roll
Stick (a rhythm stick works well)

What to do

1. Ask the children to sit in a group on the floor (this activity works best with a group of about ten children).

2. Place the empty paper towel roll with one end resting against a heavy object on the floor away from the group of children (adjust the distance depending on how many children are in the group).

3. Invite one child to stand and retrieve the roll, but explain that there are rules that must be followed in retrieving the roll—once a child stands up he can move to only one spot on the floor and must pretend that his shoes are glued to that spot so he cannot move; no child may touch the roll with his hands.

4. When the children ask how they are to retrieve the roll, suggest that they should talk about how they can help each other to reach the roll. Explain that the child who is standing can ask only one other child to help.

5. The child who is asked to help can ask one other child sitting on the floor to help. This continues until all the children are standing.

6. The object is for the children to create a line that reaches the spot where the roll is laying and to pass the rhythm stick from one child to the next until the child closest to the roll scoops it up with the stick and passes it back to the first child, touching only the stick and not the roll.

7. During the activity the teacher should encourage the children to suggest ways to retrieve the roll. If the children are having difficulty solving the problem, the teacher should ask questions to help the children talk about how to reach the torch (roll) and how to pass it back to the first child.

More to do

Art: Partner paintings—two children create a picture on one paper.

Large motor: Children walk, run, jump or move in any other way while holding hands with a partner.

Science: Assign two children each week to maintain the fish tank, plants or other project in the classroom. The children talk about how they will cooperate to do the work.

Related books

Big Al by Andrew Clements
The Rainbow Fish by Marcus Pfister
Tillie and the Wall by Leo Lionni

Related song Any song from "Teaching Peace" by Red Grammar

★ Deborah Robbins, Narberth, PA

Rainbow Fish . . . . .5+

Materials needed

The Rainbow Fish by Marcus Pfister   Paper
Crayons and markers   Confetti
Glue   Scissors

What to do

1. Read *The Rainbow Fish*, a story of a beautiful but lonely fish who is friendless until he learns to share his beautiful scales with other fish.

2. Talk about the story and the importance of friendship, sharing and cooperation.

3. Divide the children into small groups. Provide each group with supplies to create a rainbow fish. Give each group only one glue bottle and one pair of scissors to encourage sharing and cooperation. Ask the children in each group to sign their names on their fish.

4. Display the children's cooperative efforts.

More to do

During winter if snow is available create a rainbow fish out of snow in a tub or shallow pan. Provide empty shampoo bottles each filled with a different color of water for the children to use in squirting the snow fish. Talk about how the different colors blend on the snow.

Related books

Rainbow Fish to the Rescue by Marcus Pfister

★ Cindy Winther, Oxford, MI

Sharing Scales . . . . .5+

Materials needed

The Rainbow Fish
Multicolored glitter paint
Thread and needle
Yarn or cord
Scissors

White cloth (36" x 36")
Fabric paint
Velcro
Tagboard

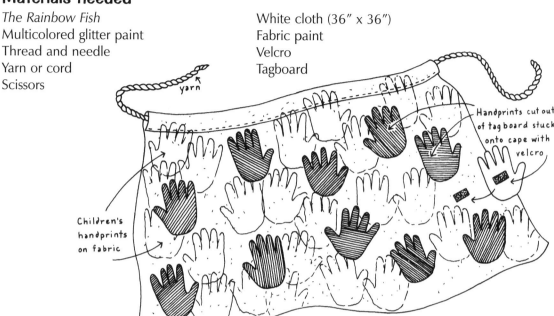

yarn

Handprints cut out of tagboard stuck onto cape with velcro

Children's handprints on fabric

What to do

1. Read The Rainbow Fish by Marcus Pfister and tell the children that together they will make a colorful cape with scales.

2. In advance, prepare the white cloth by folding over a large triangular corner to make a casing so that a piece of yarn or cord can be run through it to provide a tie for the cape. Sew the casing in place.

3. Provide fabric paint for the children to use in painting their hands. Ask the children to place their hands on the white cloth in the same direction. The closer the hands are placed to one another the more the handprints will look like scales. Continue until the entire cloth is filled with handprints.

4. Let the cloth dry.

5. The children wash and dry their hands and then paint their hands with the multicolored glitter paint. Each child makes one handprint on the tagboard.

6. After the handprints on the tagboard are dry, cut out the handprints to make the glittering scales.

7. Staple velcro pieces on the back of each multicolored glitter handprint.

8. Put the corresponding velcro pieces on various spots of the cape after it has dried.

9. Attach the glittering scales to the velcro on the cape.

10. Talk about the props (cape and scales) that the children have made which they can use in acting out the story of rainbow fish during circle time.

11. One child wears the colorful cape and plays the role of rainbow fish. The other children are the starfish, the octopus and the other fish in the story.

★ Christy Krueger, Evansville, IN

More and More Elephants ....3+

Materials needed
Piece of rope

What to do
1. Lay a tightrope (rope) down in the center of the circle.

2. Select one elephant (child) to stand on the rope.

3. The other children sing the following song.

> *One elephant went out to play,*
> *Out on a tightrope string one day.*
> *He had such enormous fun,*
> *He called for another elephant to come.*

(Repeat the first line of the song and the next three lines increasing the number of elephants until everyone has a turn. Then sing the following verse.)

> *Ten (or the number of children) elephants went out to play,*
> *Out on a tightrope string one day.*
> *They had such enormous fun,*
> *That the tightrope broke and they all fell down!*

4. Each child walks the length of the rope and stands on it. After the last line of the song is sung all the children fall down.

More to do
Game: Go on a peanut hunt.

Large motor: Toss peanuts into a pail.

Math: Count, sort and eat peanuts.

Water table: Wash plastic elephants in the water table.

★ Ann Scalley, Wellfleet, MA

Memory Match Game ....3+

Materials needed
16 note cards (3" x 5")
Wrapping paper with 8 different shapes, characters or designs
Clear self-adhesive paper or laminating film

What to do
1. Cut out two of each design from the wrapping paper so that you have a total of sixteen pieces.

2. Glue one design piece on each note card.

3. Laminate or cover the cards with clear self-adhesive paper.

4. Talk with the children about how to play the game. Lay all the cards face up for the children to see.

5. Place all the cards face down in the middle of the circle.

6. Each child takes a turn turning over two cards to find a match. The cards are left turned face up so the children can more easily make matches. (For older children turn the unmatched cards face down.)

7. Each child takes a turn until all the cards are turned over and the matches are found.

8. Tell the children that by working together they found all the matching cards.

★ Laura M. Claire, San Jose, CA

Mystery Box .3+

Materials needed
Cardboard box
Item from classroom
Chart paper and marker

What to do
1. Place a familiar classroom item in a box.

2. Pass the box to all children, asking them to shake the box and listen to the sound it makes.

3. Ask the children what they think the mystery item is. Talk about the size of the box and what they have played with in the classroom that could fit into a box that size. You may want to give the children clues as they are guessing.

4. Record their guesses on a chart.

5. Open the box and reveal the mystery item.

★ Lisa Sunbury, Cambridge, MA

Mystery Picture . . . . .3+

Materials needed
Large magazine pictures
Poster board
Tape

Glue
Easel or chalk board
Scissors

What to do
1. Mount the pictures on the poster board.

2. Cut each picture into four or five pieces. Place a rolled piece of tape on the back of each puzzle piece.

3. At circle time show the children one piece of the puzzle and explain the game.

4. Attach the first piece to an easel or chalk board in its relative place in the puzzle.

5. Attach each piece of the puzzle, pausing for children to guess what the picture is after each piece is placed.

6. Ask the children to talk about the clues that the puzzle pieces gave them to help them guess what picture is in the puzzle.

More to do

Math: Provide puzzle pieces from two or three mystery pictures on a table, each picture a different color. Children sort the pieces by color before constructing the puzzles.

★ Susan R. Forbes, Holly Hill, FL

Question Box . . . . .3+

Materials needed

Cardboard box with item inside
Tape

What to do

1. Place a familiar item that relates to the current theme in a box.

2. Discuss with the children that the item is something that is used in the classroom to help children learn about the current theme.

3. Pass the box around the circle so the children can shake the box and feel its weight.

4. Tell children to ask questions because your answers may give them clues to guessing what is in the box.

5. After the children have finished guessing open the box and talk about which clues helped the children guess the correct item.

6. Put the open box on a table for all the children to see.

7. Change the item in the box periodically to give children practice in asking questions and guessing what is in the box. Place a sign, "What is in the box today?" on the table to remind children to guess what is in the box.

Related books

Brown Bear, Brown Bear, What Do You See? by Bill Martin, Jr.
Who Sank the Boat? by Pamela Allen
Whose Mouse Are You? by Robert Kraus

★ Andrea Clapper, Cobleskill, NY

Shoe Bag Match-Ups . . . . .3+

Materials needed

2 clear plastic multipocket shoe bags
2 matching sets of plastic tools (hammers, pliers, screwdrivers, drills, wrenches)
Easel

What to do

1. At circle time set up the easel in the middle of the circle. Hang the two shoe bags on the easel, one on each side.

2. Insert a tool in each pocket, one set of tools on each side of the easel.

3. Ask two children to play the game. One child stands on each side of the easel, facing the shoe bag.

4. The teacher asks the children to find a tool. Each child looks at the shoe bag in front of her, finds the tool and holds it in the air. Continue until the children have found all of the tools.

5. If the children are not familiar with the names of the tools, have an extra set of tools or pictures of the tools to show the children when you ask for a tool.

6. Repeat the game until all the children have played.

More to do
Instead of tools use musical instruments, shapes, plastic food items.

★ Deborah A. Cole, Ashtabula, OH

What Was There? . . . . .3+

Materials needed
Tray
Scarf or cloth to cover the tray
Assortment of items
Chalk board and chalk or chart paper and marker

What to do
1. Ask the children to sit in a circle.

2. Place the tray on the floor in the middle of the circle.

3. Ask the children to look at the items.

4. Tell the children they need to look very carefully at the items because in a few minutes you will remove the tray and ask them what is on the tray.

5. Take the tray away after an appropriate amount of time. Cover it with the cloth.

6. Ask children to tell you what they remember seeing on the tray.

7. Write the items down on the chalk board or on chart paper.

8. When the children have named all the items they can remember, show the tray again and ask the children if they see any items that they did not remember.

More to do
Play a game where the children close their eyes and one child from the group disappears. The other children try to guess who is missing. The teacher plays the tune to various songs and the children can try to guess the songs.

★ Melissa Browning, West Allis, WI

What's Missing? . . . . .3+

Materials needed

Various colored boxes, cans, containers
Collections of items with a similar theme (blue box containing 6-10 different blue items)

What to do

1. At circle time show the children each item (unusual items are interesting and introduce new vocabulary words).

2. Talk about and describe each item.

3. Place all the items in a row so that all the children can see them.

4. Ask the children to cover or close their eyes.

5. Remove one item.

6. Say, "1-2-3, look and see, something is not there that used to be."

7. The children guess what is missing. Continue playing as long as the children are interested in the game.

8. After the children have played several times, ask the children to try to remember all the items that are in the box before showing the box to them.

More to do

Play this game with different themes. Use a box for each of the primary and secondary colors, and for seasonal or holiday items.

Related books

Green Eggs and Ham by Dr. Seuss
The Rainbow Fish by Marcus Pfister
Red Leaf, Yellow Leaf by Lois Ehlert

★ Theresa J. Nos, Baltimore, MD

Bean Pot . . . . .4+

Materials needed

Various colored beanbags (1 per child)

What to do

1. The children stand in a circle with their hands cupped behind their backs.

2. One child is outside the circle holding a container of beanbags. This child is named the cook.

3. As the cook walks outside the circle the children chant:

> *Colored beans for our pot*
> *We will cook to make them hot.*
> *Around the circle in your hand*
> *A colored bean for our pan.*

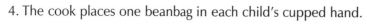

4. The cook places one beanbag in each child's cupped hand.

5. The cook comes to the center of the circle (bean pot) and chants:

> *Bean pot, bean pot*
> *Stir it till it's nice and hot.*
> *Bean pot, bean pot*
> *What color have you got?*

6. The cook says the name of a color. If a child's beanbag is that color, the child (or children) tosses the beanbag into the bean pot (center of the circle), trying to miss the cook. If it hits the cook or the cook catches it, the child throwing the beanbag comes to the center of the cirlce to be the cook's assistant. The children without beanbags sit down and lead the children in the chants.

7. The cook chants again naming a new color until only one child with a beanbag remains. He becomes the new cook and the game begins again.

More to do

Give each child in the circle two different colored beanbags; the child does not sit down until he has tossed both beanbags.

★ Connie Wade, Watauga, TN

Comparison Companions . . . . .4+

Materials needed

Construction paper shapes cut into 2 puzzle pieces
Pictures cut from magazines (mounted on construction paper and cut in pieces)

What to do

1. Cut heart shapes out of construction paper (cut one-half the number of shapes as the number of children playing the game since each shape will be cut in two pieces).

2. Cut each heart into two puzzle pieces (see illustration).

3. Mix up the pieces and place them in a bag.

4. At circle time each child draws one piece.

5. Children compare their pieces to see if their pieces will fit together.

6. The children with the two pieces that make a heart are partners.

More to do
This game encourages children to talk with one another and it is a way to pair partners. Make puzzle pieces that relate to a theme. Also cut puzzle pieces from pictures or advertisements. Increase the size of the puzzle shape and the number of puzzle pieces to group children in teams. For a permanent set of puzzle pieces, cut pictures of nature photographs from magazines. Mount the pictures on one color of construction paper. Cover the pictures with clear self-adhesive paper. Cut the pictures into the same size rectangular pieces. Store the puzzles in a large envelope with the pieces to each picture paper clipped. When playing the game mix the cards and distribute them face down. Children move about the group to find the other children who have pieces to the same picture (see illustration).

★ Linda Ann Hodge, Minnetonka, MN

Musical Spots . . . . .4+

Materials Needed
Tape recorder
Markers
Scissors

Tape of children's songs or other music
Construction paper (various colors)

What to do
1. Make enough shapes (squares, triangles, rectangles, circles, ovals) of various colors for each child in the class. They should be large enough for a child to stand on.

2. At circle time talk about the shapes and colors with the children.

3. Give one shape to each child. Ask the children to place their shapes in a circle on the floor. This circle should be large enough for the children to walk in a circle without touching the next child. Ask the children to stand on their shapes.

4. Explain that this game is played like musical chairs. When the music starts the children begin to walk outside the circle of shapes. When the music stops the children will step on the shape that is closest to them. Only one child may stand on a shape. There is one less shape than children each time the game is played.

5. The child who does not have a shape to stand on is asked to sit down and hold the shape that is taken away.

6. The game continues with a shape being removed each time the music stops.

More to do
The game can be played with shapes of animals, transportation vehicles or with vinyl placemats.

Related book
Shapes and Things by Tana Hoban

★ Karen Megay-Nespoli, Massapequa Park, NY

Small, Medium, Large . . . . .4+

Materials needed

3 brightly colored circles (6", 12", 18") labeled with the words small, medium or large
Sets of 3 similar items that are small, medium and large (nesting cups, stuffed animals, mittens, brushes, envelopes)

What to do

1. At circle time show the three circles to the children and discuss small, medium and large. Hang the three circles at eye level on the wall.

2. Invite a child to select one item from the box that contains all of the items.

3. Ask two other children to each select an item that is in the same category as the first item chosen.

4. The three children then compare their items and decide which of the three items is small, medium and large.

5. Ask the three children to stand under the appropriate size circle that corresponds to the size of their item.

6. Ask the other children if they agree with the three children.

7. Continue the game until all the children have had a turn to select an item.

More to do

Blocks: Ask children to sort blocks into groups of small, medium and large blocks.

Dramatic play: Include items that are small, medium and large (small plate, medium plate, large plate).

Math: Ask the children to sort other objects in the classroom, such as transportation vehicles on the small, medium and large circles.

Related books

Deep in the Forest by Brinton Turkle
Goldilocks and the Three Bears by James Marshall
Somebody and the Three Blairs by Marilyn Tolhurst
The Three Bears by Paul Galdone

★ Ann Wenger, Harrisonburg, VA

Undercover . . . . .4+

Materials needed

Large blanket or sheet

What to do

1. After the children are sitting in a circle ask them to close their eyes.

2. When the children have closed their eyes, wrap yourself in the blanket leaving only your face uncovered.

3. Ask the children to open their eyes and that you will play a guessing game.

4. Ask the children questions about what you are wearing under the blanket, such as "Do I have buttons on my shirt? Do my shoes have laces? What color are my socks?"

5. After listening to the children's answers, remove the blanket and discuss the questions and their answers.

6. The children may want to have a turn going undercover, having the other children try to remember what they are wearing.

More to do
Talk about colors by focusing the children's attention on the colors of the clothing you are wearing.

★ Vicki L. Schneider, Oshkosh, WI

What Do You See? . . . . .4+

Materials needed
Familiar objects

What to do
1. The children sit in a circle and the objects are displayed in the middle of the circle.

2. The children choose an object to be passed around the circle.

3. The challenge is for each child to give a word to describe the object as it is passed to the next child. Encourage careful listening so that the descriptive words are not repeated.

More to do
To extend the activity ask the children to say a descriptive sentence about the object. For example, if the object passed is a milk carton, possible descriptions could be: "The colors of the carton are red and white;" "The side of the carton looks like a rectangle;" "The carton feels smooth."

★ Iris Rothstein, New Hyde Park, NY

Play Cards . . . . .4+

Materials Needed
2 decks of playing cards

What to do
1. The children sit in a circle on the floor and each child receives a few cards.

2. Ask the children to help you separate the numbered cards from the rest of the deck. Use only the numbered cards to play the game.

3. The more children in a group, the fewer number of cards each child receives. (In a group of twelve, each child receives five cards to play the game.)

4. The children look at the numbers on their cards.

5. The teacher uses the second deck to select one card and announces the number she has selected.

6. The children who have that number on a card put that card on the floor in front of them.

7. The game continues until everyone has placed all their cards on the floor.

More to do
As a follow up activity the children can look around the room to see if any of the shapes that are on the cards are in the room.

★ Elmida Baghdaserians, Glendale, CA

Mystery Questions . . . . .5+

Materials needed
None needed

What to do
1. The game encourages children to consider clues in solving a mystery by identifying a specific object in the classroom. The game can be adapted to focus on a theme that is introduced. At circle time talk about playing a mystery game with the children.

2. A sample mystery question: "What hangs on the wall and has numbers on it?" Additional clues would include that it has a face and that it has numbers from 1 to 12. The answer is the clock on the wall.

3. Each day a child could ask the mystery question and think of clues to help the other children guess the answer.

★ Jyoti Joshi, Framingham, MA

Describe That Picture . . . . .5+

Materials needed
Large picture with details (page from a big book or magazine)
Chart paper
Marker

What to do
1. At circle time divide the children into groups or teams of four or five children each.

2. Show the children a page from a big book or magazine and tell the children to look at the picture carefully. Display the picture where all the children can see it.

3. Explain that in playing the game a child from each team will describe something in the picture. The child can talk with his team about what to say about the picture. Each team will have a turn.

4. The teacher writes the comment on the chart and other teams cannot repeat the same description.

Games

5. When a team cannot think of a new comment they must pass and wait until their next turn to give another description.

More to do
A variation of the game is to show the children a picture for a few seconds and then remove the picture. The children then give descriptive words of what they saw in the picture.

★ Sandra Garrison, Piedmont, MO

Puzzle Mystery . . . . .5+

Materials needed
Poster board
Marker
Scissors

What to do
1. Draw a large picture of something that is related to a theme, such as a bear.

2. Cut the bear (or other picture) into as many pieces as there are children. Use the outline of the picture as the puzzle frame in which children place their puzzle pieces. (This game is designed for a small group so that each child receives a piece or with larger groups give one puzzle piece to two or three children to share.)

3. At circle time distribute the puzzle pieces.

4. Explain that together the children will make a picture of something that is related to the theme. Ask the children to guess what the picture will be after each child places her piece in the puzzle. Talk with the children about the clues that each piece provided in helping them guess what the picture is.

5. Sing a song or read a story about what the picture revealed, such as a song or story about a bear.

★ Maxine Della Fave, Raleigh, NC

Inventions . . . . .5+

Materials needed
Familiar objects (plastic bottle, seashell, hair brush)

What to do
1. The children sit in a circle and the objects are displayed in the middle of the circle.

2. The children choose an object to be passed around the circle.

3. As each child holds the object she invents a new use for it. The new way of using the object may be described or demonstrated.

4. If a child cannot think of a new use he may pass and take a turn later.

★ Iris Rothstein, New Hyde Park, NY

Pass the Secret . . . . .5+

Materials Needed
None needed

What to do

1. The teacher chooses two children sitting beside each other in the circle to pass two different secrets.

2. The teacher then chooses two children who are sitting across the circle from the secret starters to be the secret reporters who will hold up their hands when the secret reaches them.

3. The teacher whispers a secret to one of the secret starters. This child whispers to the child on her right and that child whispers to the next child until the secret reaches the secret reporter.

4. The teacher then whispers a different secret to the other secret starter. That child then passes the secret to his left.

5. When both secrets are passed half way around the circle to the children who raise their hands everyone listens to the secrets and compares them with the secrets that the teacher whispered.

6. The teacher or a child starts two new secrets in another place in the circle, to the right and to the left. New secret starters and reporters are chosen with each new game.

★ Sandra Garrison, Piedmont, MO

Find Your Team . . . . .5+

Materials needed
Note cards (3" x 5")

What to do

1. Create a set of cards by stamping, drawing or gluing a picture on each note card, one per child. A set of cards is made for each category or theme, such as for a pet category the cards would include pictures of dogs, cats, fish. Create two or more sets of cards depending on the number of children so that the children will group themselves in teams by the picture on their cards.

2. At circle time each child receives a card and is told to move about the circle to find other children who have picture cards that are in the same category as their picture card.

3. After the children locate other children who have picture cards in the same category they go to an area where they can practice acting out behaviors that give clues about the name of their category.

4. After the children return to the circle each team acts out clues and the other children try to guess the category of the picture cards that the team had.

More to do
Other picture cards could include farm animals, zoo animals, movement (swimming, jumping, crawling) or emotions (happy, sad, excited). Ask the children for ideas.

★ Bev Schumacher, Ft. Mitchell, KY

April Fools' Game . . . . .5+

Materials needed
Construction paper
Scissors
Tape
Markers

What to do
1. On April 1st in France children try to fasten a paper fish to a friend's back. That child becomes the April Fish. The game can be adapted as a guessing game.

2. In preparation, cut out five fish shapes from construction paper and draw a fruit on each of the five fish, such as an apple, orange, banana, pear, pineapple.

3. Ask five children if they would play the game by having a fish shape taped to their backs.

4. Gather all the children in a circle and explain that no one is to tell the five children what picture of fruit is taped to their backs.

5. Ask the five children to sit in the center of the circle. Each child stands and turns around so all the children can see her picture. Each of the five children may take turns asking questions of the other children that will help them guess what fruit they represent. "Am I red?" "Am I round?" "Am I juicy?"

6. When the five children have guessed what fruit they represent, the fish shapes are removed from their backs and the game is repeated with five other children.

More to do
This game can be played any time of year with different shapes and drawings that relate to a theme.

Related books
One Fish, Two Fish, Red Fish, Blue Fish by Dr. Seuss
The Very Hungry Caterpillar by Eric Carle

★ Karen Megay-Nespoli, Massapequa Park, NY

Frog Jump . . . . .5+

Materials needed
Poster board
Black markers and pens
Clear self-adhesive paper
1 die
4 player markers

What to do

1. In preparation for the activity make a game board by drawing large squares that make a path on the board and write directions in each square. Write one of the following directions in each square:

✓ Crabwalk (player walks on hands and feet with her stomach facing upward).
✓ Do five jumping jacks (player jumps feet apart and hands together overhead, then jumps feet together and brings arms down by his sides).
✓ Frog jump (player squats and puts hands on floor in front of her, moves hands forward and then squat jumps ahead).
✓ Do five donkey kicks (player stands on hands and feet, then kicks legs up and out while balancing on hands).
✓ Do three pushups (player stands on knees and hands with back straight and pushes body up and down using arms only).
✓ The last square is marked as the finish line.
✓ Cover the board with clear self-adhesive paper.

2. Ask the children to sit in a circle and show them the board that you made to play a game called "Frog Jump."

3. Explain the rules of the game: each child takes a turn rolling the die and moving the play marker to a square. After reading the directions on the square the child does the movement that is indicated. The game continues until all the children have reached the finish line.

★ Nicole C. Foust, Madison, CT

Hermit Crab Habitat . . . . .3+

Materials needed

Aquarium
Small containers for food and water
Hermit crab
Book about hermit crabs
Shells of assorted sizes
Sand
Sponge (natural sponge preferred)
Hermit crab food
Driftwood

What to do

1. Read a story about hermit crabs or look at pictures of hermit crabs.

2. Talk about where hermit crabs live and what they like in their habitat.

3. Show the children the aquarium and sand.

4. With the help of the children, place the sand in the aquarium.

5. Place driftwood, shells and small containers of food and water in the aquarium. (Place a sponge in the water container to enable the crab to drink from the sponge and to protect it from drowning in the water.)

6. Show the hermit crab to the children and talk about how to hold the crab to avoid being pinched.

7. The crab can be placed in water briefly to make it more alert and to encourage it to walk.

More to do

Language: Children keep a journal describing the movements of the hermit crab.

Math: Children record the movements of the crab by drawing a map and compare its movements on different days.

Science: Children experiment with feeding the hermit crab various vegetables and fruits and graphing the food preferences of the hermit crab.

★ Melissa Browning, West Allis, WI

Over in the Meadow . . . . .3+

Materials needed

Flannel board animals or puppets to accompany song

What to do

1. Make up a new version of the song "Over in the Meadow" to fit a theme. Children help compose new verses, such as

> *Over in the farmyard,*
> *By the big red barn,*
> *Lived an old mother cow and her little cow one.*
> *"Moo," said the mother.*
> *"I moo," said the one,*
> *And they moo-ed and were happy by the big red barn.*

Over in the ocean,
In the deep blue sea,
Lived an old mother whale,
And her little whales two.
"Spout," said the mother.
"We spout," said the two,
And they spouted and were happy in the deep blue sea.

Additional verses

Over in the jungle....
Up in the sky....
Over in the forest....
Over in the desert....

More to do

Dramatic play: Make a cave habitat out of a large box for children to go inside to play. Children can add natural materials and paint trees for the background.

Game: Make a matching animal game with animal stickers on milk bottle lids.

Language: Cut out magazine pictures to illustrate the verses of the song and make it into a book for the listening center along with a tape of the class singing the song.

Math: Provide small toy animals for the children to use in counting when they sing the song.

Science: Display pictures of different animal habitats and sort animal pictures by the habitat the animals live in.

Related books

Home for a Bunny by Margaret W. Brown
Lazy Lion by Mwenye Hadithi
My First Book of Animals: More than 150 Animals Every Child Should Know by Turie MacCombie
Over in the Meadow by David A. Carter
Over in the Meadow by Ezra Jack Keats
Play With Me by Marie Hall Ets

★ Laura Egge Durbrow, Lake Oswego, OR

Animals Everywhere . . . . .4+

Materials needed

5 sheeets of poster board
Pictures of various animals

What to do

1. Make each sheet of poster board into an animal habitat by drawing or pasting pictures of one of the following habitats on each sheet: jungle, forest, farm, ocean and city.

2. Sing "Old MacDonald Had a Farm" at circle time.

3. Discuss the kind of animals that live on a farm.

4. Talk about how pets are different from wild animals.

5. Talk about the things all animals need to live.

6. Hand each child a picture of an animal.

7. Talk about the different places where animals live and ask the children where the animals in the pictures might live.

8. Show the children the habitat posters.

9. Ask the children to put their animal pictures on the posters that represent the habitat where their animals might live.

More to do
Art: Paint with feathers. Make an eggshell mosaic.

Field trip: Visit a pet store. Take a trip to the zoo or a farm.

Snack: Make an animal snack by spreading a graham cracker with cream cheese or peanut butter and place a few animal crackers on top.

Related books
The Big Pets by Lane Smith
Tigress by Helen Cowcher

★ Teresa J. Nos, Baltimore, MD

Habitat Home . . . . .4+

Materials needed
Collection of miscellaneous items
A House Is a House For Me by Mary Ann Hoberman

What to do
1. Read *A House is a House For Me* at circle time.

2. Discuss the pictures as the story is read to make sure the children are aware of the author's intent and to enhance their sense of observation.

3. Pass the objects around the circle, giving each child the opportunity to explain how the item is "housed." Examples may include a cereal box, a card and an envelope, a bag of pretzels and a box of paper clips.

4. After passing the objects around the circle, ask the children to survey the room and make up houses for classroom objects, such as a desk is a house for papers and books.

More to do
Create a diorama of an animal's habitat.

★ Cathlene M. Hedden, Livionia, MI

Where I Live . . . . .4+

Materials needed

A House Is a House for Me by Mary Ann Hoberman

What to do

1. At circle time read and talk about *A House Is a House for Me*.

2. Ask children to talk about where they live. Discuss houses for pets and other animals. Point out that we all live in different homes.

More to do

Art: Ask the children to draw homes and their occupants including animals, seeds, cars, boats. Note: There are many dual relationships such as a boat that can be a home (houseboat) and also have a home (dock).

Field trip: Walk around the neighborhood.

Social studies: Help the children enlarge their concept of where they live by talking about the community, state and country in which they live.

Make a page for each child with the following information:

I live with my family (write names)_____

at this address_____

in this city _____

in the state _____ zip code _____

in the country _____

in the World

on the planet Earth

Each child draws a picture of his home on the page.

Related books

The Biggest House in the World by Leo Lionni
The Little House by Virgina Lee Burton
A Very Special House by Ruth Krauss

Houses and Homes by Ann Morris
This Is My House by Mercer Mayer

★ Wendy Pfeffer, Pennington, NJ

Peep Show Box . . . . .5+

Materials needed

Shoebox
Real or plastic plants
Colored cellophane
Cardboard cutter or scissors

Miniature toy animals
Glue or glue gum
Markers
Finger puppet (optional)

What to do

1. Cut a hole in one end of a shoebox to look through.

2. In the opposite end of the box cut a window and add colored cellophane.

3. Cut a large window in the lid and tape colored cellophane to cover the window.

4. With glue or glue gum attach small animals to the floor of the box. Add plants, pebbles, sand and other natural material to the habitat. Children can add details to the environment with markers.

5. If desired, cut a hole in the bottom of the box to allow a finger puppet to stick up.

6. Pass this box around the circle for the children to see before reading one of the books listed below.

7. Use this box to extend a story or to acquaint children with the habitat of different animals.

More to do

Art: Ask children to bring in shoeboxes to make their own peep show boxes. Use drawings, stickers or magazine cutouts instead of small animals.

Field trip: Take a walk to hunt for pebbles, pine cones and other natural material to make peep show boxes.

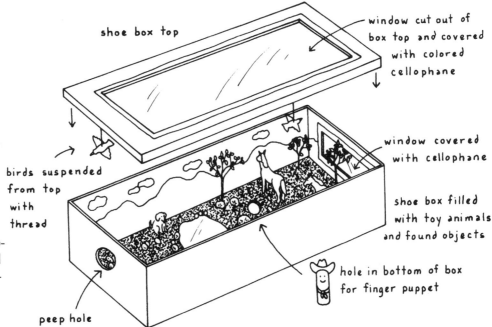

shoe box top

window cut out of box top and covered with colored cellophane

birds suspended from top with thread

window covered with cellophane

shoe box filled with toy animals and found objects

hole in bottom of box for finger puppet

peep hole

Language:
Encourage the children to make up stories about what they see in the peep show boxes and dictate their stories to the teacher. If you use a finger puppet ask the children to imagine themselves in its place and make up a story.

Music: Make a peep show box to use when singing a song about animals, such as "Over in the Meadow," and "Old MacDonald."

Related books

Anansi and the Moss-Covered Rock by Eric A. Kimmel
Quick As a Cricket by Don Wood
Lazy Lion by Mwenye Hadithi
Animals Born Alive and Well by Ruth Heller
In the Forest by Marie Hall Ets
Ask Mr. Bear by Marjorie Flack

★ Laura Egge Dubrow, Lake Oswego, OR

How Animals Protect Themselves . . . . .5+

Materials needed
Pictures of animals (turtle, porcupine, chameleon, rabbit, opossum, skunk, deer, cheetah, tiger, polar bear, chimpanzee)
Large box (flattened and cut into an oval shape to look like a turtle shell)

What to do
1. Open with a discussion about how different animals protect themselves from other animals called predators or from people. Some animals can run very fast if they are frightened. Some animals have a very sensitive sense of smell or hearing. Some animals have special markings that prevent them from being seen in their natural habitat. Some animals have other special ways to protect themselves.

2. Hold up pictures of animals and have the children guess what special traits or skills each animal has to escape harm (do not show the picture of the turtle).

3. Now hold up the picture of the turtle. Discuss what special protection this animal has.

4. Put the turtle shell (the flattened box) in the middle of the circle. Ask one child to crawl under the box and pretend to be the turtle. Ask the children, "What does the turtle do to protect itself if something tries to get it?" (Pull its head, arms and legs into the shell.) As time allows, ask other children to take turns being the turtle.

5. Explain that even though turtles move relatively slowly and have very sensitive skin, they have their own special form of protection.

More to do
Art: Chameleon—give the children colored paper (limited to the colors of playdough or clay available). Ask them to choose playdough or clay based on the color of their paper to make their chameleon (it should be the same color since the chameleon changes color to blend into its environment). Porcupine—give the children clay and toothpicks and ask them to make porcupines.

Original song
(Tune: "Twinkle, Twinkle, Little Star")

> *Animals have lots of ways*
> *To protect themselves for all their days.*
> *Some have quills and some have shells*
> *Some have noses that smell well.*
> *Animals have lots of ways*
> *To protect themselves for all their days.*

Related books
A Color of His Own by Leo Lionni
The Great Kapok Tree by Lynne Cherry

★ Kathryn Yeaton, Vernon, CT

Happy Tooth Glove Puppet Song . . . . .3+

Materials needed
White poster board (outlines of a tooth, toothbrush, toothpaste tube, dental floss package and glass of milk)

Chart paper   Markers
Velcro   Work glove

What to do
1. Cut outlines (2" high) of the items listed above from poster board and draw in details with markers. Glue velcro pieces to the poster board pieces and the ends of each finger of the glove to make a hand puppet.

2. At circle time talk with the children about ways to take care of teeth properly and ask them how they care for their teeth.

3. Record what each child says on chart paper and discuss their responses.

4. Sing the following song.

"Happy Tooth" (Tune: "Twinkle, Twinkle, Little Star")

> *I'm a happy tooth, you see, (place tooth piece on thumb of glove)*
> *Always taking care of me.*
> *I am brushed every day. (place toothbrush and toothpaste pieces on two glove fingers)*
> *Keeping clean as I play.*
> *Eating healthy, yes I do. (place glass of milk piece on glove finger)*
> *Flossing daily helps me too. (place dental floss piece on glove finger)*

More to do
Art: Place cardboard teeth patterns on a table and ask the children to trace a tooth pattern and cut it out. Ask the children to paint their tooth with a toothbrush and toothpaste. Explain as they go why we brush our teeth. (For a very young child you may want to precut the teeth.) Provide materials for children to make playdough teeth with white playdough. Bake the playdough teeth in the oven at low temperature or dry overnight. After completely dry children can paint the playdough teeth with clear varnish (with teacher supervision).

Game: Make a tooth matching game. Make 20 poster board squares (2" x 2"). Draw two identical pictures of different shapes and kinds of teeth (shiny teeth, dirty teeth, rotten teeth). Children match the pairs of teeth.

Related books
My Tooth Is About to Fall Out by Grace Maccorone
The Prince's Tooth Is Loose by Harriet Ziefert

★ Deborah L. Stuck, Reeds Spring, MO

Tooth Brushing Song . . . . .3+

Materials needed
None needed

What to do
1. At circle time repeat the poem during the week so the children will learn the poem. Add motions for the children to do as you say the poem.

Everybody brush your teeth
Up and down and all around.
First you get the bottom ones
Don't forget the side teeth
And the back teeth.

Use your cup to get a drink
From the faucet, not the sink.
Don't forget to rinse your spit
No one likes to look at it.

Brush away the sugar bugs
Before they eat up all your teeth.
Rinse about and spit them out
There they go on down the drain.
Glub glub glub.

Rinse and rap and tap your brush
And don't forget to put it up.

★ Dani B. Rosensteel, Payson, AZ

Sudsy but Dry . . . . .3+

Materials needed
My Hands by Aliki

What to do
1. At circle time read *My Hands* and ask the children to mimic the actions of the hands in the book.

2. Ask the children to stand and identify different parts of their bodies.

3. Explain that the children are going to pretend to wash their bodies.

4. Encourage the children to mimic you as you pretend to wash various parts of your body (feet, knees, legs, arms, elbows, hands, tummy, neck, ears, face and hair).

More to do
This activity can lead to a discussion of why and when to wash hands.

Original song

"Teeny, Tiny Fingers" (Tune: "Eensy, Weensy Spider")

Teeny, tiny fingers wiggling in the air.
Teeny, tiny fingers snapping here and there.
Teeny, tiny hand waving to and fro.
Teeny, tiny hands now up and down they go.

Related books

My Feet by Aliki
Everyone Poops by Taro Gomi

★ Christina Chilcote, New Freedom, PA

Take a Bath . . . . .3+

Materials needed

Scarves, sponges or pieces of fabric

What to do

1. As the children are standing in a circle give them each a scarf, sponge or piece of fabric.

2. Ask the children to mimic you as you pretend to take a bath.

3. Pretend to get into the bathtub and take a bath, washing each body part as you name it. Don't forget to use soap.

4. Wash and rinse your hair.

5. Pretend to splash and kick in the water.

6. Get out of the bathtub, dry your body and get dressed, pantomiming actions and naming body parts.

More to do

Water table: Put washable dolls in the water table for the children to bathe.

Related book

Harry the Dirty Dog by Gene Zion

★ Brenda Miller, Olean, NY

Heartbeat Feet . . . . .3+

Materials needed

Book about fitness, such as *Bunnies and Their Sports* by Nancy Carlson
Large red heart stickers
Poster or page in a book showing the location of the heart in the body
Collection of pictures of physical activity (from newspapers and magazines)
Fast-tempo music

What to do

1. Introduce health and fitness by talking about our muscles and the different activities that help our muscles become stronger. Ask children if they can feel their heartbeat. (Younger children will need help.) Children place heart stickers on the spot where they feel their heartbeat.

2. Read *Bunnies and Their Sports* or discuss exercising with the children. Practice a variety of exercises and activities that the children suggest. The teacher may begin with warm-up stretching and bending followed by the activities the children may suggest, such as walking, jogging, swimming, basketball, aerobics, dancing, ice skating, bicycling.

3. Invite the children to participate in a fitness challenge. Ask the children to feel their heartbeat and note how it feels. The challenge is to keep moving to the fast-tempo music which is played. The children can try any of the above activities or they may choose to gallop, jump or hop while the music plays. When the music is over, everyone sits down and feels their heartbeat and listens to their breathing.

4. Provide a short cool-down for the children through stretching, bending and twisting movements that children suggest.

5. Encourage the children to exercise everyday.

More to do

Art: Children create a Fitness Mural with pictures that they collect and that they draw.

Music: Talk about how rhythm inspires us to dance.

Science: Talk about how we help ourselves stay healthy through exercise.

Related book

The Human Body by Jonathan Miller and David Pelham

★ Gisela Loeffler, Bellingham, WA

The Earthquake Song . . . . .3+

Materials needed

None needed

What to do

1. Sing the following song with accompanying motions.

"The Earthquake Song" (Tune: "Row, Row, Row Your Boat")

Shake, shake, shake the ground
Uh-oh an earthquake's here.
Get under a table,
Away from glass,
There's really nothing to fear!

More to do

Ask the children to walk around the classroom looking for areas to stay away from during an earthquake (such as windows, glass doors, shelves) The children can practice getting under a sturdy table and covering the back of their heads and necks with their hands.

Related book

Earthquakes by Ruth Radlauer

★ Donna Borges, Jackie Sapp, Dallas Rodriquez, Crescent City, CA

A Working Stop Light . . . . .4+

Materials needed

1 piece of black construction paper per child (12" x 4")
1 square of red, yellow and green construction paper per child (4" x 4")
1 margarine tub lid
Glue

What to do

1. In preparation trace circles on the black paper using a margarine tub lid as a pattern. Cut around the circle but leave a 1" section at the top of each circle that is not cut so each circle is still attached to the black paper.

2. Ask the children to glue the red square to the back side of the black paper to cover one circle (the top one). Only dots of glue in the four corners is necessary.

3. Attach the yellow square over the center circle.

4. Attach the green square over the bottom circle. Turn the paper over and lift the circles to reveal the colors underneath and make the traffic light work.

5. At circle time discuss the use of the light to regulate traffic and pedestrians crossing the street. Play games to practice crossing with the light.

More to do

Art: Paint with red, green and yellow at the easel. Print with circle or square shaped objects.

Large motor: Use the traffic light to give the children directions to go, slow down, stop as they march, clap, flap arms, jump. Also use the traffic light to regulate the traffic of tricycles and other riding toys.

Math: Go on a treasure hunt for squares and circles. Sort circle objects from other shapes or sort circles by size. Match various sized jars with lids.

Related book

Red Light, Green Light by Margaret Wise Brown

★ Sandra Gratias, Perkasie, PA

Stop, Drop and Roll . . . . .4+

Materials needed
None needed

What to do
1. At circle time discuss fire safety and the stop, drop and roll procedure. Demonstrate and practice this procedure.

2. Practice crawling on the floor and how to feel a closed door for signs of heat before opening it.

3. Talk about establishing a safe meeting place in the event of fire and the reason to wait near a window for a firefighter rather than hiding.

More to do
Field trip: Visit a fire house and talk with the firefighters.

Large motor: Practice stop, drop and roll on a mat. Practice crawling under a sheet (representing smoke close to the ground).

Science: Demonstrate that fire needs air to burn by lighting a candle and covering it with a jar. Watch the candle go out and explain that when we roll over fire we stop air from reaching the fire and the fire goes out.

★ Sandra Gratias, Perkasie, PA

Fire! Fire! Fire! . . . . .4+

Materials needed
Red and orange paper or felt cut in flame shapes
Tape

What to do
1. Ask the children to stand in a circle an arm's length apart.

2. Holding the flame shapes in your hand, walk slowly around the inside of the circle while singing or chanting the fire song.

"The Fire Song" (commemorating the Great Chicago Fire of October 1871)

> *One dark night while we were all in bed*
> *Mrs. O"Leary left the lantern in the shed.*
> *When the cow kicked it over,*
> *She winked her eye and said:*
> *There'll be a hot time in the old town tonight!*
> *Fire! Fire! Fire!*

3. As you sing the last line of the song tape the paper or felt flames on one child and ask the child what she should do if her clothing caught on fire.

4. Encourage the appropriate response that the child should stop, drop and roll while holding both hands over her eyes.

5. Talk about the need for a quick response in putting out a fire. Repeat the song giving the children practice with the stop, drop and roll procedure.

More to do

After singing the song ask the children to talk about: what did Mrs. O'Leary do to cause the fire, how could the fire have been prevented and what would you do if you discovered a fire.

Dramatic play: Add props to the dramatic play area to encourage role playing fire fighters. Use plastic fire chief hats, yellow or red rain coats, walkie-talkies made out of small individual size cereal boxes, cut up garden hose and axes made out of cardboard and short sticks.

Large motor: Ask the children to walk slowly in a circle as they sing "The Fire Song." When they reach the end of the song, all of the children should stop, drop and roll.

Social studies: Invite the fire chief from the local fire department to visit the class and talk about fire safety. Many fire departments have "Sparky, the Fire Dog" videos available.

★ Virginia Jean Herrod, Columbia, SC

Emergency! Emergency! . . . . .4+

Materials needed

Poster board
Markers
Rug or mat
Unconnected telephone

What to do

1. During circle time talk about what an emergency is and discuss what the children should do in a fire emergency.

2. Show a poster board on which a large telephone with a number touch pad is drawn. Draw the numbers—9 and 1— in a bright color.

3. Ask a child to touch the 9, the 1 and the 1 (a second time) to dial 911.

4. Explain to the children that you are asking them to pretend that a fire begins while they are asleep and then to role play what they would do to protect themselves in a fire.

5. In the role play make a beeping noise like a smoke detector to awaken the children.

6. Ask the children to role play—crawling on the floor to a door and feeling if the closed door is cool before opening it.

7. Practice stop, drop and roll, the procedure for extinguishing burning clothes, on the mat or the rug.

8. Ask a child to dial 911 on an unconnected telephone and talk about what to say on the phone.

9. Reinforce that 911 is only to be called in an emergency. Ask the children to identify emergencies. "Is a splinter an emergency? Is a fire an emergency?"

10. Encourage the children to locate the smoke detectors in their homes and to practice drills with their families. (Send a note to parents explaining the recent focus on emergencies in the class and ask them to discuss family emergency plans with their children.)

Note: Some children may be frightened by activities that focus on emergencies and fire. Address those feelings when they occur. Talk with colleagues and the local fire chief about the appropriateness of this activity for the children.

More to do

Invite the local fire chief to visit the school and conduct a school fire drill.

Art: Paint a fire picture with red, yellow and orange paint.

Related books

Curious George Visits the Fire Station by H. A. Rey
Red Light, Green Light by Margaret Wise Brown

★ Teresa J. Nos, Baltimore, MD

First Aid . . . . .4+

Materials needed

Potatoes (1 per child)
Adhesive bandages (1 per child)
Potato peeler

What to do

1. At circle time give each child a potato. Explain that the potato has skin which covers the inside of the potato and that a person has skin that covers their body.

2. Tell the children that they will take care of their potato while they learn about first aid. Explain that if the skin on their potato is scratched they will pretend that it is similar to the scratched knee of a child who fell and skinned his knee. Ask the children to find the place on their potato where it is scratched (scratch or peel a piece of each potato beforehand).

3. Ask the children what they would do it they skinned their knees. Talk about how to care for a skinned knee. Discuss the importance of telling an adult, washing the area and applying a bandage.

4. Ask each child to care for the scratch on his potato. Let each child show you where his potato is scratched. Help the child wash the area and apply an adhesive bandage.

5. Ask each child to take his potato home and tell his parents how he cared for his potato.

More to do

Art: Create a collage of first aid supplies using bandages of assorted sizes, gauze, tongue depressors, swabs, cotton balls.

Dramatic play: Add dolls and first aid supplies to the area for the children to practice first aid.

Social studies: Visit a clinic or invite a doctor or nurse to visit the class.

★ Susan Rinas, Parma, OH

Seat Belt Bear . . . . .4+

Materials needed
1 piece of poster board per child (6″ square)
1 strip of vinyl plastic per child (1″ x 8″)
Velcro
Markers
Glue
1 paper bear per child (cut from brown construction paper)

What to do
1. To prepare, the teacher cuts two slits (1 1/4″ each) in each piece of poster board, spaced so that the bear's tummy fits between the slits.

2. At circle time ask the children if they wear a seat belt in the car. Explain the seat belt's function and demonstrate using a doll in a chair. Push the chair and stop suddenly with the doll first unbelted and then belted.

3. Explain that the children will make a bear wearing a seatbelt.

4. Provide precut bears and markers for the children to decorate their bears by drawing a face and clothing.

5. Glue the bear on the poster board between the two slits.

6. Thread the vinyl strip through one slit, around the back of the poster board and through the other slit so the ends of the strip overlap on the bear's tummy.

7. Staple velcro to each end of the strip so the ends will overlap and fasten.

8. Talk to the children about keeping their bear in their car to remind them and their parents about using a seat belt.

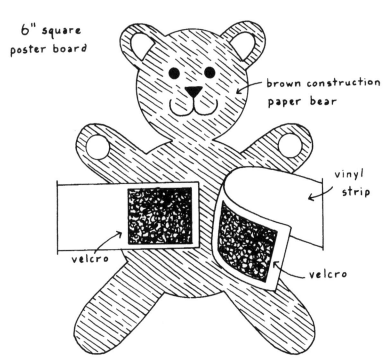

6″ square
poster board

brown construction
paper bear

vinyl
strip

velcro

velcro

More to do
Math: Ask the children to count the number of seat belts in their cars and to identify the color of the seatbelts. Create a graph of the number of blue, gray, black or other colored seat belts. Ask children to look at their shoes to help the class graph the number of velcro vs. tie shoes.

Science: Try sticking velcro to a variety of things in the room. Why does only the rough side of velcro stick to objects? Why does it stick only to fuzzy objects? Look at both sides of a velcro strip under a magnifying glass. Ask children to bring an object from home to see if it will stick to velcro.

★ Sandra Gratias, Perkasie, PA

Snaggletooth Club . . . . .4+

Materials needed

Large tooth drawn on white tagboard labeled "Snaggletooth Club"
Snaggletooth graph with the months of the year recorded on the tooth
Three-ring binder with paper for the Snaggletooth book

What to do

1. When a child looses a tooth she records the month the tooth was lost on the graph, writes a story about losing a tooth for the Snaggletooth book and writes her name on the large tooth drawn on the tagboard.

More to do

Math: Make tally marks to record the number of teeth lost during the year and periodically compare the number with the monthly record of another class.

Related book

Little Rabbit's Loose Tooth by Lucy Bate

★ Patti Jones, Monroe, NC

Wash My Hands . . . . .4+

Materials needed

Hand soap
Water
Paper towels
Chart paper
Marker

What to do

1. At circle time ask the children why they wash their hands. Make a list of their answers on chart paper. Discuss with the children the importance of washing hands.

2. Demonstrate the correct way to wash hands:

Step 1: Wet your hands.

Step 2: Soap your hands.

Step 3: Scrub your hands, top, palms, between fingers and finger tips.

Step 4: Rinse your hands.

Step 5: Turn the water off.

Step 6: Dry your hands with a paper towel.

Step 7: Place the paper towel in the trash can.

Allow time for all the children to wash their hands.

3. Sing the following song and do the appropriate hand motions to each verse.

"Wash My Hands" (Tune: "Shake My Sillies Out")

Gotta wash, wash, wash my hands clean,
Wash, wash, wash my hands clean,
Wash, wash, wash my hands clean,
And I wash my hands today.

Gotta soap, soap, soap my sudsies up,
Soap, soap, soap my sudsies up,
Soap, soap, soap my sudsies up,
And wash my hands today.

Gotta scrub, scrub, scrub my dirt away,
Scrub, scrub, scrub my dirt away,
Scrub, scrub, scrub my dirt away,
And wash my hands today.

Gotta rinse, rinse, rinse my germs away,
Rinse, rinse, rinse my germs away,
Rinse, rinse, rinse my germs away,
And wash my hands today.

Gotta dry, dry, dry my water away,
Dry, dry, dry my water away,
Dry, dry, dry my water away,
And wash my hands today.

Gotta wash, wash, wash my hands clean,
Wash, wash, wash my hands clean,
Wash, wash, wash my hands clean,
And wash my hands today.

More to do

Art: Soap bubble painting—use a straw to blow bubbles in a tub of soapy water to which food color has been added. Lay paper gently down on the bubbles, remove the paper and allow it to dry.

Language: Children design their own books on how to wash hands. Children write a story about what the world would be like without soap. Children make posters that illustrate the steps of hand washing to use at home.

Math: Ask children to bring bars of soap from home. Count the bars. Classify the soap bars by shape, color, size. Compare the soap bars by weight and length. Make a graph using the findings obtained in the study of the soap bars.

Water table: Provide soap and paper towels at the water table for children to play with the soap in the water. Provide wands and bubble blowing solution in the water table.

★ Frances A. Ferguson, Tampa, FL

Stethoscope .... .5+

Materials needed

Elizabeth Blackwell: First Woman Doctor by Carol Greene
2 long black pipe cleaners per child
1 piece of aluminum foil per child (4" x 4" square)   Cotton balls
Glue   Stethoscope

What to do

1. During circle time show the children a stethoscope and ask them if they have seen a stethoscope before, who was using it and how was it used.

2. Read *Elizabeth Blackwell: First Woman Doctor* and discuss the life of Elizabeth Blackwell.

3. To make a pretend stethoscope, give each child two long, black pipe cleaners and ask the children to twist the pipe cleaners together beginning at a point about one-third down the length of the pipe cleaners.

4. Bend the upper one-third part of the pipe cleaners into a U-shape and fasten a cotton ball to each end.

5. Fold the aluminum foil square in half and cut out two circles each 2" in diameter (but do not cut through the folded edge so the circles will be double in thickness).

6. Bend the edges of the aluminum foil circle so the double thickness of foil will stay together. Glue a circle on each side of the end of the twisted length of pipe cleaner.

cotton
balls

2 black
pipe cleaners

2 pieces of aluminum foil

More to do

Art: Make a collage by using first aid supplies, such as bandages, gauze, tongue depressors, cotton balls and related pictures from magazines or boxes.

Math: Weigh and measure the children using a health scale. Mark the height of each child on a wall chart emphasizing the inch as the unit of measurement. Make a class graph of the weight and height of each child.

Social studies: Collect items that a doctor or nurse would use and discuss each.

Related book

Elizabeth Blackwell: The Story of the First Women Doctor by Shari Steelsmith

★ Sandi Fisher, Kutztown, PA

Holiday Celebrations . . . . .3+

Materials needed
Pictures of holiday celebrations (Kwanzaa, Hanukah, Christmas)
Chart paper
Markers

What to do
1. At circle time talk with the children about celebrations.

2. Ask the children what holidays they celebrate at their homes and list the celebrations on a sheet of chart paper.

3. Talk about the variety of celebrations that families have in the community.

4. Show the children pictures that represent holiday celebrations and describe what is happening in each picture.

More to do
Art: Make holiday cards to give to persons in the community who celebrate the holiday represented.

Cooking: Prepare and share foods that are eaten at various celebrations.

★ Holly Dzierzanowski, Austin, TX

Halloween—Pumpkin Kids . . . . .3+

Materials needed
Send a note to parents (to provide a child-sized shirt and pair of pants)
Newspaper   Safety pins
Orange paper plates   Black markers

What to do
1. At circle time talk with the children about making pumpkin kids.

2. The children roll newspaper into balls to use in stuffing the shirt and pants that they brought from home. Attach the shirt and pants with safety pins.

3. Each child draws a face on an orange paper plate using a black marker.

4. Attach the face to the shirt with safety pins.

5. Involve the children in playing with their kids throughout the day.

More to do
Math: Weigh and measure each child and then the pumpkin kid that each child made. Make a graph comparing the sizes of children with the sizes of the pumpkin kids.

Outdoors: Take the pumpkin kids outdoors at recess and using duct tape put the pumpkin kids on the climber, swing set, sandbox. When the parents arrive the children can hide and the parents will only see the pumpkin kids.

★ Cindy Winther, Oxford, MI

Halloween—Pumpkin Power! . . . . .3+

Materials needed

1 large pumpkin
Carving knife
Candle
Small plastic cups and pumpkin stickers
Large spoon
Newspapers

What to do

1. Place the newspapers in the center of the circle and set the pumpkin on top of them.

2. At circle time talk about how to carve a scary jack-o-lantern with the children.

3. Cut the top off the pumpkin and then ask one child at a time to scoop out some of the pulp and seeds with a spoon. Provide cups for the children to decorate with pumpkin stickers and to put seeds in to take home.

4. Continue until all children have had a chance to scoop out seeds.

5. Carve the eyes, nose and mouth of the pumpkin.

6. Place a candle inside the pumpkin and turn out the lights in the room.

7. Sing the song on the next page with the children adding motions to the words.

More to do

Art: Give each child a paper pumpkin and materials to use in decorating it, such as moveable eyes and black feathers. Encourage the children to name their pumpkins.

Language: Encourage the children to make a "How to Carve a Jack-o-Lantern" book in which they illustrate the steps in carving a pumpkin (see illustration).

Original song

(Tune: "I'm a Little Teapot")

> I'm a little pumpkin round and fat.
> I have two eyes now look at that.
> You can light me up, put a candle within,
> Turn out the lights and watch me grin!

★ Lisa Lang, Parkersburg, WV

Halloween—Stuffing Pumpkins . . . . . . .3+

Materials needed

Pumpkin lawn leaf bag
Recorded music

Newspaper to crumble
Chart paper and marker

What to do

1. At circle time play music and talk about how all the children will work together to stuff the pumpkins.

2. Give children paper to crumble and put in the pumpkin lawn leaf bag.

3. Stuff the pumpkins with newspaper until full.

4. Ask the children to help write a story about how they made the pumpkins. Ask them to tell you what they did to help stuff the pumpkins. Record their comments with their names in writing the story on the chart paper.

5. Display their story and pumpkin.

More to do

Game: Start and stop the music—when the music stops, the children stop stuffing the pumpkin. When the music starts, they begin stuffing again. Fast and slow music—children stuff the pumpkin faster or slower to correspond with the tempo of the music.

★ Rae Ann Brodie, Silver Spring, MD

Halloween—Counting Pumpkin Seeds . .3+

Materials needed
Pumpkin seeds (save from Halloween—Pumpkin Power, see page 218)
Bowl or basket
Paper plates
Markers

What to do
1. For younger children, write the numerals 1 through 5 on five paper plates. Also draw the same number of dots on each plate. For example, on the plate with numeral 3 draw three dots. For older children, write the numerals 1 through 10 on ten paper plates.

2. At circle time place the plates and bowl filled with pumpkin seeds in the middle of the circle.

3. Ask one child at a time to take a paper plate, count the number of dots on the plate and then count out the same number of pumpkin seeds from the bowl.

4. Continue until each child has a turn counting out the pumpkin seeds on a plate. After each child takes her turn return the seeds to the bowl so each child can choose the plate she wants to use.

5. On another day ask the children to fill the plates in numerical order.

More to do
Art: Carve a pumpkin as a class project and ask the children to make drawings of their class jack-o-lantern.

Field trip: Visit a pumpkin patch where the children can pick their own pumpkins.

Math: Sequencing. Take pictures of the children carving a pumpkin (use a camera, such as a Polaroid® camera so the children can sequence the pictures of carving the pumpkin on the day it is carved).

Science: After Halloween put the jack-o-lantern in a glass terrarium so the children can observe how it decays. Record the children's descriptions of what they see. The decayed pumpkin makes excellent fertilizer for planting seeds later in the year.

Related books
How Spider Saved Halloween by Robert Kraus
Pumpkin Moonshine by Tasha Tudor

★ Cory McIntyre, Crystal Lake, IL

Halloween—Witch's Brew . . . . .3+

Materials needed
Large pot (cauldron)
Cups
Milk (1 1/2 cups)
Vanilla (2 teaspoons)

Ladle
Orange juice concentrate (12-ounce can)
Water (1 1/2 cups)

What to do

1. At circle time talk about the witch's brew and how the children together will make a lucky witch's brew.

2. The children take turns putting the ingredients in the cauldron and stirring. (You may want to ask the children to pretend to be witches and that the ingredients represent items associated with Halloween, such as the orange juice concentrate could be pumpkin guts; the milk could be juice from a milkweed plant, etc.)

3. Ladle the witch's brew into a cup for each child.

More to do

Art: Make and wear witch hats made from construction paper.

Original song

"The Witch's Brew Song" (Chant or make up your own tune)

> Stirring and stirring and stirring our brew
> Ooooo-ooooo-ooooo-ooooo-ooooo
> Stirring and stirring and stirring our brew
> Ooooo-ooooo-ooooo-ooooo-ooooo

Related book

Candy Witch by Steven Krol

Related fingerplay

"The Five Little Pumpkins"

> The five little pumpkins sitting on a gate. *(hold up five ringers)*
> The first one said, "Oh my it's getting late." *(hold up one finger and gesture to look at watch)*
> The second one said, "There are witches in the air." *(hold up second ringer and wave hand through air)*
> The third one said, "But we don't care." *(hold up three fingers)*
> The fourth one said, "I'm ready for some fun." *(hold up four ringers)*
> The fifth one said, "Let's run and run and run!" *(hold up five ringers)*
> Then Wooooooooo went the wind,
> And out went the lights. *(clap hands)*
> And the five little pumpkins ran out of sight! *(hold up five fingers and hide them behind your back)*

★ Anne Bonstead, New Hartford, NY

Halloween—Jack-O-Happy . . . . .3+

Materials needed

14 paper plates
Scissors
White glue
Stapler (optional)

7 orange circles cut from construction paper
Black marker
7 tongue depressors

What to do

1. To prepare for the activity, the teacher (with help from the children) cuts seven orange construction paper circles to fit on the paper plates. Cut the seventh circle much smaller than the rest.

2. Draw seven jack-o-lantern faces with the black marker, one on each orange circle. Draw the faces to be: happy, sad, sleepy, mad, puzzle pieces, small, pie (see illustration).

3. Glue each orange circle to a paper plate. You will have seven plates with circles and seven plates left over.

4. Next, glue a tongue depressor to the back of each of the plates with orange circles. (see illustration). Staple the tongue depressor to the plate for extra strength, if desired.

5. Dry completely.

6. Glue or staple another paper plate to the back of the first seven plates with orange circles, covering the end of the tongue depressor like a sandwich. This gives the plates extra strength for heavy use by children.

7. On the back of each plate print the word that corresponds to the orange jack-o-lantern face: happy, sad, sleepy, mad, pieces, small, pie.

8. At circle time say the following poem, reciting the words and holding up the pumpkin faces in front of your face. Use voices that match the type of pumpkin you are holding, such as: bright happy voice, sad almost crying voice, sleepy yawning voice, growling mad voice, broken staccato voice, teeny tiny squeaky high voice and a normal very proud voice for the pie.

"Jack-o-Happy"

> I am Jack-o-Happy
> I am Jack-o-Sad
> I am Jack-o-Sleepy
> I am Jack-o-Mad.
>
> I am Jack-o-Pieces
> I am Jack-o-Small
> I am Jack-o-Pie
> The Best of Them All.

9. Ask for volunteers to hold the jack-o-faces. Give one pumpkin face to each of seven children. All the children can say the poem together changing their voices with each line or the child holding the specific pumpkin face may say her line alone as her turn comes up in the poem.

More to do

Language: One child may wish to dramatize the Jack-o-Happy poem for the entire group. Children love to make their own characters, voices and dramatizations. Other jack-o-faces could include: Jack-o-Kitty, Jack-o-Earth, Jack-o-Baby, Jack-o-Giggle, Jack-o-Grumpy.

Math: Make a second set of faces. Children can match the faces. Fill an egg carton with little cut-out jack-o-faces with different attributes, such as sad, happy, large, small that the children can sort.

Related books

Little Witch's Big Night by Deborah Hautzig
Strega Nona by Tomie dePaola
The Teeny Tiny Woman by Paul Galdone

Related songs

"Five Little Pumpkins Sitting on a Gate"
"The Witch Is on Her Broomstick"
"Oh, Do You Know the Pumpkin Man ?" (Muffin Man)

★ MaryAnn F. Kohl, Bellingham, WA

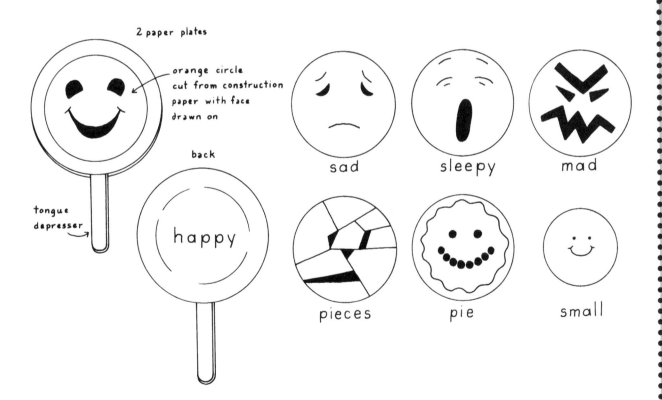

2 paper plates

orange circle cut from construction paper with face drawn on

back

tongue depresser

happy

sad

sleepy

mad

pieces

pie

small

Holidays

Halloween—Evan's Halloween . . . . .4+

Materials needed

Flannel board
Felt family figures (Mother, Father, Evan and Peter)
Felt clown costume, hat and mask for Peter
Felt cowboy hat, boots, neck scarf and vest for Evan
Felt ghost costumes for Mother and Father
Felt trick or treat bags for Evan and Peter

What to do

1. At circle time tell the children that you will be telling them a story about Evan's Halloween using the flannel board.

2. Place the felt figures of Mother, Father, Peter and Evan on the flannel board and begin to tell the story.

3. "This is Evan, a boy just about your age. He has a big brother named Peter and this is his Mother. Evan and Peter were playing and Mother called, 'Peter, tomorrow is Halloween. You should try on your costume to see if it fits.' Evan asked, 'What's a costume?' Mother replied, 'A costume is clothing that you usually don't wear and that makes you look like someone else. Sometimes the costume even makes you look funny or scary.' 'I'm going to be a clown,' said Peter. Evan watched as Peter put on his suit. (Place the clown suit on Peter, then the hat and mask.) Then Peter put on his hat and finally his clown mask. 'You don't look like Peter anymore, you scare me.' said Evan. Peter pulled off his mask and said, 'But I still am Peter! See my face?' 'Yes, you are Peter. Mommy, can I have a costume too?' asked Evan. 'Yes, Evan. What would you like to be for Halloween?' Evan replied,'I want to be a cowboy and wear my new cowboy hat and boots.' 'You can wear my vest,' said Peter. (Place the items on

Evan.) 'Here is a scarf you can wear around your neck,' said Mother. 'What kind of mask do you want to wear, funny or scary?' 'I'm not sure I want a mask,' said Evan. 'Do I have to wear one?' 'No,' said Mother, 'You don't have to wear a mask, but maybe we could paint your face. You can think about it.' 'Are you and Daddy going to wear costumes?' asked Evan. 'Yes,' said Mother, 'But you and Peter will have to wait until tomorrow to see our costumes.' (Leave Peter and Evan dressed on the felt board and remove Mother.) The next day, Peter and Evan waited for Mother and Father to come into the room. 'Close your eyes,' said Mother. (Tell the children to close their eyes. Place Mother and Father dressed in their ghost costumes on the flannel board. Tell the children to open their eyes.) Suddenly two friendly ghosts appear and shout, 'Happy Halloween!' Mother gave Evan and Peter trick or treat bags and the family went trick or treating in the neighborhood."

4. Discuss the story with the children and talk about Halloween. Encourage the children to talk about their experiences with costumes and trick or treating.

More to do
Make the flannel board available during playtime so the children can experiment with the felt pieces and dress the family in their costumes. Encourage the children to retell the story or make up a new one.

★ Irene A. Tegze, Waldwick, NJ

Shining Stars .3+

Materials needed
Yellow construction paper stars (1 per child)
Yarn

What to do
1. Send a letter home to parents similar to the sample letter (after you have discussed the holiday season with the children to include their responses in the letter):

> Dear Parents,
> The holiday season is upon us! This means excitement is in the air. The boys and girls have expressed some of the changes this season brings in their homes. The children have talked about putting up a tree, hanging wreaths, watching a special show, baking cookies. Over the next few weeks, we will keep the routine fairly consistent, but we will talk about and do activities that relate to specific family traditions. Please take a few minutes to reflect on this season with your family and write down something your family does together that is a family tradition. Try to be specific in your description. Thank you for helping to make this season a unique and special one for the children.

2. Make one large yellow construction paper star for each child. Punch a hole in one of the points.

3. Find a special spot in the room to hang each shining star as it is introduced.

4. Make a list of each child's family tradition as you receive it.

5. On one side of the star put the child's name. On the opposite side write the family tradition and illustrate the tradition with the child's help.

6. Laminate the stars and tie long pieces of yarn through the holes.

7. Each morning during circle time introduce one or more shining stars. (Consider the number of children in the class when planning the schedule to include all the children.) Ask the child to talk about the family tradition. During the day incorporate the tradition as a group experience, such as sending holiday cards, reading a story together, baking, making ornaments.

Note: The group experiences will need to be planned in advance when the list of family traditions is compiled.

More to do

Art: Provide materials in the area that relate to the family tradition.

Home connection: Invite parents to the classroom to share and demonstrate the family tradition.

Language: Favorite family stories can be checked out of the library and placed in the reading center.

Music: Favorite family songs can be recorded on tape and placed in the listening center.

★ Anne Lippincott, New Hartford, CT

Dreidel Game and Activities . . . . .4+

Materials needed
Plastic dreidel
Peanuts

What to do

1. At circle time divide the children into groups of about five children each.

2. Each child counts out 20 peanuts.

3. Before each child takes a turn, the children each put one peanut in the middle of the group.

4. Each child in turn gets a chance to spin the dreidel. Depending on what Hebrew letter the dreidel lands on the child must do the following: (see illustration)

> HAY—take half
> GIMEL—Take all
> NUN—do nothing
> SHIN—put one in

(If possible give each child a bag of peanuts, a plastic dreidel and directions on how to play the game to take home for a family gift.)

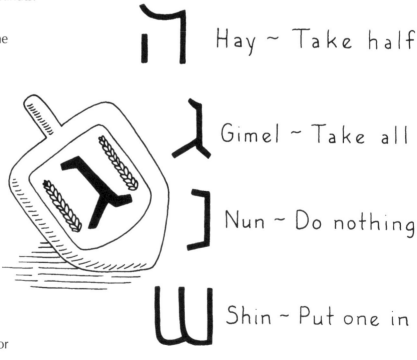

Hay ~ Take half

Gimel ~ Take all

Nun ~ Do nothing

Shin ~ Put one in

More to do

Art: Put paint on the tip of the dreidel and spin on paper towels or roll the dreidel in paint and then roll it on paper.

Cooking: Make dreidel cookies with a package of sugar cookie dough, dreidel shaped cookie cutters and sprinkles. Bake and eat.

Math: Ask the children to make a graph of the number of peanuts that each child has at the end of the game.

★ Ann Scalley, Wellfleet, MA

Jingle Bell Blanket . . . . .4+

Materials needed
Blanket or sheet
Small jingle bells

What to do

1. At circle time ask the children to stand around the perimeter of a blanket and hold the blanket waist-high.

2. Place jingle bells in the center of the blanket.

3. As the children sing "Jingle Bells," ask them to wave the blanket up and down to make the bells bounce and jingle on the blanket.

4. For a challenge, ask the children to try to keep the bells on the blanket without falling off throughout the singing of the song.

More to do

Art: Small jingle bells can be purchased from craft stores and strung on to strings to make jingle bell bracelets and necklaces. Ask older children to make jingle jars by placing pennies in baby food jars and screwing on the lids.

Science: Place different size and types of bells in the discovery center for children to listen to and determine which makes the loudest or softest sound which has the highest or lowest pitch.

★ Suzanne Pearson, Winchester, VA

Little Drummer Girls and Boys . . . . . . .3+

Materials needed
Little Drummer Boy by Ezra Jack Keats
Tin or cardboard cylinder boxes (coffee cans, oatmeal containers)
Paper
Glue
Collage materials (styrofoam peanuts, glitter, cotton, paper scraps)

What to do

1. At circle time read the story *The Little Drummer Boy* and talk about sharing and the gift that the Little Drummer Boy gave, the gift of music.

2. Talk with the children about making drums and that each child will choose a container and make a drum.

3. Provide the materials including paper, glue and collage materials.

4. Wrap the paper around the container and decorate the drum.

More to do

Field trip: Visit a nursing home and play the song while the children play their drums. Following the field trip talk with the children about the responses they received to playing their drums. How did they feel in sharing their drum playing with others?

Music: Play "The Little Drummer Boy" song and ask the children to play their drums when they hear the sounds "par-rum-pum-pum-pum."

★ Regina Curtis, Stamford, CT

Musical Christmas Present Surprise ...3+

Materials needed

8 to 10 boxes in graduated sizes (small to large)
Small items for presents, such as children's rings, seasonal erasers
Wrapping paper, ribbon and tape
Recorded music

What to do

1. Wrap the presents in the smallest box.

2. Put each box inside the next larger box and wrap with wrapping paper and ribbon.

3. At circle time, pass the present around the circle as music is playing. When the music stops the child holding the present opens it. Continue until the last present is opened.

More to do

Surprise gifts could be adapted to any theme throughout the year.

★ Ann G. Glenn, Memphis, TN

Christmas Recordings . . . . .4+

Materials needed
Tape recorder with cassette tape

What to do
1. Pretend to be a reporter for the Holiday Gazette and explain that a reporter's job is to ask people questions. Tell the children that as a reporter you will ask them questions about how they celebrate the holiday season and then tape their responses.

2. Ask questions that encourage extended responses (avoid questions to which the children could give yes or no responses). Suggestions include: How does your family celebrate Christmas (or holiday the child celebrates)? What is your family's favorite food to make at Christmas (or holiday the child celebrates)? How is the food prepared?

3. After interviewing the children, play the tape and discuss the variety of family celebrations. Listening to the tape can also provide a game for the children, to guess who is speaking.

4. Send the tape home with the children on a rotating basis for the children to share the tape with their parents.

More to do
Language: Place the tape in the listening center so the children can listen to the tape periodically. Ask a child to be the reporter and interview other children.

★ Valerie Chellew, Marshfield, WI

Chinese Dragon Parade . . . . .4+

Materials needed
1 paper grocery bag
Assorted paper scraps
Scissors
Glue
1 twin sheet or 2 yards of 45" wide material
Wooden blocks or rhythm sticks

What to do
1. To prepare for this activity, cut off the bottom of the bag and cut down one side. Cut the resulting long rectangle into an oval. Cut out two large oval eye holes from the center of the oval. Attach the two ends of the strip of paper bag next to the outside corner of each eye to form handles. Make sure the handles are on the printed side of the bag (if one side has print). Turn the bag over to the plain side.

2. Encourage the children to add decorations to the bag to create a dragon face, including cheeks, eyebrows, lashes, beard, hair, teeth, nose and a mustache.

3. At circle time show pictures of China and talk about the people who live in that country. Explain their New Year traditions and explain that each new year is given the name of an animal. Talk about the significance of the dragon in the celebration.

4. Have a dragon parade. One child holds the handles and peers through the eye holes of the dragon. Six to nine children line up behind the head and hold the shoulders of the person in front of him. Cover the line of children with a sheet. The child at the head of the dragon leads the line of children around the room and through the hallways while the other children in the class follow banging blocks to chase the dragon away. Ask the children to take turns playing each of the roles.

More to do

Art: Have red paint at the easel (a Chinese color for good luck).

Movement: Dance with scarves or ribbons to Chinese music.

Music: Play Chinese music and talk about the sounds and the tempo.

Snack: Serve chow mein noodles (available in most grocery stores) and a variety of dipping sauces.

Related book

Ming Lo Moves to the Mountains by Arnold Lobel

★ Sandra Gratias, Perkasie, PA

Cut off bottom of bag and down one side.

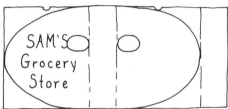

Open and cut into large oval. Cut ovals for eyes.

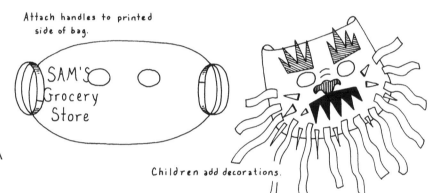

Attach handles to printed side of bag.

Children add decorations.

Groundhog's Shadow . . . . .4+

Materials needed

Overhead projector or large flashlight

What to do

1. Using the overhead projector (or flashlight), shine the beam light on a blank wall. Make sure the light is narrow enough so that a child standing up will only see the shadow of his upper body.

2. Turn out the lights and ask one child to squat below the overhead beam.

3. As the rest of the children sing the following song, the child slowly rises up until the shadow of her head and shoulders are seen on the wall. The child then quickly squats as though she is afraid of her shadow.

"Mr. Groundhog" (Tune: "Frere Jacques")

> *Mr. Groundhog, Mr. Groundhog,*
> *Take a peek, take a peek.*
> *If you see your shadow*
> *The weather will be awful*
> *For six more weeks, six more weeks.*

4. Ask the children to take turns playing the role of the groundhog.

More to do

Science: Show the children how a shadow changes when moving closer or farther away from the wall. On a sunny day take the children outside and let them experiment with shadow play.

★ Dotti Enderle, Houston, TX

What Is a Shadow? . . . . .4+

Materials needed

Overhead projector
Screen or large blank area (to view projected image)
Objects with distinct silhouettes (scissors, pencil, glue bottle, cardboard shapes)

What to do

1. At circle time talk about Groundhog Day and explain that traditionally it is said that groundhogs come out of their holes in the ground. If a groundhog sees its shadow, it runs back into its hole and hides indicating that six more weeks of cold weather is expected. If the groundhog does not see its shadow, it is believed that there will be an early spring.

2. Talk with the children about shadows and ask them to describe when they have seen their shadows.

3. Illustrate the concept of shadows by placing familiar objects on an overhead projector and ask the children to guess what the objects are.

4. Ask the children to make hand shadows in front of the projector.

5. Ask several children to select objects in the classroom to place on the overhead projector. The other children guess the object by looking at its shadow.

More to do

Art: Prepare cups of black and white paint for shadow painting. Staple white and black pieces of paper together. Cut the same design out of sheets of white and black paper simultaneously. It will look like a picture and its shadow. Put a transparency (with shapes, pictures, numbers) on the overhead projector and project the image onto a large piece of bulletin board paper. Children trace the outlines of the projected shapes onto the paper and color them.

Blocks: After children build with blocks, turn off the lights and ask them to use flashlights to make shadows of their structures.

Outdoors: Have the children look at shadows on the sidewalk. Ask them, "Is your shadow in front of you, beside you or behind you? Why?"

Sand table: Children stand sand toys of varying heights up in the sand. Children can then hold flashlights at different angles to experiment with shadows when the lights are turned off.

Science: Ask children to use flashlights to create shadows when the lights are turned off. On a sunny day experiment with making shadows on a sidewalk or paved area.

Original song
"Pop Goes the Weasel" (substitute "groundhog" for "weasel"). Children begin singing in a swatted position and jump up when the line, "Pop, goes the groundhog!" is sung.

★ Lauren Zimmerman, Reisterstown, MD

Passover . . . . .4+

Materials needed
Our Holidays by Miriam Schlein
Haggadah (book that tells the story of Passover)
Sedar plate
Matzo

What to do
1. At circle time read the story of Passover in *Our Holidays* to the children.

2. Show the children the seder plate and talk about the symbols and what they mean (see the Haggadah for explanations).

3. Read from the Haggadah and encourage discussion.

4. Explain the significance of matzo and pass around pieces for the children to taste.

More to do
Invite parents and others in the community who celebrate Passover to discuss the holiday and have a seder with the children.

★ Debbie Bokor, Richmond Hill, Ontario, CA

Plaster Eggs . . . . .5+

Materials needed
Large plastic Easter eggs   Plaster of Paris
Water   Large bowls
Spoons   Tape
Petroleum jelly, such as Vaseline®   Markers or tempera paint

What to do
1. At circle time talk with the children about eggs and that they are a symbol of new life, especially meaningful in the springtime. Explain that they will make eggs from plaster of Paris.

2. Cut off a small part of the bottom half of each plastic egg with a sharp knife or craft saw to make a hole (teacher does this before the activity).

3. Ask each child to rub the inside of the two halves of the plastic egg with petroleum jelly.

4. Ask the children to tape the two egg halves together after making sure they fit tightly.

5. Following the directions on the box, mix the plaster of Paris with water in a large bowl.

6. Ask the children to quickly pour the wet plaster in the hole in their eggs using spoons (small pitchers and funnels may be helpful). After the eggs are filled with plaster tell them to tap the eggs to remove any air bubbles and place the eggs upright in an egg carton to dry and harden.

7. When the plaster of Paris is completely hard remove the tape and open the two halves of the plastic egg to reveal the plaster egg.

8. Decorate the eggs with markers or paint.

More to do
The decorated eggs can be used for an Easter egg hunt or as paper weights.

★ Manisha Segal, Burtonsville, MD

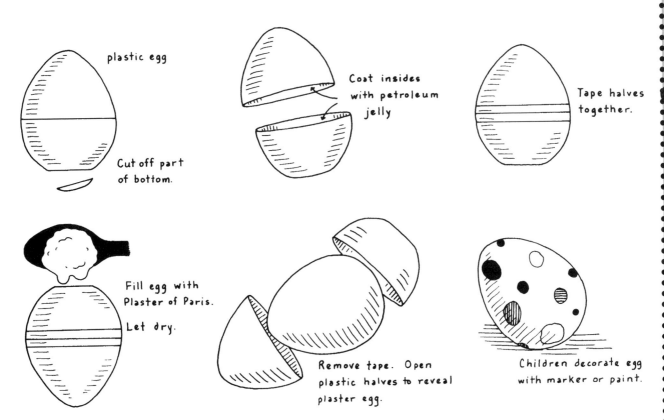

plastic egg

Cut off part of bottom.

Coat insides with petroleum jelly

Tape halves together.

Fill egg with Plaster of Paris.

Let dry.

Remove tape. Open plastic halves to reveal plaster egg.

Children decorate egg with marker or paint.

Cinco de Mayo Celebration . . . . .4+

Materials needed

Sombrero hat
Mexican flag

What to do

1. Group children in a circle around a sombrero and talk about the Cinco de Mayo celebration (5th of May) which is Mexico's day of independence. It is a major holiday for Mexicans and Mexican Americans.

2. The children dance around the sombrero while singing the following song, "Cinco de Mayo Song," to the tune of "The Mexican Hat Dance."

> *Olé, olé, olé,*
> *It's Cinco de Mayo day.*
> *Olé, olé, olé*
> *It's Cinco de Mayo day.*
>
> *Olé, olé, olé*
> *It's Cinco de Mayo day.*
> *Olé, olé, olé*
> *It's Cinco de Mayo day.*
>
> *Enchiladas, burritos and tacos,*
> *Empanadas and macho nachos*
> *Fried beans and guacamole*
> *For a day that's olé, olé.*

More to do

Art: To make pretend tacos cut medium size circles from tan construction paper (for tortillas). Crumble dark brown paper up in small balls (for ground beef), cut strips of green (for lettuce) small strips of orange (for cheese) and cut red wedges (for tomatoes). Children make the tacos by gluing the paper ingredients on the paper tortilla. Fold the taco in half and clip with a paper clip to hold it together. Glue the taco to a paper plate. Using red and green markers write "Cinco de Mayo" on the plate.

Cooking: Prepare tacos and other Mexican foods.

Language: Talk about foods that are typically eaten in Mexico and ask the children to describe any Mexican foods they have eaten. Discuss the Cinco de Mayo Celebration, the clothing people wear and the types of dancing they enjoy at the celebration.

★ Penni Smith and Donna Karnes, Riverside, CA

Flag Day Activity . . . . .3+

Materials needed
American flag

What to do
1. At circle time show the children the American flag and discuss its significance. Talk about the design of the flag, the stars and strips, the colors and how the first flag was made.

2. Discuss the ways we show respect for the flag.

3. Ask one child to carry the American flag and lead the children in a flag parade. The children stand in a circle and march while singing the following song, "I Love My Flag," to the tune of "Yankee Doodle."

> *I love my flag*
> *Oh yes I do.*
> *It's red and white and blue.*
> *I stand up tall when it goes by*
> *And I salute it too.*
>
> *Fifty stars and thirteen stripes lead*
> *As we march along.*
> *Follow now around the room*
> *And sing our happy song.*

More to do
Art: Make flags—provide cardboard tubes from paper towels, construction paper, glue, scissors, gummed stars. Each child designs his own flag and glues the flag to the cardboard tube.

Bulletin board: Provide a large piece of white bulletin board paper, red paint, blue construction paper and gummed stars. The children paint broad red stripes on the bulletin board paper. When the paint dries, place a square of blue construction paper in the top left corner of the striped paper and ask the children to add gummed stars. (Accept the number of stripes and stars the children put on the flag.)

Language: Each child draws a picture of a flag and dictates a few sentences about his drawing for the teacher to write on the paper. Compile the drawings in a book titled "Our Flags."

Movement: After the children complete making the flags, each child holds his flag and marches to recorded parade music.

Snack: Serve fresh blueberries and strawberries with whipped topping for a red, white and blue snack.

Related books
Parade by Donald Crews
Stars & Stripes by Leonard E. Fisher

★ Barbara F. Backer, Charleston, SC

Bugs . . . . .3+

Materials needed
None needed

What to do

1. Talk with the children about bugs, what they do for us, how they move, names of different kinds of bugs.

2. Say the following poem and then repeat it with the children.

"Bugs"

> Big bugs, little bugs, thin bugs, fat.
> Creepy, crawling, creepy, crawling. Just like that!
> Black bugs, brown bugs, green bugs, too.
> Leaping, jumping, leaping, jumping right past you!

3. Tell the children that they will pretend to be bugs and act out the movements.

4. Ask half of the children to be creepy, crawly bugs and the other half of the children to be leaping, jumping bugs.

5. When the children say the words "creepy, crawling" half of the children act like creepy, crawly bugs.

6. As the poem continues and the children say the words "leaping, jumping" the other half of the children act like leaping, jumping bugs.

7. After saying the poem a few times ask the children to choose which type of bug they would like to be and to act out the movements when the children repeat the poem and say the words describing their type of bug.

More to do

Art: Make ink blot bugs by folding a sheet of white construction paper in half and opening it again. Using bright colors of tempera paint, put several dots of paint near the fold on one side of the paper. Fold the paper in half and rub. Open the paper to reveal the bug.

Large motor: Move like insects: butterflies, spiders, grasshoppers, worms, bumblebees.

Math: Make an insect memory game using bug stickers on cards.

Science: Start an ant farm. Add soil and insects to the science table.

Related books
The Grouchy Ladybug by Eric Carle
The Very Busy Spider by Eric Carle
The Very Hungry Caterpillar by Eric Carle

★ Cory McIntyre, Crystal Lake, IL

Caterpillar and Butterfly . . . . .3+

Materials needed

The Very Hungry Caterpillar by Eric Carle
Butterfly (cut from felt)
Velcro
Fabric paint
Caterpillar puppet
Leaf shape (torn from wallpaper)
2 pompoms
Plastic fruit

What to do

1. To make the caterpillar puppet, use a sock or cut the bottom off an old pair of tights. Use two pompoms for eyes. Sew one onto the caterpillar's face in the appropriate place. Attach the other eye with a small circle of velcro. To make the butterfly, cut a butterfly shape from felt. Decorate it with fabric paint to match the color of your sock caterpillar. To make the leaf, tear wallpaper samples in shades of green to create a collage effect. To create food props, use plastic fruit or create collage props similar to the leaf. The pompom that has a velcro piece on it can also be used as the egg sitting on the green leaf. (When the egg hatches into the caterpillar in the story attach the pompom to its place as the caterpillar's eye on the sock puppet.)

2. At circle time read the story of *The Very Hungry Caterpillar*.

3. When the caterpillar goes inside its chrysalis fold the bottom of the sock caterpillar over your fist.

4. When the butterfly emerges pull your hand out of the sock puppet to reveal the felt butterfly that was hiding in the palm of your hand throughout the story.

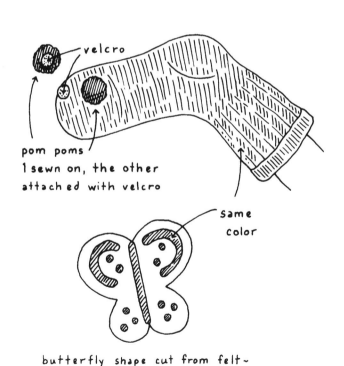

velcro

pom poms
1 sewn on, the other
attached with velcro

sock folded over hand
to form crysallis

same
color

butterfly shape cut from felt –
decorated with fabric paint

Pull hand from sock to
reveal butterfly hidden
in palm.

More to do

Art: The children can bring socks from home to make their own puppets. Fabric or felt scraps can be used to make the children's butterfly puppets.

Language: Place the caterpillar puppet, butterfly and leaf in the reading center to encourage the children to use them in retelling the story.

Related books

Amazing World of Butterflies and Moths by Louis Sabin
The Butterfly Hunt by Yoshi
The Caterpillar and the Polliwog by Jack Kent
The Very Hungry Caterpillar by Eric Carle

★ Ann Wenger, Harrisonburg, VA

Cricket Habitat . . . . .3+

Materials needed

Aquarium with screen cover
Cotton ball
Grass seed
Crickets (from a pet store)
The Very Quiet Cricket by Eric Carle or other book about crickets

4 soda bottle caps
Cereal
Dirt
Containers with clear plastic lids

What to do

1. Gather the children around the aquarium (outside if possible).

2. Talk about making a home or habitat for crickets in the aquarium.

3. Prepare soil in the aquarium to plant grass seed. Each child puts in a scoop of dirt. After the top of the dirt is smoothed each child scatters a pinch of grass seed over the dirt.

4. The soil in the aquarium is kept moist (place plastic wrap over the top of the aquarium until the grass seed sprouts. Explain to the children that the grass will provide an excellent habitat or environment for crickets.

5. After the grass in the aquarium is an inch high (about a week later) talk with the children about crickets and read a story about crickets.

6. Place the crickets in containers with clear plastic lids and pass them around the circle so the children can see the crickets.

7. After looking at the crickets the children carry the containers to the aquarium and open the lids releasing the crickets into their new home or habitat.

8. Place cereal in soda bottle caps and water-soaked cotton balls in other soda bottle caps. Place the caps in the aquarium.

9. Observe the crickets daily and ask the children to talk about what they see.

★ Melissa Browning, West Allis, WI

Five Little Flies . . . . .3+

Materials needed

Glove puppet (can be made by sewing the soft side of velcro to fingers of a glove)
5 flies cut from poster board (attach the hook side of velcro to the backside of each fly)

What to do

1. In advance, make the glove puppet (see illustration).

2. At circle time talk about insects and ask the children to act out the ways insects might move about, for example, caterpillars creep, flies buzz, ants march.

3. Put on the glove puppet and say the following fingerplay, "Five Little Flies."

Five little flies buzzing through a hive,
One snuck some honey,
And took a deep dive.
Four little flies buzzing through a door,
One slipped and fell,
Crash! on the floor.
Three little flies buzzing through the
*   trees,*
One bumped the bark
And bloodied his knees.
Two little flies buzzing through a shoe,
One held his nose
And PEE! YOO!
One little fly buzzing through a bun,
The swatter goes SPLAT!
Now there are none.

pattern for fly glove puppet

body – black
wings – white
eyes – red

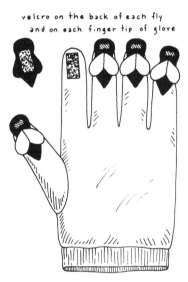

velcro on the back of each fly
and on each finger tip of glove

More to do

Art: Do fly swatter painting. Pour a thin layer of paint into shallow pans. Dip the fly swatter in the paint, scrape off excess paint and swat large sheets of paper.

Games: Make memory and lotto games using bug stickers. Cut out 2" squares and attach a sticker to each one. Laminate.

Science: Make an entomology (study of insects) center in the classroom. Include plastic bugs and magnifying glasses. Add pictures and books about insects. Encourage children to find live insects (collect with the help of an adult) to bring to the center to observe for a day or two.

Related books

In the Tall, Tall Grass by Denise Fleming
Old Black Fly by Jim Aylesworth
A Picture Book of Insects by Joanne Mattern

★ Debora L. Stuck and Frances Youngblood, Reeds Springs, MO

Worker Ants . . . . .4+

Materials needed

Blanket (optional)
300 white cotton balls
Container large enough to hold cotton balls
Stopwatch

What to do

1. Scatter cotton balls on the floor (or blanket) and ask one child to pick the cotton balls up and put them in the container. Using a stopwatch time how long it takes the child to pick up all the balls.

2. Scatter cotton balls on the floor again and ask a small group of children to pick them up and put them in the container. Time how long it takes the group of children to pick up the cotton balls and compare results.

3. Discuss why it took less time for the group of children than for the individual child to pick up the cotton balls.

4. Talk about ants and how they work together to accomplish a task rather than working alone. Compare how ants work together with how the children worked together picking up the cotton balls.

More to do

Art: On a large sheet of paper create an ant community with tunnels and hills. Sprinkle tunnels and hills with glue and cover with sawdust or punched paper holes. Children add fingerprint ants by pressing a finger on a stamp pad or in paint and pressing the finger on the paper. Ant legs can be drawn on each of the fingerprints.

Science: Construct an ant farm and observe the ants. The children record and document their observations through drawing in an Ant Farm Journal that remains on the science table.

Snack: Eat ants on a log (celery spread with peanut butter and raisins).

Related book

Two Bad Ants by Chris Van Allsburg

★ Kimberle S. Byrd, Wyoming, MI

Cooperative Camouflage ....5+

Materials needed
None needed

What to do
1. At circle time talk about camouflage in nature and how insects are protected when their color blends with the environment and cannot be easily seen by a predator.

2. Talk about the different ways insects move. Ask the children to pretend to be either a butterfly, moth or caterpillar. Together decide what areas of the room will be bushes, grass, tree, sand and a garden.

3. Ask the children to move about the room pretending to be one of these insects. Talk about what the insects do, such as gathering nectar with their proboscises, munching on a leaf, laying eggs, flying in the air or crawling on the ground.

4. Tell the children that a predator is looking for the insects that they are pretending to be.

5. Each child must find something in the room that matches the colors of his clothing so he will not be easily seen and will become as close a part of the environment as possible. Children with similar colored clothing can huddle together to hide and to use their imaginations in trying to keep the predator from seeing them. (Children develop problem solving skills through finding a way to camouflage their appearance.)

More to do
Language: Ask the children to talk about what they did to camouflage themselves and to compare what they did with what other children did.

Movement: Encourage children's own dramatizations, such as opening up from the chrysalis, moths exerting pressure to work their way up to the surface from deep under ground. Practice the Yoga position, "The Butterfly" that is achieved by sitting up straight on the floor, bringing the knees up and letting them fall outward to the left and to the right, putting the soles of the feet together and the knees like wings.

Science: Look for evidence of butterflies, moths and caterpillars, such as leaves with holes, missing leaves or flower petals, eggs on leaves and camouflaged pupae or chrysalises. Attract day butterflies and moths with a sugar-water solution, rotten fruit, flower plantings such as marigolds, petunia, zinnia, butterfly bush or butterfly weed. Attract night moths in winter and early spring by painting large splotches on tree trunks of the following mixture: one can of beer, 3/4 lb. sugar, molasses and mashed fruit. Moths are also attracted to lights. Moths should appear in a few minutes.

Related books
A Color of His Own by Leo Lionni
The Caterpillar and the Polliwog by Jack Kent
A Golden Guide—Butterflies and Moths, a Guide to the More Common American Species by
    Robert Mitchell and Herbert Zim
An Instant Guide to Butterflies by Pamela FitzSimmons Forcy
The Very Hungry Caterpillar by Eric Carle
Where Butterflies Grow by Joanne Ryder

★ Jill Putnam, Wellfleet, MA

Insects

Beanbag Balance ....3+

Materials needed

Beanbags (1 per child)

What to do

1. At circle time ask the children to stand in a circle. Distribute the beanbags and talk about playing a balancing game with beanbags.

2. Ask the children to place the beanbags on different parts of their bodies, such as head, shoulder, elbow, knee, nose, wrist, hand, foot.

More to do

Social skills: Ask the children to work in pairs balancing one beanbag together using parts of their bodies. Ask the children to try as many different ways as they can think of to balance a beanbag.

Spatial relationships: Ask the children to place the beanbags above their shoulder, below their knees, on their left side, on their right side, behind their back, inside the circle, outside the circle.

★ Margery A. Kranyik, Hyde Park, MA

Body Part Cube ....3+

Materials needed

6 pictures of body parts (head, hand, foot, arm, knee, nose)
Small square box (cube)   White paper
Glue

What to do

1. Cover a box with white paper. Glue one picture of a body part on each side of the cube. Label the picture with the name of the body part.

2. Each child takes a turn rolling the cube. All the children point to the part of their body that corresponds to the picture of the body part that appears on the top of the cube.

3. Sing the following song to the tune of "Put Your Finger in the Air."

> *There's a beanbag on my nose, on my nose.*
> *There's a beanbag on my nose, on my nose.*
> *I'm walking very slow 'cause it's very hard to go,*
> *With a beanbag on my nose, on my nose.*

4. After singing the song a few times give the children beanbags to place on the part of their body that corresponds to the picture of the body part that appears on the top of the cube. Continue rolling the cube and singing the song naming that part of the body that appears on the top of the cube.

5. The children then try to move around the room with a beanbag balanced on the part of their bodies that appears on the top of the cube.

6. Roll the cube to find different ways to move objects—using the part of the body that appears on the top of the cube. Give each child an object to move. Each child takes a turn rolling the cube.

★ Mary Paciocco, Appomattox, VA

Circle Time Movement Game . . . . .3+

Materials needed
None needed

What to do
1. Ask the children to stand in a circle.

2. The teacher stands in the center of the circle and demonstrates a movement for the children, such as jumping up and down, touching your toes, spinning around, imitating an animal, pretending to be a ballerina, pretending to skate.

3. Ask the children to mimic the movement demonstrated while chanting the following poem.

> *This is my movement,*
> *My movement I'll do.*
> *This is my movement,*
> *I will show it to you (do movement)*
> *Can you do it too?*

4. Choose a child to enter the circle and repeat the chant substituting her name.

> *This is (child's name)'s movement,*
> *His (her) movement we'll do,*
> *This is (child's name)'s movement,*
> *(Child's name) will show it to you*
> *Can you do it too?*

5. Continue until all the children who wish to participate have a turn. This is a good way for children to learn each other's names.

More to do
After the children are familiar with the game, a child can start the game by saying the poem. You can expand this game by using only movements that begin with a specific letter, such as S. For example, children could skate, swim, skip, squirm, sneeze (covering their mouths, of course).

★ Connie Heagerty, Trumbull, CT

Wood Times Four . . . . .3+

Materials needed
Wood block or drum

What to do
1. Ask the children to walk to the sound of the wood block and to freeze when the sound stops. The teacher plays a wood block four times (in a steady beat). Children freeze when the sound stops.

2. Children continue to move with the sound of the block and freeze when the sound stops.

3. Once the children understand the game, suggest a variety of movements, such as jumping, crawling, running, rolling, walking.

4. A variation of the game is to play the four beats in an unpredictable way. Try playing the block three times very quickly and then delaying the fourth beat so that the children have to listen carefully.

5. Ask the children to take turns being the leader playing the four beat patterns. The leader also chooses the movement for the children to follow.

★ Deanna Davis Peters, State College, PA

Shake and Wobble Like a Bowl Full of ... . .3+

Materials needed
Large area

What to do

1. At circle time ask the children to stand in a circle and follow your directions. Tell them to walk around the circle and then stop. Walk backward, walk forward, walk sideways, walk high, walk low. Introduce words, such as stretch, leap, creep.

2. After the children understand the game, tell them to walk and make a shape with different parts of their body touching the floor and then to flop down staying in that shape .

3. Talk about gelatin (such as Jell-O®), how it is made, how it looks, how it feels.

4. Shake and wobble, pretending to be a bowl of Jell-O®. The children take turns showing how they wobble and shake.

5. Describe the process of making Jell-O® while the children act out the actions, such as water boiling, Jell-O® being poured into a bowl, being stirred, becoming firm.

6. The children shake, wobble and wiggle and then flop down on the floor.

7. The children lie down on the floor and relax. Ask each child to imagine that he has a balloon in his tummy. Fill it up with air and let it out. Sink into the floor and relax. Relax your legs. Lift them up and shake them out and relax. Do the same with the arms. Relax your shoulders and your head. Sit up when relaxed.

More to do

Cooking: Make Jell-O® and ask the children to talk about how they moved when they pretended to be Jell-O®. Enjoy eating it for snack.

★ Debbie Bokor, Richmond Hill, Ontario, Canada

Move Just a Little Bit . . . . .3+

Materials needed
None

What to do
1. Explain to the children the difference between moving just a little bit and moving a lot. Practice little and big movements.

2. Practice each of the following movements for a just a little bit: standing, jumping, crawling, hopping, skating. End with sitting just a little bit.

3. Practice each of the same movements for a long time. End with sitting a long time.

More to do
This activity can be adapted to a variety of playground games including the game of "Mother May I." Ask the children for suggestions of how to move.

★ Melissa Browning, West Allis, WI

Movement Cube . . . . .3+

Materials needed
Square box
White paper
6 drawings or pictures showing different movements
Glue

What to do
1. Cover a box with paper. Glue one movement picture to each side of the box to make a movement cube. Label each movement picture with a word describing the movement.

2. The children take turns rolling the cube.

3. Name the movement picture that lands on the top of the cube and ask the children to move this way.

4. The children say a simple chant, such as "Jumping, jumping all around, we are jumping all around," while doing the movement.

★ Mary Paciocco, Appomattox, VA

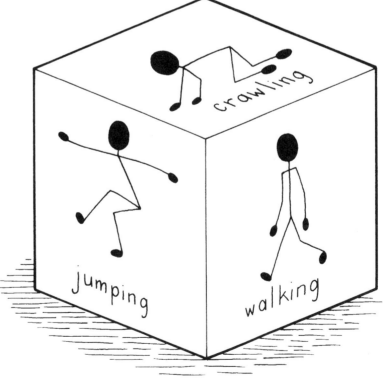

Movin' . . . . .3+

Materials needed
Record or cassette tape of instrumental music

What to do
1. Ask children to stand in a circle.

2. Play the music and give the children the following directions to move while listening to the music: wiggle your body, hop on one foot, do the bicycle, reach up high, reach down low, jump up and down, shake your body, boogie down low, shake your body, boogie down low, jump up and down, shake your body, boogie down low. Repeat movements and then ask the children to move to the music in any way they would like to move.

More to do
Use slow relaxing music and pretend to fly, swim, skate, surf.

Transitions: This activity is also good for moving from one activity to the next by hopping, skipping or making a train.

★ Mary Ramirez, Chamblee, GA

Olympic Obstacle Course . . . . .3+

Materials needed
Hand puppet (or ball) and box
Masking tape
2 or 3 chairs
Adult helpers
Gold medals made from yellow tagboard and yarn (1 per child)

Get Set and Go! by Eric Feldman
Table or student desk
2 or 3 carpet squares

What to do

1. Use the puppet (or a small ball) and the box to familiarize the children with the concepts of in, out, over, around and through. For example, the puppet goes in the box, around the box, through the box.

2. Read the book, *Get Set and Go!*

3. Take the children to the location of the prearranged obstacle course. The course might include: stepping or jumping from carpet piece to carpet piece, walking around or between two or three chairs, crawling under a table or desk, and crossing a finish line (marked by tape on the floor). Children go through the obstacle course one at a time.

4. Arrows made of tape can be placed on the floor to help the children move in the right direction.

5. It is important to have a responsible adult at each section of the course to help the children and to make sure that an accident doesn't occur.

6. Cheer each child as she crosses the finish line. A gold medal can be given to each child as she crosses the line.

★ Christina Chilcote, New Freedom, PA

Paper Dancing . . . . .3+

Materials needed
Crepe paper cut into 3' lengths (various colors)
Clear packing tape
Dance music (tapes or records)

What to do

1. Each child chooses three colors of crepe paper. An adult helps her to tape the crepe paper together with the clear packing tape. Cover approximately 3" of the streamers to make a handle for the child to hold onto while dancing.

2. Play the music (Yanni or George Winston are great choices). Vary the type of music on different days.

3. Children create their own dance movements to the music.

4. Talk with the children about how they moved the crepe paper streamers to the music.

More to do

Art: Make movement collages by cutting out pictures illustrating different types of movement from magazines. Make collages from scraps of crepe paper.

Related book
Color Dance by Ann Jonas

★ Deanna Davis Peters, State College, PA

Searching for Corduroy's Button . . . . . 3+

Materials needed

Corduroy by Don Freeman

What to do

1. Read the story to the children and involve the children in talking about the story.

2. Tell the children they are going to pretend to be Corduroy searching for his button.

3. Review the spatial relationship concepts that are a part of the story: up the escalator, on top of the bed, on the shelf.

4. Tell the children the area in the room in which they can move while searching for the button.

5. Ask the children to act out the movements as you retell the story about Corduroy searching for his button. Expand on the story adding words describing spatial relationships, such as jumps off the shelf to search for his button; walks up the escalator; searches (looking on the floor); searches under, on top of, behind and between furniture; squeezes between furniture; climbs on the mattress and falls off; hears (put hand to ear) the lamp crash; climbs back onto the bed and falls asleep; blinks because the night watchman's flashlight shines in his eyes; gets carried back down the steps; plops back on the shelf; and smiles when he gets carried home by his new friend.

More to do

Game: Play "Button, Button, Who's Got the Button?"

Language: Discuss the events in the story and encourage children to talk about their favorite part of the story.

Music: Create a song about Corduroy using one of the following tunes: "Twinkle, Twinkle, Little Star," "Mary Had a Little Lamb" or "I'm a Little Teapot."

Science: Talk about bears, hibernation, habitats, circus, zoo.

Original song

(Tune: "Are You Sleeping?")

> *Corduroy, Corduroy*
> *Searched for his button. Searched for his button.*
> *He looked on the floor, He looked on the floor*
> *Of the department store, of the department store.*
> *Corduroy, Corduroy*
> *Searched for his button. Searched for his button.*
> *He walked up the escalator, he walked up the escalator*
> *To the furniture department, to the furniture department.*

Add other verses to sing the sequence of the story.

★ Kay McAlpine, Dunkirk, OH

Shadow . . . . .3+

Materials needed
None needed

What to do
1. Ask the children to be your shadow and watch what you do carefully so they can repeat it, but without talking.

2. Movements could include touching body parts, shaking your head, sticking out your tongue, wiggling fingers, jumping up and down. The children can take turns being the leader with the other children and you following their movements.

More to do
This activity can extend a discussion of shadows on Groundhog Day or incorporate it as a transition activity after observing real shadows on a sunny day. Darken the room and turn on a bright light source, such as an overhead projector so the children can make shadows on the wall as they follow a leader's movements.

★ Brenda Miller, Olean, NY

Steady Beat .3+

Materials needed
None needed

What to do
1. Sit in a circle and ask the children to clap their hands following your beat.

2. When the children are clapping in time sing the following song to the tune of "Mary Had a Little Lamb."

> *We can keep a steady beat, steady beat, steady beat.*
> *We can keep a steady beat, let's do it (child's name).*

3. Then one child creates a new movement and the children sing the song again.

4. Go around the circle so each child gets a turn. The children copy the leader's movements. Suggested movements include shrugging shoulders, rubbing hands, swaying side to side.

More to do
Change the words of the song to "We can be a little dog (cow, car)."

★ Ivy Sher, Sherman Oaks, CA

Stretch It! . . . . .3+

Materials needed
None needed

What to do
1. While sitting in a circle ask the children to do the following motions.

2. Reach up with your arms as far as you can. Stretch! Sway from one side to the other side.

3. Stretch one arm up high. Now stretch the other up high. Alternate stretching first one arm and then the other arm (to the count of 8—1 2 3 4 5 6 7 8).

4. Stretch your arms out to the side. Stretch your arms out in front of you. Stretch your arms out behind you.

More to do
Ask the children to move other parts of their bodies, such as make your hands move in circles; try your elbows; try your shoulders; move your head from side to side.

Original song
"Stretching" (Tune: "Twinkle, Twinkle, Little Star")

> *Everybody reach up high, stretching, stretching to the sky.*
> *Swaying left and swaying right,*
> *Stretching up with all our might.*
> *Everybody stretching high, 'til we nearly reach the sky.*

★ Margery A. Kranyik, Hyde Park, MA

The Seeds and Flowers Dance . . . . . . .3+

Materials needed
Packet of flower seeds
Flower pot
Soil
Watering can

What to do
1. At circle time involve the children in planting flower seeds in a flower pot. Fill the pot with soil and pat the soil. Make several indentations with the tip of a pencil and drop a seed into each hole. Pat the soil over the seeds.

2. Ask the children what the seeds will need before they can sprout. Talk about watering the seeds and putting the pot in a window for light. Explain that it will take at least ten days before the flower seeds will sprout (marigolds are recommended).

3. Ask the children to pretend to be seeds so they can do "The Seeds and Flowers Dance." First, ask the children to make their bodies small and round like tiny seeds. Tap each child on the back and explain that you are planting them in the soil and pressing soil on top of them. Tell the children that you have the watering can and that you will pretend to water them (walk to each child and tickle the

Movement

250

child's back lightly with your fingers as if you are watering them). Explain that the seeds need to be in the light for a long time before they will sprout (count to ten very slowly). Tell the children that after pretending to wait ten days the seeds are beginning to sprout and that when you count to three they should poke one finger out of the soil up toward the sky (1 2 3). Continue counting and tell the children that when you reach 10 the tiny sprouts will have grown into tall plants (children slowly stand up). Walk around the room pretending to water the plants and tell them that as you count to 10 the flowers will begin to bloom (children raise their arms above their heads). Tell the children to look around the room and see all the beautiful flowers. There are marigolds, zinnias, pansies, roses and snapdragons. What a beautiful garden you've made.

4. Continue the role play by telling the children that there is a gentle wind (children move their arms slowly, swaying in the wind). Explain that the wind is blowing harder (make the whoosh-whoosh sound of the wind with your voice). Tell the children to keep their roots (feet) planted in the soil and move their body from side to side. Explain that sometimes the wind carries seeds from the flowers to different parts of the garden and they will pretend that the wind will gently scatter these seeds to different spots in the garden (count to 3 and tell the children to gently blow (move) to another place and land gently on the ground). Tell the children that they just danced "The Seeds and Flowers Dance."

More to do

Art: Draw pictures of different flowers and describe the flowers.

Field trip: Take a field trip to a local nursery or garden.

Music: Listen to songs about flowers and plants.

Science: Look at pictures of different types of flowers and identify them. Look at pictures of tropical environments and northern environments and discuss the differences in plants and flowers.

★ Karen Kaufmann, Missoula, MT

The Balloon Dance . . . . .4+

Materials needed
1 colorful balloon for each child
Tape of instrumental music (light and airy)

What to do
1. Ask the children to describe what happens when someone blows up a balloon and what happens if the air escapes.

2. Tell the children to make-believe they are holding a tiny balloon and that you will give the followings directions: stretch the balloon a few times, put it in your mouth and blow, take three breaths to blow the balloon up big (blow and expand hands bigger and bigger and bigger), let the air out (hands contract smaller and smaller).

3. Explain that now the children are to pretend to make their bodies into the balloons: begin by lying on the ground in small, limp shapes; take three breaths to blow your bodies into big, round shapes on the floor (1, 2, 3); feel how big your balloon is (make body big, round and wide), let the air out (quickly become small again making a blowing sound as you contract).

4. Tell the children to blow up their balloons (bodies) while they are standing up into large round shapes: Take three breaths (1, 2, 3), then let the air out and slowly fall to the floor.

5. Ask the children to form a circle holding hands and pretend to make one big balloon with the circle: begin by standing close together in a small circle, Take three breaths and blow the circle up big, (1 we're getting bigger, 2 we're growing, 3 we're really big), now let the air out and make the circle small again (ssssssssss).

6. Give each child one balloon (blow them up in advance and keep them in large plastic garbage bags). Tell the children that when they hear the music start lightly tap their balloons to keep them up in the air and when the music stops to grab their balloons in two hands and hold them still. Turn the music on and after a short time turn it off. Repeat several times.

7. Explain to the children that they will do a variation of the balloon dance by not touching the balloon with their hands but will instead use their elbows, knees, head or feet.

More to do

Science: Discuss helium and the effects it has on a balloon. Show the difference between a balloon with and without helium. Dance the helium balloon dance by floating and drifting. Discuss air and air pressure and how it affects us. Ask the children if they can see air (their breath on a cold morning), can feel the air (on their face when it's windy), know when the wind is blowing (feel the wind against their body).

★ Karen Kaufmann, Missoula, MT

Funny Footsteps . . . . .4+

Materials needed
1 flat sheet or shower curtain
24 adhesive footprint shapes (used in tubs for nonskid surface)

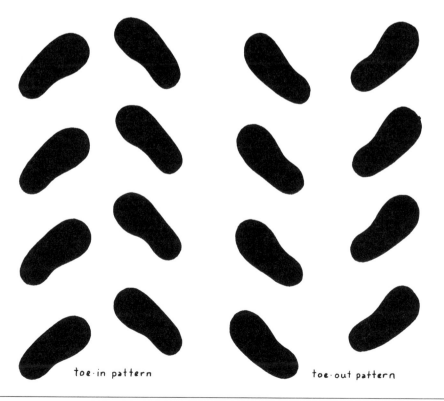

toe-in pattern   toe-out pattern

What to do

1. In advance prepare walking patterns, such as a toe-out pattern using eight footprints placed on the sheet and a toe-in pattern using eight footprints placed on the sheet.

2. Turn the sheet over for another footprint pattern. Cut eight footprint shapes in half creating eight balls from the footprints and eight heels from the footprints for a heel-toe pattern; place eight balls of the footprint shapes in a straight walking pattern, then eight heels. (This pattern is more challenging due to the weight shift of the feet.) A variety of patterns can also be created by placing footprints far apart or close together.

3. At circle time ask the children to stand in front of the sheet and take a turn walking across the sheet or use the footprints as a way for the children to walk to the circle.

4. To make it more challenging give the child an open umbrella to hold while walking (another thing to concentrate on in addition to walking).

More to do

Talk about different ways animals walk and ask children to practice the ways, such as duck walk, crab walk.

★ Yvonne Thompson, Ashtabula, OH

Can You Guess? . . . . .4+

Materials needed

None needed

What to do

1. At circle time tell the children that you will do an activity using only motions and not words.

2. Demonstrate a pantomime for the children to guess (read a book, pretend to eat, brush your teeth). Ask the children to guess what you are doing.

3. Ask individual children to think of an activity that could be acted out without using words. The children take turns pantomiming an activity and asking the other children to guess what they are doing.

More to do

Language: Explore the motions we use to communicate with others, such as come here, I'm cold, stop.

Social skills: Ask the children to pantomime an activity working in pairs or in a small group.

Related book

Talking Without Words by Marie Hall Ets

★ Margery A. Kranyik, Hyde Park, MA

Outer Space Song and Dance . . . . . . .4+

Materials needed

I Want to Be an Astronaut by Byron Barton

What to do

1. Read *I Want to Be an Astronaut* or another book about astronauts.

2. Ask the children to pretend to be astronauts by pantomiming how to put on a space suit, space helmet, boots and gloves.

3. Ask the children to sit in a circle and do a countdown: 10-9-8-7-6-5-4-3-2-1 BLAST OFF!

4. The children follow the teacher and skip around the circle singing the original song below.

More to do

Language: Ask the children to pretend that they are flying in a rocket and to describe where they will go and what they will see. Write down their responses and make a class book about their pretend adventure.

Science: Talk about and look at pictures of the stars, moon, sun, comets and astronauts.

Original song

"We're on the Way to Outer Space" (Tune: "Grandpa's Farm")

Chorus

> *We're on the way (children skip around the circle)*
> *We're on the way*
> *On the way to outer space.*
> *We're on the way*
> *We're on the way*
> *On the way to outer space. (stop skipping and face the center of the circle)*
> *In outer space there is a rocket (hands above head in triangle)*
> *Zoom Zoom. (move triangle shape toward sky)*
> *In outer space there is a rocket*
> *Zoom Zoom.*

Repeat chorus and then face the circle.

> *In outer space there is an astronaut*
> *"Hi, Captain." (salute)*
> *In outer space there is an astronaut*
> *"Hi, Captain."*

Repeat chorus and then face the circle.

> *In outer space there is the moon (make circle with arms)*
> *I'm cold. (hug body)*
> *In outer space there is the moon*
> *I'm cold.*

Repeat chorus and then face the center of the circle.

In outer space there is the sun (make circle with arms)
I'm hot. (wipe brow)
In outer space there is the sun
I'm hot.

Repeat chorus and then face the circle.

In outer space there are the stars
Twinkle, twinkle. (move fingers together like twinkling stars)
In outer space there are the stars
Twinkle, twinkle.

Repeat chorus and then face the circle.

In outer space there is a comet (make a whoosh sound, moving hands from high to low
*   like a comet from sky to earth)*
In outer space there is a comet.

Repeat chorus and then slowly land your rocket on a spot in the circle.

★ Diann Spalding, Santa Rosa, CA

The Boa .4+

Materials needed
2 pillowcases (green or gray)
2 big black buttons
1 piece red felt

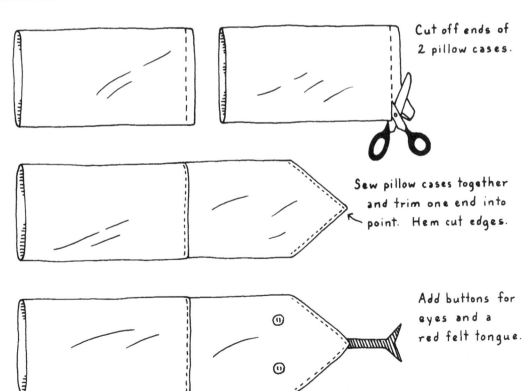

Cut off ends of 2 pillow cases.

Sew pillow cases together and trim one end into point. Hem cut edges.

Add buttons for eyes and a red felt tongue.

Movement

What to do

1. Cut the ends off both pillowcases. Sew the pillowcases together, end for end so that it is open all the way through. Hem the cut edges. Attach buttons to the top portion of the pillowcase for eyes. Make a red felt tongue and attach it beneath the eyes.

2. At circle time talk about and show the children the boa that you made to help the children act out the motions of the song "I'm Being Swallowed by a Boa Constrictor."

3. Each child is asked to take a turn being swallowed by a boa constrictor while the other children sing the song. The child steps into the pillowcase and the teacher slowly pulls up the pillowcase as each body part is named until the child's body is completely swallowed.

More to do
Science: Show pictures and talk about snakes.

Related book
A Nice Walk in the Jungle by Nan Bodsworth

Related song
"I'm Being Swallowed by a Boa Constrictor"

★ Melanie B. Brain, Salem, OH

Turn Your Scarf into a Leaf . . . . .4+

Materials needed
Scarves (1 per child)
Paper bag

What to do

1. At circle time talk with the children about leaves blowing in the wind. Ask the children what it would feel like to be blowing in the wind.

2. Show the children the bag of scarves and ask each child to take a scarf.

3. Tell the children to pretend the scarves are blowing in the wind.

4. Make the scarves blow back and forth from side to side.

5. Pretend the scarves are the wind that blows the leaves off the tree. Blow harder and harder, then stop.

6. Pretend the scarves are leaves, let them fall from the tree and then pick them up.

7. Throw the leaves up in the air and try to catch them with your hands.

8. Throw the leaves up in the air and try to catch them on your head.

9. Throw the leaves up in the air again and let them fall to the ground.

10. Pretend to hold a rake and rake all the leaves on the ground into a pile.

11. Each child picks up a leaf (scarf). The teacher makes a larger circle with her arms and the children put the leaves in the basket (teacher's arms).

★ Diann Spalding, Santa Rosa, CA

Take Two Turtle Steps . . . . .5+

Materials needed
None needed

What to do
1. Ask the children to stand side-by-side in a line facing the opposite wall and to listen closely to the directions of a game. Explain that the game differs from the traditional "Mother, May I?" because all of the children advance together (no competition or winner).

2. Tell the children to take 10 tiny steps forward. Count in a tiny, squeaky voice.

3. Tell the children to take 3 giant steps and count in a giant, loud voice.

4. Continue with the directions, take 6 zigzag steps and demonstrate what a zigzag is.

5. Hop 3 steps, turn around twice, 5 fast steps in the other direction, 6 very slow steps, 2 backward steps, 8 dancing steps.

6. Run slowly across the room. Hop on 1 foot.

7. Talk about which steps were the most difficult to take, which were the easiest, which were the most fun.

More to do
To add variation to the game, tell the children to take 8 kitty cat steps, 4 monster steps, 3 butterfly steps, 5 kangaroo steps, 7 basketball steps. Play lively music. Use the above directions and demonstrate how to take various steps to the beat of the music.

Related book
Johnathan and His Mommy by Irene Smalls-Hector

★ Cathy Chenoweth, Columbia, MO

Movement

We Are Friends . . . . .3+

Materials needed

Magazines
Scissors
Glue
Paper

What to do

1. Talk with the children about what all people need to live. List the children's ideas. Discuss basic needs, such as food, water, shelter and love.

2. Talk about the similarities and differences in the appearance of the children. Ask them to share their observations about hair, eyes, height, glasses and other physical characteristics of the children in the class. How are they alike? How are they different?

3. Cut out pictures of people from magazines to make a collage.

4. Encourage the children to share observations about the people in their collage.

5. Teach the following song to the tune of "Frere Jaques."

We are alike, we are alike.
We are different, we are different.
We are friends, we are friends.
We are neighbors, we are neighbors!

★ Angela Williamson, Greensboro, NC

We All Eat Bread . . . . .3+

Materials needed

Bread, Bread, Bread by Ann Morris
Different types of bread (French baguette, bagel, tortilla, matzo, Russian pumpernickel, foccaccia, pita, Navaho Fry bread)
Paper plates

What to do

1. Read *Bread, Bread, Bread* at circle time.

2. Point out the different types of bread shown in the pictures.

3. Tell the children that people living in all parts of the world eat bread but that the bread doesn't always look like the bread we eat.

4. Show them the different types of bread that you brought to share with them.

5. Discuss the differences in the breads and the cultures that they have come from.

6. Invite the children to taste the different types of bread (provide small pieces of the bread for tasting).

7. Talk about differences in the taste of the bread and which type of bread the children liked best.

8. Ask the children what type or types of bread their family eats.

More to do

Cooking: Bake bread or soft pretzels and eat for a snack.

Field trip: Visit a bakery.

Social studies: Set aside days (or weeks) that feature a culture and sample the foods, stories and customs of that culture.

Related books

Bread, Bread, Bread by Ann Morris
Hats, Hats, Hats by Ann Morris
Houses and Homes by Ann Morris
Loving by Ann Morris
Shoes, Shoes, Shoes by Ann Morris
Tools by Ann Morris

★ Teresa J. Nos, Baltimore, MD

Friendship Chain . . . . .4+

Materials needed

Multicultural crayons
2 white paper strips for each child (5" x 2")
Tape
We Are All Alike, We Are All Different by Cheltenham Elementary School Kindergartners or similar book

What to do

1. At circle time read *We Are All Alike, We Are All Different*.

2. After reading the book, the teacher places her hands in the middle of the circle and asks the children to describe her skin color.

3. Encourage the children to compare their skin colors using words such as lighter, darker, same color.

4. After comparing all of the skin colors ask the children to match their skin color to those of the multicultural crayons.

5. Each child selects a crayon and colors two paper strips to represent his skin color.

6. After the strips are completed make a Friendship Chain (interlocking and stapling the strips), proudly displaying the children's skin colors.

7. When the chain is complete ask the children where to display it.

8. Discuss how the chain looks, how all of the skin colors look together, how each link is special and unique and what can be accomplished when we all work together.

More to do

Science: Obtain flesh tone paint chips and place on a table with magnifying glasses so children can examine them closely.

Manipulatives: Make a matching game using flesh tone paint chips.

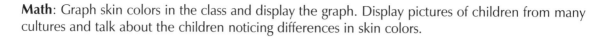

Math: Graph skin colors in the class and display the graph. Display pictures of children from many cultures and talk about the children noticing differences in skin colors.

Related books
We Are All Alike, We Are All Different by Cheltenham Elementary School Kindergartners
We Are All Different and That's Okay! by Shelia Holden
Why Am I Different? by Norma Simon

★ Latrina K. Baldwin, Bordentown, NJ

The Talking Stone . . . . .4+

Materials needed
1 stone (about the size of a child's palm, too big for mouths, small enough to hold)
Drawstring bag to hold the stone (optional)

What to do
The Talking Stone is a variation of a Native American tradition. A person who is holding a Talking Stick or Talking Stone is the designated speaker in settling disputes. I use an adaptation of this idea to encourage language and listening skills.

1. Introduce the Talking Stone at group time. If desired it could become a daily circle activity. The only rule is: "Whoever holds the stone gets to talk about anything, for as long as she likes." The other children listen or look at books, but the child holding the stone is the only child that talks.

2. The teacher gives the stone to a child who may talk about any subject.

3. After talking the child gives the stone to another child who has not had a turn. Use this as a listening time for yourself as well as the children since only one child may talk at a time.

4. Throughout the year children may ask for the Talking Stone when they have something to say at circle time.

More to do
Special days or special themes can be attached to the Talking Stone time.

Related book
Noisy Nora by Rosemary Wells

★ Tracie O'Hara, Charlotte, NC

Stick Power . . . . .4+

Materials needed
Branches from tree (1 per child)
Yarn (nature colors, such as green, brown, orange, yellow)
Beads (same colors as yarn)
Feathers (same colors as yarn)

What to do
1. Go outside and hunt for sticks. Help the children check for the appropriate length and thickness.

2. Make sure the branches are dry and that they will not bend or snap.

3. Explain to the children that they will each make a Talking Stick that represents power and respect. The Talking Stick is a variation of a Native American tradition. The only person permitted to speak is the one who is holding the stick. Children can take their sticks home and use them in family discussions. (Send a note to parents explaining the use of a Talking Stick.)

4. Introduce the use of the Talking Stick to the children by holding it while you are speaking. If a child has a question or comment she must raise her hand and wait until the stick is placed in her hand before speaking.

5. Decorate the sticks. Wrap the entire stick or only the base with yarn. String beads to hang from the top or sides. Place feathers on the top.

6. Provide a Talking Stick for the children to use during circle time.

★ Kim Gardner, Cleona, PA

Matryoshka Dolls . . . . .4+

Materials needed
2 dolls of different sizes
Set of the paper matryosha dolls (with felt or a magnet on the back)
Magnet or felt board

What to do
1. At circle time show the children two dolls from the classroom and ask which of the two is larger and which is smaller.

2. Talk about the many different kinds and sizes of dolls that children are familiar with.

3. Show the children two of the paper matryoshka (pronounced mah-tree-osk-kuh) dolls. Explain that these are paper pictures of the real dolls that are usually made of wood and are a folk art of Eastern Europe. If a globe or map is available point out eastern Europe and show pictures of people living in this region. If possible show a picture or samples of these stacking dolls that are often painted with the bright colors of the local clothing and are made in sets of odd numbers such as three, five or seven. Tell the children that the scarves worn on the dolls' heads are called "babushkas." This word also means "grandmother" in the Russian language.

4. Place three of the paper matryoshka dolls on the board. Ask the children which is largest, which is smallest and which is the size in between the other two dolls. Ask older children to put five or seven dolls in order by size.

5. Provide the paper dolls for the children to play with during choice time.

More to do

Dramatic play: Place clothing similar to that of the dolls' costumes, such as long flowered dresses and scarves in the dramatic play area.

Fine motor: Provide patterns of paper dolls so each child can cut out a set.

Note: Plastic matryoska dolls are available through Eichorchen Cimmer, Eichorn-Germany. They may also be available in some local toy stores.

Related books

Babushka's Doll by Patricia Polacco
Count Your Way Through Russia by Jim Haskins
Russian Girl: Life in an Old Russian Town by Russ Kendall
The Turnip: An Old Russian Folktale by Pierr Morgan

★ Sandra Nagel, White Lake, MI

Spanish Lesson (La lección de español) 5+

Materials needed
None needed

What to do
1. Begin circle time by introducing a few basic Spanish words, such as "hola" (hello), "buenos dias" (good morning), "adiós" (goodbye) and counting from one to ten.
2. If there is a calendar in the room print the days of the week in Spanish on paper above the English words. Learn to sing the days of the week in Spanish as well as in English.
3. Incorporate a few new Spanish words every day, as well as reviewing previously learned words, such as the season, the month, colors and short phrases.
4. Learn to sing familiar circle time songs in Spanish.

More to do
Home connection: If there are parents who speak Spanish, invite them to visit the classroom regularly to speak Spanish with the children and share their culture.

Language: Print the word in Spanish on a chart paper strip and put a picture of what the word describes above it, such as "gato" and a picture of a cat. Label everything in the classroom with its English name. When the children learn a new Spanish word of an object in the classroom, also label it with the Spanish name.

Related books
Buenas noches, luna by Margaret Wise Brown, Spanish version of *Goodnight Moon*.
La oruga muy hambrienta by Eric Carle, Spanish version of *The Very Hungry Caterpillar*.
Un sillón para mi mamá by Vera B. Williams, Spanish version of *A Chair for My Mother*.

Related songs
"Here We Are Together" in English (to the tune of "The More We Get Together")

> *Here we are together, together, together*
> *Here we are together on this sunny day.*
> *With (child's name) and (child's name) and (child's name).*
> *Here we are together on this sunny day.*

"Here We Are Together" in Spanish

> *Aquí estamos reunidos, reunidos, reunidos.*
> *Aquí estamos reunidos, en este día de sol.*
> *Con (child's name) y (child's name) y (child's name).*
> *Aquí estamos reunidos en este día de sol.*

Days of the week
Sunday (domingo)   Monday (lunes)   Tuesday (martes)
Wednesday (miércoles)   Thursday (jueves)   Friday (viernes)
Saturday (sábado)

★ Jennifer Scott-Greenfield, Philadelphia, PA

Life in Japan . . . . .5+

Materials needed

Origami paper
String
Markers

What to do

1. At circle time tell the children that you will talk about the people and culture of Japan. Show pictures and talk about Japan or read a book about Japan. Explain that the children will make a fan from origami paper that is common in Japan.

2. Give each child a square of origami paper and talk about how it is different from other types of paper.

3. Ask the children to make lengthwise accordion pleated folds across the paper.

4. Tie a piece of string around the folded pleats about one-half inch from the bottom. Provide markers for the children to use in decorating the fans.

5. Sing the following song to the tune of "A Hunting We Will Go." The children hold their fans and add motions to the song while singing.

> *My fan can make the waves. (move fan in wave-like rhythm in front of body)*
> *My fan can make the waves.*
> *When I move my fan like this.*
> *My fan can make the waves.*

> *My fan can make the wind. (move fan swiftly back and forth over head)*
> *My fan can make the wind.*
> *When I move my fan like this.*
> *My fan can make the wind.*

> *My fan can make the leaves. (move fans in a fluttering motion above head to floor)*
> *My fan can make the leaves.*
> *When I move my fan like this.*
> *My fan can make the leaves.*

More to do

Dramatic play: Remove the tables and chairs and replace them with cushions. Provide a low cardboard box for a table and on it place a small teapot, cups, plates and chopsticks. Include a wok with the cooking utensils. Place Japanese clothes in the dress-up center and encourage the children to take off their shoes before entering this area.

Language: Display samples of Japanese writing. On a nearby table place Q-tips, small cups of black paint and rectangular pieces of construction paper for children to use in copying Japanese words. Incorporate Japanese terms into the daily routine, such as

Konnichiwa—Hello

Ohayo—Morning

Saynora—Goodbye

Arigato—Thank you

Hai—Yes

Lie—No

Math: Write the following numerals on chart paper and then write the Japanese word for each numeral. Use the chart in teaching the children to count in Japanese.

1—Ichi		2—Ni	
3—San		4—Shi	
5—Go		6—Roku	
7—Shichi		8—Hachi	
9—Ku		10—Ju	

Snack: Make Ramen soup. One packet will probably be enough for two or three children. Small pieces of tofu or bok choy may be added. Provide chopsticks for children who would like to use them. Serve with rice crackers and a small cup of warm tea.

一 ichi (1)
二 ni (2)
三 san (3)
四 shi (4)
五 go (5)
六 roku (6)
七 shichi (7
八 hachi (8)
九 ku (9)
十 ju (10)

夏 natsu (summer)
冬 fuyu (winter)
春 haru (spring)
秋 aki (autumn)

Related books
Trees of Crane by Allen Say
Grandfather's Journey by Allen Say
Umbrella by Taro Yashimo

★ Patricia A. Jackson, Dublin, OH

This Friday—Korea! . . . . .5+

Materials needed
Posters, maps, clothing, chopsticks, pictures (reflecting the culture of Korea)
Poster board and markers or chalk board and chalk

What to do
1. Tell the children that on the following day they will pretend to travel to Korea and talk about life in that country. (This activity focuses on Korea but the focus could be on any country, especially one representing the nationality of people in your community).

2. Before the children arrive on Friday, decorate the bulletin board with the following items:

✓ Map of Korea
✓ Poster pictures and a paper flag (available free from Korean Embassy and some travel agencies)
✓ Any items from the country
✓ A sample of writing in Korean
✓ Pictures of Korean children, men and women in traditional dress (magazines obtained from Korean embassy)

3. At circle time talk about each item on the bulletin board and show the children the location of Korea on a globe or world map.

4. On the chalk board write the numerals 1, 2, 3 and then write the Korean name for each numeral.

1—hana
2—dul
3—seit

5. Teach the children to count in Korean and to say a few words in Korean (if possible, invite a person from Korea to visit).

6. Read a story or folktale from Korea.

Note: The Oregon International Council, Salem, Oregon 97303 rents a discovery kit with lunch boxes, games, paper and other assorted items from Korea.

More to do

Language: Children talk about what they learned about Korea (teacher writes what each child says on a separate piece of paper). Each child illustrates his page and helps to compile the pages into a class book about Korea.

Snack: For snack serve the children Kim Chee (available in many grocery stores).

Related books

Blindman's Daughter by Edward B. Adams
Sun and Moon by K. Seros (folktales from Korea)

★ Barbara J. Vogel, Soldotna, AK

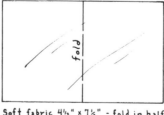

Soft fabric 4½" x 7½" - fold in half.

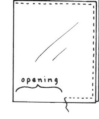
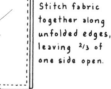

Stitch fabric together along unfolded edges, leaving ⅔ of one side open.

opening

opening

Turn inside out and fill ½ full with beans through opening.

Sew opening closed.

Bands . . . . .3+

Materials needed

Musical instruments or pictures of instruments
Toilet paper rolls
Wax paper
Rubber bands

What to do

1. Show children pictures of musical instruments.

2. If possible, invite student musicians from a nearby school to visit. Ask the musicians to play a few notes on the instruments showing the children how they make different tones and music with their instruments. Ask them to play songs that the children know so they can sing along.

3. Make instruments with the children by placing wax paper over the end of a toilet paper roll. Hold the wax paper in place with a rubber band. Children blow into the wax paper and make a humming sound. Other instruments that the children could make include string instruments made with rubber bands, tin cans played with spoons or blocks to bang together for a rhythm instrument. Children can play their instruments along with the visiting musicians.

★ Marilyn Harding, Grimes, IA

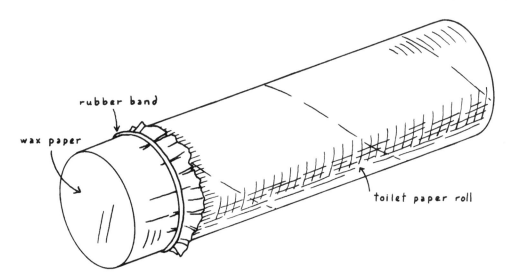

rubber band

wax paper

toilet paper roll

Trash-A-Musical Instrument . . . . .3+

Materials needed

Tissue boxes
Rubber bands
Tape
Small plastic containers with lids
Beads, buttons, dried beans, rice, paper clips, pebbles
Large plastic or metal containers

What to do

1. Talk with the children about making musical instruments from recycled materials and listening to the sounds the instruments make.

2. To make tissue box guitars: stretch rubber bands across the hole in the box and tape the rubber bands on all sides of the box. If desired, decorate the guitars with stickers and markers. Ask the children to listen to the sounds the rubber bands make as they strum the guitars.

3. To make shakers: put a few beads, buttons, dried beans, rice, paper clips or pebbles into empty plastic or metal containers and screw on the lids. See-through spice containers and dish detergent bottles work well. Tape the lids on securely. Listen to the sounds the shakers make.

4. To make recycled drums use an empty container with a plastic or metal top (cans of potato chips, coffee, cocoa, oatmeal).

Note: Always check for sharp or rough edges. Containers and cans can be used without the lids if the edges are wrapped with duct tape.

5. Ask the children to tap a rhythm with hands, a spoon or stick and listen to the sounds.

Caution: With young children who still put things into their mouths, be sure items are large enough so that they cannot be swallowed.

★ Linda Ann Hodge, Minnetonka, MN

Sticky Dancing . . . . .3+

Materials needed

Duct tape
Dancing music (fast tempo)

What to do

1. At circle time tell the children they are going to do a sticky dance.

2. Roll a piece of duct tape (sticky side out) around your shoe to demonstrate.

3. Put the duct tape around the children's shoes.

4. Have the children take a few steps to get used to the feeling of the duct tape.

5. Start the music and invite the children to dance.

6. When the children are finished dancing, turn off the music and remove the duct tape.

More to do

Art: Add strips of duct tape to the art area. The children can make collages by sticking scraps of paper to the duct tape that is rolled with the sticky side exposed.

★ Glenda Manchanda, Huber Heights, OH

Vocal Recording . . . . .3+

Materials needed
Blank cassette for each child
Tape recorder

What to do
1. Each month after the children have learned new songs, record the children singing the songs.

2. Always play the tape for the children after each monthly recording. They love to hear their voices on the tape and look forward to the next recording.

3. Arrange to have multiple copies of the tape duplicated.

More to do
Give the recording as a family gift. The tape is also an excellent gift at the end of the school year for children to play during the summer so they can sing along with the songs.

★ Joyce Montag, Slippery Rock, PA

Barefoot Musical Marching Band . . . . .3+

Materials needed
Marching music
Clear self-adhesive paper
Carpet square
Musical instruments (1 per child)
Cardboard
Tape

What to do
1. In advance tape a sheet of clear self-adhesive paper, sticky side up, to the floor in an area of the room where the children are not playing.

2. At circle time explain that the children will become a barefoot marching band.

3. Ask the children take off their shoes and socks (help if necessary).

4. Show the children that you are taping a piece of cardboard and a carpet square to the floor.

5. Ask the children to choose a musical instrument they will play in the marching band.

6. Start the music and march around the room, playing the instruments while marching. The teacher leads the band and marches over the cardboard and carpet square.

7. Then lead the children to the self-adhesive paper and march over it.

8. Enjoy their reaction to marching on the sticky paper.

9. When the children are finished marching, turn off the music and ask them to join you in the circle time area.

10. Talk about how walking on the sticky paper felt. Discuss the different textures the children felt with their feet as they marched around the room.

More to do

Language: Talk about the different textures the children felt with their feet while marching and list the words they use to describe the textures on chart paper.

★ Glenda Manchanda, Huber Heights, OH

Jingle Bells and Rhythm Sticks . . . . . .3+

Materials needed

1 pair of rhythm sticks for each child (rhythm sticks are easy to make from dowel rods)
1/2" or 3/4" jingle bells for each rhythm stick
Recording of the "Parade of the Wooden Soldiers"
1 tie from a plastic bag for each rhythm stick
1 rubber band for each rhythm stick

What to do

1. In advance, attach each jingle bell to a rhythm stick by using a tie and then wrapping a rubber band over the tie to hold the bell in place.

2. At circle time invite the children to use the rhythm sticks as they march to the "Parade of the Wooden Soldiers."

More to do

Play a variety of marching music while marching with the rhythm sticks (or lummi sticks). Also make rhythm patterns by tapping the sticks together or tapping them on the floor.

★ Shirley MacDonald, Troy, MI

Music . . . . .3+

Materials needed

Cassette player
Cassette tapes of classical, jazz, funk, rock and roll, reggae and rap music

What to do

1. Talk about different types of music with the children.

2. Listen to the different types of music and ask the children which music is their favorite and how they feel when listening to the different types of music.

3. Encourage discussion about the different types of music.

4. Ask the children to dance or move to the various types of music.

More to do

Art: Play different music while the children are drawing and tell them to feel the beat of the music and draw to the rhythm of the music. Use different media, such as paint, pastels, chalk.

★ Debbie Bokor, Richmond Hill, Ontario, Canada

Musical Hoops . . . . .3+

Materials needed
Music (fast tempo)
6-9 hula hoops

What to do
1. At circle time explain that when the music is playing, the children may dance and move to the music. When the music stops, they need to stand inside a hula hoop.

2. Start the music.

3. Stop the music. Encourage the children to help each other find a hula hoop.

4. When everyone is standing inside a hula hoop, remove one of the hoops.

5. Repeat Steps 2 and 3 until there are only three hula hoops left. This game encourages cooperation and no one should be left out.

Note: When doing this activity with a large number of children, increase the beginning number of hula hoops and the number left at the end to ensure the game will be safe.

More to do
Art: Make paper tube shakers or paper plate shakers. The teacher records the children playing their shakers and uses this music when playing the game.

★ Glenda Manchanda, Huber Heights, OH

Pop Goes the Weasel . . . . .3+

Materials needed
Metal lids from jars with a safety pop-up button (about 2" in diameter)

What to do
1. In advance collect jar lids that fit inside a child's hand (ask parents for contributions).

2. At circle time ask each child to choose a lid. Show the children how to hold the lids and pop the button with their thumbs. Talk about the noise that it makes.

3. Explain that as the children sing a song together they can make the popping noise as they sing the words of the song. Ask the children to suggest songs to sing. "Pop Goes the Weasel" is an excellent one because of the popping sound. Sing the songs the children suggest and pop the lid to the words.

More to do
Home connection: Ask parents to save the lids for the children to use in art projects such as a popping, musical lid collage.

Math: Sort lids according to color, size, loudest pop.

Science: Ask the children to predict which lid will pop the loudest, softest or not at all.

★ NeVada Lynn Runnebaum, Leavenworth, KS

Music

Musical Water Glasses . . . . .4+

Materials needed
8 water glasses
Water
Spoon or small mallet

What to do
1. Teach the song "Do, Re, Mi."

2. Place eight tall water glasses in a line on a table.

3. Fill the first one with water. In the next glass put less water, less in the next one and so on. Make sure the glasses are in tune.

4. Use a spoon to demonstrate how to play "Do, Re, Me" on the glasses. For simplicity, just go up the scale. Do not attempt to play all the notes of the song. Demonstrate other songs, such as "Mary Had a Little Lamb."

5. Let the children experiment with the musical glasses.

6. Add food coloring to the water in the musical glasses to make a different color (or shade of color) in each glass.

More to do
Play a duet with a xylophone and the water glasses. Note the Do, Re, Mi pattern. Make up new words for a familiar tune, such as "Mary Had a Little Lamb" and sing the new words while playing the musical glasses. For example, "This is how we play a song, play a song, play a song. This is how we play a song. Won't you sing along?"

Related books
Push, Pull, Empty, Full by Tana Hoban
Mary Had a Little Lamb by Sara Hale

★ Wendy Pfeffer, Pennington, NJ

Be a Conductor . . . . .4+

Materials needed
Baton for conducting (chopstick, pencil)
Musical instrument for each child

What to do
1. At circle time give each child a musical instrument (initially, use rhythm sticks).

2. Allow time for the children to explore the instruments.

3. Ask the children to copy a slow rhythm that you begin.

4. Talk about the role of the conductor who helps the musicians work together to play a certain song. Ask the children to watch you while they are copying the rhythm.

5. Demonstrate a signal for "begin," such as both hands raised, then quickly brought down together. Demonstrate a signal for "stop," such as both hands quickly moved apart. (Initially use verbal as well as manual signals.)

6. Establish a rhythm with the children. Encourage them to keep their eyes open for the "stop" signal.

7. When the children are comfortable following the conductor practice the "begin" signal.

8. Invite the children to take turns conducting.

More to do
Record the children's music and place the tape in the listening area.

Large motor: Play a Stop and Go Game to music (when music stops, children must "freeze").

Related book
Musical Max by Robert Kraus

★ Sharon Dempsey, Vineland, NJ

Follow the Director . . . . .4+

Materials needed
Picture of an orchestra or band
Rhythm instruments for the children

What to do
1. Introduce the activity by showing the children the picture of a musical group. Describe the instruments shown in the picture. Tell the children that in a band there is one person in charge and she is called the director. This person shows the players when they should play and helps them play the music together. Ask the children what would happen if the band members played their instruments at any time they wanted or as fast as they could play.

2. Invite the children to be a part of a clapping band. Ask the children to clap their hands when you hold your hands up high. Have them stop clapping when you lower your hands to your lap. (Have a clearly defined point at which they should stop.) Ask the children to practice clapping while they watch you raise and lower your hands at irregular intervals.

3. Explain that today they will play together as a band following a director. Talk about the importance for everyone to watch the director while they are playing an instrument.

4. Distribute the instruments and ask the children to play the instruments when you raise your hands and stop playing when you lower your hands. Invite volunteers to take turns to be the director leading the band.

5. When all volunteers have had a turn directing the band collect the instruments and ask the musicians to take a bow.

More to do

Field trip: Visit the rehearsal of a local music group.

Social studies: Invite musicians to the classroom to demonstrate their instruments and to talk to the children about their music.

Related books

Musical Max by Robert Kraus
Loudmouth George and the Cornet by Nancy Carlson

★ Karen Wojahn, Windom, MN

Gadget Orchestra . . . . .4+

Materials needed

Kitchen gadgets that make noise (each child brings 1 from home)
Pictures of musical instruments
Cassette tape recorder and tape

What to do

1. Send parents a note requesting that their child bring a kitchen gadget that makes noise to school on a specific day.

2. Ask the children to bring their kitchen gadgets to circle time.

3. Talk about an orchestra and that it has four sections including strings, woodwinds, brass and percussion. Show the children instruments or pictures of instruments.

4. Ask each child to describe his kitchen gadget and to show how it makes noise.

5. Group the children according to how their gadgets make noise. Try to arrange the orchestra into four sections.

6. Talk to the children about the role of the conductor and that as the conductor you will signal each group when it is time to play their instruments.

7. Allow time for the children to practice playing their instruments at the direction of the conductor.

8. Record the children playing their instruments and play the tape for the children to hear. Ask the children to listen to identify the sound of their instruments.

★ Kimberle S. Byrd, Wyoming, MI

Maestro, if You Please ....4+

Materials needed
The Maestro Plays by Bill Martin, Jr. and Vladimir Radunsky
Pictures of musical instruments
Recorded classical music

What to do
1. Show the children pictures of the musical instruments. Ask the children to pantomime how to play the instruments.

2. Read *The Maestro Plays* at circle time.

3. Ask the children to name the instruments they saw in the book.

4. Reread the book and ask the children to pretend to play each instrument moving like the musician in the picture.

5. Invite the children to play pretend instruments as they listen to classical music.

More to do
Art: Make shakers and drums to create a band. Ask each child to draw a picture of himself playing an instrument. Combine the pictures to create a class book.

Language: Read books about musical instruments and draw pictures of the instruments.

Music: Listen to recordings that highlight the specific instruments that the children have drawn pictures and have talked about.

Related songs
"Tubby the Tuba"
"Peter and the Wolf"

★ Deanna Davis Peters, State College, PA

Sing Along Time ....4+

Materials needed
Toilet paper roll
Aluminum foil
Black construction paper or tissue paper
Glue or tape

What to do
1. To make a hand microphone wrap the empty paper roll with foil. Crumble the black paper into a ball and attach it to the top of the roll with glue or tape.

2. At circle time provide the microphone for children to use as they sing a favorite song. (If children would like to make their own microphone, provide materials at the art center.)

More to do

Place the pretend microphone in the music area with a tape recorder. Encourage the children to make a recording of a song with friends. Teach children the following song to sing at circle time while holding the microphone.

Original song

"Singing Song" (Tune: "Frere Jacques")

> *I am singing, I am singing, Hear my song? Hear my song?*
> *Sing around the circle, sing around the circle,*
> *Sing my song. Sing along.*
> *We are singing, we are singing. Hear our song? Hear our song?*
> *Sing around the circle, sing around the circle,*
> *Sing our song. Sing along.*

The soloist sings the first verse. The other children sing the second verse. The soloist then hands the microphone to another child who becomes the soloist.

★ Margery A. Kranyik, Hyde Park, MA

Sound Effects . . . . .4+

Materials needed

Tape recorder and blank tape
Items that produce sound effects (rhythm instruments or common objects)
Character necklaces (way to designate characters)

What to do

1. Choose a well known, predictable story (for example, *The Three Bears*).

2. Talk with the children about each character and ask them to choose a musical sound that will represent each character.

3. After deciding on a musical sound for each character, ask the children to choose the character they want to be and to wear the corresponding necklace or other character identification.

4. Explain that as you read the story, you will signal which character's turn it will be to make the musical sound to designate that character. (For example, "My porridge is too hot" would be accompanied by the Mother Bear's music, playing tambourines; "My porridge is too cold" by Father Bear's music, playing drums; "Mine is just right" by Baby Bear's music, ringing jingle bells.) The more frequently this activity is repeated, the more proficient the children will become at anticipating their turns.

5. Read the story and ask the children to practice their parts. When the children are ready record the story with the accompanying musical sounds. Play the recording and ask the children to listen for their parts. With the children plan and create the musical sounds to accompany other familiar stories.

More to do

Game: Record sounds throughout the day and later play the recording for the children to guess what made the sounds in their classroom.

Language: Record a variety of common sounds on a tape and place it in the listening area. Children can identify the sounds and write a story about what is making the sounds.

★ Sharon Dempsey, Vineland, NJ

Rhythm Memory . . . . .5+

Materials needed
None needed

What to do

1. At circle time begin a rhythm by clapping three times or a similar rhythm that the children can follow.

2. The child sitting next to the first person copies the rhythm and adds another rhythm with three beats.

3. Continue around the circle until everyone has had a turn. Repeat the rhythm together challenging the children to remember the entire rhythm.

More to do

Vary the activity by asking each child to add a body movement rather than a rhythm to the pattern. Continue around the circle until everyone has had a turn and then ask the children to repeat all the body movements.

★ Stephanie Person, Kingsburg, CA

Everybody Needs a Rock . . . . .3+

Materials needed

Everybody Needs a Rock by Byrd Baylor
1 rock

What to do

1. At circle time tell the children that you have something very special in your hand that you will pass around the circle. Describe how you hunted and searched until you found the perfect one.

2. Ask the children to guess what is in your hand. After several children guess show them the rock in your hand.

3. Pass the rock around the circle and then read *Everybody Needs a Rock*.

4. Go outside and allow time for the children to search for their own rocks. Bring a bucket of water outside so they can see what their rocks look like when they are wet. Do they look different? How? How do the rocks smell? Feel?

More to do

Art: Make a home for the rock by decorating a small box and adding cotton, grass or twigs for the rock to rest on. Rock and Roll—Marble Paint with a small rock (round pebble). Put a piece of paper in a pan. Dip a rock in a container of paint. Place the small rock in the pan and move the pan back and forth to move the rock making a paint design on the paper.

Home connection: Encourage children to bring in interesting rocks from home to display in the classroom. Invite parents in to view the rocks in the class museum. Ask the children to be tour guides in the museum.

Language: Make signs for the museum display of rocks.

Science: Rub two rocks together over a piece of white paper. What happens? What does it make? How does the spot feel where the two rocks are rubbed together? Start a Rock Museum.

★ Ann Scalley, Wellfleet, MA

A Rock Place  ....3+

Materials needed
Rocks (collected by children)
Large shallow pan or tray

What to do
1. At circle tme ask the children to place their rocks in a shallow pan.

2. Discuss the rocks with the children. Ask the children to describe their rocks and tell where they found their rocks. Talk about the different colors, shapes and textures of the rocks.

3. Count and sort the rocks according to sizes, colors or textures.

4. Arrange the rocks in the Rock Place in categories or by mixing the different types of rocks together.

5. If desired, add water to cover the rocks for a rock aquarium or let the rocks dry for a rock garden. Display the rocks in a place where the children can handle them.

More to do
Home connection: Ask parents if they know a person in the community who collects rocks and would talk with the children.

Science: Encourage the children to continue adding to the collection and take the time to talk about each new rock. Allow the children time to explore the rocks and touch, count, sort and look at the rocks with a magnifying glass and then to return them to the Rock Place. If you have a rock tumbler, tumble a few of the rocks for about one month and make periodic observations.

★ Susan Rinas, Parma, OH

Which One Is Heavier? ....3+

Materials needed
Polished and unpolished rocks
Water
Paper towels

Paper and markers
Containers

What to do
1. At circle time talk with the children about the different kinds of rocks.

2. Explain how rocks are tumbled around and around by water in the ocean or in a river and become smooth. Show samples of polished and unpolished rocks. Let the children feel the difference in the rocks.

3. Take a walk where children can collect rocks.

4. Place a scale with different types and sizes of rocks where children can weigh the rocks. Include several types of rocks, such as crystals, granite, pumice.

Nature

5. Ask the children to predict which rock will be heavier and to weigh the rocks to test their predictions.

More to do

Place a container of water on a table and let the children discover if the rocks will sink or float. Include pumice in the collection of rocks (a light porous lava rock that will float). Grow salt crystals by pouring warm water into a jar until it is half full. Add three tablespoons of salt and stir until the salt is dissolved. Tie a string on a stick placed across the mouth of the jar and let the string hang in the water. Let the jar stand several days until crystals form.

★ Linda S. Andrews, Sonora, CA

Make-A-Tree . . . . .3+

Materials needed

Paper bags (1 per child)
Large sheet of paper
Glue
Tape
Crayons or markers

What to do

1. Prior to taking a nature walk provide each child with a bag that she can decorate. While walking encourage the children to collect materials, such as leaves, tree bark and twigs.

2. After the walk ask the children to sit in a circle and place the materials they collected on the floor in front of them.

3. Explain to the children that together they will create a picture of a tree on the large sheet of paper. Draw a large outline of a tree on the sheet of paper.

4. Ask each child to contribute something they found on the nature walk to help create the group tree picture.

5. Help each child glue or tape her contribution to the outline of the tree.

6. If desired, add pictures of bird nests and animals to the tree.

More to do

Art: Provide pictures from nature magazines to develop a collage with a tree theme.

Math: Measure the circumference of several trees and compare the measurements. Count the number of rings on a cross section of a log to determine the age of the tree.

★ Tom Gordon and Nancy McKnight, Slippery Rock, PA

Tree Stories Bulletin Board ....4+

Materials needed

30 Tissue paper rolls (6 rolls for tree trunk and 24 rolls for branches)
Glue
Tape
1 clothespin per child
Tempera paint (variety of colors)
Paintbrushes
Mat board (40" x 32")
Magazine pictures or children's artwork of birds, bird nests, squirrels, insects
Paper, pencils, crayons and scissors
Twigs

mat board 32" x 40"

What to do

1. Talk with the children about creating a bulletin board for their "tree stories."

2. Invite the children to take a walk where they can collect twigs for the border of the bulletin board.

3. Explain that the children will create the branches of the tree at tables in the art center and after the branches are dry they will put all the branches together to create a tree.

4. Involve the children in painting the paper rolls. Allow the paper rolls to dry.

5. Place the mat board on a table or on the floor in the middle of the circle.

6. With the children's help construct the tree. To make the trunk glue or tape six rolls (placed vertically) on the mat board. To make the branches use the following pattern: for the top branch place one roll on each side of trunk; for the second and third row of branches place two rolls on each side of trunk; for the fourth row place three rolls on each side of trunk; for the fifth row place four rolls on each side of trunk.

7. Glue or tape the tree formation to the mat board.

8. Ask the children to design a twig border and glue the twigs to the mat board.

9. While the glue is drying ask the children to cut out magazine pictures of squirrels, birds, bird nests, insects or to draw their own illustrations.

10. Using tape attach each picture to a clothespin.

11. Ask the children to create "tree stories" about the pictures they attached to the clothespins. Invite each child to clip her picture to a tree branch and tell a story about the picture.

More to do

Math: Display pictures of apples on the tree. Count the apples and graph the number of apples, comparing size and color.

Outdoors: Create apple garlands from apple wedges using blunt embroidery needles and yarn. Thread the apples onto the yarn and tie the ends of the yarn together to form a garland. Help the children hang the garlands on tree branches for birds to eat.

Science: Bring a variety of apples to school. Invite children to feel and smell the apples. Introduce each apple by its name. Cut the apples into wedges and serve the apples for snack.

Related books

The Seasons of Arnold's Apple Tree by Gail Gibbons
A Tree Is Nice by Janice May Udry

★ Jill Loveless, Lee's Summit, MO

Natural Surprises . . . . .4+

Materials needed

Natural object (leaves, acorns, seed pods, pine cones, dead wood)
Chart paper

What to do

1. Talk about how children explore and learn about nature through their senses such as sight, hearing, touch and smell. (Unless you are introducing a safe and clearly edible food, such as an apple, tell the children not to taste the natural objects.)

2. Encourage the children to use their senses to explore the collection of objects from nature. Encourage creativity by imagining the objects to be other than they are (for example, a prickly seed pod could be a green porcupine).

3. Give a natural surprise to each child. On the top of the chart paper write the words "Nature is...." Ask each child to describe their special surprise by using one word, such as soft, sticky, fuzzy. Record words and compose a class poem using the words.

More to do

Large motor: Act out the "Nature Walk Action Rhyme" below. Ask the children to repeat each line and act out the motions with you.

Original poem

"Nature Walk Action Rhyme"

> We're going on a nature walk (walk in place)
> To see what we can see. (hand over eyes)
> We might smell some flowers (sniff)
> We might hear some bees. Buzz!
>
> The sun is mighty hot (wipe brow)
> So let's find a shady tree.
> Oh look, there's a perfect one (point)
> Hey, come follow me!
>
> Shhh! Whisper!
> I see a rabbit eating grass. (point)
> So we don't disturb him
> Let's tiptoe as we go past. (tiptoe in place)
>
> Now, on to the tree
> And there we'll take a rest.
> Let's just lie down there (lie down, heads together)
> Hey, look up! I see a nest. (point to sky)
>
> Birds are flying over me (hands flutter as wings)
> As they look for bits of twig.
> To add to their nest
> To make it nice and big.
>
> A squirrel is climbing down the trunk (fingers down arm)
> Let's try not to make a fuss.
> If we are very quiet (whisper)
> He might crawl over to see us.
>
> Keep still, here he comes! (only leader begins to creep)
> Creeping nearer and nearer to you.
> Close your eyes, listen for him.
> Can you feel his tickle too? (tickle kids with soft object)
>
> We fall asleep under the tree (pretend to sleep)
> And soon the afternoon is gone. (stand up)
> And as we walk towards home again (walk in place)
> We can count as stars turn on. (point skyward and count to ten)

Related book

Nature Spy by Shelley Rotner and Ken Kreisler

★ Kathryn Sheehan, Cape Elizabeth, ME

Nature

Canoeing . . . . .4+

Materials needed
Chairs
Environmental sound tape (optional)

What to do
1. In the middle of the circle set up a pretend canoe by putting chairs in a line, four chairs per canoe.

2. Each child will sit on a chair and pretend to hold a paddle by making a fist with both hands, putting her fists together and make a paddle motion with her fists.

3. Explain to the children that they are on a river in a canoe and they need to paddle to move the canoe down the river.

4. Act out paddling motions while listening to the environmental sound tape or singing the following song.

"A Canoeing We Will Go" (Tune: "A Hunting We Will Go")

> A canoeing we will go
> A canoeing we will go
> We'll dip our paddles in the water
> And down the river we'll go.

More to do
Art: Glue a popsicle or craft stick on blue construction paper to represent a canoe and glue items collected on a nature walk on the paper for a nature scene picture.

Related book
Antler, Bear, Canoe: A Northwoods Alphabet Year by Betsy Bowen

★ Dianne Leschak-Halverson, Chisholm, MN

From Seed to Tree . . . . .4+

Materials needed
Magnifying glass
Paper

Acorns, maple seeds, pine cones
Crayons and markers

What to do
1. Take a walk in the neighborhood and observe the different trees. Collect acorns, maple seeds, pine cones. Look at these items using a magnifying glass.

2. Explain to the children how seeds from the trees are planted. Discuss how squirrels store acorns in the ground for winter, maple seeds have wings like a helicopter and whirl to the ground, pine cone seeds sprinkle out when tossed about. Show the children pictures of different trees that grow in the area.

3. Pass out paper and ask the children to draw a picture of the following story as you tell it: "One day Gray Squirrel found an acorn. He knew he could enjoy this delicious nut next winter when there was

no other food around to eat. So he quickly buried it in the ground. (Ask each child to draw an acorn. Encourage them to listen and draw each thing that happens to the acorn.) Soon, little roots begin to appear; a stem starts to grow; more roots sprout; a tree trunk shoots up and gets wider and wider; branches appear and grow longer and longer; small acorns appear. They get larger and larger. Acorns fall from the big oak tree until the ground is covered with them. One day Gray Squirrel comes along again and what do you think he does?"

Related books
The Carrot Seed by Ruth Krauss
City Leaves, City Trees by Edward Gallob
Eat the Fruit, Plant the Seed by Millicent Selsam
Gift of the Tree by Alvin Tresselt
A Tree Is Nice by Janice Udry

★ Wendy Pfeffer, Pennington, NJ

Snakes . . . . .4+

Materials needed
Model of a snake or a live snake
Tempera paint
Paintbrush
Tape

Pictures of snakes
Paper towel rolls
Construction paper scraps
Pipe cleaners

What to do
Prior to this activity pour different snake-like colors of paint into containers.

1. At circle time show the children a model of a snake or a real snake in a clear container.

2. Observe the snake and discuss the characteristics of a snake—color, size, how it lives, where it is found, how it moves.

3. Show pictures of different snakes and describe them.

4. Ask each child to decide how long she wants her snake to be and give her that many paper towel rolls to paint.

5. When the rolls are dry hook the pipe cleaners together and insert them through the rolls. This allows the snake to bend and move.

6. Using construction paper scraps, make a head and tail for the snake and tape them to the first and last roll.

7. If the child desires, she can paint spots, lines or diamonds on the snake.

8. Display the snakes in an environment setting.

More to do
Language: Ask the children to describe the snake and list their descriptive words on chart paper.

Large motor: For creative movement sing the song "Sally the Swinging Snake."

Science: Observe and feel the molted skin of a snake.

Related books

The Day Jimmy's Boa Ate the Wash by Trinka Noble
Take a Look at Snakes by Betsy Maestro

Related song

"Sally the Swinging Snake" by Hap Palmer

★ Sandi Fisher, Kutztown, PA

The Great Kapok Tree Village . . . . .5+

Materials needed

The Great Kapok Tree by Lynne Cherry
Magazine pictures of rainforest plants and animals
Large brown or white roll of paper
Paint, brushes, newspaper
Chart paper
Markers

What to do

1. During circle time read *The Great Kapok Tree*.

2. On chart paper list the rainforest vocabulary discussed in the book.

3. Categorize the list of words.

4. Using the roll of paper construct and paint a large kapok tree (several feet tall). Paint the leaves, trunk, add animals and plants.

5. On following days add additional rainforest animals to the tree and the area surrounding it.

6. If desired, hang blue polyester film, such as Mylar® from the top of the chalk board or bulletin board to resemble a waterfall area.

More to do

Art: Design rainforest animals, paint and stuff with newspaper and place near the tree.

Math: Record the measurement of the tree the children created and of trees in the neighborhood. Compare and graph the heights of trees (average measurements of trees are provided in various resource materials).

★ Doris Jane Smith, Lincolndale, NY

Blast Off . . . . .3+

Materials needed
The Magic School Bus Lost in the Solar System by Joanna Cole
Large number cards 1-10

What to do

1. At circle time read *The Magic School Bus Lost in the Solar System*.

2. Ask ten children to stand in a line facing the other children. Give each child who is standing a number card, placing the cards in descending order.

3. Tell the ten children to listen for their number and to crouch down when they hear it and get ready to BLAST OFF. Begin counting backwards from ten.

4. After you reach one shout "BLAST OFF" and tell the children to jump in the air.

5. Repeat the activity so all the children will have a chance to BLAST OFF.

More to do

Language: Count down to BLAST OFF in different languages. Replace the cards with number words in other languages and place them in descending order before count down begins.

Math: Ordinal numbers can be used (first, second, third, etc.). Odd or even numbers can be used by counting down only the odd numbers (nine, seven, five, three, one, BLAST OFF) or even numbers.

Transitions: Give each child a turn to be the rocket and after each count down he gets to BLAST OFF to wash hands for lunch, exit to the playground or move to the next activity.

Original song

(Tune: "London Bridge Is Falling Down"

> *See the rocket taking off, flying high, flying fast,*
> *See the rocket in the sky, now it's landing.*

Related book

Moja Means One: A Swahili Counting Book by Muriel Feelings

★ Ann Gudowski, Lake Forest, CA

Copy Clapping . . . . .3+

Materials needed
None needed

What to do

1. Start a clapping pattern, such as clap two fast and two slow; clap one high, one low, one to the left and one to the right; clap twice in the air, pat knees twice.

2. Allow time for the children to practice the pattern.

3. Ask a child to clap a pattern.

4. The other children follow this pattern. If the group is small ask each child to repeat the pattern before moving onto a new pattern. Say the pattern out loud to add emphasis. Practice the patterns to music.

More to do
Art: Using a stamping object (sponge, rubber stamps, potato prints) make a pattern on the paper and repeat it.

Large motor: Make patterns out of large motor actions, such as jumping, hopping, sitting, standing.

Math: Notice the patterns all around us, such as in the tile on the floor, on wallpaper, on clothing.

★ Catherine Shogren, Eagan, MN

Do Things Four Times . . . . .3+

Materials needed
None needed

What to do
1. At circle time explain that the children will repeat a movement four times.

2. Begin by asking the children to hop four times.

3. Then ask the children what action they would like to do next.

4. Continue the activity until all the children have a turn naming the movement. Count to four as you repeat each movement, such as clapping, touching your nose, sitting down.

More to do
During each day of the week increase the number of times the children do a movement, such as on Monday do it one time, on Tuesday, two times, etc.

Language: Find the numeral four on the wall, in a book, etc.

Math: Count a variety of objects into groups of four.

Outdoors: Play a game outdoors hunting for four things of the same kind.

Related books
Ten Black Dots by Donald Crews
One, Two, One Pair by Bruce McMillan

Related song
"Four Little Monkeys"

★ Billiana Miteva, Pomona, NJ

How Does Popcorn Add Up? . . . . .4+

Materials needed

Popcorn
Popcorn popper
Napkins

What to do

1. Pass unpopped popcorn kernels around the circle. How do the kernels feel? Soft or hard? Is the texture smooth or rough? Are they large or small? How will heat change the popcorn?

2. Pop the popcorn in a popper for the children to smell and hear the corn as it pops. Pass the popped popcorn around the circle so the children feel the popcorn and compare the unpopped and popped popcorn.

3. Ask the children to describe the changes in the size, texture and shape of the popcorn.

4. Serve the popcorn to the children and count each kernel as it is eaten.

Related books

Popcorn by Frank Asch
The Popcorn Book by Tomie dePaola

★ Ruth M. Stevens, Aberdeen, OH

Bag of Numbers Game . . . . .4+

Materials needed

Drawstring bag
Wooden or cardboard numerals

What to do

1. Children take turns drawing one numeral from the bag and identifying the numeral or the children can say the number together.

2. The child who drew the numeral announces a movement, such as clapping hands.

3. The children say the following chant and repeat the action while counting to the number drawn from the bag.

> *I can move*
> *You can too*
> *(Chosen movement) is what I choose to do.*

4. The bag is then passed to another child until everyone has had a turn.

More to do

One child draws a numeral from the bag and then brings that number of objects from the room to the circle to be counted. Another child chooses a numeral from the bag and then finds a similar numeral in the room.

Art: Use wooden numerals and paint for printing or place the numerals under sheets of paper on the table to make crayon rubbings. Group the corresponding number of crayons in crayon bundles to use in drawing, such as with the numeral 4 use four crayons held together with a rubber band.

Dramatic play: Use the numerals as price markers in the stores, such as vegetables on a shelf with the numeral 3 will cost three dollars.

Math: Place the numerals on a table and ask the children to sort that number of small objects into groups.

Outdoors: Take a walk and place a numeral in the bag. Collect that number of items in the bag. Place each of the numerals in a container on the playground and ask the children to collect the corresponding number of rocks or leaves in the container.

★ Elaine Keville, Spotsylvania, VA

The Number Game ....4+

Materials needed
Large number cards 1-10

What to do
1. At circle time give each of the children a number card.

2. Sing the following song and ask the children who are holding the cards with the number identified in the song to follow the song's directions.

"Number Song" (Tune: "Hokey Pokey")

> *The one steps in.*
> *The one steps out.*
> *The one holds up his number*
> *And he waves it all about.*
> *The one brings me his number*
> *Then goes to wash his hands. (or goes to another activity)*
> *Where is the two?*
> *The two steps in*
> *The two steps out....*

3. Sing the numbers in order and repeat until all the children have a turn.

More to do
Language: Give each child a sheet of paper that has a numeral written on it and ask the children to draw or paste that number of items on a sheet. Compile the sheets to make a class number book.

Related songs
"Seven Little Rabbits"
"Five Little Ducks Went Out to Play"
"Three Monkeys Swinging in a Tree"

Related books

Seven Little Rabbits by John Becker
I Can Count by Dick Bruna
Ten Apples Up on Top by Theo LeSieg
Ten in the Bed by Penny Dale
You Can Name 100 Dinosaurs by Randy Chewning

★ Sandy Scott, Vancouver, WA

Number Quilt .4+

Materials needed

Square pieces of material
Number cards 1-10
Number cards 1-10 (each cut in two pieces)
Old blanket
Glue

What to do

1. Show the children the number cards from 1 to 10 and display them where the children can see them .

2. Divide the children into two groups. Give each group five number cards (each number card cut into two parts, a total of ten pieces). Make sure each child has a piece. If you have less than ten children in each group, the extra number cards will be shared by the group.

3. The children in each group show their number cards to the other children in their group to find the missing half of their numbers.

4. When the children have found the missing half of their number ask them to put the pieces together and lay the completed number on the floor.

5. Give each pair of children a square piece of material and ask them to glue their number card onto the material.

6. After all the numbers have been matched place an old blanket on the floor. Ask each pair of children to glue their number card on the blanket in order from 1 to 10.

7. Talk with the children about how they made a number quilt. Display the quilt in the classroom.

More to do
Art: The children cut small number cards into two pieces, match the number cards and glue the number cards from 1 to 10 to make a smaller version of the quilt.

Related books
Mouse Count by Ellen Stoll Walsh
One Cow Moo Moo by David Bennett
One, Two, Three by Tana Hoban

Related songs
"Ten Little Flowers" and "Ten Little Seagulls," included in *Tunes for Tots* by Dr. Laverne Warner and Paulette Berry
"One, Two, Three, Four, Five" collected by Malcom Jones, in *JUMBO: The Children's Book*.
"One, Two Buckle My Shoe"

★ Kathy Brand, Greenwood Lake, NY

Estimation Station . . . . .5+

Materials needed
1 large resealable plastic bag
Small pieces of paper
Overhead projector (optional)

What to do
1. On the Thursday before Estimation Station Week, send a note to parents of the child selected to bring a number of items for the Estimation Station the following Monday (suggest an appropriate range of numbers from which to choose, probably not higher than twenty). Give the child a large resealable plastic bag to put the items in.

2. On Monday, the child only tells the teacher the number of items in the bag. Place the bag at the Estimation Station. During the week the other children make estimates of the number of items in the bag and the estimates are recorded on the pieces of paper.

3. On Friday, count the number of items in the bag with the children. If available, count the objects on an overhead projector because the children can more easily see the small objects if they are projected on the wall.

More to do
Encourage children to collect items from outside to use for the Estimation Station.

Related book
The Doorbell Rang by Pat Hutchins

★ Patti Jones, Monroe, NC

Grocery Ad Numeral Game ....5+

Materials needed
Grocery ad
Crayon or marker
Glue

What to do
1. Tape a grocery ad to the chalk board, bulletin board, table top or floor.

2. Ask the children to sit so they can easily see the ad.

3. The teacher (or a child) begins the game and identifies a numeral and circles it. She chooses the next player until each child has had a turn.

4. If a child cannot identify a numeral she asks the other children for help in identifying a numeral.

Related books
Anno's Counting Book by Misumasa Anno
More Than One by Tana Hoban

★ Ruth M. Stevens, Aberdeen, OH

Uncovering the Sequence ....5+

Materials needed
4 or 5 colored building blocks or pattern blocks
Scarf to cover the blocks

What to do
1. At circle time place four or five colored blocks in a sequence (red, blue, red, blue, red).

2. Ask the children to look closely at the blocks while you both repeat the sequence together. Tell the children that you will cover the blocks with a scarf and will mix the blocks up and they will need to put the blocks back in the original sequence.

3. Mix the blocks up and then remove the scarf. Choose one child to arrange the blocks in the same sequence.

4. When the child has completed this task, ask the other children if the blocks are in the original sequence. If not, ask the children to help arrange the blocks in the original sequence.

5. Repeat Steps 1-6, changing the sequence each time until all the children have a turn.

6. Continue the activity and increase the number and colors of blocks.

7. Build a simple structure with the blocks and ask the children to recreate it.

More to do

Art: Encourage the children to create repetitive pattern designs using a variety of colored shapes on paper. Sponge paint patterns on paper to use as gift wrap. Use eyedroppers filled with different colors of tempera paint to drop on a sheet of paper creating interesting patterns.

Large motor: Enjoy jumping, hopping and marching in time to music. Place colored mat squares or colored construction paper in a pattern on the floor. Ask children to jump on certain colors naming the pattern as they jump.

Math: Use pattern blocks to explore different shapes and their relationship to one another.

Related book

Changes, Changes by Pat Hutchins

★ Barbara Fischer, San Carlos, CA

Making a Missing Teeth Graph . . . . .5+

Materials needed

Poster board
Ruler
Markers

What to do

1. Prior to this activity make two bar graphs similar to the one illustrated. Use two pieces of poster board, each 12" x 24". Use a ruler and black marker to draw a blank graph with columns for graphing the number of teeth children loose. Adjust the number column on the left according to the number of children in the class.

2. At circle time near the beginning of the school year tell the children that at about age five children begin to lose their baby teeth. Explain that the children will make a graph together to show the number of teeth they have lost.

3. Show the graph and date it with the current date.

number of teeth lost: _____ date: _____					
17					
16					
15					
14					
13					
12					
11					
10					
9					
8					
7					
6					
5					
4					
3					
2					
1					
	0	1	2	3	4 or more

4. Discuss the choices on the graph, zero teeth lost, one tooth lost, two teeth lost, three teeth lost, four or more teeth lost. (The zero category sometimes requires careful explanation so that children understand that if they have not yet lost a tooth they will still be included in the graph.)

5. Before recording information invite the children to predict which category will have the largest number of children.

6. Ask each child to make an entry on the graph. Do this by first asking the child how many teeth he has lost, then asking the child to write his or her name in the lowest empty space in the correct column using a marker. For example, a child who has lost two teeth writes his name in the lowest space in the column labeled two, another child who has also lost two teeth writes her name directly above the first child's name in the same column.

7. Pause several times to count the numbers of children appearing in each column. You may wish to ask whether anyone would like to make a new prediction based on this information.

8. Continue until all the children have recorded their names on the graph.

9. Occasionally a child may be unsure of how many teeth he has lost. The teacher may help these children with a quick "Open wide—let's take a look!" If the number is still uncertain, a best estimate is certainly acceptable.

10. Count the number of names recorded in each category. Discuss which category has the most names and which has the least.

11. Discuss how the graph could change in the future. Explain that in the spring near the end of the school year the children will make a new graph and children's names may be in different categories. Invite the children to predict which category their names will appear in the spring.

12. Hang the graph in the classroom.

13. Near the end of the school year repeat the activity with another blank graph. You may wish to use different colored poster board for the fall and spring graphs to make it easier for the children to remember which graph is which.

14. After completing the second graph compare the two graphs. Discuss the differences between the two graphs.

15. Hang both graphs side by side in the classroom where the children may examine and discuss them.

More to do

Make other graphs, such as number of siblings in the child's family, number of birthdays falling in each month of the year, number of children having different kinds of pets, favorite colors—offer a choice of several colors and ask each child to choose a favorite.

★ Susan Jones Jensen, Norman, OK

We Are the Number Train . . . . .5+

Materials needed

20 rectangles (5" x 9") in a variety of colors
40 black circles
20 strings

What to do

1. Prior to this activity write the numerals 1 to 5 (four of each numeral) on the rectangles. Glue two black circles on the bottom of each rectangle for the wheels of the train car. (Involve the children in making the train cars.) If possible, laminate the train cars before attaching the strings.

2. At circle time the teacher distributes one train car to each child and asks him to put the string over his head and wear it like a necklace.

3. The teacher explains that each child will identify the numeral on his train car and then join the other children in forming a number train. They will march around the circle chanting: "We are the number train. Watch us say our number name."

4. The teacher walks around the circle saying the chant. At the end of the chant, she stops by a child and asks him to identify his number. If he names the number correctly the child stands up and holds onto the teacher to form a train. (If the number is incorrectly named other children tell the child the number name.) The train continues around the circle adding other children until all the children are marching.

5. After all the children are attached to train, the chant becomes: "We are the number train. We all know our number name."

More to do

Adapt the activity to make a color train with children naming the color of the train car they are wearing and chant, "We are the color train, watch us say our color name."

★ Eileen L. Kaplan, Miramar, FL

Paper Pizza .5+

Materials needed

Sheets of construction paper (red and brown)
Small scraps of colored paper (yellow, green, black)
Scissors
Glue

What to do

1. Prior to the activity make a paper pizza by cutting out a 6" circle from red paper and a 7" circle from brown paper and gluing the circles together.

2. Use yellow, green and black scraps of paper for cheese, peppers and olives.

3. Show the children the paper pizza during circle time and ask them how to divide it in half, in quarters and in eighths.

4. Compare the different size of pieces and talk about their relationship to the whole pizza.

Related book

The Doorbell Rang by Pat Hutchins

★ Cathy Chenoweth, Columbia, MO

Measuring With Worms . . . . .5+

Materials needed

Inch by Inch by Leo Lionni
Tagboard
Clear self-adhesive paper

Green paper
Glue
Chart paper and marker

What to do

1. At circle time read *Inch by Inch*.

2. Talk with the children about measuring.

3. Give each child one green inch worm. (Prior to the activity glue green paper on tagboard or use green tagboard. Cut out the inch worms and cover with clear self-adhesive paper.) Talk about how to use the worms to measure things in the classroom.

4. Give each child an inch worm and ask the children to find objects in the room that are two worms long, six worms long, etc.

5. Make a list of the objects and their measurements.

6. Talk about which objects needed the most worms to measure them, which objects used the least worms.

7. Ask the children to take their inch worms home to use in measuring objects at home.

★ Deb Barbuch, Sheboygan, WI

The Big Fat Worm .... .5+

Materials needed
Construction paper (blue and brown)
Black marker
Scissors
The Big Fat Worm by Nancy Van Laan

What to do
Prior to the activity trace and cut out birds from the blue construction paper (one for each child). Trace and cut out thirty worms from the brown construction paper. (Involve the children in cutting out the worms.) Number the birds from 1 to 10 with the black marker (repeat numbers if there are more than ten children).

1. Tell the children that you are going to tell them about a very crafty worm who manages to get away from every bird that tries to catch it. Read *The Big Fat Worm*.

2. After the story pass out the paper birds, one to each child. Place the paper worms in the middle of the circle. Tell the children that their birds are trying to catch as many worms as the number written on their birds. As each child goes to the middle of the circle and catches the number of worms corresponding to the number written on her bird, the other children help her by counting to the number written on her bird.

More to do
Language: Read the story a second time and ask the children to play the part of the worm by saying what the worm says in the story.

Science: Collect several live earthworms and put them in a large tub and place it on a table. Ask the children to observe the worms and describe what they see. Talk about the worms: what worms eat, where they live, what they do. Return the worms to the earth.

★ Joy M. Tuttle, London, OH

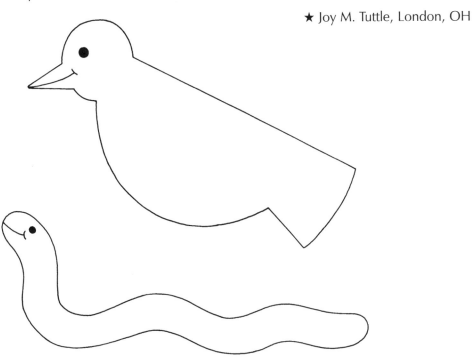

Counting With Cards . . . . .5+

Materials needed

1 or 2 decks of cards (the ace through 10)
Poker chips (5 to 12 per child)

What to do

1. At circle time talk with the children about playing the card game.

2. Give each child the same number of poker chips and ask them to leave the chips on the floor until it is time to "Place your bets."

3. Show the children the cards holding up a card representing each number. Explain that each card has the same number of symbols on the card that corresponds to the number written on the card. To help determine the number on a card tell the children to count the number of symbols on that card. Point out that the ace equals number one.

4. Explain that each child will receive a card face down on the floor and he is to leave the card on the floor until the teacher says "Place your bets." Each child picks up the card and determines the number on the card.

5. Once the child determines the number on the card, he puts that number of chips on the floor in front of him and places the card face down beside the chips.

6. When the teacher says "Show me your hand," the child turns over the card. The teacher asks each child in turn to hold up his card and asks the other children to agree or disagree with the number of chips the child has counted out. If needed, children are asked to help each other count the correct number of chips.

7. Collect the cards, shuffle the deck and play another round.

Related books

Mouse Count by Ellen Stoll Walsh
One Cow Moo Moo by David Bennett
One, Two, Three by Tana Hoban

Related songs

"Two Little Blackbirds"
"Five Little Ducks"

★ Kelly J. Sickle, Richmond, MO

Counting Blocks .5+

Materials needed
Blocks

What to do
1. At circle time tell the children that they will add and subtract numbers while counting blocks. Ask two children to each count out a few blocks and place them in a stack. Tell the children to touch each block as they count it.

2. Ask the children to then put their stacks of blocks together and count the total number of blocks.

3. Ask two other children to work together to count a stack of blocks and then ask the children to take some of the blocks away and to count the blocks that were removed and the blocks that remain in the stack.

4. Talk with the children about how they have added and subtracted numbers and encourage them to add and subtract numbers using other objects when they are working in the centers.

★ Rayne Reese, Glendale, MO

Nursery Rhymes . . . . .3+

Materials needed
Nursery rhyme posters (child-made)
Props for each character

What to do
1. Make props for each character in the rhyme. For example, for "Jack Be Nimble" draw a picture of Jack and a picture of a candlestick. Cut the pictures out and mount them on a poster board. Rather than using pictures the children dramatize the rhyme. For example, one child wears a sign that says "Jack" and jumps over a real candlestick at the appropriate time in the rhyme.

2. To begin the dramatization a child announces the rhyme and holds up the child-made sign that identifies the name of the nursery rhyme.

3. All the children say the rhyme while the actors dramatize the rhyme using the props.

More to do
Art: The children make a class nursery rhyme book with each child illustrating or drawing a page. The teacher attaches the words of the rhyme to each page and compiles the book.

Cooking: Prepare foods that relate to the nursery rhymes the children are learning, such as a plum pie.

Home connection: The children take the book home to share with their families on a rotating basis. Children may also make individual books to give their parents.

Related books
Let Loose on Mother Goose by Terry Graham

★ Kaethe J. Lewandowski, Centreville, VA

Miss and Mr. Muffet . . . . .3+

Materials needed
Chair
Plastic bowl and spoon

What to do
1. At circle time place a chair, a plastic bowl and a spoon in the middle of the circle. Explain that a few of the children will act out the nursery rhyme while the other children say the rhyme and make up the audience.

2. Ask one child to be Miss Muffet or Mr. Muffet and a few children to be the spiders.

3. Miss (Mr.) Muffet sits on the chair with her back to the rest of the children.

4. The spiders get on their knees and begin to crawl towards Miss (Mr.) Muffet as the other children say the nursery rhyme.

Little Miss (Mr.)Muffet sat on her (his) tuffet, (pretends to eat)
Eating her (his) curds and whey.
Along came the spiders and
Sat down beside her (him), (spiders crawl very close)
And frightened Miss (Mr.) Muffett away. (drops bowl and spoon and runs away)

5. Vary the dramatization to include several children playing the role of Miss Muffet and only one child pretending to be the spider.

More to do

Art: Provide string, scissors and tape for the children to make spider webs.

Music: Sing the "Eensy, Weensy Spider."

★ Ann Scalley, Wellfleet, MA

Hickory, Dickory Dock . . . . .3+

Materials needed
Musical instruments (wood blocks, triangle)
Chair

What to do

1. At circle time choose one child to be the clock, one child to be the mouse and two children to play the instruments. The other children say the rhyme.

"Hickory, Dickory Dock"

> *Hickory, dickory dock, tick-tock*
> *The mouse ran up the clock, tick-tock.*
> *The clock struck one.*
> *The mouse ran down.*
> *Hickory, dickory dock, tick-tock.*

2. The child who is the clock stands on the floor.

3. As the other children say the rhyme the child playing the mouse responds by standing on the chair to run up the clock and steps down from the chair to run down.

4. Each time the children say, "Tick-tock" the child holding the wood blocks pounds them together two times.

5. When the clock strikes one, another child hits the triangle one time.

★ Joyce Montag, Slippery Rock, PA

Humpty Dumpty ....3+

Materials needed

Eggs (hard boiled)
Markers
Forks and plates

What to do

1. Say the nursery rhyme, "Humpty Dumpty," with the children.

2. Dramatize the rhyme by asking the children to make their hands into two fists touching each other and to pretend that their fists are Humpty Dumpty. Tell the children to pretend that their arms are the wall. At the end of the rhyme ask children to open their fists and spread their fingers to represent the cracked egg.

3. Give each of the children a hard boiled egg and invite the children to draw faces on the eggs. Allow the children to drop their eggs on the floor to see how Humpty Dumpty cracked.

4. Help the children peel the eggs and save the shells to be dyed and used for collage projects. Eat the eggs for snack.

5. Talk about other ways that eggs are prepared and the different foods that contain eggs.

More to do

Math: Store a dozen colored cardboard eggs (cut in half) in an egg carton. The children match the halves.

Science: Talk about the baby animals that hatch from eggs (frogs, chickens, turtles, birds) and the different sizes of the eggs.

Related books

Egg to Chick by Millicent Selsam
Horton Hatches an Egg by Dr. Seuss

★ Wendy Pfeffer, Pennington, NJ

Old Woman in the Shoe ....3+

Materials needed

Construction paper and markers
Dish pan of warm, soapy water
Large piece of tagboard with "The Old Woman in the Shoe" nursery rhyme printed on it (optional)

Tempera paint and brushes
Towels

What to do

1. Read "The Old Woman in the Shoe" nursery rhyme aloud.

Note: Change the next to last line to "She kissed them all soundly and sent them to bed."

2. Repeat the rhyme encouraging the children to say it with you.

3. Ask the children to remove their shoes and socks.

4. Make three or four headings on construction paper, such as shoes with velcro, shoes with ties, slip-on shoes, boots.

5. Put the headings on the floor and ask the children to put their shoes under the appropriate heading to make a floor graph.

6. Discuss which category has the most, least, same.

7. Ask the children to sit in a chair, one at a time. Place a large piece of construction paper under their feet.

8. Paint the bottoms of their feet or ask them to stand in a shallow pan of paint.

9. Make the children's footprints on the paper by having them stand up.

10. Ask the child to sit down and put their feet into a bowl of warm soapy water.

11. Wash the paint off the children's feet and ask them to dry their feet with a towel.

12. Display the footprints on a wall and talk about the differences in the footprints.

More to do
Fine motor: Teach older children how to tie shoes. Provide a large shoe with laces for the children to practice with.

Math: Ask the children to cut out their footprints (precut for younger children) and use them to measure objects by placing them heel to toe. For example, measure how may footprints across a table, how may footprints from the table to the door.

★ Barbara Saul, Eureka, CA

Roll a Rhyme . . . . .3+

Materials needed
1 empty half-gallon milk carton
Construction paper
Glue
Marker
Titles or pictures of 6 songs,
    fingerplays or nursery rhymes

What to do

1. Construct one large die from the milk carton. Cut off top of the carton, cut the carton in half and slide one half into the other to form a cube (see illustration).

2. Glue construction paper on all six sides.

3. Draw the title or pictures depicting a song (fingerplay, nursery rhyme) on each side of the cube.

4. Roll the cube (die) and sing the song that shows on top of the die.

More to do

Games: Add other dice games to the classroom. Create other games to play using the die that you made.

★ Debbie Moran, Brownsville, OR

Three Bags Full . . . . .3+

Materials needed

3 grocery bags (each numbered 1, 2 or 3)
Sets of 3 items (similar classroom items, such as 3 books, 3 different colors of blocks)

What to do

1. Say or sing "Baa, Baa Black Sheep."

2. Show the children and count the three empty bags.

3. Ask one child to choose three things that belong together.

4. Ask the other children why these items belong together.

5. The child drops one item at a time into each of the three bags while the children count 1, 2, 3.

6. Continue until all the sets of three items have been placed into the bags.

7. Talk with the children about having three bags full, just like in the nursery rhyme.

★ Ann Wenger, Harrisonburg, VA

Candlestick Craft . . . . .4+

Materials needed

Toilet paper roll (1 per child)
Yellow and orange tissue paper
Glue
Stapler

6" paper plates (1 per candle)
Markers
Scissors
2 paper clips per child

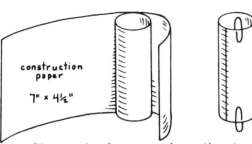

construction paper

7" × 4½"

Glue construction paper to cardboard roll and secure with paper clips until dry.

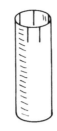

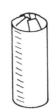

Cut ½" slits every ½".

Push slits into center and glue.

Cut 2 diamonds of yellow and orange tissue paper, 1½" wide and 3" long each. Overlap the layers of tissue and twist together at one end.

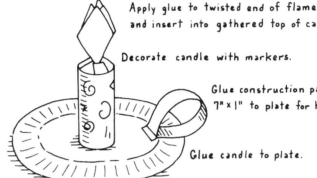

Apply glue to twisted end of flame and insert into gathered top of candle.

Decorate candle with markers.

Glue construction paper strip 7" × 1" to plate for handle.

Glue candle to plate.

What to do

1. At circle time teach the children the rhyme "Jack Be Nimble" and tell them that they will each make a candlestick to use in acting out the rhyme.

2. Involve the children in making the candlesticks in the art center (help children as needed).

3. Cut construction paper or use an index card for the candle (5" × 7").

4. Cut two rectangles of yellow and orange tissue (6" × 8" each).

5. Cut one construction paper strip for handle (1" × 6").

6. Glue construction paper or index card to the toilet paper roll and hold in place with paper clips until dry.

7. Make four slits (1/2") at one end of the candle, spread slits out and glue or staple to the paper.

8. Overlap the two squares of tissue paper to form the candle flame and push the tissue paper about 2" into the top of the candle.

9. Decorate the paper plate (candlestick) with markers.

10. Make a loop with the paper strip and glue it to make the handle of the candlestick.

11. During circle time on the following day say the rhyme "Jack Be Nimble" with the children and ask them to act out the rhyme by jumping over their candlesticks.

More to do

Make larger candles by using paper towel rolls and large paper plates.

Science: Teach about fire safety and the need to use caution with real candles.

★ Mary Brehm, Aurora, OH

Shoe House ....4+

Materials needed

Large cardboard appliance box
Paint and brushes
Twine

Small cardboard box
Mat cutter (for teacher only)
House furnishings

What to do

1. At circle time say the rhyme, "The Old Woman in the Shoe" with the children.

2. Ask the children to help you build a shoe that they can use in dramatic play.

3. Tape a small box (for the toe of the shoe) to a large appliance box.

4. Cut an entrance and windows in the large box.

5. Provide paint and brushes for the children to use in painting the shoe.

6. Cut holes along the front center of the shoe and lace a long piece of twine through the holes for shoe strings.

7. Add furnishings and decorate the inside of the shoe.

More to do

Dramatic play: Set up a shoe store with old shoes, shoe boxes, bags, laces, ruler, small mirror, cash register and pretend money. Create a shoe shining shop for pretend play and to encourage children to tie shoes.

Related books

The Elves and the Shoemaker by Paul Galdone
My Feet by Aliki
What Neat Feet! by Hana Machotka

★ Janice Bodenstedt, Jackson, MI

Circle Time Walks . . . . .3+

Materials needed
None needed

What to do

1. During circle time take the children outdoors for a nature walk. Look for seasonal changes, talk about the weather and the neighborhood.

2. If there are businesses or stores in your neighborhood go on a community helper walk.

3. Visit various businesses and stores. Call the merchants in advance and ask them to greet the children or arrange a tour.

More to do

Art: Ask the children to draw something they thought was interesting from the walk. Put the pictures together and make a class book.

Language: Ask the children to tell you about their drawings and write what they say on the pages of the book.

Original song
(Tune: "The ABC Song")

> *Let's join hands and take a walk*
> *With our friends we can talk.*
> *About the things that we will see*
> *People, houses and some trees.*
> *Hold my hand and walk with me*
> *I wonder what we will see.*

★ Susan Myhre, Bremerton, WA

Come Visit Us . . . . .3+

Materials needed
Send the following note home to parents:

Dear Parents:

Our class is learning about community helpers. We invite you to visit us and talk about your job. If you wear a uniform please wear it and if you use equipment on your job that you could bring and show us we would like to see it. Please return the bottom portion of this note or call me to arrange for a time to visit.

Sincerely,

Teacher' Name
Telephone Number:

Name:
When I Can Visit:

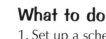

What to do

1. Set up a schedule of parents to visit during circle time, preferably one parent each day while you are discussing community helpers.

2. In advance talk with the parents asking them to show materials that would interest the children and tell them the preferred length of time for their discussion with the children.

3. After each visit ask the children to talk about the experience and record their comments on paper. Also provide paper for the children to draw pictures about the visitor. Ask the children to tell you about their pictures and you will write down their responses. Compile the pages into a class book that can be given to the visitor.

More to do

Field trip: Arrange a field trip to visit a place where community helpers work, such as a fire station, grocery store, hospital, fast food restaurant, police station, bakery.

Home connection: Ask parents to write a short story about their jobs and to attach photographs. Make a class book with the stories. Invite the children to take turns bringing the book home to share with their parents.

Related books

What's It Like to Be a Bus Driver by Judith Stamper
What's It Like to Be a Police Officer by Michael J. Pellowski
What's It Like to Be a Doctor by Judith Bauer
What's It Like to Be a Nurse by Judith Bauer
What's It Like to Be a Chef by Susan Poskazer
What's It Like to Be a Grocer by Shelley Wilks

★ Barbara Saul, Eureka, CA

Mail a Letter .3+

Materials needed

None needed

What to do

1. At circle time sing the following song, "Mail a Letter," to the tune of "Frère Jacques."

*Mail a letter, mail a letter
To a friend, to a friend.
Going to the mailbox, going to the mailbox
Around the bend, around the bend.
Get a letter, get a letter
From a friend, from a friend.
Look inside your mailbox, look inside your mailbox.
What did they send? What did they send?*

Is it a letter? Is it a letter?
Addressed to you, addressed to you?
Do you know who sent it? Do you know who sent it?
Do you have a clue? Do you have a clue?
(Name) sent a letter, (Name) sent a letter
Just for me, just for me.
I will write a letter, I will write a letter
Wait and see, wait and see.

More to do

Dramatic play: Set up a corner of the room to be the Post Office. Children use pretend money to purchase stamps and post their letters. The postmaster cancels their stamps at the Post Office. The children take turns being mail carriers, delivering letters to the children's mailboxes in the room.

★ Penni Smith and Donna Karnes, Riverside, CA

The Mail Carrier . . . . .3+

Materials needed

Pictures of mail carriers, mail trucks, a post office
Bag (mailbag)
Large envelope with address, stamp and return address clearly labeled

What to do

1. At circle time display the pictures and talk about them with the children.

2. Introduce the words mail carrier, post office and mail truck.

3. Show the large envelope and highlight the address, stamp and return address on it.

4. Ask if the children have ever written or received a letter.

5. Talk about how a letter that a mail carrier delivers traveled in a mail truck and possibly on an airplane before reaching a local post office and then being delivered to your home (point to the pictures).

6. Play the mail carrier game and ask one child to be the mail carrier and wear the mailbag while carrying a letter. The children stand in a circle and sing the following song. As the song ends the mail carrier drops the letter behind a child who picks up the letter and tries to catch the mail carrier.

"The Mail Carrier" (Tune: "London Bridge")

Who delivers mail to you?
Mail to you?
Mail to you?
Who delivers mail to you?
It's our mail carrier.

More to do

Dramatic play: Set up a post office complete with props. Use boxes with dividers for mailboxes. Provide recycled envelopes, stamp pads, packages, a cash register and pretend money.

Original poem

The letter carrier brought a valentine.
The envelope was white,
A stamp was in the corner,
And my name was printed right.

★ Diana Reed and Debi Behr, New Wilmington, PA

Field Trip Sequence Book . . . . .3+

Materials needed

Camera and film
Tagboard
Rubber cement
3-ring 1" binder

What to do

1. On a field trip take photographs throughout the day including getting on the bus (van or car) at the beginning and off the bus at the end of the trip.

2. After the photographs are developed select photos depicting the major activities that occurred throughout the day.

3. Glue the photographs on 8" x 11" pieces of tagboard with rubber cement.

4. Punch three holes in the tagboard pages and put the pages in a binder in the order in which the activities occurred during the day, beginning with getting on the bus and ending with getting off the bus.

5. At circle time look at the Field Trip Sequence Book with the children talking about the order of the activities during the field trip.

6. Ask the children what activity came first? What happened next? What happened last?

7. Rearrange the pages in the book and ask the children to put them in the correct sequence.

More to do

Language: The children take turns "reading" the book to the other children. Read the book backwards starting with leaving the site of the field trip. Ask each child to describe their favorite activity of the trip and to find the corresponding photograph.

★ Deborah Bauer, Tempe, AZ

Can You Guess What I Do? . . . . .4+

Materials needed

8-10 photographs of community workers (police officer, teacher, auto mechanic, waiter or waitress, doctor, veterinarian, grocery store worker, farmer, carpenter)
1 or 2 items that are a part of each worker's job (hammer and nails for carpenter; stethoscope and tongue depressor for doctor)
Box

What to do

1. At circle time display the photographs (with young children show fewer photos).

2. Place the job-related items in a box.

3. Ask each child to take turns pulling out one item from the box and matching it to the worker who uses it.

More to do

Game: Play a memory game using about ten of the job-related items. Show the children the items on a tray, cover the tray, remove an item and ask the children which item is missing.

Home connection: Make a bulletin board displaying the variety of jobs that the children's parents have. Request parents to send in a photo of themselves at work either at home or on the job.

Social studies: Include photographs, posters and books that depict men and women in a variety of jobs that are not stereotypical.

Original song

(Tune: "Hi Ho, Hi Ho, It's Off to Work I Go")

> *Hi Ho, Hi Ho,*
> *It's off to work I go*
> *To be a (carpenter) and (build a house)*
> *Hi Ho, Hi Ho*

★ Anne Hartmann, St. Paul, MN

What Worker Am I? . . . . .4+

Materials needed

Tape recorder
Recorded job descriptions of community helpers

What to do

1. At circle time talk with the children about the different types of jobs that adults have.

2. Ask the children to listen carefully to the voices on the tape about community helpers as they describe the work they do. (For example, I help protect people and buildings. I wear a helmet and heavy coat and boots to protect myself.)

3. After each community helper speaks turn off the tape and ask the children to identify the community helper.

★ Leleña L. Williams, Beacon, NY

What's In a Bag? . . . . .4+

Materials needed

Bag

Community helper tools (paintbrush, magnifying glass, hammer)

What to do

1. At circle time talk about the different tools community helpers use to do their work.

2. Explain that each child will choose a tool from the bag and identify which community helper uses that tool.

3. Ask the children to also describe the tools and explain how they are used.

More to do

Review items that were in the bag. Make riddles about various community helpers.

★ Cindy L. Knutson, Vermillion, SD

My Home . . . . .4+

Materials needed

Building a House by Byron Barton

What to do

1. At circle time talk about how carpenters build a house. Ask the children to describe their homes—how many floors does it have, how many rooms, color of the house and of the front door.

2. Talk about the differences in houses, townhouses and apartments.

3. Read *Building a House*. Describe the role of an architect (planning) versus the builder (construction). Review the different parts of a house.

More to do

Art: Ask the children to draw pictures of their houses. Encourage them to label the parts of the house—roof, door, window.

Blocks: Provide construction materials, such as Legos® and blocks to build houses. Discuss the similarities and differences of the buildings.

Language: Provide books describing other types of houses, such as igloos and huts. Talk about their similarities and differences.

Related book

Houses and Homes by Ann Morris

★ Gail Dezube, Vienna, VA

Occupational Musical Chairs . . . . .5+

Materials needed
Chairs
Pictures of workers
Recorded music and player

What to do
1. Ask the children to sit in chairs that are arranged in a circle.

2. Tape a picture of a person doing a different type of work on each chair.

3. Ask each child to describe the type of work depicted in the picture taped to her chair.

4. Ask the children to stand. Start the music and remove one chair from the circle.

5. Allow time for the children to walk around the chairs as they look at the pictures. Stop the music. The child that doesn't have a chair chooses a chair and names the job in the picture taped to the chair and then removes it from the circle.

6. Continue playing the game until all the children have had a turn removing a chair from the circle.

★ Sandra Hutchins Lucas, Cox's Creek, KY

Building a Town . . . . .5+

Materials needed
Large sheet of butcher paper
Various sizes of envelopes
Marker or crayons
Glue (optional)

butcher paper

What to do

1. At circle time place the sheet of butcher paper in the middle of the circle and explain that together the children will create a town.

2. Provide different sizes of envelopes from which the children choose one, open the envelope flap, lick the gummed part (or provide glue) and stick it on the butcher paper (streets are mapped on the paper in advance to provide a line on which the children place their envelopes). The envelopes represent different size buildings and houses (remember the school building).

3. The children use crayons and markers to draw windows, a door and other details on their buildings (remind the children that the envelope flap is the roof).

4. Ask the children to lift their envelopes up, bend them back and draw the interior of their buildings on the butcher paper.

5. Add people, cars, roads and signs to the paper.

More to do

Art: Provide envelopes and construction paper for the children to make individual buildings.

Related books

The Day the Teacher Went Bananas by James Howe
Grover Goes to School by Dan Elliot
I Like School by Bobbie Kalman
My Teacher Sleeps in School by Leatie Weiss
Shawn Goes to School by Petronella Breinburg

★ Julie W. Lawhorn, Gaithersburg, MD

My Letter .5+

Materials needed

Pencils and paper
Self-addressed, stamped envelope for each child (ask parents to provide)

What to do

1. At circle time talk with the children about writing letters to themselves. Explain that they will mail the letters and that they should check the mail that their families receive at home to see when it arrives.

2. Provide sheets of paper and pencils for the children to use in writing and signing their letters.

3. The children folds their letters and place the envelopes their parents provided.

4. Walk to a nearby mailbox or to the mailbox in the school office so that each child can personally mail his letter.

More to do

Dramatic play: Set up a post office in the classroom, complete with a window (use puppet theater), mailboxes (child-made) and appropriate clothes and hats for the post office workers. The children write letters and mail them at the post office.

Field trip: Visit the local post office and talk with the Postmaster and mail carriers.

Related book

The Jolly Postman by Janet and Allan Ahlberg

★ Terri Pentz, Melbourne Beach, FL

Field Trip Stories . . . . .5+

Materials needed

Camera (Polaroid® and film)
Chart paper
Markers
Tape

What to do

1. Take one instant photograph of each event or activity during a field trip.

2. After returning to school divide the class into three groups. Ask a parent who accompanied the children on the field trip to serve as a recorder for a group.

3. Divide the photographs from the field trip into three sets (beginning, middle and end of trip) and give each set to the parent in one of the groups.

4. The children in each group talk about their photographs and arrange them in the order in which the events in the photographs took place. The children dictate what was happening in each photograph (parent records on chart paper to tell a sequential story about the field trip).

5. Tape the photographs on the chart paper after the sentence which describes the photograph.

6. Display the sheets of chart paper and read the entire story with the children.

★ Kimberle S. Byrd, Wyoming, WI

Making Waves . . . . .3+

Materials needed

1 plastic bottle (2 liter) per child
Water
Blue food coloring
Vegetable oil
Tape

What to do

1. Rinse bottles well and add water to fill the bottles half way.

2. Add several drops of food coloring per bottle

3. Add 1/2 cup vegetable oil to each bottle.

4. Screw on the cap and tape it securely to the bottle.

Note: Involve the children in helping assemble the bottles.

5. At circle time distribute the bottles and ask the children to make waves by gently rocking the bottle. Ask the children to describe what happens with the oil and the water mixture.

More to do

Language: Ask the children to describe the steps involved in making their "wave machines" and to talk about how they made waves. Write down their responses on chart paper.

★ Jodi Sykes, Lake Worth, FL

Mixing Different Things . . . . .3+

Materials needed

Objects (different in 1 characteristic, such as texture)
Glass jar with lid
Water colored with food coloring
Vegetable oil
Exactly the Opposite by Tana Hoban

What to do

1. At circle time talk about the word "different."

2. Show examples of things that are different, such as a hard rock and a soft cotton ball.

3. Talk about different kinds of liquids and that although they are all liquid they are also different. Show the children vegetable oil and ask them to describe it (watery, liquid, runny).

4. Show the children water colored with food coloring and ask them to describe it (watery, liquid, runny). Note the difference in color and ask if there are any other differences.

5. Tell the children that oil and water may look similar but are also different.

6. Show how oil and water are different by pouring colored water into a glass jar until the jar is filled 1/3 full.

7. Add an equal amount of oil to the same jar.

8. Place the lid on the jar and ask the children what will happen when you shake the mixture in the jar.

9. Shake the jar. Watch how oil and water mix for a short time, but eventually the oil rises to the top. Explain that oil and water may look similar but are also different .

10. Following the experiment read *Exactly the Opposite* or any book about opposites and talk about differences.

More to do

Art: Oil and water painting. Mix tempera paint and oil in a cup until creamy. Spoon a few drops of the oil paint on top of a pan filled with water. The oil paint lays on top of the water. Float a piece of paper on top of the oil paint and lift the paper off carefully.

Science: Mixing egg carton rainbows—fill plastic egg carton compartments with water. Add blue, yellow and red food coloring to three of the twelve compartments. Use an eyedropper to drop the colored water into the other nine compartments filled with water, creating new colors.

Original song

"Oil and Water" (Tune: "Frère Jacques")

> *Oil and water, oil and water*
> *They don't mix, they don't mix!*
> *Oil floats to the top*
> *Water's on the bottom.*
> *Mix, mix, mix!*
> *Mix, mix, mix!*

Related book

Of Colors and Things by Tana Hoban

★ Debi Behr and Diana Reed, New Castle, PA

The Shadow Game . . . . .3+

Materials needed

White sheet
Overhead projector or bright lamp
Familiar objects

What to do

1. Set up the sheet and light so shadows can be made behind the sheet.

2. At circle time use different objects to create shadows.

3. Ask the children what objects are making the shadows.

More to do

Fine motor: Ask the children to use their hands to make different shadows. Encourage the children to experiment with making shadow animals with their hands.

Language: Ask the children to make up a story to go with their hand shadows.

Outdoors: On a sunny day experiment with shadow play. Explain the game of shadow tag where one child steps on another child's shadow.

Science: Extend the activity by experimenting with different types of shadows and talk about how light creates shadows.

Related books

Shadows Here, There and Everywhere by Ron Goor
What Makes a Shadow? by Clyde Bulla

★ Wanda K. Pelton, Lafayette, IN

Which Is Heavier? . . . . .3+

Materials needed

Balance scale
Various objects (chalk, block, paper scraps, paper clip, eraser, crayon, scissors)

What to do

1. At circle time show the children the scale and talk about weighing a variety of objects to determine which is heavier.

2. Select any two objects and ask the children to predict which object will be heavier.

3. Place the objects on the scale and test the children's predictions.

More to do

Science: Encourage the children to continue this activity working in pairs and record the results of their experiment by drawing a picture of the two objects and indicating the object that is heavier. The results of each group's conclusions could then be compared or graphed during another circle time.

★ Barb Lindsay, Mason City, IA

Magnets .3+

Materials needed

Assorted magnets
Paper clips

What to do

1. At circle time introduce the magnets and explain that the children will experiment to see what objects in the room the magnets will stick to.

2. Give each child a magnet and ask them to walk around the room trying to stick their magnet on different objects.

3. Allow time for experimentation and then ask the children to come to the circle to discuss their results.

4. Experiment with other materials. Will a magnet work under water? Through glass? Through paper? How many paper clips (in a paper clip chain) will the magnet lift?

More to do
Math: Sort objects into two categories: will stick or will not stick to a magnet. Record and graph the results.

★ Sandra Gratias, Parkasie, PA

Jack and the Beanstalk . . . . .4+

Materials needed
Jack and the Beanstalk by Paul Galdone
Markers
Potting soil
Newspaper
Spoon

Chart paper
Plastic ant farm container
Bean seeds
Eyedropper

What to do
1. Read *Jack and the Beanstalk* and talk about how the beans grew in the story.

2. Discuss what is needed to grow bean seeds (soil, water, sunlight).

3. Place a large two-sided plastic ant farm on a table covered with newspaper.

4. Ask the children to use a spoon to add soil into the ant farm until it is 3/4 filled.

5. The children plant bean seeds in the soil near the side of the plastic wall so the bean seeds are visible.

6. Add water using an eyedropper and place the ant farm near a window.

7. The children observe the beans daily and record their observations.

8. As the beans begin to sprout the children can chart the growth of the beans on a paper taped near the planted beans. Allow time for the children to talk about their observations.

More to do
Language: Encourage the children to describe their observations (teacher records their dictation). Ask the children to make up a story about the bean seed that grows into a beanstalk describing where the beanstalk takes them as they climb it.

Math: Measure and graph the height of the bean plant and the length of the roots (if visible) on a regular basis.

★ Doris Jane Smith, Lincolndale, NY

Good Vibrations . . . . .4+

Materials needed
Styrofoam meat tray (1 per child)
Markers
Assorted rubber bands

What to do
1. At circle time show the children an autoharp, guitar or violin. Pluck strings and watch the strings vibrate.

2. Ask the children to touch the front of their throats to feel the vibration when they talk.

3. Strike a tuning fork and listen to the sound. Hold the tuning fork close to each child's ear so each child can hear the sound clearly and feel the tickle of the vibration. Strike the fork and hold the handle on a block or wood shelf (sound is louder because the wood vibrates).

4. Experiment with holding the tuning fork on other surfaces. Dip the vibrating tuning fork into a cup of colored water and watch the water splash. Touch the tuning fork to a paper with styrofoam pieces scattered on it and watch the pieces dance.

5. Give the children the styrofoam trays and ask them to decorate the trays using markers.

6. Put four or five rubber bands of different thickness on the trays.

7. Ask the children to strum the rubber bands, listen to the different tones and watch the bands vibrate. Ask the children if they feel the trays vibrating in their hands.

More to do
Art: Decorate toilet paper rolls with markers and stickers. With a rubber band attach wax paper over one end of the roll. Ask the children to hum into the wax paper and feel it vibrate.

★ Sandra Gratias, Perkasie, PA

assorted
rubber bands

styrofoam meat tray
decorated with markers

Science

Ice Is Nice . . . . .4+

Materials needed
Clear pitcher of water
Cylinder container (coffee can)
Rubber mold or latex glove
Shallow pan

What to do
1. At circle time show the children the water in the pitcher and tell them they will explore water to learn more about water. Invite the children to dip their fingers in the water and describe how it feels. Pour the water into the shallow pan and note that water takes the shape of whatever container it is in. Ask the children what will happen when the water is frozen.

2. Take the rubber mold (a rubber animal mold used for centerpiece ice sculptures can be used rather than a glove) and place it in the can for support. Fill the glove with water and show the children that the water in the glove cannot stand by itself. Place the mold and can in the freezer.

3. Show the glove (mold) of frozen water at circle time the following day. Ask the children if it looks different and place it on the floor to see if it will keep its shape. What happened to the water? What will happen if the mold is pulled off? Pull off the mold and see if the ice will hold its shape.

4. Place the sculpture in a shallow pan and ask the children to feel the ice and describe how it feels comparing it to the water they dipped their fingers into the day before.

5. Place the ice sculpture where the children can look at it throughout the day to observe the ice melting.

More to do
Art: Experiment with ice painting using an ice cube for a paintbrush. Pour tempera powder on paper and brush the ice cube over the tempera—watch what happens.

Language: Read *The Cloud Book* and *Danger—Icebergs*. Encourage questions and talk about the books. Make a time line of an iceberg and its journey.

Science: Place different size chunks of ice in a tub of water and observe them melt throughout the day.

Related books
The Cloud Book by Tomie dePaola
Danger—Icebergs! by Roma Gans

★ Barbara Fischer, San Carlos, CA

The Great Magnet Playoff ....4+

Materials needed

3 or more magnets
Paper clips
Chart paper
Marker

What to do

1. At circle time show the children three or more different types of magnets (bar, horseshoe, round).

2. Ask the children to predict each magnet's strength based on how many paper clips each magnet can hold.

3. List the magnets on chart paper and the number of paper clips each is predicted to hold.

4. Test each of the magnets by making a paper clip chain by attaching paper clips one at a time to each magnet.

5. Keep adding paper clips until the magnet will no longer hold the chain when the magnet is raised.

6. Record the number of paper clips held by each magnet and graph the results.

Related book

The Mystery of Magnets by Melvin Berger

★ Wanda Pelton, Lafayette, IN

Magnetic Prediction Game ....4+

Materials needed

Magnets
Chart paper and markers
Objects (1 per child) such as paper clips, key, knitting needle, plastic fork, cotton ball, metal fork, nail, rubber band)

What to do

1. At circle time ask the children to identify the different objects.

2. Prepare a prediction chart on chart paper, listing each object.

3. Ask each child to pick an object and make a prediction. "Will the magnet be attracted to your object?" The child will predict yes or no. Record the prediction on the chart.

4. After each child has made a prediction on the chart, ask her to test her prediction with a magnet and record the results. Compare the results.

5. Talk about and compare the results listed on the chart. Ask the children what material the objects are made of that are attracted to a magnet (iron and steel, not all metals).

More to do

Ask the children what objects in the room might be attracted to a magnet. List the objects on chart paper and ask the children to test their predictions. Make hand magnets for testing objects. Give each child a craft stick and a piece of magnetic tape. Glue the magnetic tape to the craft stick. Children can decorate the craft stick with markers.

Related book

Experiments With Magnets by Helen Challand

★ Gina M. Duddy, Arlington, MA

Magnet Boxes . . . . .4+

Materials needed

Box with a clear lid
Tape

Iron shavings (only for teacher)
Magnet

What to do

1. At circle time explain that you will make a magnet box. Cover the bottom of the box with iron shavings.

2. Place the lid on the box and secure it with tape.

3. Show the children how to run a magnet across the bottom of the box. Ask the children to look through the clear top to can see the iron shavings move.

4. Make the box available for children to experiment with and see what they discover.

More to do

Put different amounts of shavings in different boxes. Also use different size magnets. Add other objects to the boxes.

★ Sandra Hutchins Lucas, Cox's Creek, KY

Wet and Dry . . . . .4+

Materials needed

Various wet objects, such as wet sponge, ice cube, mud, wet paintbrush
Various dry objects, such as dry sponge, paper, block, dry paintbrush
Chart paper and markers

What to do

1. At circle time show children several objects that are wet and several objects that are dry.

2. Ask the children to touch each of the items and describe how they feel, how they look and how the items are similar or different from each other.

3. Pass the objects around for the children to touch and talk about.

4. Make a chart and ask the children to classify the items into categories by how they feel.

More to do

Art: Salt Painting—mix 1/8 cup liquid starch, 1/8 cup water, 1 tablespoon tempera and 1/2 cup salt. Paint the mixture on stiff cardboard. Painting will crystallize when dry. Shiny Paint—mix a variety of tempera paint with white glue. Paint on paper, wood or cardboard. This looks wet even when dry.

Cooking: Peanut Butter Playdough—Mix 1/2 large jar peanut butter, 2 tablespoons honey and 2 cups powdered milk. Talk about the ingredients being either wet or dry.

Original song

"Messy Children" (Tune: "For He's a Jolly Good Fellow")

> *Oh, we are messy children,*
> *Oh, we are messy children,*
> *Oh, we are messy children.*
> *Now what do you think of that?*

Related book

Water by Carme Solve Vendrell

★ Diana Reed and Debi Behr, New Wilmington, PA

Plants . . . . .5+

Materials needed

4 plants
Water
Window
Paper and marker

What to do

1. Ask the children what plants need to grow (their predictions). List their responses and encourage the children to test their predictions (include water and light).

2. Plan an experiment with the children that will test a plant's need for water and light. Talk about how the experiment will be conducted. Ask the children to consider the following variables: put one plant in the window and ask a child to water it, put another plant in the window with no watering, put a third plant in a closet or box with no light and ask a child to water it and put a fourth plant in a closet or box with no watering.

3. Check the plants daily and record the children's observations.

4. After two weeks discuss their predictions and the condition of each plant.

5. Graph the results on chart paper.

★ Angela Williamson, Greensboro, NC

Water Changes Form . . . . .5+

Materials needed

Hot plate
Small pan
Measuring cup
Chart paper

Freezer or cold outside temperature (below 32° F)
Bowl of ice cubes
Water
Marker

What to do

1. Measure one cup of water and put it in the pan and heat the water to boiling. Talk about what causes heat and if the water will become hot.

2. Ask the children to observe what happens as the water begins to boil and continues to boil.

3. Hold a glass plate or mirror over the boiling water and ask the children to describe what they see. Talk about the steam and ask the children how the water changed. Observe if the amount of water in the pan is less that when the water began to boil (mark the water level on the pan before and after the experiment).

4. Display an ice cube tray filled with water. Place it in the freezer or outside on a day when the temperature is below freezing. Talk about what happens to the water when it becomes very cold.

5. After the water has frozen place it on a table where children can observe the ice melting during the day. Talk about the changes they observe.

More to do

Science: Ice Sculpture: place lines of rock salt on a block of ice to melt it in interesting patterns. Use eyedroppers and food coloring to add color to the melted parts of the ice to emphasize the patterns.

Water table: Add ice cubes and chunks of ice to the water table. Talk about why things melt and what happens to the water during and after the ice melts.

Related books

Snow and Ice by Stephen Krensky
What Can it Be? Riddles About the Senses by Jacqueline A. Ball
★ Diana Reed and Debi Behr, New Wilmington, PA

Benjamin Banneker's Clock . . . . .5+

Materials needed

Book about Benjamin Banneker (see related books)

What to do

1. Introduce Benjamin Banneker through reading a book or telling the story about the many contributions he made.

2. Ask the children to describe the clock in the room and explain that Benjamin Banneker invented the first clock. Discuss what it would be like if there were no clocks.

3. Say the following poem with the children.

"Benjamin Banneker"

> *Hickory, dickory dock, tick tock*
> *Benjamin made a clock.*
> *Hickory, dickory dare,*
> *At the stars he liked to stare,*
> *Hickory, dickory that,*
> *He wrote the Almanac,*
> *Hickory, dickory be,*
> *Benjamin drew D. C.*
> *Hickory, dickory dock, tick tock*
> *Benjamin made a clock.*
> *Benjamin made a clock.*

Related books

Benjamin Banneker: Scientist by Garnet N. Jackson
Benjamin Banneker by Kevin Conley

★ Patricia Murchison, Chesapeake, VA

My Shadow . . . . .5+

Materials needed

Overhead projector or gooseneck lamp
White paper
Pencil
Crayons

What to do

1. Hang a piece of white paper on the wall.

2. Place an overhead projector or lamp a short distance from the wall.

3. Ask a child to take a pencil and trace around another child's shadow (the whole body or the profile of the head). With young children the teacher or an older child can trace around the shadow.

4. The children color their shadows and talk about how the shadow was made.

More to do

Show the children how to make shadow animals with their hands.

★ Sandra Hutchins Lucas, Cox's Creek, KY

Salt Crystals . . . . .5+

Materials needed
Water
Salt
Yarn
Clear plastic container

What to do

1. On Friday, mix hot water and salt in a clear plastic container. Tie a piece of yarn to a pencil and lay the pencil across the top of the container. Talk with the children about the experiment and ask the children to predict what changes they expect to see on Monday.

2. At circle time on Monday ask the children to describe any changes and to compare their observations with what they expected to see. Observe and talk about the formation of crystals throughout the week.

3. Explain that the children will act out the formation of crystals. Ask for volunteers to raise their foot if they want to play the role of water and to raise their hand if they want to play the role of salt.

4. Ask the children who are pretending to be salt to stand outside the circle.

5. Ask the children who are pretending to be water to stand in a circle and hold hands.

6. Ask the children who are pretending to be salt to touch the hands of the two children in front of them and ask the children to drop their hands so they can stand between the children and hold their hands (mixing up the water and salt).

7. Lay a long piece of yarn extending from the edge to the center of the circle and explain that now the water will evaporate into the air. Walk around the circle touching the children who are pretending to be water and ask them to drop hands and walk to the center of the circle and hold onto the yarn. Ask the children pretending to be salt to move closer to the center of the circle and hold onto another child's waist so all the children are touching each other (forming solid crystals).

8. Ask the children to sit in a circle and talk about their experience of acting out how crystals are formed from salt and water.

9. Look at the crystals that were formed again and recall how the crystals were made by dissolving salt in the water to make a salt solution and leaving the solution over the weekend during which time the water evaporated and only the crystals were visible.

★ Barbara M. Bergstrom, Spokane, WA

Science

Sound-Travel Game . . . . .5+

Materials needed
3' length of string (2 per cooling rack)
Small wire cooling racks
Spoons (metal, wooden, plastic)

What to do
1. Tie string through the cooling rack so there is at least 1' of string extending from each side of the rack.

2. Ask children to work in pairs.

3. Show one child in each pair how to wrap one end of the string around his index finger on one hand a couple of times and wrap the end of the other string around his index finger of his other hand.

4. Ask the child to lean over so the cooling rack does not touch his body.

5. Ask the child to place his fingers in his ears.

6. Ask the other child in each pair to gently strum the cooling rack with each of the three spoons.

7. Ask the children who are holding the cooling racks to describe the different sounds they heard when each of the three spoons were used to strum the cooling rack.

More to do
Experiment making sound machines using string tied to other types of materials. Ask the children to identify the materials that conduct sound better than other materials. Experiment and talk about acoustical materials that absorb sound, such as insulation and rugs.

★ Cathy Chenoweth, Columbia, MO

Different Seasons, Different Clothes . . .3+

Materials needed
Scenic calendar
Scissors
Seasonal clothing
Basket

What to do
1. Take an old scenic calendar and cut off the calendar part so only the pictures are left.

2. At circle time show the pictures to the children and ask questions about the season in which the pictures were taken. Was the weather cold or hot when this picture was taken? Look at the trees in the pictures and identity the season. Talk about the different seasons and the weather of each season.

3. After talking with the children about the seasons show the children a basket of seasonal clothing. Ask each child to pick an article of clothing and tell the season she would wear it in.

More to do
Dramatic play: Place the clothing in the dramatic play area to use for dress-up.

Math: Ask the children to sort the clothing by the season in which they would wear the clothing.

★ Sandra Hutchins Lucas, Cox's Creek, KY

Nature Walk . . . . .3+

Materials needed
Paper bag
Poster board

What to do
1. During circle time discuss the temperature outside and the current season of the year. Talk about where the children will take a nature walk. Ask the children what they may see, for example, tree, grass, flowers, birds, nests, leaves, insects, rocks. Talk about what the children should look for on their nature walk.

2. Show the children the paper bag and talk about the items they may collect and put in the paper bag.

3. During the walk look for bird and squirrel nests. Talk about seasonal changes (spring—trees budding, summer—plants and flowers, fall—leaves turning colors and falling, winter—trees dormant). Discuss the textures of the items the children collect.

4. After returning to the room ask the children to describe the items they collected. Provide poster board for the children to use in gluing items collected during the nature walk. Date the collage and label with the season.

5. As the seasons change take other nature walks and collect items. Ask the children to glue the items on another piece of poster board. Date and label the collage and hang it next to the other seasonal collections.

More to do

Adopt a nearby tree to visit regularly and observe seasonal changes and how various animals use the tree. Make bird feeders using pine cones, peanut butter and bird seed. Hang the feeders nearby and watch the birds.

★ Terri B. Garroli, Lenoir, NC

A Tree for All Seasons . . . . .3+

Materials needed

Tree nearby for observation

What to do

1. Talk about the weather outside and ask if the weather will always be the same or if it will change.

2. Ask the children how the weather will change. Explain that the weather may be hot, cold, rainy, snowy.

3. Changes in weather occur in different seasons that are spring, summer, fall and winter.

4. Locate a tree nearby to visit during the four seasons.

5. As each new season arrives, visit the tree and note the seasonal changes in the tree.

More to do

Art: Draw an outline of a tree and make four copies for each child. Each season give each child a copy of the tree and crayons. Each child draws how the tree looks during that season. Ask the children what colors remind them of spring. summer, autumn, winter. Draw a large outine of a tree on butcher paper for the children to decorate each season.

Language: Compile the children's pictures of the trees and bind in a class book. Ask the children to decide on a title for the book and to design the book cover.

Related books

Caps, Hats, Socks and Mittens by Louise Borden
Over and Over by Charlotte Zolotow
The Year at Maple Hill Farm by Alice and M. Provensen

★ Wendy Pfeffer, Pennington, NJ

Four Seasons Box Mural ....4+

Materials needed
Empty refrigerator box
Seasonal tracings
Seasonal collage items
Glue

What to do
1. At circle time talk with the children about making a seasonal box mural and show them the box.

2. Talk about the current season and encourage the children to describe the season, how the seasons are different and what activities they do in each season.

3. Make a collage on one side of the box with items pertaining to the current season, for example, mitten tracings and cotton balls (winter), flower tracings and kites (spring), colored leaves and acorns from a nature walk (fall), sun, sand and beach tracings (summer).

4. Display the seasonal box mural and refer to it throughout the year reinforcing that there are four seasons.

More to do
Art: Encourage the children to make seasonal drawings for the mural.

Language: Ask the children to tell you about their pictures and write what they say on their pictures.

★ Kate West, Buckingham, PA

Seasonal Wall Collage ....4+

Materials needed
Butcher paper
Nature objects (flowers, grass, twigs, branches, leaves, sand, seashells, pine cones, acorns, pumpkin seeds)
Glue
Marker

What to do
1. Divide the butcher paper into four sections or use four sheets, one for each season.

2. Provide natural objects (not current season) and take a walk with the children to collect items from the current season.

3. At circle time ask the children to glue items on the sheet representing the season in which the item is found.

Seasons

More to do

Science: Label four shoeboxes: fall, winter, spring and summer and ask the children to sort items by season. Place a microscope or magnifying glass in the science area and encourage children to look at the texture of each item.

Related books

A Busy Year by Leo Lionni
My Favorite Time of the Year by Susan Pearson

★ Quazonia Quarles, Newark, DE

Four Seasons Flip Book . . . . .5+

Materials needed

1 1/2 sheets of light blue construction paper (9" x 12") per child
Scraps of green construction paper
Light green crayons
Tissue paper (brown, red, yellow, orange)
Glue
White laundry detergent

What to do

1. At circle time discuss the seasons and how they affect the lives of people and animals. Talk about the sequence of the seasons.

2. Tell the children that they are going to make a Four Season Flip Book.

3. Cut the whole sheet of construction paper into 4 rectangles.

4. Staple three of the rectangles to the top of a 6" x 9" piece of blue construction paper along the 6" edge.

5. Each child draws a tree trunk on the uncovered lower half of the larger bottom sheet and draws branches on the other half sheets and on the top half of the larger sheet.

6. Ask the children to decorate the tree branches for each of the seasons. For fall (top sheet) crumble squares of the colored tissue paper and glue to branches. For winter (next sheet) paint glue on the branches and sprinkle with detergent for snow. For spring (next sheet) draw light green buds on the branches. For summer (top half of large sheet) tear pieces of green construction paper and glue to branches to make leaves.

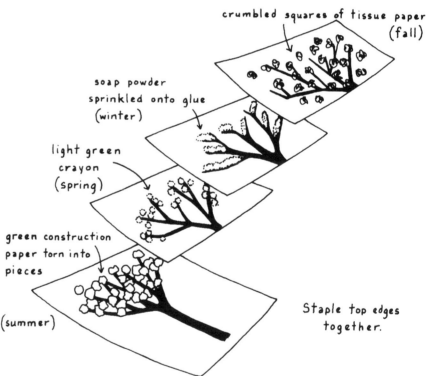

crumbled squares of tissue paper (fall)

soap powder sprinkled onto glue (winter)

light green crayon (spring)

green construction paper torn into pieces

(summer)

Staple top edges together.

More to do

Art: Make leaf rubbings or leaf prints: rub fingerpaint on a leaf. Place painted side of the leaf down on the paper. Roll over the leaf with a rolling pin. Remove the leaf to reveal the print.

Field trip: Visit a plant nursery or orchard.

Math: Sort leaves by color or shape and graph the number of leaves in each category.

Science: Use a magnifying glass to examine bark, leaves, pine needles, acorns, nuts.

Related books

Changing Seasons by Rose Greydanus
The Four Seasons by Gerda Muller
January Brings the Snow by Sara Coleridge
Look at a Tree by Eileen Curran
The Seasons of Arnold's Apple Tree by Gail Gibbons

★ Sandra Gratias, Perkasie, PA

Build a Tree . . . . .5+

Materials needed

Tree bark and leaves
Butcher paper 6' long
Construction paper (various colors)
Markers, crayons
Glue
Scissors

What to do

1. Provide samples of real bark and leaves for children to examine and use in designing their representation of bark and leaves.

2. Divide the children into four groups with each group being responsible for constructing a section of the tree—roots, trunk, branches and leaves.

3. Talk with each group about the materials they will use in making a representation of a part of a tree. Provide materials and discuss the texture and colors of the tree parts.

4. After the children have completed making their part of the tree ask them to bring their parts to the circle. Talk about the placement of the tree parts. Ask the children to glue the tree parts together by section—trunk, roots, branches and leaves. Ask the children to talk about how they made their tree parts.

More to do

Art: Attach the tree to the wall and create a "tree center" nearby with materials where children can continue adding to the tree and explore the textures using a magnifying glass. Ask the children to change the tree with the seasons. Instead of gluing the fall leaves on the tree, curl tape and stick the leaves on temporarily. Take the leaves off during winter and replace them with blossoms and leaves in the spring. On another day draw, cut out and add seasonal animals to the tree. Don't forget the hibernating animals in the winter.

Language: Label the tree parts with index cards. Make a second set of cards and encourage the children to play a word match game using a smaller picture of a tree on the table.

★ Susan R. Forbes, Holly Hill,

Every Year There Are Four Seasons . . .5+

Materials needed

Items for each season (wool scarves, beach hats, rake, snow shovel, rain boots, winter boots, seed packets, hot chocolate package, plastic jack-o-lantern, sand bucket, swimming suit, coats of different weights)
5 strips of paper labeled (Spring, Winter, Fall, Summer and All Year)

What to do

1. Place the seasonal items on the floor and ask children to sit in a circle around the items.

2. Hold up an item, such as a rake and ask the children if they have raked leaves. Ask the children in which season did they rake leaves. Hold up other items representing different seasons. As you talk about each season, place the season's label on the floor. Count the labels with the children and talk about the four seasons in each year. Tell them that a fifth label is for items that are used in more than one season. Put the label All Year next to the other four labels.

3. Ask each child to choose an item, tell which season the item is used and why, then place the item under the appropriate season label. Some items will fit into two or more categories, such as a swimming suit. The child can talk about how he goes swimming all year. He would then place this item under the All Year label.

4. After all the items have been sorted, assign children into five groups: winter, spring, summer, fall and all year. Encourage the children to plan a short skit with their props. This might be as simple as pretending to make a snowman or as elaborate as a play with individual speaking parts, depending on the ages and abilities of the children. Ask the children to present the short skits for the other children.

More to do

Art: Cut four pieces of butcher paper (or use one long piece divided into four sections) and label each one with the name of a season. Working in groups, the children create a mural using paints, crayons or markers depicting things their families do in the different seasons. For example, a child might draw a picture of a child on a sled on the winter mural.

Related books

My Favorite Time of the Year by Susan Pearson   *The Seasons of Arnold's Apple Tree* by Gail Gibbons
Sleepy Bear by Lydia Dabcovich

★ Susan Thompson, Casper, WY

Child's Picture Journal . . . . .3+

Materials needed

File cabinet
Large labels

3-prong folders (variety of colors)
Art work by each child

What to do

1. At the beginning of the year purchase folders in a variety of colors. Place a large label on the front of each folder and print the child's full name on the label.

2. File the folders alphabetically where children can easily reach them.

3. During circle time show the children a sample folder (use examples of work collected in previous years). Tell the children that it is a Picture Journal and that they will make a journal during the year.

4. Individually show each child how to find his folder and place work in it (date each paper).

5. Throughout the year ask the children to place samples of their work in their folders. Periodically talk with each child and together select the samples of work that best represent the child's individual talents and that show the progressive development of the child's abilities.

6. Periodically throughout the year arrange each child's work in order by date, punch holes in the pages and place the pages in the folder.

7. Children will enjoy looking at their art collection and so will parents.

Note: It took less than a month for children to learn to locate their folders and they loved collecting their work on a regular basis.

★ Cathy Chenoweth, Columbia, MO

Child of the Week . . . . .3+

Materials needed

Paper and markers
Bulletin board
Chair

Note to parents

Dear Parents,

Your child _____ has been chosen to be the Child of the Week for the week beginning_____. Your child will be a special person in our class during this week. Please fill out the enclosed form and send in pictures of your child for us to share and put on our special bulletin board. This would also be a great time for you to visit our room. If you have stories about your child or pets you would like to share, please call me and make arrangements for your visit. I look forward to hearing from you,

Sincerely,
Teacher's Name

Self-Concept

Child of the Week

My full name is _____

I was born on _____ at _____

I weighed _____ and I was _____ long.

My Mommy's name is _____

My Daddy's name is _____

My brothers and sisters are _____

My other relatives are _____

I like to eat _____

At home I like to _____

At school I like to _____

What to do

1. Print each child's name on a separate piece of paper.

2. Put the papers in a special Child of the Week box.

3. Once a week on designated day draw one name from the box to be the Child of the Week for the following week. After the first selection the current Child of the Week draws the name of the next child at the beginning of the week.

4. Send the note and a copy of the form to the child's parents.

5. Ask the Child of the Week to sit in the special chair at circle time and to be the special helper during the week.

6. Share pictures and information about the child that the parents provided and put the pictures on the Child of the Week bulletin board.

★ Barbara Saul, Eureka, CA

All About Me . . . . .3+

Materials needed

Tape recorder and tape
Book about self esteem (see related books)

What to do

1. At circle time read a book about things children can do and ask the children to talk about the things they like to do.

2. Show the children the tape recorder and explain that they will each have time to talk about what they like to do so you can record what they say.

3. Experiment with the tape recorder so children become familiar with listening to their voices (sing familiar songs).

4. During choice time talk with each child about something she likes to do.

5. After the children have each talked on the tape, play the tape at circle time and enjoy listening to the tape. Ask the children to guess who is talking so they will become familiar with recognizing the other children's voices.

6. Record the children's comments throughout the year and play the tape periodically at circle time.

Related books
Grover Goes to School by Dan Elliot
Little Engine That Could by Watty Piper
Look What I Can Do by Jose Aruego

★ Deborah Hannes Litfin, Forest Hills, NY

Class Photo Albums . . . . .3+

Materials needed
2 flexible 3-ring binders
Photo pages
Photographs of children

What to do
1. Take photographs of children throughout the day and tell the children that you will make two class albums and add them to the library area. Ask another adult to take several pictures of you and the children working together.

2. Arrange the photographs of the children in the album and label it "Who Do You See?"

3. Create another album with photographs showing the sequence of activities during a typical day and label it "Our Day at School."

4. Ask the children to take turns taking the albums home to share with their families.

★ Lisa Sunbury, Cambridge, MA

I Am So Tall . . . . .3+

Materials needed
Butcher paper
Markers
Various classroom objects

What to do
1. At circle time measure the children against a wall and record their heights on a long piece of butcher paper taped to the wall. Label each marking with the child's name.

2. Talk with the children about their heights and explain that they will compare their heights with several objects in the classroom.

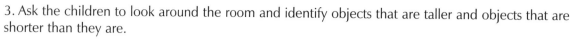

3. Ask the children to look around the room and identify objects that are taller and objects that are shorter than they are.

4. Ask the children to select an object and bring it to the butcher paper and compare its height with the mark indicating their height on the paper. Talk with the children about the difference in the heights and emphasize how much taller they are than the object they measured.

5. Ask the children who in their family is taller and who is shorter. Also compare their heights with their pets and other animals they may have seen at the zoo.

More to do

Math: Tape a large piece of paper (divided into two sections, Taller and Shorter) on the wall and after the children have measured objects and talked about the height of various animals ask them to paste pictures of objects and animals in the appropriate categories. Measure the children using string and let them take their "This Is How Tall I Am" strings home.

Related books

Growing Story by Ruth Krauss
You'll Soon Grow Into Them, Titch by Pat Hutchins

★ Wendy Pfeffer, Pennington, NJ

I Can Do So Much . . . . .3+

Materials needed

None needed

What to do

1. Discuss with the children all the different things they can do. Include routines, such as washing hands, brushing teeth; physical activity, such as running, jumping, talking; caring activity, such as loving, helping.

2. Discuss what they can do now that they couldn't do when they were younger. What would they like to do when they are older?

3. Encourage the children to act out what they can do, such as brush teeth, hug someone, comb hair. Ask the other children to guess what they are doing.

More to do

Art: Make pictures labeled "I Can Do So Much." Give each child a sheet of paper folded in half, crayons, paste and scissors. Ask the children to cut out pictures or draw the things they can do and paste these on one side of the paper labeled "I Can Do So Much." Children paste pictures or draw things they wish they could do on the other half that is labeled "I Wish I Could...."

Language: Ask each child to speak into a tape recorder saying something special she can do. Play the recording and ask the children to guess who said what, not only by the voice but by what the child said she can do.

Related books
The Chick and the Duckling by Ginsberg
Children Do, Grownups Don't by Norma Simon
Curious George Rides a Bike by H. A. Rey
Look What I Can Do by M. Doray
When I Get Bigger by Mercer Mayer

★ Wendy Pfeffer, Pennington, NJ

I'm Growing Up . . . . .3+

Materials needed
Photographs of teacher and children at different ages

What to do
1. Ask parents to loan photographs that span their child's life to show the other children.

2. At circle time show the children photographs of yourself that span many years and ask the children to put the photographs in order based on your age when the photograph was taken.

3. Show several photographs of a child and ask the children to look at the photographs and put the photographs in order based on the child's age, from the youngest to the oldest.

4. On another day show one photograph of each child and ask the children to guess who is in each photograph.

More to do
Art: In advance staple several pages together in book format for each child. Ask each child to make a book about when he was a baby, a toddler and now (label the pages accordingly). Ask the children to draw a picture of themselves on a page to represent themselves at each of the different ages. Encourage children to decorate their books and to tell you the book's title for you to write on the cover. (If any children ask to paste their photographs in the book, first check with their parents.)

Math: Show the children clothing and toys appropriate for different age children and discuss the difference in ages. Provide the children with department store catalogs and ask the children to cut out pictures of clothing and toys appropriate for each age. Ask the children to put the pictures in order from what is used by the youngest child to the oldest child.

Science: Children draw (or find pictures) of animals and talk about how they grow. Ask children who have pets if their pets are bigger than when they first got them.

Related books
The Growing Story by Ruth Krauss
The Very Little Boy by Phyllis Krasilovsky
The Very Little Girl by Phyllis Krasilovsky

★ Wendy Pfeffer, Pennington, NJ

Self-Concept

Look Who's Special . . . . .3+

Materials needed

Photo album
Small nonbreakable mirror
"I Am Special" laminated badges
Hat
Name card for each child

What to do

1. At circle time show the children the photo album (with the small nonbreakable morror attached to the first page) and tell them that a special person's picture is in the album.

2. Ask each child to open the album and look inside (remind the children they are not to say whose picture they see).

3. After all the children have looked in the album ask the children who they saw that is a special person (children reply that they saw themselves).

4. Talk with the children explaining that each of them is special because there is no one else exactly like them. Give each of the children a "I Am Special" badge to wear.

5. Place the children's name cards in a hat and ask a child to pull a name out of the hat and to say one special thing about that child.

More to do

Art: Place a mirror next to an easel and ask the children to paint their portraits. Frame each portrait using construction paper strips and display the portraits.

Math: Measure and chart each child's height. Use a variety of tools for measuring (unifix cubes, blocks, yardstick) and discuss the different methods of measurement.

Related books

Leo, the Late Bloomer by Robert Kraus
Little Gorilla by Ruth L. Bornstein
One Hundred One Ways to Make Your Child Feel Special by Vicki Lansky
You are Special: Words of Wisdom from America's Most Beloved Neighbor by Fred Rogers

★ Ann M. Ferruggia, Voorhees, NJ

Self-Esteem . . . . .3+

Materials needed

Apples (1 per child)

What to do

1. Ask each child to choose an apple to hold and feel.

2. Talk about the apples, how they feel, how they smell, their size, their color.

3. Sort the apples by color and place them into groups. Count the number of apples in each group. Talk about which group has more, which has less and if any groups have the same number.

4. Cut the apples and give the children a piece of each apple to taste. Ask the children if the different colors of apples taste the same or taste different from each other.

5. Ask the children which apple is their favorite, count the responses and graph the results.

6. Talk about how different types of apples can taste different (more sweet, more sour) and have a different texture (crisp, soft).

7. Explain that different types of apples have different characteristics but each is special. Children also have different characteristics but each is special in her own way.

More to do

Language: Read or tell the children the story about Johnny Appleseed.

Math: Count the number of seeds in each apple, record and graph the results. Compare the number of seeds in the different colors of apples.

★ Holly Dzierzanowski, Austin, TX

Self-Esteem Song . . . . .3+

Materials needed
Hand mirror
Photocopy picture of each child
Glue
Tagboard
Clear self-adhesive paper

What to do
1. Ask the children to sit in a circle and teach them the "My Friend" song (Tune: "Brown Bear").

> *My friend, my friend*
> *Who do you see?*
> *I see (child's name) looking at me.*

2. Tell the children that you will pass a hand mirror around the circle and each child will in turn look in the mirror and say his name. The children will sing the song again saying that child's name at the appropriate time.

3. Adapt the activity by photocopying a picture of each child and attaching it to a hand mirror made from tagboard. Cover the hand mirror with clear self-adhesive paper or laminate it after attaching a child's picture. Sing the following song as the children look at their pictures in their mirrors.

> *Twinkle, twinkle, little mirror*
> *Who do I see sitting near?*
> *Someone special I can see.*
> *I think that it must be me!*

More to do

Game: Photocopy each child's picture twice, laminate the pictures on poster board and use the two sets of pictures as a lotto game.

Language: Tape record each of the children talking about themselves, listen to the tape and ask the other children to guess who is talking on the tape.

Math: Make a graph of the color of the children's hair, eyes, height and weight.

Social skills: Place the children's names in a hat, draw one name, give clues about that child and ask the children to guess who the child is that you are describing.

Related songs

"Free To Be You and Me"
"I'm Something Special"

★ Patricia Moeser, McFarland, WI

The Same but Different! . . . . .3+

Materials needed

Photographs of each child

What to do

1. Give the children a copy of their photographs and ask them to suggest ways the photographs could be sorted into categories. Begin with obvious characteristics such as hair or clothing color.

2. After sorting the pictures a few times encourage the children to suggest other ways to categorize the photographs into groups (gender, child smiling or not, coat on or not, child indoors or outdoors).

More to do

Provide the photographs for pairs of children to sort during choice time.

Related books

All the Colors of the Earth by Sheila Hamanaka
Why Am I Different? by Norma Simon

★ Cheryl Devine, New Brunswick, NJ

What About You? . . . . .3+

Materials needed
Chart paper
Marker

What to do
1. At circle time ask the children to look at their clothing and the clothing of other children and say how one thing they are wearing is different from what another child is wearing.

2. List the differences the children identified on chart paper. Sort the children into two groups based on each of the items listed, for example, if tie shoes is an item ask the children with tie shoes to stand up and count the number of children, ask the children with shoes without ties to stand up and count the number of children. Record the number of children in each category. To show the difference in number more clearly ask the children in each group to stand in different lines and compare the number of children in each line.

3. Continue sorting the children into groups by the differences the children reported.

4. After sorting by different items of clothing look at the numbers and determine which type of clothing was worn by the largest number of children, which type of clothing by the smallest number of children.

More to do
Children can sort sets of objects into groups (blocks into groups by color).

★ Melissa Browning, West Allis, WI

I Am Growing . . . . .4+

Materials needed
1 baby picture of each child (4" x 6" or smaller)
Tape
Shoebox
Marker
Chart paper

What to do
1. Ask parents to loan a baby picture of their child.

2. Put the pictures in a shoebox and bring it to circle time.

3. At circle time tell the children that you are going to pull a baby picture out of the shoebox, tape it on the chart paper and ask the children to guess whose baby picture it is (the child in the picture should not tell the other children).

4. After the picture is identified write the child's name under it on the chart paper.

5. After all the pictures are displayed ask the children to talk about their pictures.

6. Talk about the things babies do, such as crawl, drink from a bottle. List the children's comments on a sheet of chart paper.

7. Read each of the comments and ask the children what they do now instead of what they did when they were babies. Write their responses next to the item being discussed, such as crawl—walk, drink from a bottle—drink from a cup.

8. Talk about and compare the lists.

More to do
Game: Put the baby pictures and recent photographs of the children on a table and ask the children to match the two pictures of each child.

Math: Obtain the birth weights and heights of the children from their parents. Measure the children's current weights and heights and record them. Compare the children's weights and heights as babies with their current measurements and graph the two sets of data.

Related book
When I Get Bigger by Mercer Mayer

Related song
"I Wonder If I'm Growing" by Raffi

★ Julia A. Masury, Raymond, NH

I Am Special Day . . . . .4+

Materials needed
Note to parents

What to do
1. Send a note to parents explaining that each child will choose a day during the year to celebrate as her special day (birthday or other day of significance). Each child will help plan and prepare for the day. Ask the parents to talk with their child and tell you the day selected.

2. In preparation for the special day ask the parents to loan a family photograph and a number of photographs of their child as a baby and a toddler. Suggest that they display the photographs on a poster board.

3. Ask the child to bring something special to show the class, such as a collection, hobby, pet.

4. The child may also invite family members or special friends to visit on her special day.

5. Invite the child and parents to give a gift, such as a book for the children to enjoy.

6. Encourage the child and parents to provide a snack that is their favorite.

7. Decorate a chair in special honor of the child and present an "I Am Special" badge, crown or balloon to wear for the day.

8. Take a photograph of each child on her special day, frame it and hang it in the hall of fame gallery in the classroom.

More to do

Language: Ask the special child to talk about what she enjoys doing and involve the other children in the discussion of things they like to do. Point out similarities in what the children enjoy.

Snack: Ask the special child to help you prepare the tables and serve the snack.

★ Jean Lortz, Seattle, WA

Marvelous Me . . . . .4+

Materials needed
White T-shirts (1 per child)
Permanent markers (various colors)
Large piece of cardboard

What to do
1. Write each child's name on the front of a T-shirt.

2. Help each child trace his handprints on his personal shirt (place a piece of cardboard inside the shirt to prevent the marker from showing through on the back of the shirt).

3. Help each child trace his footprints or shoe prints on his shirt.

4. Ask each child to draw a picture on his shirt.

5. After the shirts are completed ask the children to put on their shirts and have a Marvelous Me parade.

6. At circle time ask each child to stand and talk about the drawing on his shirt.

More to do
Ask the child to invite members of his family to draw pictures on his shirt. Make shirts with a specific theme, such as trace or sponge print leaves for fall, draw or sponge print butterflies for spring.

★ Mimi Williams, Tallahassee, FL

Pair Power .4+

Materials needed
Magazine pictures cut in half
Pairs of envelopes (each containing identical objects)

What to do
1. Give each child one half of a picture or one of an envelope pair.

2. Ask the children to find their partner who has the other half of their picture or a matching envelope.

3. After children have found their partner ask them to do several movements together, such as sitting in front of, in back of, facing each other, side-by-side, back-to-back. Provide a mirror that they can look in together and talk about what they see. Ask the partner to compare the sizes of their hands and feet. Ask them to talk about how they are the same and different from their partner.

More to do

Throughout the day ask the children to make choices with their partners. This is a good way to introduce new children in the group or to encourage children to interact with children other than their friends.

★ Andrea M. Lazzari, Richmond, VA

The Mirror I Made . . . . .4+

Materials needed

Craft sticks or tongue depressors
Glue
Assorted materials (beads, buttons, beans, sequins, glitter, confetti)
Metallic paper

What to do

1. Give each of the children six craft sticks and show the children how to glue the sticks to make a shape (square, triangle, rectangle).

2. After the sticks are dry give the children the assorted materials to use in decorating the sticks that will become a picture frame.

3. Ask the children to cut (with help if necessary) metallic paper to fit the frame made with the sticks.

4. Glue the frame onto the metallic paper. After the glue has dried, glue another stick to the back of the frame as a handle for the hand mirror.

5. Ask the children to bring their mirrors to circle time to show the other children and talk about how they made their mirrors.

6. Ask the children to look into their mirrors and to describe what they see. Tell the children that when they look into their mirrors they can begin telling a story about themselves by saying, "When I look in the mirror I see...."

Related books

Amazing Grace by Mary Hoffman
Brown Bear, Brown Bear, What Do You See? by Bill Martin, Jr.

★ Patricia Murchison, Chesapeake, VA

Which One Is Me? . . . . .4+

Materials needed
Tape recorder
Blank tape
Mirror

What to do
1. During choice time have a tape recorder and a mirror available for the children to become familiar with and use.

2. Ask each of the children to look in the mirror and talk about themselves recording what they say on tape.

3. After each child has had a turn play the tape at circle time. Ask the children to guess who is talking.

More to do
Place the tape recorder in the listening center so the children can listen to their own voice and guess the other children's voices on tape. The children can also sing songs and listen to them throughout the year.

★ Sandra Hutchins Lucas, Cox's Creek, KY

Who's Who? . . . . .5+

Materials needed
Photograph of each child
Paper and pencils

What to do
1. Send a note to parents asking them to loan a baby picture of their child (without their child's knowledge).

2. Number each of the photographs and display the photographs on the bulletin board.

3. Put slips of paper near the bulletin board for children to write the number of the photograph and the name of the child whose photograph they think it is.

4. At the end of the week ask the children to talk about their guesses and then reveal the name of the child in each picture.

More to do
Math: Ask parents to write down the age of their child when the picture was taken. Arrange the pictures in order by age and graph the ages of the children to determine at what age most of the pictures were taken.

★ Patti Jones, Monroe, NC

Self-Concept

I'm a Dandy Lion .... .5+

Materials needed

Paper plates (1 per child)
Paper T-shirt outline (1 per child)
5" piece of yarn (1 per child)
Markers, crayons or paints
Dandelion by Don Freeman

What to do

1. At circle time read *Dandelion* and talk about the story with the children.

2. Ask the children to talk about the things they can do and ask them to decorate the T-shirt by drawing pictures of what they can do and writing (or dictating to an adult) their ideas.

3. Ask each child to draw his face on the paper plate and thread the yarn through the prepunched holes on the lower edge of the plate and the upper edge of the T-shirt to fasten the face to the T-shirt.

★ Cathlene M. Hedden, Livonia, MI

No One Else Is Like Me .... .5+

Materials needed

Ink pad
Books about uniqueness (see related books)

What to do

1. At circle time talk about the unique characteristics of each child including the tone of the voice, handprints, footprints, fingerprints.

2. Ask each child to put her thumb on an ink pad and make a thumbprint on each of two large sheets of paper. Label each thumbprint on both sheets of paper with the child's name.

3. Cover the names by taping flaps of paper over the names.

4. Ask the children to compare the thumbprints on one sheet with the thumbprints on the other sheet to match each child's thumbprint.

5. Check to see if the thumbprints are a match by lifting the flaps to check the child's name.

More to do

Art: Ask the children to decorate a piece of heavy paper with their thumbprint designs. Experiment with making thumbprint people, animals, hills, forests.

Related books

Ed Emberly's Great Thumbprint Drawing Book by Ed Emberly
Fish Is Fish by Leo Lionni
I Like Me by Nancy Carlson
Just Me by Marie Hall Ets

★ Wendy Pfeffer, Pennington, NJ

Sprout Your Wings . . . . .5+

Materials needed

Charlie the Caterpillar by Dom De Luise
Glue, markers, crayons

Construction paper cut into 9" circles (various colors)
1 caterpillar face slightly larger than the 9" circle

What to do

1. At circle time read *Charlie the Caterpillar* to the children and talk about how they think Charlie felt and how it might relate to their experiences.

2. Give the children a 9" circles and ask them to draw or write something about themselves on the circles.

3. Put the caterpillar face first and assemble the children's circles behind it to form a long caterpillar.

4. Talk with the children about their caterpillar and display it on a wall.

More to do

Ask the children to write their names on a large paper outline of a butterfly and display it near the caterpillar.

★ Cathlene M. Hedden, Livonia, MI

Me Collages ... .5+

Materials needed

White construction paper
Magazines
Overhead projector
Scissors
Glue
Marker
Masking tape

What to do

1. At circle time talk with the children about their favorite things. Ask the children to cut out pictures of their favorite things (food, sports, hobbies, clothes, people, animals, games) from magazines. Ask the children to glue their pictures on white construction paper after their profiles pre traced.

2. While the children are cutting out the pictures, place the overhead projector two feet in front of a wall and tape a sheet of construction paper. Ask one child at a time to stand in front of the paper so you can trace her profile on the paper using a black marker.

3. Ask the children to write their names on the top of the paper and glue their pictures inside their profiles.

4. Ask the children to share their collage and talk about their favorite things.

More to do

Language: Create a class song or poem about the children's favorite things.

Math: Compare the collages and determine the favorite thing identified by the largest number of children.

★ Kristine Poteracki, Brookfield, IL

Matching Textures . . . . .3+

Materials needed
Shoebox
Glue
Tape

5 clean frozen juice lids
Wrapping paper or tissue paper
Scraps (corduroy, velcro—both sides, velvet, polyester)

What to do
1. At circle time pass the fabrics around the circle and talk about how each fabric feels.

2. Cover the shoebox with wrapping paper or tissue paper.

3. Cover each juice lid with a different type of fabric.

4. Cut five slits in the lid of the shoebox and place a different type of fabric above each slit.

5. Place the shoebox and lids on a table for children to feel the different types of fabric and put the juice lid in the slit marked with the matching type of fabric.

More to do
Art: Make a collage of fabrics and other materials having different textures.

★ Stephanie Spanbauer, Coal City, IL

Are You Listening? . . . . .3+

Materials needed
Candle or flashlight
A Dark, Dark Tale by Ruth Brown
Small boxes or plastic eggs (filled with either pebbles, rice, marbles, buttons, nails or water and secured with tape)

What to do
1. At circle time turn off the lights and light a candle or turn on a flashlight in the center of the room.

2. Read *A Dark, Dark Tale* and talk about the story with the children.

3. Tell the children that you will pass several boxes around the circle and ask them to guess what is inside the boxes.

4. Pass around the boxes one at a time and ask the children to guess what is inside by listening to the noise it makes as they shake the box. Allow time for all the children to guess before opening the box and showing the contents.

More to do
Art: Ask the children to decorate boxes (tissue boxes work well) with feathers, sequins, glitter to keep their treasures in.

Language: Read *The Listening Walk* and then go on a listening walk. Take a tape recorder and tape the sounds on the walk. After returning from the walk listen to the tape and ask the children to identify the sounds.

Large motor: In *The Listening Walk* by Paul Showers a woman's high heel shoes make an interesting sound. Challenge the children to make interesting sounds with their shoes (pulling velcro, tapping shoes, rubbing boots).

★ Ann Scalley, Wellfleet, MA

Aromatic Herbs . . . . .3+

Materials needed

3 types of herbs (dill, lemon balm, spearmint)
Large flat (washed) rocks or cutting boards
Small round (washed) rocks (or mortar and pestle)
Small container

What to do

1. At circle time show the children the herbs and talk about the fragrances.

2. Pass each of the herbs around the circle for the children to smell the herbs before they are crushed.

3. Each child crushes an herb on the large rock, using the small stone.

4. After crushing the herbs place each type in a bowl for the children to smell and taste.

More to do

Science: Plant an herb garden, indoors or outdoors. Herbs grow easily in a sunny area.

Snack: Make sour cream (or yogurt) and herb dip. Serve with crackers.

Related books

Rosy's Garden: A Child's Keepsake of Flowers by Satomi Ichikawa and Elizabeth Laird
Tom Brown's Guide to Wild Edible and Medicinal Plants by Tom Brown

★ Carol Patnaude, Cathy Costantino, Darlene Maloney, Lynn Camara, Warwick, RI

Feel the Clothing . . . . .3+

Materials needed

Various fabrics (wool, corduroy, velvet, knit, velour, cotton, satin, vinyl)

What to do

1. At circle time show the fabrics and pass them around the circle for the children to feel.

2. After the children touch the fabric pieces talk about how each fabric felt.

3. Ask the children to run their hands over their own clothing and talk about how their clothing feels.

4. Ask the children to compare their clothing to the other fabrics and talk about how the different textures felt.

Senses

5. Sing the following texture song. Repeat the song until all fabrics are named in the song. The tune is "Mary Wore Her Red Dress."

> *Who is wearing (holding) corduroy,*
> *Corduroy, corduroy?*
> *Who is wearing (holding) corduroy*
> *At this time?*

Note: If the children are wearing a variety of fabric types, use their clothing. If not give each child a piece of fabric to hold.

6. Place the fabrics on a table for the children to explore individually or in small groups.

More to do
Art: Make a fabric collage with different types of fabric.

Science: Make a texture or fabric match by gluing pieces of fabric on tagboard cards.

Related book
Corduroy by Don Freeman

★ Glenda Manachanda, Huber Heights, OH

Listening Game . . . . .3+

Materials needed
Song "Pause" on "Movin" recording by Hap Palmer
Jingle Sheet

What to do
1. In advance, make a Jingle Sheet by using strong quilting thread to attach jingle bells to a sheet (twin or double size) in a scattered pattern covering the center section of the sheet.

2. At circle time ask the children to sit around the sheet, putting their legs under the sheet and holding the edges. Explain that they will play a listening game and will shake the sheet while the music is playing and will stop shaking the sheet when the music stops.

3. Using exaggerated movements and facial expressions adds to the fun of this game.

4. If the sheet has a design or is multicolored ask the children to touch specific designs or colors (while waiting for all the children to join the circle).

More to do
This record is excellent for children's movement activities, such as wiggle and stop, dance and stop, or stop and start any action.

★ Linda Ann Hodge, Minnetonka, MN

Senses

Making Popcorn . . . . .3+

Materials needed

Popcorn

Oil

Napkins

Popper

Cups

What to do

1. At circle time talk about the five senses and tell the children that they will use their five senses—seeing, hearing, smelling, touching and tasting.

2. Talk about and show the children the ingredients and the popper to make popcorn.

3. Explain that since the popper will get very hot and that the oil may splatter the children need to sit away from the popper.

4. Place oil and 1/4 cup of popcorn in the popper, cover with the lid and plug the popper into an outlet.

5. While the popcorn is popping talk about and listen to what is happening.

6. Ask the children which senses they are using during each step in the process of making and eating popcorn.

7. After the popcorn is finished popping, place it in cups and give to the children.

8. As the children eat the popcorn talk about the senses they are using.

More to do

Math: Compare the size of the popcorn kernels before popping and after popping. Taste various kinds of flavored popcorn and make a graph showing the children's most favorite and least favorite.

★ Cindy L. Knutson, Vermillion, SD

Music Box . . . . .3+

Materials needed

Music box

What to do

1. At circle time show the children a music box and explain that you will hide the music box and that the children will take turns trying to find it by listening to the sound and going to the area where the sound is coming from.

2. Start the music box and ask one child to leave the room while you hide the box.

3. The child returns to the room and listens to where the sound of the music is coming from. If younger children have difficulty locating the music box, give clues to help their search.

4. Repeat the activity until all children have a turn or if the group of children is large continue the activity on subsequent days.

5. Ask the children to talk about their experience in trying to find the music box and discuss the importance of the sense of hearing.

More to do

Ask children and parents to bring a music box from home on a specific day. Compare different designs, sizes, shapes and sounds of the music boxes.

★ Cathy Badorek, Bozrah, CT

Feeling With Feet . . . . .3+

Materials needed

Plastic swimming pool
Items with various textures (leaves, pillows, wood chips, sand, bubble packing paper, fabric—velvet, corduroy, water—warm, cold, with bubbles)

What to do

1. Put the swimming pool in the middle of the circle and add one of the textured materials (provide a different material on subsequent days).

2. Invite the children to take off their socks and shoes (allow time for practicing this self-help skill) and walk in the pool (help younger children avoid slipping).

3. After each child has had time to walk on the material ask the children to sit in the circle and talk about how the material felt on their feet. How is it different from feeling the same material with their hands? Toddlers are often better at describing the texture than teachers.

★ Lisa Sunbury, Cambridge, MA

Slimy and Soft Fingerpaints . . . . .3+

Materials needed

Fingerpaints
Baby oil
Smock for each child
Sink or washing area

Cornstarch
1 container for each child
Spoon for each child
Tables

What to do

1. Introduce the activity by telling the children that you have special paints that they will explore.

2. Give each child a container and a spoon.

3. Ask the children to put one spoonful (handful) of fingerpaint into their containers (with younger children you may want to help).

4. Encourage the children to explore the fingerpaint with their hands or spoons.

5. Add one spoonful of cornstarch (special soft ingredient) to each child's container.

6. Encourage the children to explore the mixture with their hands. How does it feel?

7. Add one spoonful of baby oil (slimy ingredient) to each child's container.

8. Encourage the children to explore the mixture with their hands. How does it feel now?

9. Allow time for the children to mix and explore the ingredients and talk about how the mixture feels.

10. After the children have finished ask them to wash their hands and hang up their smocks.

More to do

Language: On chart paper record the children's descriptions of what the fingerpaint felt like after each ingredient was added.

Science: Put the leftover fingerpaint in resealable plastic bags. Add these "squish bags" to the science area. Putting tape over the seal will prevent leakage.

★ Glenda Manchanda, Huber Heights, OH

Smell Game . . . . .3+

Materials needed

Film canisters (holes poked in the top with a nail or ice pick)
Fragrant substances (vanilla, almond and peppermint extracts, vinegar, lemon juice, ammonia, soap, evergreen needles slightly crushed, chocolate)
Cotton balls (to absorb liquids)

What to do

1. Put fragrances into the film canisters shortly before circle time.

2. Pass a canister around the circle and ask the children to smell it but not to say what it smells like until everyone has smelled it.

3. Ask the children to raise their hand if they recognized the smell.

4. Listen to their guesses and identify the fragrance.

5. Pass the next canister around, possibly in a different direction or at a different starting point, so that eventually everyone gets to be first to smell the canister.

More to do

Ask the children to smell one fragrance and to identify the matching fragrance from a set of three or more canisters.

Related book

The Nose by Dr. Seuss

★ Dixie Havlak, Olympia, WA

Texture Blanket . . . . .3+

Materials needed
Blanket made from different textures
Pillow case

What to do
1. In advance, sew pieces of different fabrics together to make a texture blanket.

2. Put the blanket in the pillow case and show the children the pillowcase at circle time.

3. Talk about the special blanket as you pull it out of the pillowcase and invite the children to feel the blanket and describe the textures. Name the different textures as the children feel the textures.

4. Spread the blanket in the middle of the circle so the children can continue to explore the blanket and feel the different textures. Talk about the different textures and how they feel.

More to do
Provide the children with additional pieces of materials so that they can match the pieces with the pieces on the texture blanket.

★ Susan M. Blansfield, Wilmington, DE

The Five Senses . . . . .3+

Materials needed
Book about the 5 senses (see related books)

What to do
1. At circle time talk about and read a book about the five senses.

2. After reading the book ask the children when they use their senses.

3. Ask the children questions such as, "What do you see when you look around the room? What do you hear? Can you smell anything? Touch the floor. How does it feel?"

4. Encourage the children to take off their socks and shoes (allow time for practicing this self-help skill) and walk around the room (carpeted and uncarpeted floor). Talk about how the different textures of the floor felt on their feet.

More to do
Art: Five Senses Collage—children look through magazines for pictures of noses, mouths, eyes, ears, hands and feet. Cut out the pictures and paste them on construction paper. Hang the collages on a Five Senses bulletin board.

Outdoors: Listening Walk—take the children on a walk and ask them what they hear, see and smell. Ask them to touch the grass, sidewalk, tree and ask them how it feels.

Senses

Game: Children point to their eyes, nose, mouth, ears and hands as they say the following poem.

I have two little eyes to see the blue sky with.
I have two little ears to listen to the rain go
P-L-O-P, P-L-O-P on the roof!
I have two little hands to touch my soft blanket with.
I have one little nose to smell cookies baking.
And I have one little mouth to taste a cookie with!

Language: Senses Book—start the week with a story about all five senses and on subsequent days in the week read a book about a different sense and ask children to make a collage about that sense. Compile the collages into a Five Senses book or put the collages on a Five Senses bulletin board.

Related books

City Noise by Karla Kuskin
Country Noise by Margaret Wise Brown
Find Out by Touching by Paul Showers
Follow Your Nose by Paul Showers
How You Talk by Paul Showers
Indoor Noisy Book by Margaret Wise Brown
The Listening Walk by Paul Showers
My Hands by Aliki

★ Sheri Lawrence, Louisville, KY

What Is It? .4+

Materials needed

Blindfolds
Various objects
Diaper wipe container (putting a large sock over the end will conceal an object for children who do not want to wear a blindfold)

What to do

1. At circle time talk with the children about how they can identify objects by feeling them with their hands even when they cannot see the objects.

2. Ask a child to put on a blindfold, hold an object and guess what the object is.

3. Continue until all the children have had a turn .

4. Ask the children to talk about how they could identify the objects. Discuss the shape, size, texture as providing clues.

5. After identifying the objects the children can sort the objects into categories, such as hard and soft.

More to do

Manipulatives: Place blindfolds in the puzzle area for children to wear when completing familiar puzzles.

Outdoors: Take a blind walk with the children holding onto a jump rope.

Social skills: Group the children in pairs and ask one child in each pair to wear a blindfold and ask the children to perform various tasks, include taking a walk.

Snack: Eat snack while wearing a blindfold or with eyes closed.

★ Melissa Browning, West Allis, WI

Name That Voice! . . . . .4+

Materials needed
Blindfold

What to do
1. At circle time tell the children that they will play a game in which they will try to identify a child by only hearing the child's voice.

2. Ask one child (first child) to close and cover her eyes with her hands or wear a blindfold.

3. Point to another child (second child) to gently tap the first child on the back and say, "Hi, (first child's name) I have (describe self)." The second child returns to his place in the circle.

4. The first child uncovers her eyes and tries to guess which child said "Hi." The other children can give clues if needed.

5. The second child then becomes the next child to cover his eyes.

Related book
The Listening Walk by Paul Showers

★ Nancy L. Schwider, Glen Ellyn, IL

Exploring a Guitar . . . . .4+

Materials needed
Guitar

What to do
1. At circle time talk about the sense of hearing and ask the children to listen carefully as you play one string on the guitar. Was it a quiet sound or a loud sound? Was it a high sound or a low sound?

2. Pluck a different string. Was the sound higher or lower than the first?

3. Pluck the same string while moving a finger down the frets on the neck. What happens to the sound?

4. Ask the children to take turns strumming the guitar and exploring the different sounds it makes. It will be necessary for an adult to hold the guitar, but the children can pluck or strum the strings.

5. Explain that guitars can make one more sound and tap lightly on the wood to make the "drum" sound.

More to do

Language: Talk about the parts of the guitar. Many of the words are already familiar but have different meanings to the children (neck, key, string). Talk about the words and their different meanings.

Math: Count the number of strings, keys, frets on the guitar.

Music: Have a sing-along while someone plays familiar songs on the guitar. Let children select classroom instruments to play. Have a parade or concert.

Science: Use strong rubber bands to simulate guitar strings. Put them around a hollow box and strum them. What does it sound like? How does the sound change when the rubber bands are stretched tighter?

★ Kim Arnold, Kent, OH

Counting With Your Ears . . . . .4+

Materials needed

10 pennies
Glass jar or aluminum can

What to do

1. Show children the pennies and count the pennies by lining them up and counting them.

2. Talk with the children about using their eyes to count by looking at each penny as it is counted.

3. Tell the children they will learn to count them with their ears (children find this so silly).

4. Ask the children to be very quiet as you drop the pennies one at a time into the jar or can. Ask the children to count the "plink!" sound as each penny drops and tell the children that is how they can count with your ears.

More to do

Experiment with counting other objects that make a sound, such as a clock with chimes, keys on a keyboard or piano, marbles dropped in a cup.

★ Suzanne Pearson, Winchester, VA

Hearing Impairment . . . . .5+

Materials needed

Bell
Paper
Different types of hearing aids

What to do

1. At circle time ask children to close their eyes and focus on listening for sounds.

2. Tell the children that they will hear three sounds and ask them to identify each sound after you make it.

3. Ring a bell and ask children to guess what made the sound, rip a piece of paper and wait for guesses and pretend to sneeze (achoo). Allow time for children to talk about the sounds they heard.

4. Introduce the words "hearing impaired" and explain that if people cannot hear sounds well they are described as being hearing impaired.

5. Show children different types of hearing aids (behind the ear aid, button hearing aid, amplified box) and explain how they help people to hear better.

6. Whisper to the children and explain that this is the level of sound a person with a hearing impairment might hear and that a hearing aid would help amplify the sound and make it louder.

More to do

Music: Tape record children making different noises using various items around the room (hammer and nails, metal spoons, plastic spoons, styrofoam cups, glass and metal spoon, triangles, bells, cymbals). Listen to the recording to play a sound guessing game.

Science: Make a cone telephone. Clip 1/2" off the pointed end of two cone shaped cups and attach them with three yards of string. One child talks into one telephone cone while another child stands three yards, pulls the string taunt and puts the other cone over his ear to listen.

Related books

A Button in Her Ear by Ada B. Litchfield
I Have a Sister, My Sister Is Deaf by J. Peterson
"Forgotten Language," a poem from *Where the Sidewalk Ends* by Shel Silverstein

★ Diana Reed and Debi Behr, New Wilmington, PA

It Makes Sense . . . . .4+

Materials needed

Various objects (paper clip, button, leaf, acorn, pencil, rubber band, pine cone, lemon, ball, feather, shoelace, apple, zipper, bell, orange)
Blindfold
Decorated Box

What to do

1. Place the objects in the box prior to circle time.

2. Ask children to sit in a circle.

3. Tell the children that the box is filled with many objects and they will pay a guessing game to find out what is in the box.

4. Explain that each child will have a turn to wear a blindfold and put her hand in the box and take out an object.

5. Tell the child to use her sense of smell, touch and hearing to guess what object she is holding.

6. After the child guesses what the item is, remove the blindfold and ask her to use her sense of sight to see if her guess was correct.

7. After all the children have had a turn talk about how they were able to identify objects without seeing the objects.

8. Cut apples and oranges into slices and invite the children to use their sense of smell and taste to enjoy eating the fruit.

More to do

Lay the objects on a table and ask the children to sort the objects into categories, such as food items, office supplies, natural items.

★ Dalia Behr, Ozone Park, NY

My Book of Senses ....4+

Materials needed

Magazines
Glue
Construction paper

Scissors
Markers

What to do

1. Staple six pieces of construction paper together or punch holes in the corners of the paper and tie with a piece of string.

2. Design the cover on the first page and label each of the five pages with the name of one of the five senses.

3. Ask the children to cut pictures out of magazines and sort them into five categories, one for each of the five senses.

4. Glue the pictures that relate to one of the senses on each page of the book.

5. Ask the children to talk about their pictures on each page and why they put the pictures on that page. Ask the children to describe the pictures.

More to do

Games: Play a guessing game by describing an object in the classroom and asking the other children to guess what the object is. Ask the children to close and cover their eyes with their hands and guess what is making a sound (person knocking, bell ringing).

Science: Make six scent jars (using film canisters) and put the same item in two jars (coffee, onions, flowers) and ask the children to match the jars that smell the same.

★ Mary Dacey, Portland, ME

What Do I Hear? ....4+

Materials needed

1 egg carton
Small pictures of objects that make sounds
Round wooden bead or ball

What to do

1. Glue a picture in each section of the egg carton (telephone, airplane, musical instrument, animal, car).

2. Place a bead or ball in the carton.

3. At circle time pass carton around the circle and ask each child to shake the carton. The child opens the carton, sees what picture the ball landed on and imitates the sound it makes (ringing sound for telephone, sound the animal makes).

4. The other children try to guess the picture by listening to the sound the child makes.

More to do

The children can also pantomime or act out movements representing the picture (animal, airplane) and the children try to guess what the picture is.

★ Maxine Della Fave, Raleigh, NC

What Do You Hear? Who Do You Hear? ....4+

Materials needed

Tape cassette
Tape recorder

What to do

1. Tape the voices of the children's parents without the children's knowledge. Ask an adult to help you with the logistics of recording parents in another room. Record each parent for about 30 seconds and suggest they give clues to their identity.

2. After all the parents' voices are recorded bring the tape to circle time.

3. Tell the children that you have recorded voices of special people on the tape and the children should listen to the voices and guess who is talking on the tape.

4. Talk about the clues that each parent gave after his voice is played to assist the children in recognizing their parents' voices.

5. Tape record the children's voices (talking, telling a story, singing a song).

★ Kim Jennette-Sheffield, Atlanta, GA

Senses

What's It Like to Be Blind? . . . . .4+

Materials needed

Blindfold
Noisemakers (bell, rattle, drum, horn)

What to do

1. At circle time ask the children to close their eyes and listen to you talk and walk around the room. Ask the children to tell you where you are standing.

2. Discuss the word "blind" and talk about what it means to be blind.

3. Ask one of the children to volunteer to wear a blindfold and help him walk around the room as the other children watch. Ask the blindfolded child to describe how he feels as he walks.

4. Ask other children to stand in different areas of the room and give them each a noisemaker. Ask each child in turn to make a noise and ask the blindfolded child to point to the child who is making a noise.

5. Continue the activity to give other children a turn to experience being blindfolded.

Related book

Through Grandpa's Eyes by Patricia MacLachlan

★ Kimberley Barnes, Burnettsville, IN

Visually Impaired . . . . .5+

Materials needed

Pieces of thick plastic
Child eyeglasses (with lenses removed)
Black construction paper
Clear tape

What to do

1. At circle time give each child a piece of thick plastic and ask them to look through the plastic and describe how another child or object looks (should look blurry).

2. Introduce the words "visually impaired" and explain that some people who are visually impaired have a vision that is blurry and that they usually wear glasses to help them see more clearly.

3. Show the children three pairs of child eyeglasses (with lenses removed), one pair without any lenses, one pair with thick plastic replacing the lenses and one pair with black construction paper replacing the lenses.

4. Pass each pair of glasses around the circle. Ask the children to experiment looking through the different glasses and describe the differences in what they see.

More to do

Art: Self-Portraits Wearing Glasses—children draw a picture of themselves wearing glasses. Provide mirrors and ask the children to look at their eyes closely, seeing the detail about their eyes including eye shape, lashes, pupil, eye brows and eye color. Children draw glasses around their eyes (trace the appropriate size circles). Finish the self portraits by adding other facial features.

Game: Blindfold Guessing Game—blindfold one child and ask her to feel another child's face and hair. Ask her to guess who the child is by feeling facial features and hair.

Science: Exploring Sight—experiment with different viewing apparatus, such as binoculars, magnifying glasses, cellophane paper in frames, colored net stockings stretched over hangers, mesh screening and kaleidoscopes.

Related books

All the Better to See You With by Margaret Wild
Friends in the Park by Rochelle Bunnett

★ Debi Behr and Diana Reed, New Castle, PA

Five Senses Games . . . . .5+

Materials needed

Smell and Taste Games:
Containers (with holes punched in lid)
Cotton balls
Various spices, extracts, condiments
Crackers
Plastic knife

Tactile Game:
Pillow case
Personal items (comb, brush, toothbrush, cup, fork, spoon)
Clothing items (sock, shoe, hat, mitten)
Various textures (cotton, fur, sandpaper, feathers, plastic, suede)

Auditory Game:
Instruments, noisemakers, bells
Tape of environmental sounds (car horn, train, animal sounds, baby crying, feet stomping)

Visual Game:
Pictures of common objects
Tape
Bulletin board
Large piece of paper or cloth

What to do
Smelling Game

1. Put one item (spice or extract) in each of the containers (if using an extract pour it on a cotton ball).

2. Pass the container around the circle so each child can smell the item.

3. Ask the children to identify each item and record their responses on chart paper. Compare the number of responses and determine which response was given the most times. Open the container and see if the item was correctly identified.

Tasting Game (This game is easier to play with a small group of children.)

1. Put a sample of one condiment on crackers. Blindfold the children and ask them to taste the cracker and to identify the name of the condiment.

Tactile Game

1. Put several items in a pillow case. The items can be sorted as personal items, clothing items or textures to add variety to the game.

2. Pass the pillow case around the circle. Each child selects one item to feel and describe. The child guesses the name of the item and then pulls it from the pillow case showing the other children.

Auditory Game

1. Hide the instruments and noisemakers so the children cannot see them.

2. Sound an instrument or noisemaker and ask the children to guess what made the sound.

3. Repeat the game by playing the environmental tape and ask the children to guess what is making the sound on the tape.

Visual Game

1. Tape pictures of familiar objects to a board and cover the bulletin board so children cannot see the pictures.

2. Remove the cover to allow children to see all of the pictures.

3. Cover the pictures again and then remove one picture.

4. Remove the cover and ask the children which picture is missing.

★ Lois McEwan, Levittown, NY

Our Five Senses . . . . .5+

Materials needed
Samples of Braille

What to do
1. This activity can be extended over four or five days:

Day 1: Seeing
Day 3: Touching

Day 2: Hearing
Day 4: Smelling and Tasting

2. Talk about how we learn about what's going on around us with our five senses—seeing, hearing, touching, smelling and tasting.

3. As each sense is discussed talk about what it would be like if one could not fully use that particular sense (visually impaired, blind; hearing impaired, deaf). Talk about what could help (eyeglasses, seeing-eye dog, Braille, hearing aid, sign language). On Seeing Day show samples of Braille. On Hearing Day teach the children sign language (see pages 386-393).

More to do
Seeing Day: Toilet Paper Roll Binoculars—each child will need two toilet paper rolls to paint and draw designs with markers. Attach the two rolls together with clear tape and punch two holes at the end of each roll to run yarn through the holes to make a necklace for the children to wear the binoculars around their necks. Use the binoculars inside to look at specific objects or outside at objects in nature (do not walk while looking through the binoculars).

Hearing Day: Paper Plate Shakers—each child will need two paper plates to decorate with crayons, markers. Staple the plates together (inside edges of the plates touch to create space between the plates) and leave a small opening. Fill the space with pebbles or dry beans and staple closed. The children can compare the sounds that their different shakers make.

Touching Day: Feely Board—Trace each child's hand on a piece of poster board or construction paper and ask each child to glue a different textured item (sandpaper, cotton ball, piece of fur, small piece of tile) onto each finger outline.

Games: Each day change the game, for example, (Seeing Day) ask the children to look at another child and describe what that child looks like; (Hearing Day) describe something in the classroom that makes a sound. Describing Game—a child looks around the room and says, "I'm thinking of something that is...." (describe object, one description at a time, adding descriptions until the other children guess the object).

Home connection: Ask the children to bring an object that makes a noise (Hearing Day), an object that has a distinctive aroma (Smelling Day).

Science: Seeing Day—use a prism to reflect sunlight to see and talk about the different colors. Hearing Day—provide a tape recording of various sounds for children to identify. Make a tape recording of the children's voices and ask the children to identify the voices. Touching Day—provide samples of different textures for children to feel and describe. Make a Feely Box and use different objects for the children to feel and identify (block, toy car, comb, spoon).

Senses

Related books
Seeing Day:
Arthur's Eyes by Marc Brown
My Five Senses by Aliki

Hearing Day:
The Ear Book by Al Perkins
The Indoor Noisy Book by Margaret Wise Brown

Touching Day:
Hand, Hand, Fingers, Thumb by Al Perkins
Here Are My Hands by Bill Martin, Jr. and John Archambault

Smelling and Tasting Day:
Arthur's Nose by Marc Brown
The Popcorn Book by Tomie dePaola

★ Deborah R. Gallagher, Bridgeport, CT

Shape Fun . . . . .3+

Materials needed
Poster board
Craft sticks
Glue or tape
Clear self-adhesive paper

What to do
1. In advance, cut a set of large shapes and a set of small shapes (triangle, circle, square, rectangle) from poster board. Cover the shapes with clear self-adhesive paper or laminate. Attach a craft stick to the back of each small shape.

2. Ask the children to sit on a large poster board shape during circle time.

3. Introduce the four shapes by singing the "Shape Song" to the tune of "Frère Jacques," holding up the specific small shape. Each shape is described in a new verse of the song.

> *This is a circle, this is a circle*
> *It is round, it is round.*
>
> *This is a triangle, this is a triangle*
> *It has three sides, it has three sides*
> *1-2-3, 1-2-3. (count the sides)*
>
> *This is a square, this is a square,*
> *It looks like a box, it looks like a box*
> *1-2-3-4, 1-2-3-4. (count the sides)*

4. After singing the verse for each shape, count the number of sides on each shape.

5. Sing the song again and ask the children to stand up when the shape they are sitting on is named.

6. After the game, ask each child to find something in the classroom that looks like the shape he is sitting on and bring it back to the circle.

More to do
Art: Make a shape collage, using shapes cut out of different materials.

★ Gaye Lubell, Olney, MD

Check It Out! . . . . .3+

Materials needed
A children's book
Cut-out shapes
Masking tape

What to do

1. Before reading the book to the children, randomly tape different cut-out shapes on different pages of the story. With young children use one or two simple shapes, such as circles and squares.

2. Tell the children that you have noticed something unusual about the book and encourage them to look for something unusual while you read the book.

3. After you have read the complete story, ask the children if they noticed something unusual. Show and talk about the different shapes that were on the pages of the book.

More to do

This same activity can be adapted to colors, numbers, animals.

★ Mary Volkman, Ottawa, IL

Fun With Shapes . . . . .3+

Materials needed

Construction paper
Glue
Cut-out shapes (circles, squares, triangles, rectangles)

What to do

1. Ask each child to select a shape from the cut-out shapes that she would like to glue on paper.

2. Ask the children to find objects that look like their shapes in the classroom.

3. During circle time encourage the children to draw shapes in the air with their fingers while saying the following poem.

> *Round circle, round circle, what do you see?*
> *I see a square box looking at me.*
> *Square box, square box, what do you see?*
> *I see a triangle looking at me.*
> *Triangle, triangle, what do you see?*
> *I see a rectangle looking at me.*
> *Rectangle, rectangle, what do you see?*
> *I see all the shapes looking at me.*

4. If desired, make flannel board pieces to represent the shapes in the poem.

Related song

"Shapes" on *We All Live Together* by Greg and Steve

★ Rhonda J. Murphy, Los Angeles, CA

Mailbox Shape Sorting . . . . .3+

Materials needed

3 mailboxes drawn on poster board with a mail slot
Envelopes with a shape drawn on each

What to do

1. In advance, draw three mailboxes on poster board. Cut the slots for the envelopes to go in. Draw a square on the first mailbox, a triangle on the second and a circle on the third.

2. Draw one of the three shapes on each envelope.

3. At circle time tell the children that the mail needs to be sorted by the shape on the envelope. Distribute a few envelopes to each child.

4. Children take turns putting their envelopes into the mailboxes that are labeled with the same shapes that are on their envelopes.

More to do

Place the mailboxes and envelopes in an area where the children can continue to sort the mail and put it in the mailboxes. To renew interest, prepare envelopes and mailboxes with corresponding colors, numbers, letters or names for sorting.

★ Suzanne Pearson, Winchester, VA

Musical Circles . . . . .3+

Materials needed

Large hula hoops
Record, tape or musical instruments

What to do

1. Place the hoops in the circle time area.

2. Play music and ask the children to dance or move to the music. When the music stops tell the children to stand in a circle (hula hoop).

3. Continue to play the game but each time the music stops take away one hoop.

4. If it gets crowded standing inside a hoop ask the children to put only a part of their bodies inside the hoop, or name the part of the body (arm, elbow, foot, head) for the children to put inside the hoop.

5. As the game continues and there are fewer hoops, children learn sharing and cooperation. There are no winners or losers, just fun!

More to do

Art: Do circle printing on paper cut into circles using paper cups or circle cookie cutters dipped in paint. Make circle collages using buttons or bottle caps.

Language: Find circles in the book, *Is It Red? Is It Yellow? Is It Blue?* by Tana Hoban.

Math: Take a walk looking for circle shapes around the school, playground or neighborhood.

Snack: Serve circle crackers and oranges sliced into circles.

★ Audrey Kanoff, Allentown, PA

Round and Round the Triangle Goes . . .3+

Materials needed
10'-15' piece of yarn
Cookie cutter shape or tagboard shape

What to do

1. In advance, thread a cookie cutter or a shape cut from tagboard (with a hole in the center) onto the piece of yarn.

2. Tie ends of yarn together so you have a large circle of yarn with a shape on it (like a charm on a necklace).

3. At circle time, ask the children to sit in a circle around the yarn, each holding a section of the yarn in their hands.

4. Sing the following song as children push the shape to the next child, around and around the circle. The tune is "Pop Goes the Weasel."

> *Round and round the (triangle) goes.*
> *Pass it to your neighbor.*
> *Where it stops nobody knows.*
> *STOP!*
> *Where's the (triangle)?*

5. On the word "Stop," the child who has the shape (triangle) holds it. After singing the next line "Where's the triangle?" the children say the name of the child who is holding it.

6. Once the children understand the game, ask one child to sit in the center of the circle and close her eyes. The children sing the song and when they say "Stop!" the child holding the shape (triangle) hides it in her lap. The other children also place their hands in their lap and the child in the middle of the circle tries to guess who is holding the triangle.

More to do
Art: Use shape cookie cutters to cut shapes out of playdough, clay or cookie dough.

Game: Provide children with objects of different shapes to hide and ask other children to find the objects in the room.

★ Suzanne Pearson, Winchester, VA

I'm Proud to Know My Shapes . . . . . .4+

Materials needed
Plastic or poster board shapes (1 per child)

What to do

1. Ask the children to stand in a circle with their hands behind their backs.

2. Walk around the outside of the circle, placing a shape in each child's hands. Remind the children that they should not look at their shapes.

3. Ask the children to feel the shapes they are holding and then in turn name the shapes and show the shapes to the other children.

4. Sing the following song, "I'm Proud to Know My Shapes" to the tune of "The Farmer in the Dell."

> *I'm proud to know my shapes,*
> *I'm proud to know my shapes.*
> *Follow along as I sing my song,*
> *I'm proud to know my shapes.*

Verse 1

> *A circle looks like this, (draw in air)*
> *A circle looks like this. (draw in air)*
> *It's a shape like no other shape,*
> *A circle looks like this. (draw in air)*

Other verses

> *A square looks like this.... (draw in air)*
> *A triangle looks like this.... (draw in air)*
> *A rectangle looks like this.... (draw in air)*
> *A diamond looks like this.... (draw in air)*
> *An oval looks like this.... (draw in air)*

Ending:

> *I'm proud to know my shapes,*
> *I'm proud to know my shapes.*
> *You followed along as I sang my song,*
> *I'm proud to know my shapes.*

More to do
To make a seasonal or animal bulletin board cut out a large shape representing the theme (Jack O'Lantern, Christmas Tree, Bear) and stick-pin small shapes around the large shape. Each day ask one child to place a specific shape on the large shape.

★ Carol Taylor, Alexandria, LA

What Shape Is It? . . . . .4+

Materials needed

2 milk cartons (1/2 gallon)
Scissors
Construction paper
6 cut-out shapes
Glue
Clear self-adhesive paper

What to do

1. In advance, make a shape cube by cutting two cardboard milk cartons into a square shape. Put them together, one inside the other. Cover the cube with construction paper, glue a different cut-out shape to each side of the cube and cover with clear self-adhesive paper.

2. Ask the children to sit in a circle and take turns rolling the cube.

3. The children name the shape on the top of the cube.

4. After the children are familiar with the game, ask the children to predict which shape will be on top of the cube before the cube is rolled.

More to do

Make two cubes and roll the cubes to play a variety of games. See how often the shapes on the top of each of the cubes match after rolling them. Play this game with colors or numbers.

★ Brenda Miller, Olean, NY

Stepping Stones . . . . .4+

Materials needed

10 carpet squares
Masking tape
Markers
Cube shaped tissue box
Paper

What to do

1. Make the numerals 1-10 on the top of each carpet square with masking tape.

2. With a marker draw one shape on the underside of each carpet square (triangle, square, circle, rectangle, octagon). There will be two carpet squares for each shape.

3. Cover the tissue box with plain paper. On each side draw one of the shapes listed in Step 2. On the last side of the box draw a star.

4. At circle time explain the game to the children. Ask the children to remove their shoes to protect the carpet squares from being soiled. Tell the children that you will roll the shape cube. When the children see the shape that is on the top of the cube the children put one foot on the carpet square with the same shape. If the star is on the top of the cube, the children choose which carpet square to stand on. More than one child can put a foot on a carpet square shape (increase the number of carpet squares if the group of children is large).

5. To vary the game ask the children to turn the carpet squares over to reveal the side on which the numerals are written. Talk about one of the different games that the children can play using the carpet squares. Place the squares in order from 1 to 10 or place the squares randomly on the floor. Ask the children to walk from one numeral to the next numeral in order or to put their foot on a specific numeral. Make up rules to a variety of games that will help children develop large motor skills, shape and numeral recognition skills, social play skills, taking turns and problem solving skills.

Related songs
"Over in the Meadow"
"One for the Money"

★ Terri Hersom, Gonic, NH

Making Shapes . . . . .4+

Materials needed
Scraps of wood
Hammer
Nails
Pencils
Shape patterns

What to do
1. Ask the children to choose a piece of scrap wood and show the children the shape patterns that are available for tracing.

2. Show the children how to trace the pattern of a shape with a pencil on the wood.

3. Explain to the children that each child will take a turn using the hammer to pound the nails on the line that outlines the shape on the piece of wood (prior experience in hammering nails is helpful).

Related song
"Johnny Works With One Hammer"

★ Sandra Hutchins Lucas, Cox's Creek, KY

Napkin Shapes .4+

Materials needed
Paper napkins

What to do
1. Ask the children to sit at the tables for snack time.

2. Give each child a napkin and talk about the shape of the napkins.

3. Ask the children to unfold their napkins to make other shapes (rectangle, triangle, a large square). Talk about the different shapes that were made by unfolding or folding the napkins. Ask the children to unfold their napkins to make a large square. When all the children have unfolded their napkins serve the snack on the napkins.

More to do
Provide different colors of napkins and napkins with designs. Ask the children to unfold and talk about the colors and designs on the napkins before serving the snack.

★ Linda Brink, Brookfield, OH

Now You See a Square, Now You Don't .4+

Materials needed
1' squares cut from fabric (1 for each child)

What to do
1. At circle time give each child a square cut from fabric and ask him to lay it on the floor in front of him. Ask the children to identify the shape and talk about its characteristics.

2. Ask the children to walk around the square counting each side.

3. Ask the children to use their hands and feet to cover the four corners of the square, counting each corner as they cover it. Discuss that all squares have four sides and four corners.

4. Ask the children to fold the square in half to match the sides and ask what they notice about the sides. Discuss that all four sides of a square are the same length.

5. Ask the children to experiment with folding the square in different ways. Allow time for exploration and then ask the children to show how they folded the square and to talk about the different shapes that they made.

6. Challenge the children to fold the square to make a triangle, a rectangle and a smaller square.

More to do
Art: Make mosaic pictures out of small construction paper squares (1/2" or smaller).

Math: Explore a variety of objects and identify the objects that have four parts, such as animals with four legs, furniture with four legs, cars with four wheels.

Related book *Changes, Changes* by Pat Hutchins

★ Ann P. Raiford, Norfolk, VA

Patchwork Sewing Card . . . . .4+

Materials needed
Felt squares, 2" x 2" (at least 5 each of 3 different colors)
Flannel board
Squares of lightweight cardboard, 8" x 8" (with 9 squares drawn on 1 side and 12 holes
    punched around the edges, 1 square per child)
40" length of colorful yarn (1 per child)
Crayons
The Patchwork Quilt by Valerie Flournoy

What to do
1. At circle time read *The Patchwork Quilt* and talk about the story.

2. Show the children a nine patch color combination using the felt squares and the flannel board.

3. Allow time for the children to experiment with nine patch color combinations on the flannel board.

4. Give each child a cardboard square and crayons to use in designing his own nine patch color combination.

5. After completing their patchwork design give each child a length of yarn to thread through the holes punched around the edge of the cardboard square.

6. Arrange the children's designs on a bulletin board to form a larger quilt and talk with the children about their designs.

More to do
For the older children, additional felt squares can be cut horizontally and diagonally to produce rectangles and triangles. The new shapes can be used to create more nine patch color combinations on the flannel board.

Original song
"Sewing" (Tune: "Twinkle, Twinkle, Little Star")

> *Sewing, sewing, needle and thread.*
> *We'll make a quilt to cover our bed.*
> *Blue and green and yellow and red,*
> *A colorful quilt to cover our bed.*

Related books
The Keeping Quilt by Patricia Polacco
Sam Johnson and The Blue Ribbon Quilt by Lisa Campbell Ernst

★ Christina Chilcote, New Freedom, PA

People Shapes .4+

Materials needed

Masking tape
Paper
Glue
Scissors
Camera (optional)

What to do

1. With masking tape make very large shapes on the floor—a circle, a rectangle, a square and a triangle.

2. Show the children the shapes on the floor and ask the children how many children will be needed to lie down on the masking tape to make each shape.

3. Ask that number of children to lie down on the masking tape to make each of the shapes.

4. If a camera is available, stand on a chair and take a picture looking down at each of the child created shapes.

5. After the pictures are developed, fasten the picture to a cut-out shape that matches the shape in the picture and attach to a sheet of paper.

6. Compile the sheets of paper each having a picture and the corresponding cut-out shape to make a class shape book.

More to do

Place the shape book in the reading center for the children to look at and talk about.

★ Kimberly Barnes, Burnettsville, IN

The Sidefinders . . . . .4+

Materials needed

"Official Sidefinder" badges (1 per child)
Attribute blocks (circle, square, triangle, rectangle)
Shoebox with holes cut on each end or opaque fabric bag

What to do

1. At circle time give each child a badge labeled "Official Sidefinder."

2. Talk about what it means to be a sidefinder and explain that the children will count the number of sides on each attribute block.

3. Place an attribute block in a shoebox or in a bag.

4. Pass the box or bag around the circle so that each child can feel the block without looking at it. Tell the children to count the sides silently and not to reveal how many sides they counted.

5. After all the children have felt the block show the block and together count the number of sides.

6. Continue the activity until all the blocks are passed around the circle and the children have counted the number of sides of each. Talk about the different shapes and the number of sides each has.

7. Ask the sidefinders to find objects in the classroom (or lay items on tables) and count the number of sides each has. After they have counted the number of sides ask the children to tell you so you can record it on chart paper. Allow time for the children to count the sides and then ask the children to review the results listed on the chart paper and compare the number of sides of each object the children counted. If there are discrepancies ask the children to count the number of sides together.

More to do

Art: Make shape necklaces by cutting construction paper into 1" squares, circles, triangles and rectangles. Ask the children to place the center of each shape on a piece of yarn and glue the shape to the yarn. Turn the shape over and glue a second shape (same shape) over the first shape so the yarn is between the two shapes. Continue until the yarn is full of shapes; then tie the yarn making a necklace and wear it.

Snack: Provide foods for snack that are shaped like circles (crackers, orange or cucumber slices), squares (bread with a slice of cheese), rectangles (graham crackers, slices of frozen waffles or pizza) and triangles (cheese crackers, refrigerated crescent rolls baked flat or watermelon cut in triangles).

Original song

(Tune: "Mary Had a Little Lamb")

> *Circles have just one side, just one side, just one side.*
> *Circles have just one side, triangles have three.*
> *Squares have four equal sides, four equal sides, four equal sides.*
> *Squares have four equal sides as you can plainly see.*
> *Rectangles have four sides, four sides, four sides.*
> *Rectangles have four sides, two are long and two are short.*
> *Counting sides is fun to do, fun to do, fun to do.*
> *Counting sides is fun to do. That's how we learn our shapes.*

Related books

Shapes, Shapes, Shapes by Tana Hoban
Shapes by Jan Pienkowski
Shapes by Carol Watson
Shapes by Philip Yenawine

★ Ann M. Ferruggia, Voorhees, NJ

Well-Built Quilt . . . . .4+

Materials needed

Children's sweaters or jackets

What to do

1. Show the children how to place a sweater on the floor, smoothing it so it lies flat and folding the sleeves in so that it forms a square.

2. Ask each child, one at a time, to place her jacket or sweater on the floor, laying it close to the one next to it, like quilt blocks.

3. Continue until all the children have placed their jackets on the floor. Talk with the children about how they created a quilt design using their jackets. Ask the children if any of the blocks should be rearranged to form more pleasing color combinations.

More to do

On white paper (7" x 9") draw a 1" grid. Photocopy the paper, one for each child. Cut 1" strips of paper in a variety of bright colors. Place the strips on the table and ask children to cut the strips into 1" squares (talk about how to estimate 1"). Children glue the squares into the spaces on the grid to make a pattern. (You may color sample patterns for examples.) Ask the children to center and glue their quilt papers onto 9" x 12" sheets of construction paper. Mount each child's quilt side-by-side on a wall to form a large quilt.

★ Cathy Chenoweth, Columbia, MO

Baby Square . . . . .5+
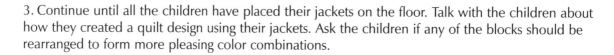

Materials needed

5" square of white paper (1 per child)

What to do

1. Using one piece of paper as a model, tell the children the following story folding the paper as you tell the story.

2. Mother Square and Father Square were very proud of their son, Baby Square (hold up square). He was such a nice boy and all of his sides were exactly the same size—just like a square should be. But Baby Square was not happy. He was tired of being a square.

3. "You could change yourself, you know," said his friend Cricket. "How?" asked Baby Square. "You are made of paper and paper folds very easily. Just fold yourself!" answered Cricket.

4. So Baby Square folded himself in half (hold up rectangle). "Look! I am a rectangle," said Baby Square. "I look just like a tall building." But Baby Square looked so different and so tall, Cricket did not recognize him and hopped away. "I didn't want to be a rectangle anyway," said Baby Square. "I'll unfold myself and try something else."

5. Baby Square unfolded himself. Then he put his top corner and the opposite bottom corner together and creased the middle. Baby Square was now a triangle (hold up triangle). "I look just like a big mountain," he thought. He was proud to be a big mountain, so he stood straight and tall and waited to be noticed. But his friends the birds flew by and never said a word.

6. "I guess no one talks to a big mountain. I will fold myself smaller." So Baby Square brought his bottom corners together and made a crease in the middle (hold up small triangle).

7. "Now I am a small mountain. Wait until everyone sees me!" Baby Square stood in the same spot for hours. More friends passed by but no one stopped. Baby Square flipped himself over and stood on his point but still no one noticed him.

8. "Humph! So much for being a mountain or even an upside-down mountain," said Baby Square. "My point is killing me. Let me fold it up." Baby Square folded his bottom point upwards until it was even with his top edge, then creased the bottom and let go of the point (hold up the paper boat that is formed).

"Look at this, I am a boat! Mother, Father come look! I am a boat and I can sail anywhere in the world!" said Baby Square.

9. Mother and Father Square cried at the sight of their Baby Square. They talked and talked but Baby Square refused to listen. They followed him to the seashore begging and pleading, but Baby Square was determined to be a boat and see the world. They watched as he set out, the waves carrying him away. "Good-bye Mother and Father," yelled Baby Square. "Oops, I'm sinking, glub, glub!" Baby Square felt himself sinking in the water, then he felt himself being lifted in the air.

10. "Baby Square," said his friends the birds, "You are paper and paper does not belong in the water. Hang on!" The birds laid Baby Square down on the seashore. Mother and Father Square unfolded him. Soon he was dry and could stand up.

11. "Let's go home," said Baby Square. "I have been a silly Baby Square. It was no fun being a tall building or a tall mountain or a small mountain. It was no fun being an upside-down mountain. And it was terrible being a boat. I am a nice square with equal sides and I am going to stay that way!"

12. Ask the children to fold their squares as you retell the story.

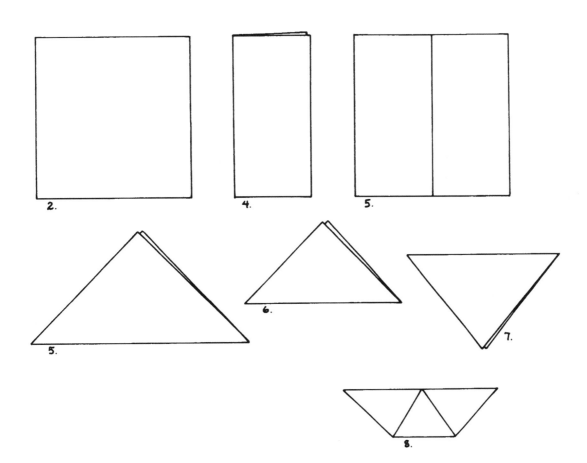

More to do

Art: Cut different shapes from poster board. Ask the children to work in groups and give each group a cut-out shape, a pair of scissors, glue and magazines. Ask the children to find pictures of objects in the magazines that are the same shape as their cut-out shape. Ask the children to cut out the pictures and glue them on the poster board shape. When completed ask the children to talk about the pictures of different objects that they cut out to match their poster board shape. Display the shape posters on the wall.

Original song

"That Is That" (Tune: "If You're Happy and You Know It")

> *A square has four sides and that is that,*
> *A square has four sides and that is that,*
> *1, 2, 3, 4 sides we name,*
> *And they are all just the same.*
> *A square has four sides and that is that.*
>
> *A rectangle has four sides and that is that,*
> *A rectangle has four sides and that is that,*
> *Two are short and two are tall,*
> *There are four of them in all,*
> *A rectangle has four sides and that is that.*
>
> *A triangle has three sides and that is that,*
> *A triangle has three sides and that is that,*
> *Come along and count with me,*
> *As you see, there's 1, 2, 3,*
> *A triangle has three sides and that is that.*

★ Carol Taylor, Alexandria, LA

Body Shapes . . . . .5+

Materials needed

Wooden or cardboard blocks

What to do

1. In advance, hang pictures of shapes in the circle time area.

2. Ask the children to choose a shape that they would like to build together.

3. Ask two children (called shapers) to be part of the shape they will build and two children (called blockers) to put the blocks where they are needed to complete the shape.

4. Ask the shapers to lie down in the middle of the circle forming two sides of the shape that was chosen. Ask the blockers to lay the blocks in places to complete the shape. Continue building shapes asking different children to be shapers and blockers.

5. As you build the shapes with the children ask them to sing the following song to the tune of "This Is the Way We Wash Our Clothes."

A triangle has three sides, three sides, three sides.
A triangle has three sides, one, two, three.

A square has four sides, four sides, four sides.
A square has four sides, all the same size.

A rectangle has four sides, four sides, four sides.
A rectangle has four sides, two short and two long.

A circle goes all the way round, all the way round, all the way round.
A circle goes all the way round in one big loop.

More to do

Art: Ask the children to use masking tape on the floor to make the outlines of different shapes. Cut shapes out of different kinds of paper.

Related song "Ring Around the Rosie"

★ Kathy Brand, Greenwood Lake, NY

Tasting Triangles . . . . .5+

Materials needed

Paper plates
Pretzel sticks

What to do

1. Talk about making shapes with pretzel sticks and give each child a plate and three pretzel sticks.

2. Ask the children what shapes they can make out of the pretzel sticks.

3. Allow time for the children to manipulate the pretzel sticks. Ask them what they are making. (Some responses I have gotten are: A, F, H, K, L, N, T, V, X, Y, Z, 4, 7, 11, triangle, arrow, hat, tent, teepee.)

4. Ask the children to make a triangle and to count the number of sides and the number of corners (angles).

5. Ask the children to take a bite out of one of the pretzels and put the remainder of the pretzel on their plate.

6. Ask the children if they can make a triangle out of the three sticks and talk about the different ways to make a triangle. Explain that a triangle is any shape that has three sides and three corners (angles); the sides do not have to be the same length.

7. Ask the children how to make a triangle out of just one pretzel stick (first they break it into three pieces). Give the children more pretzel sticks and ask them to make triangles of different sizes by breaking the sticks. After making a variety of triangles the children can enjoy the pretzels.

More to do

Language: Read or tell stories and poems that have three characters, such as *The Three Little Pigs*, *The Three Little Kittens*, or *The Three Bears*.

Related book *Circles, Triangles, Squares* by Tana Hoban

★ Ann P. Raiford, Norfolk, VA

What Am I Doing? . . . . .4+

Materials needed

None needed

What to do

1. At circle time talk about how people pantomime by using motions to act out a behavior without using words. Explain that pantomime is a way of talking without saying anything.

2. Pantomime or ask a child to pantomime an activity, such as eating, combing hair, sleeping. Other children guess what is being said. Show children another way of communicating without talking by drawing shapes in the air. Ask children to identify the shapes and talk about how they knew the shapes without hearing the names of the shapes.

3. Older children can invent their own sign language for actions or objects.

More to do

Sign language can be used in any curriculum area. The children can make up their own signs for transportation, sports, community helpers. Introduce sign language vocabulary and teach the children to finger spell their names. Any song or fingerplay that uses motions is similar to using sign language in a song or fingerplay.

★ Brenda Miller, Olean, NY

Sign Language: Please & Thank You . . .4+

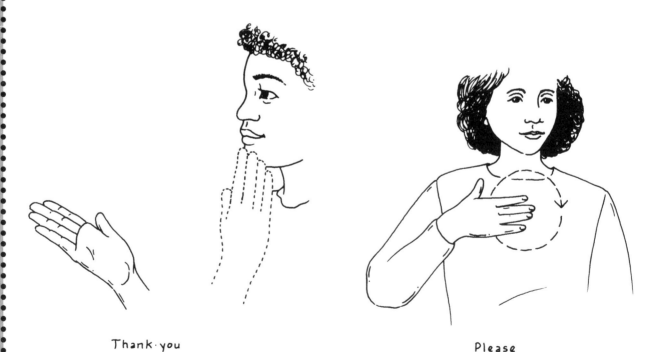

Thank-you

Please

Materials needed
None needed

What to do
1. Introduce the signs for "Please" and "Thank you."

2. Ask the children to copy you, saying and signing "Please" and "Thank you."

3. Give the children examples of different situations and ask them which sign they would use. "If you asked someone to give you a cup, what would you say and sign? If someone helped you up after you fell down, what would you say and sign ?"

More to do
Encourage children to use these signs in the classroom. Remind the children to use the "Please" and "Thank you" words and signs at home, too.

★ Nancy Dentler, Bay City, TX

Signing Hello . . . . .4+

Materials needed
Poster of sign language alphabet (optional)

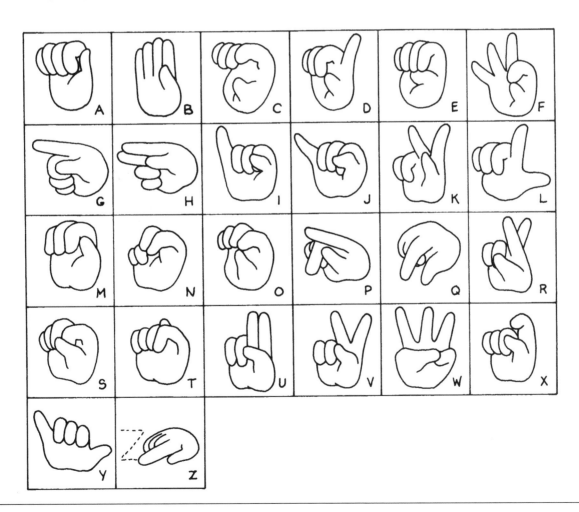

What to do

1. At circle time show the children a poster of the sign language alphabet, practicing each letter.

2. Help each child find and practice the first letter in her own name. Or ask the children to find the first letters of their names on the sign language alphabet poster and to practice signing the letters.

3. Sing the following circle hello song, allowing each child to say the first letter of her name in sign language.

Original song

(Tune: "Goodnight Ladies")

Hello (child's name),
Hello (child's name),
Hello (child's name),
It's nice to see you here.

★ Laleña L. Williams, Beacon, NY

Good Morning to You . . . . .4+

Materials needed

Recording of the song "Good Morning" by Greg and Steve
Sign language book, such as *Sign Language Made Simple* by Edgar D. Lawrence

What to do

1. At circle time play the recording of "Good Morning" and ask the children to sing along.

2. Read the book *A Button in Her Ear*, a story of a young hearing impaired girl, or a similar story.

3. Explain to the children that children who are born with severe hearing impairments cannot talk by using their voices; they learn to "talk" by making special signs with their hands to represent words. Tell the children that you know how to sing the "Good Morning" song in sign language.

4. Play the "Good Morning" song again. Encourage the children to sing along as you sign the words.

5. Show the children how to form each separate sign using their hands. Play the song again while the group sings along in sign language.

Good   morning   to   you.

More to do

Language: Animal name signs are easy to learn. Look up the sign names for familiar farm and zoo animals in *The Joy of Signing*. Copy the symbols from the book on a card and place it under a picture of the animal in the reading center. Encourage the children to visit the center and to try to form the signs. Talk about other ways we can express ourselves without using words. Ask the children to show you that they are (angry, happy, sad, afraid, surprised) without using any words. After the children have demonstrated several emotions, explain that they have been using what is known as body language. Throughout the day use body language to communicate with the children.

Related books

A Button in Her Ear by Ada B. Litchfield
Signs For Me: Basic Sign Vocabulary for Children, Parents and Teachers by Ben Bahan and Joe Dannis
The Joy of Signing by Lottie L. Riekehof

★ Virginia Jean Herrod, Columbia, SC

Sign Language: Yes and No ....4+

Materials needed

None needed

What to do

1. Show children the sign for "yes" and explain that the sign looks like a fist nodding yes.

2. Ask the children to answer "yes" in sign language to questions such as, "Is today a school day? Are you wearing shoes?"

3. Show children the sign for "no" and explain that the sign looks like a thumb and two fingers pinching.

4. Ask the children to answer "no" in sign language to questions such as, "Is today Sunday? Does a circle have four sides?"

5. Ask the children questions that can be answered by either "yes" or "no" in sign language.

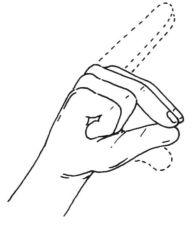

No

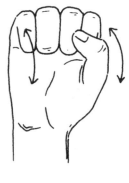

Yes

More to do

Ask children to ask each other questions that can be answered by "yes" or "no" in sign language.

Art: Children draw pictures that represent possible or impossible situations to show the other children. Each child shows her picture and asks the other children if her picture is possible (such as wearing a winter coat and hat on a snowy day) and the other children sign "yes." A child could draw a silly (impossible) picture (such as wearing a swimming suit on a snowy day) and the children sign "no." The children respond with signs for "yes" and "no" when answering questions in the classroom.

★ Nancy Dentler, Bay City, TX

Sign Language: Stop and Go . . . . .4+

Materials needed

None needed

What to do

1. At circle time introduce the signs for "stop" and "go."

2. Start counting aloud until the children tell you "stop" in sign language. Start counting again when the children tell you "go" in sign language.

3. Ask the children to clap, sing, pat their heads or any body movement until you tell them "stop" in sign language. Ask the children to start again when you tell them "go" in sign language.

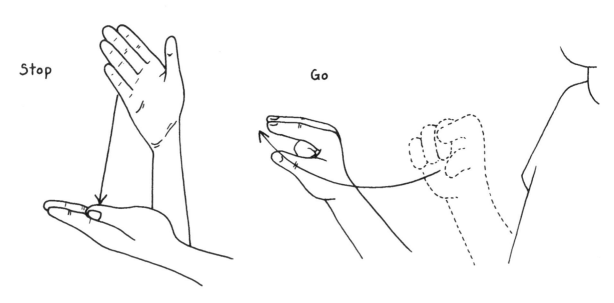

Stop

Go

More to do

When giving directions to children, use sign language for "stop" and "go." When the children are playing with toy cars or with tricycles on the playground, a child can direct traffic by signing "stop" and "go."

★ Nancy Dentler, Bay City, TX

Sign Language: Weather ....4+

Materials needed
Sign language chart of weather signs

What to do
1. Introduce weather signs to the children, such as sun, wind, rain, lightning, thunder, snow. Ask the children to sign and say the words representing weather conditions.

2. Sign the words again and ask the children to tell you what word you are signing.

More to do
Language: Place weather related items, such as sunglasses and sunscreen for sun, mittens for snow, an umbrella for the rain in a large bag. Ask the children to select an item from the bag and sign the correct weather word.

Science: Show the children the local weather forecast from the newspaper for the week. Make a weather prediction chart and ask the children to predict the weather for the week and compare their predictions with the newspaper forecast. Use the weather signs as you talk about the weather charts.

★ Nancy Dentler, Bay City, TX

Sun

Place right C against side of right eye.

Wind

Five shape both hands, palms facing, tips out. Swing back and forth.

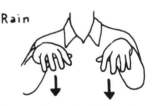

Rain

Claw shape both hands, palms down. Move down sharply two or three times.

Lightning

Hold right index finger up and zigzag down.

Thunder

S shape both hands. Draw left S back while moving right S forward. Repeat.

Snow

Five shape both hands, palms down. Wiggle fingers while moving down slowly.

Sign Language: Farms . . . . .4+

Materials needed
Sign language chart of farm signs

What to do

1. Introduce signs to the children, such as farm, farmer, barn, horse, cow, pig, sheep, duck. Ask the children to sign and say the words representing farms.

2. Sign the words again and ask the children to tell you what word you are signing.

More to do

Art: Give each child a ball of clay and ask the children to make a farm animal and tell the other children the name of the animal by signing the name.

Game: Sign the name of a farm animal and ask the children to pretend to be that animal by making the sound the animal makes, such as cows moo, ducks quack, horses neigh, sheep baa and pigs oink.

Language: Make up riddles for different farm animals, such as "I have a beak and love to quack. The water rolls right off my back. Who am I?" "I have a warm and woolly coat and sometimes I am friends with goats. Who am I?" The children answer by signing the name of the animal.

★ Nancy Dentler, Bay City, TX

Farm	Farmer	Barn	Horse
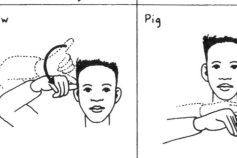	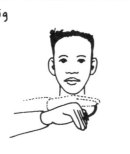	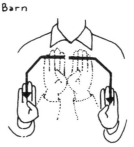	
Five shape right hand, palm in, tips left. Place thumb on left side of chin and draw across to right side.	Make sign for FARM plus sign for PERSON: palms facing, move down.	B shape both hands, thumb knuckles touching. Draw apart and down outlining shape of barn.	H shape right hand, thumb extended. Place thumb on right temple. Flap H fingers down twice.
Cow	Pig	Sheep	Duck
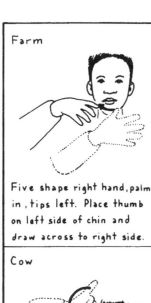	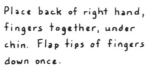	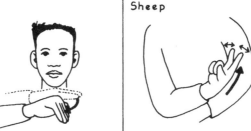	
Place thumb of right Y on right temple and twist forward.	Place back of right hand, fingers together, under chin. Flap tips of fingers down once.	Clip together tips of right V, palm up, on left forearm (as if clipping wool). Repeat.	Snap thumb and index and middle fingers together at mouth (to indicate duck quacking).

Sign Language: Counting One
Through Five . . . . .4+

Materials needed
Sign language chart of numbers, 1-5

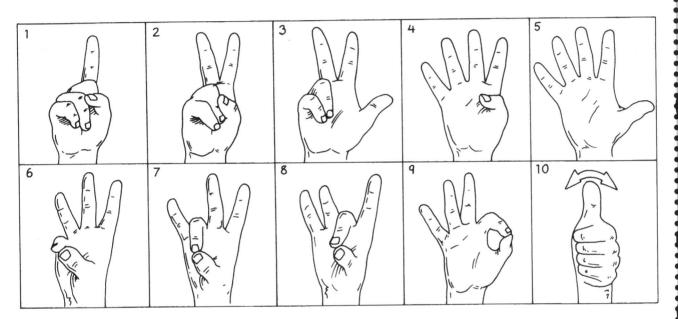

What to do
1. Introduce the signs for numbers 1, 2, 3, 4 and 5 to the children.

2. Ask the children to sign the numbers with you.

3. Show the children the signs for numbers 1 through 5 and ask the children to identify the number as you sign it.

4. Ask the children to work with a partner in counting from 1 to 5 together while making the sign for each number.

5. Ask the children to put the correct number of objects, such as seashells, milk bottle caps, plastic animals in each box.

More to do
Language: Print the words one through five on cards and ask the children to read the words and show you the number in sign language.

Math: Show children groups of objects (from 1 to 5) and ask them to tell you how many objects are in each group by signing the number. Label five boxes with pictures of hands signing numbers 1 through 5.

★ Nancy Dentler, Bay City, TX

Sign Language: Red, White & Blue . . . .4+

Materials needed

Sign language chart of colors red, white and blue
Paper and marker

What to do

1. Show the children a red piece of paper and introduce the sign for "red." Ask the children to practice making the sign with you. Do the same with the signs for "white" and "blue."

2. Show the children objects that are red, objects that are white and objects that are blue. As you show the children each object ask the children to sign the color for each object.

3. Ask the children to look at their clothing to see if they are wearing red, white or blue clothing and to make the appropriate sign for the color they are wearing. Ask the children to look for one of these colors in the classroom and ask them to sign red, white or blue when they find that color in the classroom.

More to do

Art: Make a red, white and blue July 4th fireworks display. Ask each child to use red and blue food coloring plastic drip bottles to drip red and blue food colors on a disposable white coffee filter. The filter paper will "explode" in a red, white and blue fireworks design. After the food colors have dried, punch a hole in the top of the filter paper and ask each child to sign either "red" or "blue" to choose the color of pipe cleaner to use as a hanger for her fireworks display.

★ Nancy Dentler, Bay City, TX

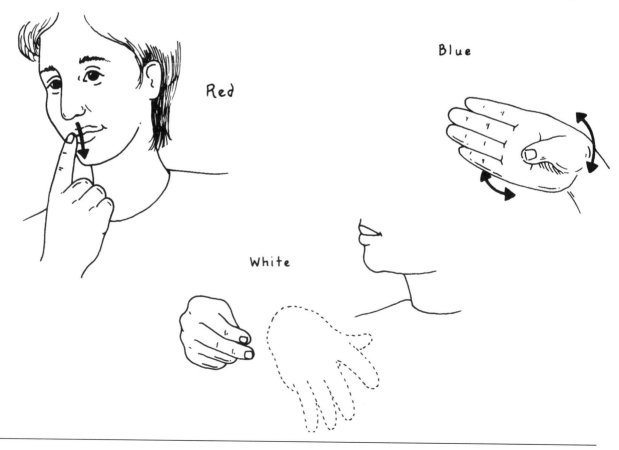

Red

Blue

White

Sign Language: Yellow, Pink & Green . .4+

Materials needed

Sign language chart for colors yellow, pink and green

What to do

1. Show the children a yellow piece of paper and introduce the sign for "yellow." Ask the children to practice making the sign with you. Do the same with the signs for "pink" and "green."

2. Show the children objects that are yellow, objects that are pink and objects that are green. As you show the children each object ask the children to make the correct color sign for each object.

3. Ask the children to look at their clothing to see if they are wearing yellow, pink or green clothing and to make the appropriate sign for the color they are wearing. Ask the children to look for one of these colors in the classroom and ask them to sign yellow, pink or green when they find that color in the classroom.

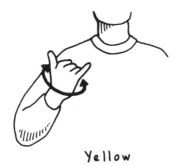

Yellow

Pink

Place middle finger tip of
right P on lower lip and brush
down to chin twice.

Green

More to do

Art: Cut springtime eggs from yellow, pink and green wallpaper sample books and ask children to sign the name of the colors of their eggs.

★ Nancy Dentler, Bay City TX

Sign a Rainbow . . . . .4+

Materials needed

Felt board
Felt pieces (red, yellow, green, blue, pink and white)

What to do

1. At circle time put each colored felt piece on the felt board as you say the name of the color and show the sign for each color. Ask the children to practice making the signs with you (see illustrations on this page and on page 394).

2. As you take each color off the felt board ask the children to make the sign with you.

3. After the children have practiced signing the names of the colors, sign the name of a color and ask the children to say the name of that color.

4. To challenge the children repeat Step 1 and then cover the felt board and remove a color. Show the children the remaining colors on the board and ask the children to sign the name of the color that is missing.

Related books

American Sign Language: A Beginning Course by Catherine Kettrick
Signing: How to Speak With Your Hands by Elaine Costello
Posters and flash cards are available from the National Association for the Deaf, 814 Thayer Avenue, Silver Spring, MD 20910 or contact the agency or organization in your area that works with the deaf.

★ Sandy Carr, Swanton, OH

Sign Language: My Telephone Number . .5+

Materials needed
Sign language chart of numbers

What to do
1. Introduce the signs for numbers 1, 2, 3, 4 5, 6, 7, 8, 9 and 0 to the children (see illustrations on page 393).

2. Ask the children to sign the numbers with you.

3. Show the children the signs for numbers 1 through 9 and 0 ask the children to identify the number as you sign it.

4. After each child can tell you his phone number and can write it, it is time to learn the phone number in sign language. Practice signing each child's phone number with the child until she can sign it alone.

More to do
Home connection: After the children take the phone book home, family members can add phone numbers important to their family. (Include a list of the category names of typically called numbers, such as drug store, library, pizza delivery service.)

Language: Make a family phone number book with each child's phone number on a different page. Photocopy the pages, add a few blank pages and staple a book for each child. Ask the children to decorate their books and give them to their families.

★ Nancy Dentler, Bay City, TX

Twelve Days of Christmas—
Sing and Sign .5+

Materials needed
Words for the song "The Twelve Days of Christmas"

What to do
1. At circle time sing the song "The Twelve Days of Christmas" using motions to act out the words.

2. After the children have practiced signing numbers ask the children to sign the numbers as they sing or listen to the numbers in the song.

More to do
Math: Review counting 1-12, then reverse 12-1, using a flannel board or fingers.

Fingerplay
"The Twelve Days of Christmas"

> *On the first day of Christmas my true love gave to me*
> *A partridge in a pear tree (fingertips touching, stretch arms over your head)*
> *...two turtle doves... (with both hands, touch thumb and forefinger several times to*
>   *imitate a bird's beak, keeping your hands by your mouth all the while)*
> *...three French hens... (put hands under each armpit and "flap your wings")*
> *...four calling birds... (pretend you are calling with both hands cupped near your mouth)*
> *...five golden rings... (show your hand, palm out, spread your fingers and wiggle them)*
> *...six geese a-laying... (squat down with arms folded like wings)*
> *...seven swans a-swimming... (pretend you are swimming)*
> *...eight maids a-milking... (pretend you are milking a cow)*
> *...nine ladies dancing... (twirl around once with a finger on your head)*
> *...ten lords a-leaping... (jump in place)*
> *...eleven pipers piping... (pretend you are playing a flute)*
> *...twelve drummers drumming... (pretend you are playing a drum)*

Related book
Talk to the Deaf by Lottie Riekehof

★ Teresa Jarmuz, Lancaster, NY

Sign Language

Mitten Day .3+

Materials needed
Mittens (1 pair belonging to each child)

What to do
1. In advance, send a note to parents asking them to send a pair of their child's mittens to school prior to Mitten Day.

2. On Mitten Day ask each child to show the other children his mittens and to describe their appearance.

More to do
Art: Paint at the easel while wearing mittens. Sponge paint with mitten shapes.

Language: Read *The Mitten* by Jan Brett and talk about the story. Ask the children to act out "The Three Little Kittens."

Large motor: Make snowballs out of white pantyhose or paper and throw snowballs while wearing mittens.

Water table: Put crushed ice in the water table and make snowballs.

★ Jennifer Joy Lee, San Antonio, TX

My Favorite Stuffed Friend . . . . .3+

Materials needed
Stuffed animals (each child brings 1 from home)
Paper, crayons, markers
Paint and brushes

What to do
1. In advance, send a note to parents asking their child to bring a favorite stuffed animal on Favorite Friend Day.

2. At circle time talk about the children's stuffed animals and ask the children to tell the other children about their animals.

More to do
Art: Ask the children to bring their stuffed animals to the art center. Provide paper and crayons for the children to trace their animals and then color the tracings with crayons, markers or paint.

Outdoors: Spread a blanket outdoors and enjoy a picnic with stuffed friends.

★ Sandra Hutchins Lucas, Cox's Creek, KY

Pool Party ･･････････････････ .3+

Materials needed
Wading pool
Lawn sprinkler
Sandbox
Water table

What to do
1. In advance, send invitations to children and their parents to attend a Pool Party.

Dear Children and Parents,

    On _____ we are having a Pool Party at school. You are asked to wear your bathing suits under your clothes to school on that day. Please bring dry clothes to change into after the Pool Party. Also bring a beach towel and beach toys, such as shovels, sifters and buckets. We will have a picnic lunch at the Pool Party.

                Sincerely,

                Teacher's Name

2. Set up the wading pool and the lawn sprinkler on a grassy area near the sandbox in the morning.

3. At circle time talk with the children about the Pool Party and the activities that will be available during the day.

4. Invite the parents to be "lifeguards" near the wading pool and lawn sprinkler.

5. Encourage the children to play in the wading pool, lawn sprinkler and sandbox. Enjoy an outdoor picnic.

6. Take photographs throughout the day to be compiled in a class book.

More to do
Home connection: Invite the children to take the class book home to share with their families.

Writing: Show the photographs to the children and ask them to dictate stories about what they did at the Pool Party. Record what the children say about the different photographs and compile the pages into a class book. Read the book to the children and then place the book in the reading center for the children to look at and talk about the Pool Party.

Related books
A Beach Day by Douglas Florian
Big Al by Andrew Clements
A House for Hermit Crab by Eric Carle
Moe the Dog in Tropical Paradise by Diane Stanley
One Morning in Maine by Robert McCloskey

★ Barbara Saul, Eureka, CA

Ribbons and Bows . . . . .3+

Materials needed

Ribbons and bows
Large box or bag

What to do

1. Place the ribbons (cut in various lengths) and the bows in the box or bag and bring it to circle time. Ask the children to guess what is inside.

2. Give the children hints, such as it is often on top of a birthday gift, it can be tied in a knot, it can be worn in a girl's hair.

3. After the children guess what is in the box or bag, show the ribbons and bows to the children and talk about how they are used, the colors, the textures.

More to do

Art: Wrap boxes and ask the children to add ribbons and bows for a three-dimensional art project. Invite the children to make collages with the ribbons and bows. Cut a whole in the center of a paper plate and then decorate the plate with ribbons and bows to create a wreath.

Fine motor: Encourage the children to tie ribbons in knots.

Math: Count and sort the ribbons and bows according to color and texture.

Social skills: Plan an Unbirthday Party with the children. Decorate the room with ribbons and bows. Bake an unbirthday cake for snack. Sing "Happy Unbirthday."

★ Susan Rinas, Parma, OH

Slumber Party . . . . .3+

Materials needed

Cotton swabs, such as Q-Tips®
Paper towels
Bedtime story
Mats or blankets

Toothbrushes
T-shirts
Recorded music (soft instrumental)

What to do

1. In advance, send a note to parents telling them about the Slumber Party and asking that their child bring a toothbrush and an adult-size T-shirt on the day of the Slumber Party.

2. At circle time, ask the children to pretend that it is very late at night and you are inviting them to a slumber party. Ask the children what they do to get ready for bed at night and talk about their responses.

3. Tell the children that first they will brush their teeth (provide Q-Tips® for any children who do not bring a toothbrush). Talk about brushing carefully (give each child a paper cup of water at a sink area if available).

4. Next talk about washing their faces and hands. Give each child a paper towel at a sink area (if available).

5. Tell the children that it is time to put on pajamas and ask them to slip their T-shirts (provide extra shirts if needed) over their clothes and pretend that the T-shirts are pajamas.

6. Ask the children to lay their mats or blankets on the floor and to lay or sit quietly on their "beds" while you read them a bedtime story.

7. Turn on soft music and ask the children to lie down and "pretend to sleep" (darken the room).

8. After about 15 minutes (depending on the age of the children), turn off the music, turn on the lights and announce "Good Morning!"

9. Ask the children to fold up the mats and blankets, take off their pajamas and "go back to school."

Related books
The Bedtime Book by Kathy Henderson
Best Friends Sleep by Jacqueline Rogers
Dirty Kurt by Mary Serfozo
The Moonlit Journey by Peter O'Donnell
We Got Here Together by Kim Stafford

★ Cathy Chenoweth, Columbia, MO

The Circus . . . . .3+

Materials needed
Books about the circus (see related books)

What to do
1. At circle time read stories and poems about the circus.

2. Sing the song below and ask the children to fill in the blank:

> *Let's go to the circus, the circus, the circus,*
> *Let's go to the circus, we can see* _____.

(Move like the animal or perform the circus act that the children identify.) To add variety to the song verses make the sound the animal makes or instead of saying the word "see" substitute "eat" or "hear."

More to do
Art: Draw pictures of events that are at the circus. Make clown puppets.

Dramatic play: Create a circus in the room.

Field trip: Visit a circus in the area.

Snack: Make popcorn for snack time.

Related books

Circus by Lois Ehlert
Jingle the Christmas Clown by Tomie dePaola
Mirette on the High Wire by Emily McCully
Paddington at the Circus by Michael Bond
Peter Spier's Circus by Peter Spier

★ Kay McAlpine, Dunkirk, OH

Camping . . . . .4+

Materials needed

Pictures of camp sites
Camping gear (canteen, mess kit, first aid kit, backpack, sleeping bag, flashlight, toilet paper, compass, tent, lantern)
Large bag

What to do

1. Show pictures of people camping and talk about what camping is like. Ask any children who have camped to tell the other children about their experiences.

2. Show the children the items of camping gear and talk about what each is used for at the camp site.

3. Place the small items of camping gear in a large bag and ask a child to feel and describe one item. The child guesses the name of the camping gear, shows the other children the item and passes it around the circle so all the children can examine it.

4. Continue the guessing game with other camping gear items in the bag.

5. Build a pretend campfire in the middle of the circle with blocks and tell stories and sing camp songs.

More to do

Art: Make stars—use white chalk to make stars (older children can draw constellations) on large sheets of blue or black paper. Tape the paper to the ceiling (if possible) or against a wall and turn off the lights. Children shine a flashlight on the stars in the darkened room.

Game: Play Whooo's There? Turn off the lights. One child holds a flashlight while other children hide in the room. When the child with the flashlight sees another child, she says "Whooo's there?" and shines the light on the other child. Children take turns with the flashlight.

Language: Environmental Sounds—play an environmental or animal tape and ask children to identify the sounds.

Science: Explore nature items, such as rocks, pine cones, branches.

★ Mary Horridge, St. Louis, MO

Autumn Hoedown . . . . .4+

Materials needed
Square dance records or tapes

What to do
1. In advance, send a note to parents telling them about the Autumn Hoedown and ask that their children wear country or western clothes, such as calico or plaid shirts and jeans. Also ask if any children are allergic to hay or straw.

2. Decorate the room for the Autumn Hoedown, with scarecrows, pumpkins and bales of straw or hay (if straw or hay is available and children are not allergic to it).

3. At circle time talk with the children about a hoedown and explain that in certain regions of the country people celebrate the end of the harvest season with a square dance party.

4. Talk about the autumn decorations in the room and about the western style clothing the children are wearing.

5. Play square dance music and show the children a simple square dance step. (Make up square dance steps if you are not familiar with square dancing. The children will enjoy just dancing to the music.)

More to do
Art: Make paper plate autumn wreaths to hang on the door. Cut the center part out of the paper plates. Glue small strips of yellow construction paper on the paper plate to look like straw. Glue cut-out orange pumpkins and fall colored leaves. For a wreath variation collect colorful leaves and acorns and tape or glue them to the paper plate.

Cooking: Invite parents to a hoedown picnic. Put checkered table cloths on the tables. Serve fried chicken, corn, cornbread, biscuits, apple cider and fruit cobbler.

Related songs
"Thank God I'm a Country Boy" and "Grandma's Feather Bed" by John Denver

★ Penni L. Smith and Donna Karnes, Riverside, CA

Pirate Treasure Hunt . . . . .5+

Materials needed
Pictures of pirates and old ships
Wooden box or container
Scraps of costume jewelry
Flattened bottle caps (for coins) or play coins
Gold spray painted play coins and stones (gold nuggets)
Treasure map

What to do
1. In advance, send a note to parents telling them about the Pirate Treasure Hunt and ask that their children dress to look like pirates on that day.

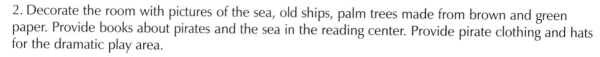

2. Decorate the room with pictures of the sea, old ships, palm trees made from brown and green paper. Provide books about pirates and the sea in the reading center. Provide pirate clothing and hats for the dramatic play area.

3. Prior to circle time bury a box of treasure (with costume jewelry, play coins, spray painted stones) outside in the sandbox or play area.

4. At circle time show pictures and talk about pirates.

5. Tell the children about the hidden treasure box and that they are going on a treasure hunt. Show the children a treasure map (that gives directions and clues) to use in hunting for the treasure. Take the children outside to the play area and help them follow the map (decipher clues, such as walk twelve steps east of the tallest tree) to where the box of treasure is buried.

6. Help the children dig up the treasure box and divide the booty.

More to do

Art: Grocery Bag Treasure Maps—tear bags apart to make pieces of paper with ragged edges and crumble the paper to make it look old. Draw landmarks (located on the play area or neighborhood) on the pieces of paper or cut out pictures of landmarks and glue them on the maps. Children can use their maps on treasure hunts.

Language: Read stories and talk about pirates, the sea, famous pirates—the ships they sailed, the way they dressed and the treasure they hunted.

Original song

"I'm Patch Eye the Pirate Man" (Tune: "Popeye the Sailor Man")

> Oh, I'm Patch Eye, the Pirate man
> I roam the Caribbean
> I sail on my ship
> Taste salt on my lips
> 'Cause I'm Patch Eye, the Pirate Man.
>
> I look for rich jewels and gold
> With an old map that I stole
> I dig and I dig
> And sweat like a pig
> 'Cause I'm Patch Eye, the Pirate Man.

★ Donna Karnes and Penni Smith, Riverside, CA

California Gold Rush . . . . .5+

Materials needed
Gold spray painted rocks
Sand
Sand table or large tub
Aluminum pie pans
Chinese food take-out boxes or containers
Paper towels

What to do
1. In advance, use gold spray paint on rocks and mix the rocks with sand in a sand table or large tub. Add water to the table or tub so that the sand and rocks are submerged.

2. At circle time talk with the children about the Gold Rush and explain how people panned for gold.

3. Show the children the technique of panning for gold (scoop some sand and water into a pie pan and swirl the water around and out of the pan to reveal the gold nuggets.

4. During choice time ask two children to pan for gold at a time. After finding the nuggets ask the children to store the nuggets in their containers.

More to do
Art: Make gold rush wall hangings from paper plates. Paint paper plates yellow and sprinkle with gold glitter. When the plate is dry, glue a gold nugget in the center of the plate. Label the plate with the current date and the name of the Gold Rush prospector.

Language: Read books and talk about the California Gold Rush in 1848, current mining for gold, how and where gold is found, ways gold is used.

Original song
(Tune: "She'll Be Comin' 'Round the Mountain")

> *She'll be fryin' eggs for breakfast when she comes (sizzle, sizzle)*
> *She'll be fryin' eggs for breakfast when she comes (sizzle, sizzle)*
> *She'll be fryin' eggs for breakfast*
> *She'll be fryin' eggs for breakfast*
> *She'll be fryin' eggs for breakfast*
> *When she comes.*

Additional verses:

> *She'll be washin' clothes on a washboard when she comes.... (rub, rub)*
> *She'll be choppin' wood for a fire when she comes.... (chop, chop)*
> *She'll be swimmin' in the fish pond when she comes.... (splash, splash)*

Related songs
"Oh, Susanna" by Stephen Foster
"Clementine"
"Sweet Betsy From Pike's"

★ Penni Smith and Donna Karnes, Riverside, CA

Winnie the Pooh Day . . . . .5+

Materials needed
Winnie the Pooh (and friends) stuffed animals
Winnie the Pooh pictures and posters
Books by A. A. Milne including *Now We Are Six*
Orange balloons and streamers
Peanut butter and honey sandwiches (cut in bear shapes with cookie cutters)

What to do
The day before:

1. Ask the children to help prepare the room for the Winnie the Pooh Day celebration. Put up posters and orange balloons and streamers.

Winnie the Pooh Day:

2. Show the children Winnie the Pooh pictures and stuffed animals and talk about the characters in the Winnie the Pooh stories.

3. Read stories about Winnie the Pooh or poems in *Now We Are Six*.

4. During choice time provide props and encourage children to act out stories based on Winnie the Pooh themes.

5. Ask the children to help prepare peanut butter and honey sandwiches for a celebration snack. Provide bear-shaped cookie cutters for the children to use in cutting the sandwiches (save the scrap pieces for eating too).

★ Margaret Howard, Northglenn, CO

Eensy Weensy and Friends . . . . .3+

Materials needed
Pictures of spiders (small, medium and large)

What to do
1. At circle time sing "The Eensy Weensy Spider" using the hand motions (see related song).

2. Explain that some spiders are medium sized like the Eensy Weensy Spider. Show pictures and talk about spiders of various sizes. Explain that some spiders are very, very tiny and ask them to make a tiny spider using their finger tips. Ask the children to sing the song again but this time ask them to make tinsy weensy motions with their fingertips and to use a high pitched tinsy, weensy voice to sing this version of the song using the words "Tinsy Weensy Spider."

3. Talk about the different way the children sang the song for each of the two sizes of spiders. Tell them that now they will sing about a hugh spider. Model a loud, deep voice for the children as you sing the song again and show the big motions to use with the song (place your hands on your opposite elbow and do a walking or alternating motion with your arms). Call this the Hugi Googi Spider. Ask the children to sing the song using the deep voice, the big motions and substituting the words "Hugi Googi Spider" for "Eensy Weensy Spider."

More to do
Show the children cutouts of small, medium and large spiders that are described in the song. Act out how the Tinsy Weensy, Eensy Weensy and Hugi Googi Spiders would act.

Original song
"There's a Spider" (Tune: "If You're Happy and You Know It")

> *There's a spider on my (arm), on my (arm).*
> *There's a spider on my (arm), on my (arm).*
> *There's a spider on my (arm), on my (arm), on my (arm),*
> *There's a spider on my (arm), on my (arm).*

Repeat the song each time substituting a different body part for "arm."

Related song
"The Eensy Weensy Spider"

> *The eensy weensy spider (touch opposite thumbs and pointer)*
> *Went up the water spout. (fingers alternate upward)*
> *Down came the rain*
> *And washed the spider out. (hands at chest level and then outward)*
> *Out came the sun, (hands meet over head, arms form a circle)*
> *And dried up all the rain. (wiggle fingers in upward motion)*
> *And the eensy weensy spider (upward thumb and pointer finger motion)*
> *Climbed up the spout again.*

For other versions of the song substitute the words "Tinsy Weensy" and "Hugi Googi" for "Eensy Weensy."

★ Sandra Nagel, White Lake, MI

Marble Roll Spider Web . . . . .3+

Materials needed

Pictures of spiders
9″ x 12″ sheet of black construction paper (1 per child)
White tempera paint
Marbles
Box lid or shallow pan (approximately 9″ x 12″)
Egg carton cups (1 per child)
Small wiggly eyes (2 per child)
Red pipe cleaners (4 per child)
Glue

What to do

1. At circle time show the children pictures of spiders, noting colors, sizes and shapes. Look at pictures of spider webs and explain how the webs are made by the spiders. Explain that spiders can be helpful by eating insect pests.

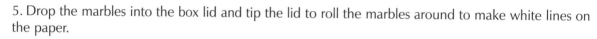

2. Talk with the children about making pretend spider webs and explain that during choice time each child will make one.

3. Show the children how to make one by placing a sheet of paper in the box.

4. Use a spoon to dip two marbles into white paint to coat the marbles.

5. Drop the marbles into the box lid and tip the lid to roll the marbles around to make white lines on the paper.

6. Glue four pipe cleaners side by side on the paper to make spider legs.

7. Glue an egg carton cup over the legs so that the eight ends stick out from the cup. When dry, bend the pipe cleaners to look like spider legs.

8. Glue two wiggly eyes on the cup to look like spider eyes.

More to do

Art: Provide yarn and paper plates (with punched holes) for children to thread the yarn through the holes to make pretend spider webs.

Language: Ask the children to name a topic they would like to know more about and show the children how to make a story web about the topic by adding a new line for each of the children's responses to a question about the topic.

Outdoors: Walk around the building, on the playground and in a field or wooded area and look for spider webs to examine.

★ Sandra Gratias, Perkasie, PA

Spider Legs . . . . .3+

Materials needed

Pictures of spiders
Large spider made from construction paper (a different colored piece of paper for each leg)
Velcro or magnetic strips (to attach each leg to the body of the spider)

What to do

1. At circle time talk about spiders—where they live, what they eat. Show pictures of different kinds of spiders and spider webs.

2. Show the children the large spider with eight long legs made from construction paper and place it in the middle of the circle. (Involve the children in making the spider the day before it is shown at the circle time.)

3. Use a ball of yarn to make a spider web over the large paper spider in the middle of the circle by tossing the ball of yarn back and forth across the circle. As each child catches the ball he holds onto a piece of the yarn and tosses the ball across the circle until all the children are holding a piece of the spider web.

More to do

Large motor: Crawl like spiders and pretend to make a spider web.

Math: Count the legs on pictures of different kinds of spiders.

Writing: Ask the children to dictate a story about a spider and then to draw a picture of the spider on a sheet of paper.

★ Jane Hibbard, Archbold, OH

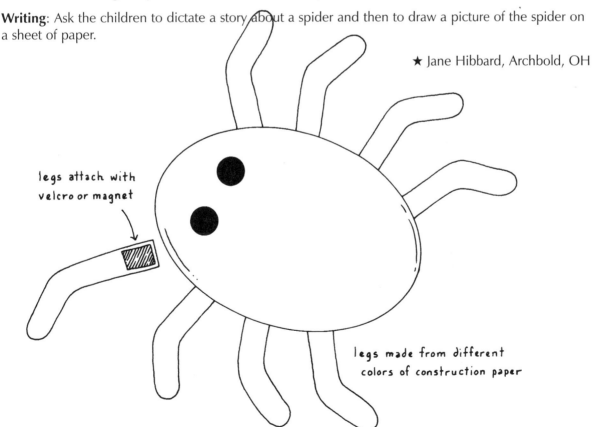

legs attach with velcro or magnet

legs made from different colors of construction paper

The Very Busy Spider Web . . . . .3+

Materials needed

1 piece of poster board
1 piece of yarn per child
Tape
The Very Busy Spider by Eric Carle

What to do

1. In advance, staple one end of each piece of yarn to the top of the poster board so that the yarn extends over the edge of the poster board.

2. At circle time read *The Very Busy Spider*. As you read each page in the story ask one child (or more depending on the number of children) to come to the poster board and make a part of the web by gently pulling one piece of yarn diagonally across the poster board and taping the end down.

3. After the story is completed and each child has helped make the web add a paper spider and talk about the story.

More to do

This activity could also be done with chalk and a chalkboard in place of yarn and poster board.

Related books

How Spider Saved the Flea Circus by Robert Kraus
How Spider Saved Halloween by Robert Kraus
How Spider Saved Thanksgiving by Robert Kraus
How Spider Saved Valentine's Day by Robert Kraus

★ Suzanne Maxymuk, Cherry Hill, NJ

Wonderful Web of Spiders . . . . .4+

Materials needed

Ball of black yarn

What to do

1. Talk about spiders and ask the children if they have seen any spiders or webs on the outside or the inside of their houses.

2. Pass a ball of black yarn (to make the spider web) from one child to the next child in the circle. Ask the children to wind off yarn from the ball and lay it across their laps. Once the yarn has gone around the circle tie it loosely and take the ball of yarn to a child across the circle, winding back and forth to create a web.

3. Sing "Eensy Weensy Spider" (or similar song "Itsy Bitsy Spider") but holding the web will prevent children from doing the hand movements.

4. Talk about and show pictures of different kinds of spiders: Daddy Long Legs (Where did they get their name?), Wolf Spiders, Tarantulas, Black Widow.

More to do

Art: Use sticky tape to make a large web on a wall. Children help make spiders using brown yarn. Cut four pieces of yarn (about 4" each) for each spider and fold the yarn loosely over a child's pinkie finger and tie the yarn, leaving 2" of yarn to tie the spider onto the web. Snip the ends. For variation use bright colors instead of brown yarn to make the yarn spiders for the class web.

Related books

Charlotte's Web by E. B. White
Miss Spider's Tea Party by David Kirk

★ Cathy Chenoweth, Columbia, MO

Freddie, the Friendly Spider . . . . .4+

Materials needed

Black playdough

Playdough recipe

2 cups flour
1 cup salt
2 Tablespoons cream of tartar
2 Tablespoons oil
2-4 Tablespoons liquid black tempera paint
2 cups water

Combine the ingredients in a pan and mix well. Bring the mixture to a boil on medium-low heat and stir constantly until the mixture pulls away from the sides of the pan and forms a ball. Pour mixture onto a bread board or table and knead. When cool put the playdough in a resealable plastic bag.

White paper
Paper punch
Colored pipe cleaners, in 4" lengths (8 per child)
Black markers

What to do

1. Put the playdough in the middle of the tables.

2. Ask each child to pull off several pieces of playdough and invite them to play with the dough.

3. Ask each child to roll the playdough into a ball to make the body of the spider.

4. Paper punch white paper circles for eyes. Use a black marker to color a pupil for each eye.

5. Place the eyes on the black spider's body (a gentle push will make the paper adhere to the playdough).

6. Ask the children to choose eight colored pipe cleaners to stick into the playdough body to make the spider's legs. The children can bend or twist the legs as they choose.

7. Allow the playdough spiders to dry.

More to do

Science: Bring live spiders in bug cages or in plastic jars with air vent lids to observe. Discuss the value of spiders in nature. Talk about web building. If you can locate an unused web, capture it on black construction paper by spraying with hair spray then bringing the paper up behind the web until it adheres.

Snack: Make spider snacks by making dark colored gelatin, such as Jell-O® in a shallow pan. Using cookie cutters, cut out circles for the body, add black licorice for legs and bits of marshmallows for eyes.

Related books

Itsy, Bitsy Spider by Iza Trapani
The Big Sneeze by Barrie Watts
The Very Busy Spider by Eric Carle

Related song

"Itsy Bitsy Spider"

★ Linda J. Becker, Rochester, MN

Spinning Spiders . . . . .5+

Materials needed

Information on web-spinning spiders
Pictures of spiders
9" heavy-duty paper plate (1 per child)
Pieces of gray or black yarn (2 pieces per child—1 piece 6 1/2' and 1 piece 5')

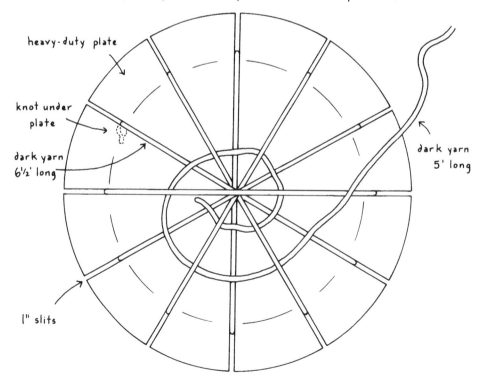

What to do

1. Show pictures and talk with the children about how spiders spin webs.

2. Give each child a paper plate (with a 1″ slit cut every 2″ around the rim of the plate) and a 6 1/2′ piece of yarn (with a knot at one end). Show the children each of the following steps in making an orb-type web.

✓ Insert the end of the yarn into one of the slits of the plate so that the knot is underneath the plate.
✓ Begin forming the web by pulling the yarn across the plate and inserting it into the slit on the opposite side of the plate. Next stretch the yarn underneath the plate and insert the yarn into the slit next to the first slit.
✓ Continue wrapping the yarn around the plate in this manner until all the slits are used and the vertical lines of the web are formed.
✓ Give each child the 5′ piece of yarn (with a knot at one end).

3. To begin weaving the web start in the center, leaving a 1″ "tail" (attach a safety pin to this end of the yarn and pin over the intersecting center pieces of the web). Weave the yarn in a circle over and under the vertical pieces of yarn, moving outward until the web is completed. Both ends of the yarn may then be knotted to the vertical pieces of the web or left loose.

Related books

The Golden Book Encyclopedia by Western Publishing Company
The Very Busy Spider by Eric Carle

★ Carol Taylor, Alexandria, LA

Spin a Spider Web . . . . .5+

Materials needed

Picture of a spider's web
Construction paper
White glue
Pencils
1/2″ round dot stickers (optional—found at office supply stores)
Watercolors

What to do

1. Show the children a picture of a spider's web. Explain how the spider starts from the center and makes lines going out and then makes the web in a circular form.

2. Give each child a piece of paper and a pencil.

3. Tell the children to make a dot in the center of the paper.

4. Show them how to make lines radiating out from the dot to the sides of the paper.

5. Show the children how to make circular lines connecting the radiating lines to make a web.

6. Show the children how to "draw" on their pencil lines with white glue.

7. Allow the glue to dry overnight.

8. When the glue is dry, show the children how to brush a watercolor wash of black, gray or blue over the web. The web made of white glue will show through the watercolor.

9. When the paint is dry, give each child one dot sticker to put on the web. Use a pencil to draw a spider's body and eight legs on the dot to make it look like a spider on the web.

More to do

Field trip: Go for a nature walk and look for spider webs.

Science: Collect a spider in a bug jar and observe it for a day. Return the spider to where you found it.

Writing: Ask the children to dictate stories about the spider they observed and to illustrate their stories. Compile the stories and make a class book about spiders. Encourage the children to take turns taking the book home to share with their families.

Related books

The Very Busy Spider by Eric Carle
Spiders by National Geographic Society
Charlotte's Web by E. B. White

★ Barbara Saul, Eureka, CA

A Little Sun .... .3+

Materials needed
None needed

What to do
1. During circle time talk about what flowers need to grow—soil, water and sunlight. Talk about the parts of a flower—roots, stem, leaves, blossom petals.

2. Say the following fingerplay with the children.

"A Little Sun"

> *A little sun (hold arms above head)*
> *A little rain (wiggle fingers in the air in a downward motion)*
> *Now pull up all the weeds (pretend to pull weeds)*
> *Our flowers grow, all in a row (hold up all ten fingers lined up like flowers)*
> *From tiny little seeds. (hold thumb and finger to show size of seeds)*

3. Encourage the children to do the motions of the fingerplay with you.

4. Repeat frequently so the children can practice the fingerplay.

More to do
Dramatic play: Set up a flower shop in the dramatic play area. Provide flower catalogs; silk, plastic and real flowers; orange juice cans (to hold flowers); telephone; pads of paper and pencils; aprons; cash register and play money.

Field trip: Visit a flower shop in the area. Take a walk in the neighborhood and look for different kinds of flowers.

Math: Make a memory game using two identical nursery catalogs. Cut out the identical pictures and glue the pictures on index cards.

Related books
My Garden Grows by Aldren Watson
The Reason for a Flower by Ruth Heller
What Is a Flower by Jennifer W. Day

★ Cory McIntyre, Crystal Lake, IL

Spring

I'm a Little Flower Seed . . . . .3+

Materials needed

None needed

What to do

1. Ask the children to choose the color of flower they would like to pretend to be.

2. Say the following rhyme with the children and ask children to act out the movements listed below.

> I'm a little flower seed.
> I'm planted in the earth.
> I feel the sun come down on me to warm this big old earth. *(children sit and tuck in their heads and knees to look like a ball)*
> The rain begins to come and gets rid of my big thirst. *(wiggle fingers in the air in a downward motion)*
> I then become a big and pretty flower so you can pick me first. *(children stand up)*

★ Cathy Wellman, Fircrest, WA

Sing a Song of Spring . . . . .3+

Materials needed

Grass
Flowers
Tree buds
Bird's nest (only abandoned nest)

What to do

1. At circle time talk about and show the children the signs of spring including grass, flowers, tree buds and an abandoned bird's nest (if available).

2. Sing the following song with the children.

Original song

(Tune: "London Bridge")

> All the grass is turning green, turning green, turning green,
> All the grass is turning green, it is springtime.

Other verses:

> See the birdies build their nest....
> All the flowers are blooming....
> Trees are budding everywhere....

★ Angela Williamson, Greensboro, NC

Rainbow Garden . . . . .4+

Materials needed
Variety of seed packets
3″ x 5″ index cards
Construction paper (variety of colors)
Tape, glue, scissors
Planting a Rainbow by Lois Ehlert

What to do
1. At circle time read *Planting a Rainbow* and talk about the story.

2. Compare the different type of bulbs, seeds and flowers, especially note the shapes and colors of the flowers.

3. Show the children the index cards (with a seed packet and sample seeds taped to each card) so the children can compare the seeds and the pictures of the flowers the seeds will become when planted.

4. Pass the index cards around the circle as you talk about each kind of flower.

5. Explain that a garden has many kinds of flowers and that the flowers are different shapes, sizes, colors. Tell the children that they will make a friendship garden of flowers.

6. Ask the children to work with a partner to trace each other's hands on a colored piece of construction paper. Add a stem and leaves to the hand tracing so it will look like a flower. Help the children arrange their flowers in a garden on a bulletin board or wall. Older children may want to design their own flowers using construction paper and torn tissue paper.

More to do
Math: Play a matching game with two identical sets of empty seed packets taped to index cards.

Science: Plant the seeds in pots or in an outside area.

★ Cathlene M. Hedden, Livonia, MI

Get Spring Fever! . . . . .4+

Materials needed
Tape of spring sounds
The Boy Who Didn't Believe in Spring by Lucille Clifton
Chart paper
Markers

What to do
1. At circle time play a short tape of spring sounds (birds chirping).

2. Talk with the children about how the weather has changed with the coming of spring. Remind the children that warm weather causes changes in nature.

3. Read *The Boy Who Didn't Believe in Spring* and review the signs of spring that were described in the story.

4. Plan a spring walk in the neighborhood. Encourage the children to use their senses—to look, listen, smell and touch to identify signs of spring. Take a notepad on the walk to write down the children's comments as they talk about what they notice.

5. Upon returning to the classroom ask the children to tell you the signs of spring that they noticed and list them on chart paper. If necessary refer to your notes to help the children remember what they had noticed on the walk. Use separate sheets of paper for visual, auditory, olfactory and tactile signs.

More to do

Art: Cut out pictures from magazines to make a spring collage including pictures of spring clothing, activities and plants.

Home connection: Ask the children to bring items from home that remind them of spring. Ask the children to show and talk about their signs of spring.

Related books

Spring by Ron Hirschi
That's What Happens When It's Spring by Elaine Good
When Spring Comes by Robert Maass

★ Lyndall Warren, Milledgeville, GA

Turn Yourself Into Mr. Bunny . . . . . . .4+

Materials needed

Home for a Bunny by Margaret Wise Brown

What to do

1. Read a book about rabbits, such as *Home for a Bunny* and talk about the story.

2. Tell the children that when you count to three they are to pretend that they are bunnies.

3. Explain that you will remind them of things that bunnies do, such as hop around the room, crawl into a hole and hide, take a nap, wake up and eat a carrot.

4. Ask the children to walk in a circle as you say the following poem to a rap rhythm. Allow the children time to practice saying the words and walking to the rhythm.

"The Swinging Bunny"

> *I'm going down the street*
> *Going hippity hop, hippity hop, hippity hop*
> *I'm going down the street*
> *Going hippity hop.*
> *Hey there, look at me. (point to self)*

5. Ask the children to pretend to be a Cool Bunny (strut and move shoulders up and down with a swinging motion) and walk in a circle snapping fingers as you say the following poem.

"The Cool Bunny"

> *I'm going down the street*
> *Going bippity bop, bippity bop, bippity bop*
> *I'm going down the street*
> *Going bippity bop.*
> *Hey there, look at me. (point to self)*

6. Ask the children to walk in a circle on their tiptoes as you say the following poem.

> *I'm going down the street*
> *Going tippity-top, tippity-top, tippity-top (walk on tiptoes)*
> *I'm going down the street*
> *Going Tippity-top.*
> *Hey there, look at me. (point to self)*

7. Ask the children to walk in a circle with their knees bent and shaking their pretend tails.

> *I'm going down the street*
> *Going dippity dop, dippity dop (bend knees and shake tail)*
> *I'm going down the street*
> *Going dippity dop*
> *Hey there, look at me. (point to self)*

8. Tell the children that the last bunny is tired and sits down to rest while you say the following poem and ask the children to do the movements as you say them.

> *Show me your bunny eyes*
> *Show me your ears*
> *Show me your nose*
> *Show me your mouth.*

When I say lippity (smile)

When I say lop (frown)

> *Lippity (smile)*
> *Lop (frown)*
> *Lippity (smile)*
> *Lop (frown)*
> *I'm going down the street*
> *Going lippity lop (smile and frown)*
> *Lippity lop (smile and frown)*
> *Lippity lop (smile and frown)*
> *I'm going down the street*
> *Going lippity lop*
> *Hey there, look at me. (point to self)*

★ Diann Spalding, Santa Rosa, CA

We Are Seeds in Springtime . . . . .4+

Materials needed

"Rocky Mountain High" by John Denver

What to do

1. At circle time ask the children to curl up in balls on the carpet and pretend to be seeds under the ground. Turn off the lights and play "Rocky Mountain High" or similar song.

2. In a low voice, tell the children to start slowly moving their arms and legs and pretend that their roots are growing.

3. As the song ends turn the lights on and ask the children to slowly stand up (coming out of the ground), raising their arms towards the lights, waving their hands like leaves in the breeze and turning their faces to the light like a flower budding facing the sun.

Original fingerplay

"Five Little Carrots"

> *Five little carrots in a veggie garden*
> *A gopher ate one, I beg your pardon.*
> *Four little carrots in the ground*
> *A gopher came along, took it to his mound.*
> *Three little carrots left in the dirt*
> *Its top was nibbled on, but didn't hurt.*
> *Two little carrots left in the sun*
> *A groundhog came along and left just one.*
> *One lonely carrot all alone*
> *'Till a farmer came along and took it home.*

★ Penni Smith and Donna Karnes, Riverside, CA

Spring Has Sprung . . . . .5+

Materials needed
Tambourine
Pink ribbons for flowers
Black ribbons for thunder
Gray ribbons for lightning
Blue ribbons for rain
Yellow ribbons for sun

What to do
1. In advance, collect enough ribbons so that each child will have one ribbon (depending on the number of children several children may play one part).

2. At circle time talk with the children about what flowers need to grow.

3. Tell the children that they will dramatize the story of how flowers grow. Explain that each child will pretend to be one of the following: flower, sun, thunder, lightning or rain. Assign the roles and give each child the appropriate color of ribbon (listed above) to wave when his part is talked about.

4. Narrate a story about how flower seeds planted in the ground begin to grow. Use the tambourine to make the sounds of thunder and rain. As you tell the story encourage the children to act out their parts.

More to do
Ask the children to narrate their version of the story of how flowers grow using the ribbons as props. Encourage the children to make up and dramatize other stories.

Related book
The Carrot Seed by Ruth Krauss

★ Debbie Bokor, Richmond Hill, Ontario, Canada

Tour the Classroom . . . . .3+

Materials needed

None needed

What to do

1. On the first day of school tell the children that you will introduce them to their new classroom. Explain that everyone will be going on a train ride to see the different areas in the room.

2. Ask the children to stand and show them how to form a human train. The teacher leads the train.

3. Begin to slowly walk around the room, stopping at each area along the way (remember to include the bathroom and drinking fountain).

4. Briefly talk about each area and explain any rules that apply to the area (or open only a couple areas the first day and gradually increase the number of areas in which the children can play after you discuss the rules for the specific area).

5. Return to the circle area and ask each child which area she would like to play in first. Remind the children that they will have time to play in other areas.

Related book

My Nursery School by Harlow Rockwell

★ Kim Anderson, Caledonia, MI

All About Our Day . . . . .3+

Materials needed

Magazines
Scissors
Construction paper
Tape or glue
Markers

What to do

1. In advance, cut pictures from magazines and catalogs representing the daily sequence of activities. Mount the pictures on construction paper and label the pictures with the activity, such as Arrival, Play Time, Snack.

2. At circle time show the children the pictures and talk about what happens in the classroom during that time of the day.

3. Talk about the daily schedule and ask the children to place the pictures in sequence according to the schedule.

★ Lisa Sunbury, Cambridge, MA

Creating a Friend Book ....3+

Materials needed
Will I Have a Friend by Miriam Cohen
Photo album
Camera
Photograph of each child
Small pieces of paper
Marker
Cup

What to do
1. Take a photograph of each child playing during the first week of school.

2. Ask each child to tell you about himself and write his response on a small piece of paper.

3. Put each photograph with the accompanying description of each child on a separate page in the photo album.

4. At circle time read *Will I Have a Friend* and talk about the story.

5. Show the children the photo album and talk about what each child said about himself.

6. Tell the children that they will each have a turn to take the photo album home to share with their family. Explain that you will put all the children's names in a cup and will draw a name to determine who will take the book home first. Emphasize that everyone will have a turn to take the book home.

7. After all the children take the book home, place it in the reading center.

Related books
Friends by Helme Heine
That's What a Friend Is by P. K. Hallinan

★ Cindy Winther, Oxford, MI

Get Acquainted Song ....3+

Materials needed
None needed

What to do
1. At circle time ask the children what it means to get acquainted with someone and talk about their responses.

2. Tell the children that you will teach them the "Get Acquainted Song" and tell them what to do during the song (point to each child in turn who will stand up and say her name). Explain that after everyone says their names (including the teacher) then all the children will say their names at the same time.

3. Sing the following song to the tune of "Alouette."

Gather 'round it's time to get acquainted.
Sing this song and I'll show you how it's done.
All you do to play this game
Is stand right up and say your name. (child says name and everyone repeats the child's name)
Ohhhh! (Repeat the song with the children and teacher taking turns to say their names. After singing the song for the last time all the children say their names together at the same time.)

More to do

Language: Use a drum or other percussion instrument when the children say their names. Beat the drum for each syllable in the name. Ask the children to stand up if their name has one drum beat (syllable). Repeat saying the names of the children whose names have one syllable. Continue saying the names of children whose names have two drum beats, three drum beats and four drum beats. After saying the children's names and beating the drum the number of times corresponding with the number of syllables in their names, allow the children to take turns playing their names on the drum when singing the song.

Social studies: Sing the "Get Acquainted Song " to introduce community helpers.

★ R. Jill Edelson, Massapequa, NY

I Have a Name . . . . .3+

Materials needed

Crayons
Scissors
Paste
Cotton balls
Yarn
Clown's face drawn on paper (photocopy for each child, then write child's name across the mouth)

What to do

1. At circle time sing "Eddie Wears a Yellow Shirt" to the tune of "Johnny Works With One Hammer." (Change the child's name and the color and name of the item of clothing to match each of the children in the group.)

Eddie wears a yellow shirt, yellow shirt, yellow shirt
Eddie wears a yellow shirt, where is Eddie?

2. When the children guess which child Eddie (or child's name) is, he comes forward and the children all sing the song to him. Repeat the song for each child using his name and color of clothing.

3. Hand out a clown picture, scissors and crayons to each child. Ask each child to look at the clown's mouth and ask what is the name written across the clown's mouth. Help the children who don't recognize their names. Ask the children to color and cut out the clown, paste cotton balls on the nose and hat, and paste pieces of yarn for hair. Tell the children that they made their own name tags. Pin or tape the name tag on each child and explain that each tag says the child's name.

More to do

Art: Encourage the children to make a name tag for each member of their family. Write the name of each family member across the mouth of the clown and give the name tags to the family members.

Music: Clap the rhythm pattern (number of syllables) of each child's name. Talk about how many names get one clap, two claps, three claps, even four.

Related book

My Name Is Alice by Jane Bayer

★ Wendy Pfeffer, Pennington, NJ

Roll That Ball . . . . .3+

Materials needed

Large ball

What to do

1. At circle time explain that you will roll a ball to one child and that child will say his name and then roll the ball to another child (only the child who has the ball may talk).

2. This activity can be varied using a different topic to learn more about the children (favorite foods, colors, toys, pets). After the children say their names, they respond to a topic, for example, "My name is Raoul and my favorite food is pizza."

Related book

My Teacher Sleeps in School by Leatie Weiss

Related song

"What Is Your Name?" by Hap Palmer

★ Suzanne Maxymuk, Cherry Hill, NJ

Rolling Balls .3+

Materials needed

Large ball

What to do

1. At circle time ask the children to sit on the floor and explain that they will play a game where they will say their names and answer a question and then roll the ball to another child sitting in the circle.

2. Ask the children a question (or ask the children to suggest a topic), such as zoo animals. The child who is holding the ball says, "My name is _____ and my favorite zoo animal is _____ because it is _____."

3. Then that child rolls the ball to another child and the game continues.

★ Amy Flick, Harrisonburg, VA

"Oh, I Went to School" . . . . .3+

Materials needed

None needed

What to do

1. At circle time sing the following song, "Oh, I Went to School." After the children learn the song, add motions using both hands pointing to eyes, ears, hands (open and out) and head.

"Oh, I Went to School" (Tune: "I Stuck My Head in a Little Skunk's Hole")

*Oh, I went to school
And my teacher said to me,
"There's a lot to do,
There's a lot to see!"
With my eyes, with my ears,
With my hands, with my head
I learn here.*

Variation for line 2 (*And my good friend said to me,*)

2. Ask the children to name their favorite activities and substitute the names of the activities in the last line of the song, such as, *I paint here, I read here, I play here.*

★ Susan Welhouse, Sheboygan, WI

Room Search Cards . . . . .3+

Materials needed
Pictures of materials found in the classroom (cut from supply catalogs, such as building blocks, easel, climber, playhouse furniture)
3" x 4" pieces of tagboard (1 per picture)
Glue
Clear self-adhesive paper or laminating film

What to do
1. In advance, make the cards gluing one picture to each of the tagboard cards and covering with self-adhesive paper for durability.

2. At circle time talk about the materials in the classroom and ask the children to name the materials they like to play with.

3. Show the children the Room Search Cards one at a time and talk about each item. Give a card to each pair of children and ask them to take the card to the area in the room where the materials are located. After the children locate the materials on their cards ask them to take turns showing the other children the materials they located.

More to do
Language: Label each card with the name of the item and place an identical label on the corresponding item in the room. The Room Search Cards help children learn the names of the different items in the room. Children take turns drawing one card at a time out of a basket and tell the name of the item. Ask the children to describe how they use this item in their play and record the children's responses on chart paper during circle time.

Social skills: The cards also help children who join the class during the year become familiar with the materials in the room (ask another child to use the cards in helping the new child locate the materials.

Related books
The Berenstain Bears Go to School by Stan and Jan Berenstain
Richard Scarry's Great Big Schoolhouse by Richard Scarry
My New School by Harriet Hains
Little Critter's This Is My School by Mercer Mayer

★ Karen Wojahn, Windom, MN

Teddy Comes to School . . . . .3+

Materials needed
Stuffed animals (1 per child)

What to do
1. In advance, send a note to parents asking their child to bring a stuffed animal to school and explain that the animal will remain in the classroom for one week.

2. Ask the children to bring their stuffed animals to circle time (if you are introducing a rule to the children). After you explain the rule ask the children to explain in their own words the rule to their stuffed animals.

3. Ask the children to put their stuffed animals in their cubbies during the day except during activities that would be appropriate for the children to hold their stuffed animals as story time or nap time.

More to do
Ask each child to draw a picture of his stuffed animal and let him take the picture home as a gift for the family.

Related books
Corduroy by Don Freeman
Paddington Bear books by Michael Bond
Pierre: A Cautionary Tale by Maurice Sendak
The Little Elephant Who Liked to Play by Naomi Sellers
This Is the Bear by Sarah Hayes

★ Cathy Chenoweth, Columbia, MO

Who's at School Today? . . . . .3+

Materials needed
Photograph of each child
Sheet of fiberboard, 2' x 3' (available at building centers)
4" lengths of 1" wide wood molding
Wood glue
Paint
Saw

What to do

1. In advance, make a schoolhouse using a sheet of fiberboard, wood molding, wood glue and paint. Saw the roof of the schoolhouse (see illustration) and glue the wood molding to school, spacing it to allow room for photographs to rest on each ledge. After the glue is dry, paint the schoolhouse and add the name of the school, if desired.

2. Take a photograph of each child to display on the schoolhouse.

3. At circle time show the children the schoolhouse and explain that each child's photograph will be on the schoolhouse.

4. Show the children the photographs and ask the children who is in each photograph.

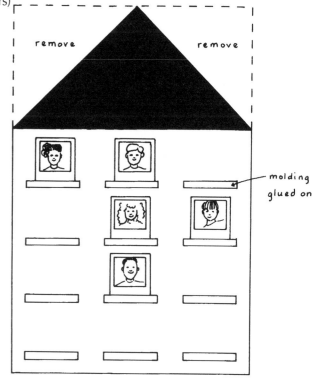

Fiber board
2' x 3'
Cut to form
and painted

remove   remove

molding
glued on

5. Each child places her photograph on one of the ledges on the schoolhouse.

6. After all the photographs are in the schoolhouse, explain that when the children come to school each morning they should place their photographs on a ledge of the schoolhouse to show that they are at school. Each morning count the number of children (photographs) at school.

★ Anne Deary, New Windsor, NY

First Day Photo Find . . . . .4+

Materials needed
Camera, such as Polaroid®
Film

What to do
1. On the first day of school take photographs of the children and the teachers.

2. At circle time give each child a photograph of a child or teacher (pair the photographs as you give them to the children so the same persons will be looking for each other).

3. Ask the children to find the person in the photograph and to talk with the person to learn his name.

4. After everyone has found their partner ask the children to sit in the circle.

5. Ask the pairs of children to introduce each other. The teacher begins by modeling an introduction. The introductions can vary depending on the age of the child. Younger children can introduce their partner by name only, while older children can interview their partner and share more information.

More to do
Language: Put each of the photographs on a sheet of paper. Ask the children to illustrate each page with a drawing that tells something about the child. Also ask the children to tell you about the child so you can write it on the child's page. Compile the pages in a class book. Children interview other people, such as school staff, neighbors, family members and share the interviews with the other children. Ask the children to illustrate their interviews with drawings and compile the pages into a book entitled "Our Neighborhood."

Related books
Angel Child, Dragon Child by Michele M. Surat
Cleversticks by Bernard Ashley

Related songs
"The More We Get Together" by Raffi (include the stanza that names all of the children in the class)
"Willoughby Wallaby Woo" by Raffi

★ Deborah Robbins, Narbeth, PA

Class Graphing  ....4+

Materials needed
Ball of yarn

What to do
1. During circle time talk about how children are similar and how children are different. Discuss appearance, play activities, family members. Tell the children that they will make a class graph of their similarities and differences.

2. Unroll the ball of yarn in a large circle on the floor and ask the girls to stand on one side of the circle and the boys to stand on the other side on the circle. Place a piece of yarn across the circle to divide the girls and the boys into two groups. Count the number of girls and the number of boys and talk about which group has more and which has less.

3. Explain that there are many ways to group the children to learn more about how they are similar and how they are different. Tell the children to divide into groups by a physical characteristic, such as hair color or eye color (designate a section of the circle for each color, such as brown, black, blue, green). Divide the circle into sections using pieces of yarn. Talk about how many children are in each section using the words as more than, less than and same.

More to do
Math: Place objects in the math center that the children can graph by different characteristics.

★ Alissa Glover, Tampa, Fl

Whose Name Is It? ....4+

Materials needed
Index cards (a child's first name printed on each card)
Recorded music (fast tempo)

What to do
1. Prior to circle time put the children's name cards in a circle on the floor.

2. As the children arrive, ask them to find their name in the circle and sit in that spot.

3. After the children are seated ask each child in turn to hold up her card and say her name.

4. Ask the children to place their cards on the floor in front of them and stand up.

5. Turn on the music and ask the children to walk around the cards in the circle until the music stops.

6. When the music stops ask each child to pick up the card in front of her and read the name on the card (or ask the teacher to read it) and hand it to that child.

7. After the name cards are identified, place the cards on the floor again and continue walking around the circle to the music.

More to do

This activity can be used with a variety of different cards to identify numbers, colors, shapes.

Original song

(Tune: "The Farmer in the Dell")

> Oh (child's name) is here today!
> Oh (child's name) is here today!
> Let's all clap our hands,
> (Child's name) is here today!

★ Jacqui Schweitzer, Effort, PA

"Who's Missing?" . . . . .4+

Materials needed

Blanket

What to do

1. At circle time explain that the children will play "Who's Missing?" and ask the children to sit on the floor and cover their eyes.

2. Cover one child with a blanket.

3. Tell the children to open their eyes and look around to see who is missing.

4. Children guess until they discover who is missing. The missing child takes the next turn covering another child with the blanket.

★ Lisa Sunbury, Cambridge, MA

Getting To Know You . . . . .4+

Materials needed

Camera and film
Construction paper
Glue
Form photocopied for each child:

My name is _____

I am _____ years old. I have _____ brothers and _____ sisters.

My pets are _____

My favorite toys are _____

My favorite book is _____

I like to _____

What to do

1. During the first day of school, take a close-up picture of each child in the class.

2. Get double prints developed.

3. During the first week of school talk with each child and fill out the above form for each child.

4. Photocopy each completed questionnaire.

5. Glue each child's photograph and questionnaire on a piece of construction paper.

6. Compile the pages and make a class book. Show the book to the children and invite them to take turns taking the book home to share with their families.

7. Use the duplicate prints and questionnaires to make a bulletin board display for the children to look at and talk about.

★ Barbara Saul, Eureka, CA

Musical Handshakes . . . . .4+

Materials needed
Recorded music

What to do

1. At circle time divide the group of children into equal groups. (If there is an odd number of children, the teacher plays too!) One group of children forms the inner circle. The other group forms the outer circle.

2. While the music plays, the inner circle moves clockwise and the outer circle moves counter-clockwise.

3. When the music stops the children stop walking. Each child in the inner circle turns to face his partner in the other circle. The partners shake hands and say their names.

4. Encourage the children to tell each other one thing about themselves, such as favorite game, number of people in family, pets.

5. Start the music again and continue. Ask the children to suggest what information they would like to share.

6. This is a great way to "break the ice" the first few weeks of school by getting to know each other.

Related book
Will I Have a Friend? by Miriam Cohen

★ Valerie Chellew, Marshfield, WI

The Tiny Tailor of Budapest . . . . .3+

Materials needed

Story text
Paper
Pencil and ruler
Highlight markers (yellow, blue, pink and green)
Scissors

What to do

1. To prepare for this activity draw one pattern on a white sheet of paper (8 1/2" x 11"). Highlight the lines in four colors. Fold the paper four times.

2. Use your hands and a pair of scissors as you tell the following story. (Trace the colored lines with your finger tip to demonstrate drawing.)

The Tiny Tailor of Budapest story is adapted from *The Tailor* by Nancy Schimmel.

Long, long ago, in the city of Budapest, there lived a tiny tailor. The tiny tailor made clothes to sell all his friends and neighbors, but he was so poor he seldom had enough money to buy cloth to set aside for himself. What the tiny tailor wanted most of all was a long wool coat to keep him warm all winter.

So the tiny tailor (unfold paper four times) saved and he saved and he saved and he saved until at last he had just enough money to buy a big piece of wool.

So he folded the cloth, drew some yellow lines, cut them very carefully and stitched them up to make a coat. It fit just perfectly! The tiny tailor was proud of his long wool coat and he wore it every day all winter long. So by the end of the winter, it was all worn out or at least it seemed to be.

But when the tiny tailor looked ever so closely, he could see that there was just enough good cloth left to make a jacket. So he folded the coat, drew a blue line, cut it very carefully and stitched it up to make a jacket. It fit just perfectly! The tiny tailor was so pleased with his new jacket that he wore it every day all through the spring. So by the end of the spring season, it was all worn out or at least it seemed to be.

But when the tiny tailor looked ever so closely, he cold see that there was just enough good cloth left to make a vest. So he folded the jacket, drew some pink lines, cut them very carefully and stitched them up to make a vest. It fit just perfectly! The tiny tailor was so pleased with his new vest that he wore it every day all summer long. So by the end of the summer, it was all worn out or at least it seemed to be.

But when the tiny tailor looked ever so closely, he could see that there was just enough good cloth left to make a cap. So he folded the vest, drew a green line, cut it very carefully and stitched it to make a cap. It fit just perfectly! The tiny tailor was so pleased with his new cap that he wore it every day all through the fall. So by the end of the fall season, it was all worn out or at least it seemed to be.

But when the tiny tailor looked ever so closely, he could see that there was just enough good cloth left to make a tie. So he folded the cap, drew a black line, cut it very carefully and stitched it up to make a tie. Then, the tiny tailor gave it to me to tie around my finger to remind me to tell this story to you!

More to do

Note: The value of conservation is cleverly hidden as a theme in this story. Bring this concept to the children's attention through talking about the story.

Art: Follow up with a scrap-art project. Use a box of classroom scraps (paper, fabric, yarn) to extend the story activity. Say, "Look! There's just enough good stuff left to make a collage!"

Cooking: Explain that the story of the Tiny Tailor is based on a Yiddish Folk Song called "I Had a Little Coat" and that Yiddish is a language spoken by some people of the Jewish culture. Mention that something the Tiny Tailor might enjoy eating is a potato latke (pancake). Make latkes for snack. (If a recipe is unavailable, prepared mixes with directions can usually be found at major supermarkets.)

Math: Provide a jar containing a large assortment of buttons for the children to sort by color or size.

Caution: With young children who still put things in their mouths, be sure items are large enough so they cannot be swallowed.

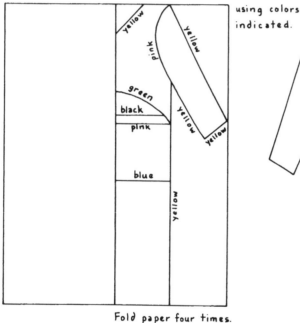

Draw pattern onto right half of 8½"×11" sheet of paper, using colors indicated.

Fold paper four times.

★ Susan A. Sharkey, La Mesa, CA

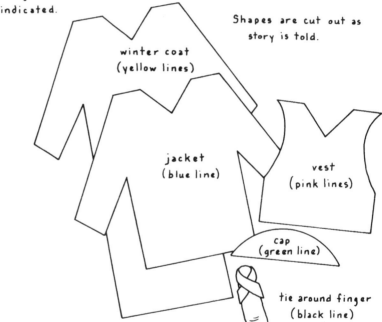

Shapes are cut out as story is told.

winter coat (yellow lines)

jacket (blue line)

vest (pink lines)

cap (green line)

tie around finger (black line)

Day and Night . . . . .3+

Materials needed

Just Like Everyone Else by Karla Kuskin

What to do

1. At circle time read *Just Like Everyone Else* or tell a similar story.

2. Ask the children to dramatize the story, how Jonathan James gets up just like everyone else, gets dressed just like everyone else, eats breakfast just like everyone else and so on. The children love dramatizing the story especially when they get to the surprise ending.

3. Ask the children to describe what happens during their days.

More to do

Art: Talk with the children about what they do during the day and what they do at night. Talk about the differences between day and night. Provide catalogs and magazines and ask the children to cut out pictures of things they could use during the day, such as clothes, wagon, food. Paste the pictures on a white sheet of paper. Then ask the children to cut out and paste pictures of things they could use at night, such as bed, lamp, pajamas on a dark sheet of paper. Talk about and compare the pictures on the two sheets of paper.

Related books

Alexander and the Terrible, Horrible, No Good, Very Bad Day by Judith Viorst

★ Wendy Pfeffer, Pennington, NJ

Feed This Hungry Caterpillar . . . . .3+

Materials needed

The Very Hungry Caterpillar by Eric Carle
Plastic food (listed in the story)
Large sock

What to do

1. Wear a large sock on your hand, pushed in to make it look like a big mouth. Introduce this sock to the children as a very, hungry caterpillar.

2. Give each child a piece of plastic food.

3. Ask the children to feed the caterpillar as you read the story.

★ Lisa Sunbury, Cambridge, MA

Finish That Thought . . . . .3+

Materials needed

None needed

What to do

1. At circle time tell the children that you will say an open ended sentence, such as "When my birthday comes, I would like...." or "When I grow up I will...."

2. Allow time for the children to think about how they would complete the sentence.

3. Ask the children to finish the sentence.

★ Iris Rothstein, New Hyde Park, NY

Our Microphone .3+

Materials needed

9" square of tagboard
Soft ball, such as a Nerf® ball
Glue

What to do

1. To prepare for this activity make a microphone by twisting the tagboard into a cone shape and tape it making the opening the same size as the ball.

2. Put the ball into the open circle of the cone and glue the ball in place.

3. The children share the microphone during circle time.

4. The person with the microphone talks, everyone else listens.

Related book

The Giving Tree by Shel Silverstein

★ Monica Hay-Cook, Tucson, AZ

The Mitten . . . . .3+

Materials needed

The Mitten by Jan Brett
2 white stretchy knee socks
Scissors
Needles and thread
Items to represent animals in the story, such as stuffed bear, stuffed white rabbits, small hedgehog, fur piece (for the fox), toy mouse (for the mole)

What to do

1. In advance, cut the two knee socks down the middle, open them flat and sew the edges together to make a long stretchy mitten.

2. Fill the mitten with the animals listed above.

3. At circle time tell the children the story of *The Mitten* rather than reading it.

4. Occasionally show the illustrations in the book to the children.

5. When finished telling the story hold up the stuffed mitten and say, "Here is Nikki's mitten. Let's see what animal crawled inside to get warm!"

6. Ask each child to take a turn reaching inside the mitten and retrieving an animal.

More to do

Science: Place one of the animals inside the mitten. Ask the children to feel the outside of the mitten (or inside the mitten) and guess what animal is inside.

Related books
Amy Loves the Snow by Julia Hoban
The First Snowfall by Anne and Harlow Rockwell
The Snowy Day by Ezra Jack Keats
A Winter Day by Douglas Florian

★ Peggy Eddy, Johnson City, TN

Hands Together . . . . .3+

Materials needed
Polaroid® camera

What to do
1. Ask the children to hold up their hands and to look at them very carefully.

2. Ask the children to examine their skin for freckles, marks, skin color and to examine their fingernails. Encourage to compare their hands with another child's hands sitting next to them.

3. Divide the children into groups of about five children and ask the children to place one of their hands together on a table (either palms up or down). Take a photograph of their hands.

4. Show the children the photograph of their hands and talk about how their hands are similar and how they are different.

5. Ask the children to talk about things they can do with their hands. Encourage the children to make up a story about their hands.

More to do
Manipulatives: Provide self-help boards (or clothing and shoes) for children to practice snapping, zipping, buttoning, tying and lacing.

Science: Ask the children create shadows on the wall using an overhead projector.

Related books
Here Are My Hands by Bill Martin, Jr. and John Archambault
Bright Eyes, Brown Skin by Cheryl Hudson and Bernette Ford
Loving by Anne Morris
All the Colors of the Earth by Sheila Hamanaka

★ Jean Lortz, Seattle, WA

Storytelling

The Hungry Thing . . . . .4+

Storytelling

Materials needed

Large cereal box
Tape or glue
String
Markers
The Hungry Thing by Jan Slepian and Ann Seidler

Blue paper
Scissors
Index cards
Pictures of food (cut from magazines)

What to do

1. In advance, make the Hungry Thing. Take a large cereal box and cover it with blue paper. Cut a large hole near the top of the box for the mouth (big enough to put index cards in). Add eyes and black wavy lines for scales. Hang a sign on the Hungry Thing with string (or attach a sign to a craft stick and place the sign nearby) that says FEED ME on one side and THANK YOU on the other side.

2. On one side of an index card write "dilk" and on the other side attach or draw a picture of a glass of milk. On another card write "ramwitch" and on the other side attach or draw a picture of a sandwich. Continue making food cards until you have a card for each child.

3. At circle time show the children the Hungry Thing you created and read *The Hungry Thing* or tell a story about The Hungry Thing who came to school one day.

4. If you tell the story about the Hungry Thing explain how it came into the room wearing a big sign that said FEED ME and it looked very hungry. So the children asked him what he wanted to eat and he said, "Bandy." Well, the children really wanted to help him but they didn't know what kind of food bandy was until suddenly one of the children shouted, "It means candy." The children got a piece of candy and put it in its mouth. And the Hungry Thing turned its sign around and it said THANK YOU.

large cereal box covered with blue paper

FEED ME

5. Explain that now The Hungry Thing needs the children's help to figure out what it wants to eat. Read the rhyming word on an index card and ask the children to identify a word that is the name of a food and rhymes with that word. When a child identifies the word she can feed the Hungry Thing by putting the picture of the food in its mouth. Continue reading the cards. Tell the children that the pictures on the back of the cards will help them if they cannot identify the rhyming word.

★ Ann Scalley, Wellfleet, MA

Three Pigs Stick Puppets . . . . .4+

Materials needed

Pink egg carton cups (3 per child)
3" pink paper circles (3 per child)
Markers
Toothpicks
3" cardboard triangle

Popsicle sticks (4 per child)
Pink strips of paper 1/2" wide
Glue
4" x 6" piece of gray construction paper (1 per child)
Paper circle punches (green, brown and blue)

What to do

1. Tell the children that they will make Three Pigs Stick Puppets they can use to act out the story of the Three Little Pigs.

2. Show the children how to make the puppets following the steps as outlined.

3. Glue the sticks to the backs of the three pink circles.

4. Dip the cut edges of the egg carton cups in the glue and stick each cup to the front of one of the circles.

5. Snip small triangles from the pink strip of paper and glue two of the triangles on the pink circle for ears. Make two small circles with a black marker for the snout.

6. Use toothpicks to put two glue dots on each circle above the snout and below the ears.

7. Stick on the paper circle punches for the eyes. Use different colored eyes for each pig.

8. Trace the cardboard triangle pattern on the gray construction paper and cut it out. Fold down two corners of the triangle for ears, draw a wolf face on the triangle and glue it to a stick.

9. Allow the puppets to dry.

10. The following day ask the children to place their puppets on the floor in front of them at circle time. Ask the children to use their puppets to act out the role of each of the characters as you tell the story of the Three Little Pigs.

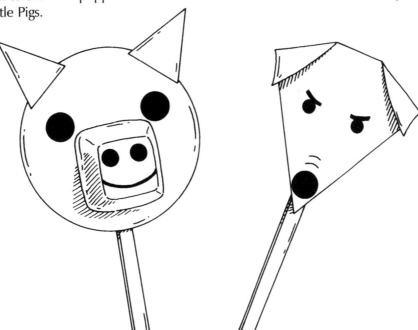

More to do

Blocks: Make blocks from clay. Cut the clay into bricks using a ruler to make straight edges. Let the blocks dry or bake them in the oven at low heat. Use the clay blocks to build the pig's brick house.

Dramatic play: Provide a variety of puppets and encourage the children to act out their stories.

Manipulatives: Provide house building materials, such as Legos®, Lincoln Logs® and unit blocks. Make blocks from half gallon milk cartons. To make a block open the tops of two half gallon milk cartons. Stuff one carton with newspaper and place the open end of carton into the empty milk carton. Cover the block with contact paper. Make at least twenty blocks for building a structure.

Science: Put straw, sticks and bricks on the Science table. Use a balance scale to weigh the materials and compare the differences. Try to break, bend and blow each of the materials.

Related books

A Day in the Life of a Carpenter by John Harding Martin
How a House Is Built by Gail Gibbons
The Three Little Pigs by Paul Galdone

★ Sandra Gratias, Perkasie, PA

Sharing Books . . . . .4+

Materials needed

Library books

What to do

1. Ask the children to bring their library books to circle time. Sing the following song with the children.

"The Library Song" (Tune: "If You're Happy and You Know It")

> *It's quiet in the library, sh-sh.*
> *It's quiet in the library, sh-sh.*
> *We must be quiet.*
> *We must use whispers.*
> *'Cause it's quiet in the library! Sh! Sh!*

2. Each child holds a book with the title showing so everyone can see it. Each child says the name of his book (or the teacher reads the title and the child repeats it).

3. After children have shared the title of their books, they take turns showing the other children their favorite page in the book and talk about that page. Encourage the children to express what they liked about the story. After the children have shared their books ask the children which of the books they would like you to read during the week.

More to do

This activity and words of the song can be adapted to the theme of any sharing activity.

★ Debra Keery, Mishicot, WI

The Vacation Book . . . . .4+

Materials needed

Photo album (with plastic covered pages)
Pictures from travel brochures and magazines

What to do

1. If you plan to be away from the children on a vacation make a Vacation Book using pictures from travel brochures and magazines to describe your upcoming trip: how you will travel (car, plane, train), things you will do on your trip (swimming, sight-seeing, visiting family), people who will travel with you, when you will return.

2. Bring the book to circle time and share your vacation plans with the children by showing them the Vacation Book.

3. Put the book in the reading area so the children can look at it while you are gone.

4. When you return from your trip, replace the cut-out pictures with some photos from your vacation and share the book while you tell the children stories about your vacation.

5. Place the Vacation Book in the reading area for children to look at. The book promotes sharing, increases vocabulary and encourages storytelling.

More to do

Adapt the idea of making a book to help prepare children for a visit to the doctor, dentist or the hospital.

★ Deborah A. Cole, Madison, OH

We're Going on a Vacation . . . . .4+

Materials needed

Suitcase
Vacation clothing
Maps, camera

What to do

1. At circle time talk about going on a vacation. Ask the children to describe vacations that they have taken.

2. Ask the children for suggestions of things to pack in the suitcase for a trip.

3. Do the following action poem with lots of energy.

"We're Going on a Vacation" (establish the beat by slapping thighs for the first three verses)

> *We're going on a vacation*
> *Would you like to come?*
> *We're going on a vacation*
> *Let's go have some fun!*

We'd better pack a suitcase
Don't forget your clothes!
And don't forget some shoes
To cover up your toes!

Now let's go outside
So we can get some sun.
Let's go on an adventure
You'd better be ready to run!

(Remainder of poem adapted from versions of "The Dragon Hunt" and "Bear Hunt")

Let's go on a dragon hunt!
Uh, oh, I see some tracks! (hand to forehead as if looking)
They lead into a swamp!
Can't go over it, Can't go under it, (make motions with hands)
Have to go through it.
Better put on our boots! (pretend to put on boots)
Ready? Let's go—slosh, slosh, slosh, slosh, slosh (pretend to wade through mud and rub hands
together to make sloshing sound)

Uh, oh! I see a stream!
Can't go over it, can't go under it,
Have to go through it.
Better put on our swimsuits! (wiggle into swimsuits)
Ready? Let's go!

Uh, oh! I see a tree!
Can't go over it, can't go under it,
Let's climb it! (imitate climbing up and then down)

We're on a dragon hunt, don't be afraid!
Oh, no! I see a cave!
Can't go over it, can't go under it,
Let's go inside. (creep into cave)
It's dark! I think I hear something! (hand to ear)
I think I feel something! (feel with hand)
I think I see something! (hand to forehead)
It's a dragon! Let's run! (rapidly slap hands on thighs as if running)

Reverse verses while rapidly slapping thighs

We're out of the cave!
Uh, oh! There's the tree! Let's climb it!
There's the stream. Let's swim through it! (swimming motions)
There's the swamp. Hurry! (make sloshing sound by rubbing hands together)
There's our school! Quick, run inside! Slam the door, (name of child).
Are we all here? Let's count to make sure. (count children)
Whew!

★ Pat Davis, Jenny Carter, Cindy Savage, Phil Carter, Spokane, WA

Washing with a Washboard . . . . .4+

Materials needed

Washboard
Soap
Clothesline and clothespins

Basin of wash water
Rinse water
Doll clothes

What to do

1. At circle time tell the children that many of their grandparents or great-grandparents probably made soap and used a washboard for washing.

2. Wash an item of doll clothing as you tell how people washed their clothes in "the good old days."

3. Give each child a chance to rub the clothes on the board, rinse and wring out. As the children rub the clothes, sing the following song to the tune of "Row, Row, Row Your Boat."

> *Wash, wash, wash the clothes.*
> *Wash them nice and clean*
> *Rub and rub up and down*
> *'Till no more dirt is seen.*

More to do

Dramatic play: Wash baby doll clothes and hang them to dry on the clothesline.

★ Phyllis Esch and Helen Hamlin, Export, PA

Storytelling With Earthlings . . . . .5+

Materials needed

5 Wooden clothespins (rounded tops)
Felt (various colors)
Glue gun or craft glue
Scissors
Permanent marker (optional)

What to do

1. In advance, make five Earthlings that will be the characters in stories that you will tell the children. (When making the Earthlings match the color of the hat and cape of each Earthling so you can distinguish them by their colored clothing and associate the color with a specific food.)

2. Cover each clothespin with a half circle (2" diameter) of felt for a cape and glue it in place.

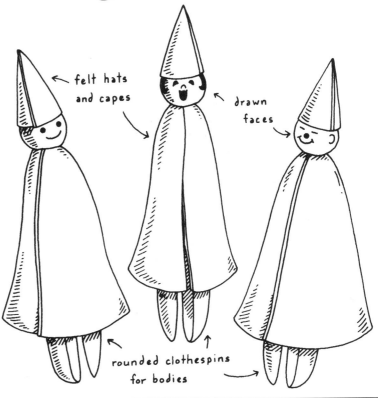

← felt hats and capes

← drawn faces

rounded clothespins for bodies →

3. Cut a triangle piece of felt large enough to wrap around the rounded knob of the clothespin for a pointy elf hat and glue it in place.

4. Add a face with a permanent marker, if desired.

5. At circle time introduce each Earthling by name and tell the children about its special characteristic, for example, Purple Earthling wears its favorite color purple because it loves to eat eggplant.

6. Tell the children a story about Earthlings that relates to the theme or to teaching children to care by showing cooperation, sharing and respect. In the stories show how the Earthlings solve problems together.

7. Select a topic such as, gardening and discuss what each Earthling wanted to plant and how they had to compromise in order to plant all the vegetables they wanted by helping each other dig, water and weed the garden.

8. Use events that have happened in the classroom and have the Earthlings act out a similar event to help the children problem solve in positive ways.

Note: The Earthling stories that I have developed originated from childhood memories that I wrote down later. The story about the Earthlings is simply one told about little elf-like people who live beneath the forest who work together to protect the wildlife and trees from danger.

More to do

Art: Provide materials for children to make Earthlings including precut felt, clothespins and a nontoxic craft glue. Allow children to explore and create.

Math: Make two of each different color of Earthling and play a matching game. Children can create patterns and record the pattern on strips of paper with stick people drawings that the children color to match their pattern sequence.

Writing: Children can write or dictate their own stories about what they would do if they were an Earthling.

Related books

Frog and Toad Are Friends by Arnold Lobel
A House for Hermit Crab by Eric Carle
Jamaica Tag-along by Juanita Havill
Miss Rumphius by Barbara Cooney

★ John A. Attanasio, Franklin, MA

Key Words . . . . .5+

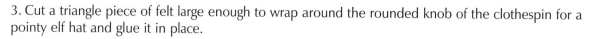

Materials needed

Chalkboard and chalk or chart paper and markers
Index cards (cut in the shape of keys)

What to do

1. At circle time draw ten rectangles on the chalkboard or chart paper and explain to the children that the rectangles represent doors that they need to unlock with keys.

2. Explain to the children that words will be the keys to unlock the doors. Begin by selecting any word, for example, "pickle" and writing it on the door.

3. Ask a child what word she thinks of when she hears the word you have written. Her response may be directly related to the word selected or somehow associated with it. (For example, sour, green, bumpy, sweet, cucumber or jar may be a response for pickle). Write the child's response on the next door.

4. Ask another child what word he would think of when he hears the word (first child's response). Continue until all the doors have words written on them and review the words listed with the children. The sequence of words may sound funny!

More to do
Younger children may select a few favorite words to be written on an index card to keep in a file box. The words can also be written on tagboard that has been cut into the shape of keys and collected on a metal key ring. The word can be used in writing and language activities. Older children may write sentences or a story using the key words listed in the activity.

★ Cathlene M. Hedden, Livonia, MI

Places to Go and Things to See . . . . . . .5+

Materials needed
Travel brochures (featuring state and local attractions)
Chart paper
Markers

What to do
1. In advance, send a note to parents asking their children to bring a photograph or a souvenir of a trip to school.

2. Display the photographs and souvenirs with the children's names and the trip locations.

3. At circle time talk about the display of photographs and souvenirs and ask the children to talk about their trips.

4. Ask the children where they would like to go on a vacation and record their suggestions on chart paper.

5. Share state and local brochures with the children that show places in their community and surrounding area that they might visit.

6. Ask the children to sit in a comfortable, relaxed position, to close their eyes and to imagine themselves preparing for a trip. Talk the children through waking up in the morning, stretching and dressing for a trip. Guide them through packing their suitcases and packing the car. (The pretend trip can take any direction as the teacher describes the events of the trip. Be sure to bring the children back from the trip by talking them through their returning travel arrangements.)

7. Ask the children to talk about the experiences they imagined while you guided them through the trip.

More to do

Place travel brochures in the dramatic play area and ask children to choose a place where they would like to travel. Encourage the children to role play taking their vacations. Provide travel props, including suitcases, clothes and play cameras.

Related books

The Perfect Ride by Lady McCrady
The Relatives Came by Cynthia Rylant
Sand Cake by Frank Asch

★ Lyndall Warren, Milledgeville, GA

What a Trip! .5+

Materials needed

Travel brochures (from travel agencies)

What to do

1. Allow time for children to look at travel brochures and ask the children to choose a brochure that describes a place where they would like to travel.

2. At circle time ask each child to advertise the vacation spot.

3. Ask the children to include information, such as location, special attractions to visit, weather.

4. Encourage the children to write stories about their imaginary vacations.

★ Melanie Lemen, Clear Spring, MD

The Three Billy Goats Gruff Visit . . . . .5+

Materials needed

The Three Billy Goats Gruff by Paul Galdone
The Three Little Pigs by Paul Galdone

What to do

1. At circle time read or tell the children the two stories listed above.

2. Ask the children how the stories are similar. (Both stories have animal characters, both have three animals, both stories have farm animals, both are make-believe stories, both have only one character to fear, both have repetitive phrases, "Trip-trap" and "I'll huff and I'll puff and I'll blow your house down.")

3. Ask the children how the stories are different. (In one story the troll lives under a bridge and in the other story the pigs live in houses. In one story the bad troll wants to keep the good goats away and in the other story the good pigs want to keep the bad wolf away.)

4. With the children make up one story using all of the characters from both stories. For example: One day three Billy goats went out for a walk to look for green grass. They saw a house of straw. "This house looks good to eat," they said. So they started to eat the straw house. An angry pig came out of the house and chased the goats away. Soon they came to a house of wood. "This house looks good to eat," they said. So they started to eat the wooden house. An angry pig came out and chased them away. Soon they came to a house of bricks. "That house looks good to eat," they said. So they started to eat the brick house. They had only eaten a few bricks before they each had a terrible stomachache (fill in dialogue). The little pig came out and instead of chasing them he told them to go see the old troll that lived under a nearby bridge.

5. Encourage the children to make up the story and to give the story a title, such as "The Three Billy Goats Gruff Visit the Three Pigs."

More to do
After reading or telling the children the two stories, "Little Red Riding Hood" and "Peter Rabbit," invite the children to make up one story with all the characters. First ask the children to identify the similarities and differences in the stories (both characters disobeyed their mothers, both main characters learned lessons, both stories are make-believe).

Dramatic play: Dramatize the stories, both the traditional and the combined stories.

Language: Cut out or draw pictures of the characters in both stories. Put flannel on the backs of the pictures and place on a flannel board. Ask the children to use the characters to tell their original stories and to tell the traditional stories.

Related books
English Fairy Tales by Joseph Jacobs
The Hungry Billy Goat by Rita Milios
Mother Goose by Tomie dePaola
The Three Little Pigs by Lorinda Cauley

★ Wendy Pfeffer, Pennington, NJ

What Would You Do? . . . . .5+

Materials needed
None needed

What to do
1. At circle time ask the children the question, "What would you do if... (fill in a situation, such as you were outside at a picnic and it started to rain?)"

2. Encourage the children to answer the question and then to use all the children's answers to tell a story.

3. Encourage the children to ask the other children a question that they can answer by telling a story.

★ Iris Rothstein, New Hyde Park, NY

The New Peter Rabbit . . . . .5+

Materials needed

Paste
Scissors
Peter Rabbit by Beatrix Potter

Crayons
6" x 9" manila paper (2 for each child)

What to do

1. At circle time read or tell the story *Peter Rabbit*.

2. Ask the children how they would change the story to make a different ending.

3. Ask the children to make up a story with the characters in the book, but to change the setting and the plot.

4. Ask the children to make a book by putting several sheets of paper together and folding them in half to make a book.

5. Ask them to write or dictate the title "The New Peter Rabbit Story" on the first page. (For younger children make books with only one or two pages prior to the activity for the children to use in drawing their stories.)

6. Ask the children to draw pictures as they make up new stories and to dictate the story so you can write it on the pages.

7. Ask the children to share their stories with each other.

More to do

Dramatic play: Cut out bunny ears and paste them on a headband for children to use in dramatizing the original story, children take turns acting out the story and being in the audience.

Snack: Wash rabbit food, such as carrots (scrape with plastic knives), lettuce and celery to eat for snack.

★ Wendy Pfeffer, Pennington, NJ

Storytelling

Lion and Mouse Finger Puppets . . . . . .5+

Materials needed

Wooden ice cream spoons (2 per child)
Nickel-sized gray circles (2 per child)
Yellow or gold yarn chopped into
    1/2″ pieces
Fine point markers
Tacky glue
1/2″ x 2″ felt strip (1 per puppet)

What to do

1. Tell the children that they will make puppets to use in acting out the fable about the lion and the mouse. Explain the following steps in making the puppets.

2. Glue the felt strip into a loop and glue the loop to the narrow part of each of two wooden spoons.

3. Ask the children to draw a face on the round end of each of the spoons, one lion face and one mouse face.

4. On the mouse spoon glue two gray circles for mouse ears.

5. On the lion spoon glue yarn for a mane. Allow the puppets to dry.

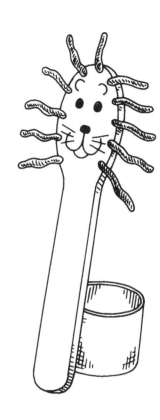

6. Ask the children to bring their puppets to circle time. Ask each child to slip the loop of one puppet on the pointer finger of one hand and to slip the loop of the other puppet on the pointer finger of the other hand. Read or tell the story to the children and encourage the children to act out the story using their puppets.

7. Talk about the story and discuss what the lion learned in the story. Explain that a story that teaches a lesson is called a fable.

More to do

Art: Make hand puppets using socks.

Dramatic play: Provide a variety of puppets to retell stories or ask children to make up their own stories.

Language: Discuss opposites described in the story, such as big and little, brave and scared, wise and foolish. Ask the children to suggest other words that are opposites. Introduce other stories with morals, such as other Aesop's fables and classics, such as *Little Red Riding Hood* and *The Little Red Hen*.

Problem solving: Ask the children what other materials could they use to make a finger puppet. Try tissue over a finger, thimble, peanut shell, discarded marker lids.

★ Sandra Gratias, Perkasie, PA

The Story of My Vacation . . . . .5+

Materials needed

Poster board
Index cards
Masking tape

Markers
Pictures from magazines, catalogs, travel folders
Clear self-adhesive paper or laminating film (optional)

What to do

1. Create a storyboard using a large sheet of poster board and print the following story:

This year for vacation my____(red)____and I took a __(gray)__ to __(green)__. We had a lot of fun __(blue)__, __(blue)__ and__(blue)__, and I got to meet__(red)__. I also saw something I had never seen before, a__(red)__! During the vacation the weather was __(yellow)__. Next year we hope to go to__(green)__. Above each blank line mark a dot the same color as the color in the parentheses in the story above.

2. Collect pictures of people, animals, outdoor scenes, buildings, fantasy characters, modes of transportation, anything that could be experienced on a vacation and a few things (for fun) that probably couldn't. Add pictures depicting different weather conditions. Attach the pictures on one side of a 3″ x 5″ index card and color code the back of each card as follows:

    red—objects or people
    green—destinations (outdoor scenes, buildings)
    blue—pictures of activities
    gray—modes of transportation
    yellow—weather conditions

3. Cover each card with clear self-adhesive paper or laminate for durability.

tagboard

This year for vacation (my) ___(red)___ and I took a ___(gray)___ to ___(green)___. We had a lot of fun ___(blue)___, ___(blue)___, and ___(blue)___ and I got to meet (a) ___(red)___! I also saw something I'd never seen before, a___(red)___! Next year we hope to go to ___(green)___!

Above each blank line draw a dot the corresponding color of the printed word in parentheses.

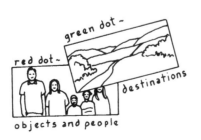

red dot~
green dot~
destinations
objects and people

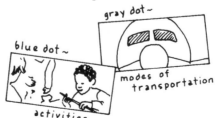

blue dot~
gray dot~
modes of transportation
activities

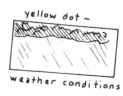

yellow dot~
weather conditions

4. At circle time ask a child to make up a story about a vacation matching the colored dots on the back of each picture to the colored dots on the storyboard. Use a loop of masking tape on the back of each card to make the pictures stick on the storyboard.

5. Ask the child to read the story to the other children (assist if needed).

6. Continue with another child making up a different vacation story.

More to do
Art: Leave out blank index cards for the children to draw their own pictures to put on the storyboard.

Language: Place the storyboard in the reading center for children to use during choice time.

★ Leslie Kuehn Meyer, Austin, MN

Alike and Different . . . . 5+

Materials needed
The Three Bears (traditional story)
The Three Bears (modern version)
Chart paper
Markers

What to do
1. At circle time read or tell the traditional version of *The Three Bears* and talk about the story.

2. The next day at circle time read or tell a modern version of *The Three Bears* and talk about the story. Review the traditional version and compare the two stories.

3. Ask the children the ways the two stories were alike and record their responses in the appropriate section of a Venn diagram on chart paper.

4. Ask the children the ways the two stories were different and record their responses in the appropriate section of the same Venn diagram on chart paper.

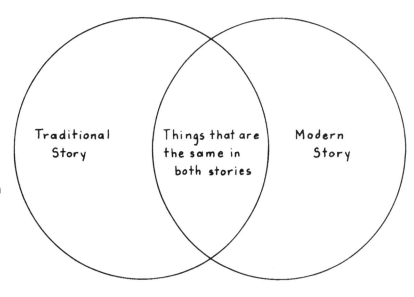

5. Talk about what is listed in each of the sections of the Venn diagram that summarizes the similarities and differences in the stories. Explain the purpose of a Venn diagram in helping to illustrate similarities and differences.

★ Patti Jones, Monroe, NC

On the Road Again! . . . . .3+

Materials needed

Masking tape
Toy cars and trucks
Scissors

What to do

1. At circle time show the children toy cars and trucks and talk with the children about different kinds of transportation.

2. Tell the children that they will make a road to drive the cars and trucks on.

3. Cut pieces of masking tape and ask the children to help you place them on the floor joining them at angles to make turns in the road.

4. Talk with the children about the road and invite them to use the cars and trucks to play on their road.

More to do

Build a city around the road by adding buildings of various shapes and sizes. Provide a variety of boxes that can be painted or covered with paper. Windows and doors can be cut out of construction paper and glued on the boxes. Involve the children in constructing the buildings and deciding where to place them along the road.

★ Jodi Sykes, Lake Worth, FL

Hurry, Hurry, Fire Truck . . . . .3+

Materials needed

None needed

What to do

1. As part of a study of fire fighters sing the following chant with motions at circle time. Encourage the children to do the motions and then to say the words with you.

"Hurry, Hurry, Drive the Fire Truck"

Hurry, hurry, drive the fire truck, (hands on steering wheel)
Hurry, hurry, drive the fire truck,
Hurry, hurry, drive the fire truck,
Ding, ding, ding, ding, ding. (ring bell)

Hurry, hurry, turn the corner, (lean to the right)
Hurry, hurry, turn the corner, (lean to the left)
Hurry, hurry, turn the corner,
Ding, ding, ding, ding, ding. (ring bell)

Other verses:

Hurry, hurry, climb the ladder....(climb the ladder)
Slowly, slowly, back to the fire station....(lean slowly to the left and to the right)

★ Linda Ann Hodge, Minnetonka, MN

Cars . . . . .3+

Materials needed

Toy car
Fill It Up by Gail Gibbons
Magazines
State road map
Scissors
Glue

What to do

1. At circle time show the children a toy car and talk about how a car works. Encourage the children's comments about their family cars.

2. Read *Fill It Up* and discuss the story.

3. Show the children a road map and talk about how to use a map when they are traveling in a car.

4. Provide magazines for the children to cut out small pictures of cars.

5. Display the map on a table and ask the children to locate the places on the map where they want to glue their cars.

More to do

Provide a variety of cars and sort the cars by color, size or type (van, sport, 2-door, 4-door).

Related book

Richard Scarry's Cars by Richard Scarry

★ Sandi Fisher, Kutztown, PA

Cars, Boats and Planes . . . . .3+

Materials needed

3 large pieces of cardboard or poster board
Construction paper (light blue, white, brown, turquoise)
Pictures of transportation vehicles
Glue
Clear self-adhesive paper or laminating film (optional)

What to do

1. In advance, prepare boards representing air, land and water settings for children to use in sorting transportation vehicles by air, land and water. To make the air setting cover a piece of cardboard with light blue paper and cut clouds out of white paper and glue on the board. To make the land setting cover a piece of cardboard with brown paper. To make the water setting cover a piece of cardboard with turquoise paper.

2. Cut pictures of air, land and water transportation vehicles and mount on poster board. For durability laminate or cover with clear self-adhesive paper.

3. At circle time talk with the children about the different kinds of transportation vehicles that travel by air, land and water. Show the children the three boards and the variety of transportation vehicles. Ask the children to take turns choosing a picture and placing it on the board where it belongs—air, land or water.

4. The vehicles can be attached with loops of masking tape on the appropriate board for a permanent display or the vehicles can be placed on the board (not attached) for a sorting game.

More to do

Transportation toys can be used rather than pictures. Use pictures of animals that live in the air, on the land or in the water.

Related books

Boats by Anne Rockwell
Boats by Gallimard Jeunesse
Cars by Anne Rockwell
I Want to Be a Pilot by Teddy Slater
Wheels: A Pictorial History by Edwin Tunis

★ Yvonne Thompson, Ashtabula, OH

How Did You Get to School Today? . . .3+

Materials needed

Outlines cut from white paper (truck, car, train, bus, shoe and bicycle)
Crayons or markers
Poster board
Tape

What to do

1. At circle time ask the children how they traveled to school. Give each child an outline representing his mode of transportation to school.

2. Ask the children what color is the vehicle or shoe that they used to get to school. Provide crayons or markers for the children to use in coloring their outlines the appropriate colors.

3. Write the name of each child on their outline and use the outlines to make a class graph of how the children traveled to school. Ask each child to tape his outline in the column on the graph that has the same outline labeling that column. Talk about the different ways that the children traveled to school and compare the number of outlines in each column on the graph.

4. Sing the following song to the tune of "Mary Wore Her Red Dress."

> *Johnny (child's name) took a blue bike, (mode of transportation)*
> *Blue bike, blue bike*
> *Johnny took a blue bike*
> *To get to school today.*

The shoe variation is:

Cindy used her purple shoes,
Purple shoes, purple shoes
Cindy used her purple shoes
To get to school today.

Ask the question:

Who took a red truck,
Red truck, red truck
Who took a red truck
To get to school today?

Continue singing a version of the song until all the children have been named in the song.

More to do

Math: Count, sort and graph shapes representing a theme.

★ Glenda Manchanda, Huber Heights, OH

Peekaboo Pictures ....3+

Materials needed

Pictures of transportation vehicles
Construction paper
Scissors
Glue

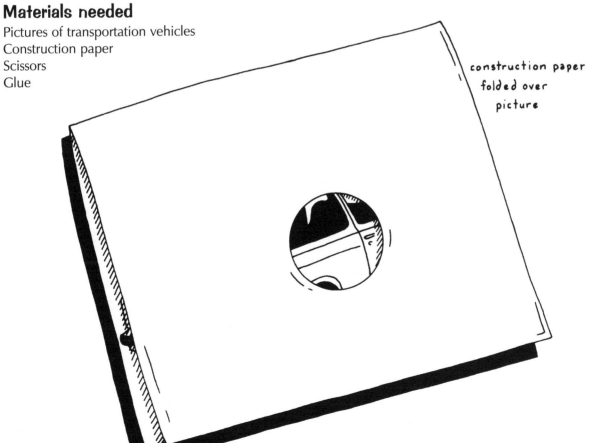

construction paper
folded over
picture

What to do

1. Talk with the children about the variety of vehicles used for transportation and show the children pictures in magazines.

2. Ask the children to cut a picture of a vehicle out of a magazine and glue the picture on the bottom half of a piece of construction paper.

3. Fold the top half of the construction paper over the picture (for younger children prefold the construction paper before they glue their picture).

4. Cut a hole (decrease the size of the hole for older children) in the top flap of the construction paper to reveal a portion of the picture.

5. At circle time ask the children in turn to hold up their piece of construction paper with the flap covering the picture.

6. Ask the other children to identify the transportation vehicle by the part of it they can see through the hole in the paper.

Related book

Look! Look! Look! by Tana Hoban

★ Shandra Urlaub, Sault Ste. Marie, MI

Transportation . . . . .3+

Materials needed

Chairs (1 per child)

What to do

1. Arrange the chairs in a curvy line.

2. Ask the children to sit in a chair and tell them that the train is about to leave. Blow a whistle, calling, "All aboard! Train is leaving! All aboard!

3. Chant the following song:

> *I'm a train, I'm a train*
> *I'm a choo-choo train.*
> *I ride in the sun.*
> *I ride in the rain.*
> *My wheels go slow.*
> *It depends, it depends*
> *On where I go.*
> *Chugga chugga, chugga (continue going faster and faster)*
> *Choo! Choo!*

4. Tell the children that the train is going to deliver food to grocery stores and the train will travel up mountains and down mountains. Emphasize that there are lots of curvy and bouncy tracks for the train to ride over. Repeat the song being animated and enthusiastic. (As the train goes uphill, lean back and chug slowly. As the train goes downhill, lean forward and chug fast. On the curvy track, lean left or right, exaggerating the chug-g-g-g. On the bouncy track, bounce up and down in the chair and make the chug-g-g-g bounce too.)

5. At the end of the train ride tell the children that the train has arrived at a grocery store and they should get off the train and sit in a circle on the carpet.

6. Talk with the children about the train ride. Ask the children what groceries the train brought to the grocery store. Explain that groceries are often shipped by train and then loaded into trucks to be delivered to the grocery stores.

Related book

The Caboose Who Got Loose by Bill Peet

★ Diana Thomas, West Hills, CA

Transportation Time . . . . .3+

Materials needed

Large sheet of white paper
Pictures or patterns (train, airplane, school bus and truck)
Tape
Books about transportation (see related books)

What to do

1. Attach a large sheet of white paper to a wall near the circle time area and place the pictures (cut from magazines or drawn using the patterns) of transportation vehicles on a table nearby.

2. Each morning read a book about transportation. Talk about the kinds of transportation in the story and ask the children to choose pictures of vehicles in the story and tape them to the mural paper.

Related books

Flying by Donald Crews
Freight Train by Donald Crews
School Bus by Donald Crews
Truck by Donald Crews

★ Tina M. Taylor, Johnson City, TN

Airplane Song and Activities ....4+

Materials needed

None needed

What to do

1. At circle time sing "The Airplane Song" to the tune of "The Wheels on the Bus."

> *The pilot on the airplane says fasten your belts (fasten seat belts)*
> *Fasten your belts, fasten your belts.*
> *The pilot on the airplane says fasten your belts*
> *When flying through the sky.*

Additional verses:

> *The children on the airplane go bumpity bump.... (move up and down)*
> *The babies on the airplane go waa, waa, waa.... (rub eyes and pretend to cry)*
> *The signs on the airplane go ding, ding, ding.... (point to signs)*
> *The drinks on the airplane go splish, splash, splish.... (pretend to hold a glass and move it)*
> *The luggage on the plane goes up and down.... (pretend to be luggage going up and down)*

2. At the end of the song, say, "We have now reached our destination. You may unbuckle your seat belts!"

3. Ask the children to name other things on an airplane that you could add to the song. Write additional verses with the children.

More to do

Dramatic play: Set up an airplane in the classroom with chairs and headphones (from listening center) for the pilot and co-pilot who sit in the first two chairs. Ask the children what is their destination. The flight attendants serve food (from the housekeeping center) on trays. Babies (dolls) are welcomed as long as they are accompanied by an adult (child). Luggage should be stored under the seat.

Language: Children write and illustrate stories of their flight in the dramatic play area or imagine a place where they would like to fly if they could go anywhere in the world. Compile their papers and make a class book.

Science: Make paper airplanes and fly the planes inside, outside, from the top of stairs and near a fan. Ask the children to measure and record the distance each plane travels. The distance can be graphed to help the children compare the differences in distance.

★ Ann Scalley, Wellfleet, MA

Going on a Big Airplane . . . . .4+

Materials needed
Carpet squares

What to do
1. At circle time sing the following song to the tune of "The Wheels on the Bus."

> *The wheels on our car go 'round and 'round (repeat)*
> *Going to the airport.*
> *We walk and we walk down the ramp, down the ramp, down the ramp (repeat)*
> *Going on a big airplane. (walk your hands on your knees)*
> *The ticket taker reads our pass, reads our pass, reads our pass (repeat)*
> *Going on a big airplane. (pretend reading, hands together, palms up)*
> *We find our seat with little windows, little windows, little windows (repeat)*
> *Going on a big airplane. (make a window with your thumbs and pointer fingers)*
> *The flight attendant says, "Buckle your belt, buckle your belt, buckle your belt" (repeat)*
> *Going on a big airplane. (put hands across tummy and bump fingers together)*

2. Say to the children, "I think we're starting to move. I think the wheels are starting to go around very slowly." (make a slow wheel moving motion with your hands)

> *The wheels on the plane go 'round and 'round, 'round and 'round, 'round and 'round (sing and repeat slowly)*
> *Going on a big airplane.*

3. Say, "The airplanes wait their turn to use the runway, while they wait they get their engines going really fast. Get those motors going. Ready?" (make engine noises)

> *The wheels on the plane go 'round and 'round, 'round and 'round, 'round and 'round, (repeat)*
> *Going on a big airplane. (make a wheel moving motion with your hands)*
> *WHEEEEE (move arms out)*
> *Now I'm flying through the air, through the air, through the air, (repeat)*
> *Now I'm flying through the air on a big airplane! (move arms out and sway)*

More to do
Make an airplane from a toilet paper tube. Staple tagboard wings to the tube (or cut slits and insert craft sticks). Paper punch a hole for a piece of yarn or string. Provide a newspaper covered work table for the children to paint their airplanes. Dry the airplanes at the airport hanger (large paper with areas marked where each child can park her plane).

★ Linda Ann Hodge, Minnetonka, MN

Transportation

How Wheels Help Us . . . . .4+

Materials needed
Shoebox
2 Tinkertoy® sticks (6"-8" long)
4 Tinkertoy® wheels
3-foot piece of string

What to do
1. In advance, make a wagon by punching two holes on each long side of a shoebox, approximately 1" above the bottom edge of the box. Push the sticks through the holes and add the wheels at the end of the sticks. Punch a hole in the middle of one of the short sides of the box, 1" from the top edge of the box and tie the string through the hole.

2. At circle time show the children the wagon and explain how you made the wagon while you take it apart and put it together.

3. Push the wagon to a child across the circle while saying the child's name.

4. The child pushes the wagon to another child.

5. Continue until all the children have taken a turn.

6. Take the wheels off the wagon and push it across the floor. Ask the children why the wagon does not move as easily. Talk about the use of wheels on wagons, cars, bicycles.

More to do
Fill the wagon with different materials. Try pulling the wagon with and without the wheels. Use square wheels made out of cardboard instead of the Tinkertoy® wheels and discuss the results. Take wheels off other toy vehicles. Discuss how they move with and without wheels.

Related book
Wheel Away! by Dayle A. Dodds

Related song
"Wheels On the Bus"

★ Deborah Bauer, Tempe, AZ

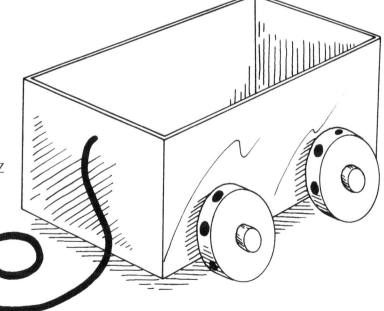

Oh, the Places I Can Go . . . . .4+

Materials needed
Transportation stencils (car, truck, bus, train, boat, airplane, helicopter)
3 half sheets of white paper (per child)
Construction paper (various colors)
Crayons, markers, pencils
Scissors

What to do
1. Talk about different modes of transportation and ask the children to choose a transportation stencil to use in making a book.

2. Ask each child to choose a sheet of construction paper and fold it in half to make a book cover. Ask each child to choose a stencil and trace the outline on the sheet of construction paper and cut out the book cover.

3. Ask the children to use the same stencil to trace on three pieces of white paper for the pages of their books.

4. On each page of the book ask the children to draw pictures of their transportation vehicles traveling to different places. For example, the train travels on a track in the country and in a city.

More to do
Block area: Encourage the children to build a road through a city and to pretend they are driving through the city.

Dramatic play: Arrange chairs to create an airplane or bus and add props such as, pilot's or driver's hats, uniforms, tickets.

Related books
First Flight by David McPhail
Freight Train by Donald Crews
How Many Trucks Can a Tow Truck Tow? by Charlotte Pomerantz
Train Song by Diane Siebert
The Wheels on the Bus by Maryann Kovalski

★ Quazonia J. Quarles, Newark, DE

Transportation

Transportation Play Day . . . . .5+

Materials needed

Transportation toys
Building materials
Masking tape

What to do

1. Send parents a note asking their children to bring a transportation toy on a specific day. Explain that the toys will be shared with other children during the day.

2. As the children bring the toys label each with the child's name.

3. At circle time ask the children to sort and categorize the toys. Make a floor graph grouping the toys into transportation categories by the type of transportation vehicle. Ask the children to determine which categories to use. Talk about the different categories and compare the number in each category.

4. Provide a variety of building materials (blocks, Legos®, Tinkertoys®) in a large space where children can build the places where their transportation vehicles will travel. Encourage the children to work in pairs and to talk about what they are building.

5. After the structures are completed ask the children to talk about what they built. Encourage the children to travel from one structure to another in their vehicles.

Related books

School Bus by Donald Crews
Truck by Donald Crews.
Freight Train by Donald Crews

★ Ann Harsh, Spring Green, WI.

Cloud Mobiles . . . . .3+

Materials needed
Construction paper (white)
Scissors
Glue
Cotton balls
String
Wooden dowel (1 per child)
Recorded instrumental music

What to do
1. At circle time talk about the clouds in the sky and tell the children that they will make cloud mobiles.

2. Ask the children to cut four or five cloud shapes from white construction paper.

3. Ask the children to spread glue on the clouds and to stick cotton balls on them.

4. Punch a hole in each cloud and tie one end of a piece of string onto the cloud and the other end of the string onto the wooden dowel to make a cloud mobile.

5. After the mobiles are completed ask the children to hold their mobiles by the wooden dowel and slowly move the mobiles to the sound of soft instrumental music.

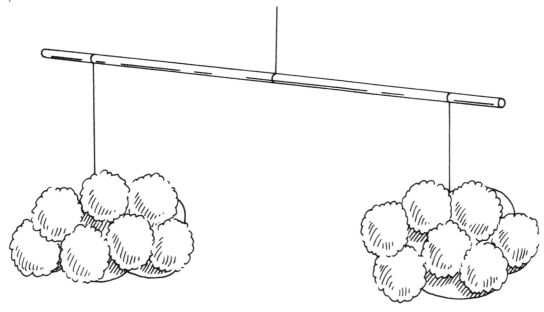

More to do
Art: Ask the children to make birds to add to their cloud mobiles.

Outdoors: Go outside and watch the clouds in the sky and talk about the different shapes of the clouds. Talk about how it would feel to float in the sky like a cloud and ask the children to pretend to be the clouds swaying in the breeze.

★ Cynthia A. Maloof, South Easton, MA

It Looked Like Spilt Milk ....3+

Materials needed

White felt
Scissors
Flannel board
It Looked Like Spilt Milk by Charles Shaw

What to do

1. In advance cut the following shapes from white felt: rabbit, pig, mitten, tree, lamb, squirrel, ice cream cone, birthday cake, bird, spilt milk and a big white cloud. Read the book and rehearse the sequence of the story.

2. At circle time talk about clouds, how they form and how they move in the wind changing shape.

3. Tell the story of *It Looked Like Spilt Milk* using the flannel board and the felt shapes.

4. Begin with the shape of spilt milk and end with a big white cloud shape.

5. Talk about the different shapes that clouds make.

More to do

Art: Sponge paint with white paint on light blue paper cut like clouds.

Related books

Clouds by Roy Wandelmaier
The Cloud Book by Tomie dePaola

★ Cory McIntyre, Crystal Lake, IL

Rain Clouds ....3+

Materials needed

Bucket or tub
Water
Sponge

What to do

1. At circle time sing the following song, "I'm a Little Rain Cloud" to the tune of "I'm a Little Teapot."

> *I'm a little rain cloud fat and round. (extend arms out and clasp hands)*
> *When it thunders, I make this sound. (cover ears with hands)*
> *Boom! Boom! Boom! Rolling around (sing loudly, roll arms in front of you)*
> *Splash! The rain comes tumbling down. (close hands in front of you, spread fingers and move fingers down like raindrops)*

2. Using a sponge and a bucket of water as props talk about how clouds are formed. Explain that the air fills with moisture (dip the sponge in the water) that clings to tiny particles of dust in the air (too tiny to see). When the cloud gets too full to hold any more moisture, the moisture or rain falls from the sky (squeeze the water out of the sponge).

More to do

Art: Provide a variety of materials for the children to make rain collages (tinsel, paper punched holes, cotton balls, glue).

Dramatic play: Provide props including raincoats, boots, umbrellas.

Water table: Add sponges and eyedroppers to the water table. Encourage the children to squeeze water from the sponges.

Writing: Encourage children to write and illustrate stories about rain.

★ Frances Youngblood, Reeds Spring, MO

Weather Clothes ....3+

Materials needed

Weather cards (sun, rain, snow)
Basket with a variety of clothes

What to do

1. At circle time show and talk about the weather cards.

2. Place the weather cards on a ledge where the children can see the cards.

3. Ask each child to choose a piece of clothing from the basket and tell the other children what it is.

4. Ask the child to match the piece of clothing with the weather card that best represents the weather when one would wear the piece of clothing.

5. Place the clothing in a pile under its matching card. Continue until all the children have taken a turn.

More to do

Dramatic play: Provide a variety of clothes for dress-up and different types of baby clothes to put on large dolls.

Related book

What Will the Weather Be by Lynda De Witt

★ Susan R. Forbes, Holly Hill, FL

Where Are We Going, Bear? . . . . .4+

Materials needed

Bear Gets Dressed by Harriet Ziefert

What to do

1. At circle time read *Bear Gets Dressed* and tell the children that Bear will be picking them up in a few minutes to take them for a trip. Explain that we aren't sure where they will be going or what the weather will be like so they should be prepared. Ask the children that if it is chilly outside how should they dress? Ask the children to pretend to dress for chilly weather.

2. Using pages in the book as a guide, ask the children to decide where they are going with Bear, how they will dress and what they will do. For example, if Bear takes us to the grocery store, what should we buy? Which aisle is it in? Ask the children to act out the situations that you describe, such as It's raining—quick, load the groceries in the car. Let's go visit the ducks at the park. I think they like playing in the rain. (Pretend to feed the ducks, walk like ducks.) Ask the children what they would wear in the rain. Continue the story using the following or similar description: It's getting colder, it's snowing, what should we wear? Should we play in the snow, make snow angels, how about a snowman? Why doesn't Bear take us somewhere sunny? How about the beach, what do we wear? What can we do? How about sailing? The wind is picking up, we're blowing this way and that way, hold on! Whew! I'm tired, let's go home and get ready for bed!

More to do

This activity can focus on pantomiming the movements or on discussing the question raised. Either way the children will have fun going to the circus, beach, other countries, police station, fire station, hospital. Ask the children to decide what they would do in the following situations: What will we do if it rains at the beach? What games will we play with grandma? What do we do if the tiger escapes at the zoo.

★ Shannon Mumper, Woodbridge, VA

I'm Listening to the Rain . . . . .4+

Materials needed

Recording of rain

What to do

1. At circle time talk about rain and explain to the children that you have a recording of the sound of rain that you would like them to listen to.

2. Ask the children to close their eyes and listen to the recording of the rain.

3. After listening to the recording talk about the sound of rain. Tell the children to pretend that they are outside walking in the rain, what do they hear? (thunder, wind) Do cars sound different in the rain (windshield wipers, tires on wet road) Can they hear the splashing when they walk in puddles? Can they hear birds chirping in the rain? Ask the children to tell about an experience they had in the rain.

Related books

Rain by Peter Spiers
Rain Talk by Mary Serfozo

★ Cathy Chenoweth, Columbia, MO

What Will the Weather Be? ....4+

Materials needed

Pictures of sun, rain, clouds, snow, wind,
Pictures of different weather conditions (1 per child)
Felt
Flannel board
Box
Pretend microphone

What to do

1. In advance, divide the circle into five areas (using felt strips or yarn) with a picture of the sun, rain, clouds, snow or wind in each of the areas.

2. Place the flannel board, microphone and box containing weather pictures (backed with felt) in the circle area.

3. At circle time ask the children to pretend to be weather forecasters giving the weather report. Explain that they will each draw a weather picture from the box, describe the picture and place the picture in the area of the circle that identifies the weather condition of the picture.

4. Model giving the weather report based on the weather picture drawn from the box. Remember to use the microphone when you give the forecast.

5. Children take turns giving the weather report and placing the pictures in the divided areas on the flannel board.

More to do

Dramatic play: Provide props for weather fashion shows with children wearing clothes for various weather conditions.

Language: Read stories in which there are different weather conditions. Sing weather related fingerplays and songs.

Original song

(Tune: "Oh Dear, What Can the Matter Be")

Oh my, what will the weather be?
Oh my, what will the weather be?
Oh my, what will the weather be?
It will be (rainy, cloudy, sunny, snowy, windy) today.

Original poems
"Good Morning, Mr. Sun"

Good Morning, Mr. Sun
How bright you are today!
I think you are smiling at me
As I run and jump and play.
You watch me wherever I go
And warm me from head to toe.
You make the dew drops sparkle
And help the flowers grow
In winter when the snow is white,
You make things glow and gleam.
And all the lovely, lovely land
Is like a delightful dream.
The fluffy clouds say hello
As they pass you by,
And you bow so politely
Or just wink your eye.

"Watching Snowflakes"

I like to watch the snowflakes
Failing to the ground.
They look so soft and gentle
And never make a sound.
Where does snow come from
Away up there so high?
I think it's like confetti
Failing from the sky.

"Thunder and Lightning"

I used to be afraid of
Lightning and thunder,
But now I just play pretend
And wonder and wonder.
Could the lightning be ribbons
Floating up so high,
Or firecrackers or a magic slate
Making pictures in the sky?
The thunder makes lots of noise
Like my daddy bowling.
A lion tamer with his whip
Or barrels bumping and rolling.
It's lots of fun to pretend
And things aren't so frightening.
Just try it the next time
There's thunder and lightning.

★ Mary Brehm, Aurora, OH

What a Storm! . . . . .4+

Materials needed

Thunderstorm by Mary Szilagyi
Drum

What to do

1. At circle time read *Thunderstorm* and talk about the story.

2. Review how the storm began, developed and ended.

3. Introduce the idea of making a storm in the classroom by beginning to rub your hands together making a soft sound. Tell the class to imagine that it is beginning to rain softly. Continue the development of the storm by snapping fingers. Follow this by patting your legs. Reverse the actions to have the storm subside.

4. Ask the children to follow your actions in making a storm. Begin, develop and end the storm. Add thunder by asking a child to beat the drum at a given signal. Drum beats should be soft at the beginning of the storm, louder as it develops and soft again as it subsides.

More to do

Language: Record parts of a real thunderstorm and ask the children to listen to the tape. Encourage the children to describe the storm using descriptive words.

Music: Use rhythm instruments to develop and end the storm. Sand blocks may be used to begin, then rhythm sticks followed by tone blocks to develop the storm. As the storm subsides, reverse the sequence.

Related books

Rain, Drop, Splash by Alvin Tresselt
Thunder Cade by Patricia Polacco

★ Lyndall Warren, Milledgeville, GA

Rain Formation . . . . .5+

Materials needed

Flannel board
Pictures of raindrops, river, sky, clouds

What to do

1. At circle time use the flannel board and pictures to tell the story of how rain is formed.

2. Begin by talking about how raindrops fall from the clouds and run into small creeks that flow into larger rivers.

3. Show the picture of the river and talk about how the rivers flow into an ocean or a lake.

4. Add the picture of the sky and explain that water (raindrops) evaporate into air and become part of the sky.

5. Add the pictures of the clouds and explain that vapor (evaporated raindrops) in the air becomes colder as it moves to higher elevations in the sky and turns into clouds filled with raindrops. When the clouds cannot hold any more moisture the raindrops fall to the earth and the cycle begins again.

More to do

Art: On a day when there is light rain ask the children to sprinkle dry tempera on construction paper. Set the paper outside for a few minutes. Bring the paper inside and talk about what happened.

Math: Measure rainfall. Set a glass container outside for a week. Check each day and mark any rainfall accumulation with tape marked with the date. Make a graph showing the rainfall accumulation.

Related book

Rain by Robert Kalan

★ Cindy Winther, Oxford, MI

Cloud Mural . . . . .5+

Materials needed

Now I Know Clouds by Roy Wandelmaier
Cotton batting for clouds
Markers
Wallpaper
Paint
Large sheet of paper for mural
Tape recording of weather sounds (optional)

What to do

1. At circle time read *Now I Know Clouds*. Talk about the different types of clouds there are and what kind of weather they bring. Stratus clouds bring rain or drizzle, cumulus clouds bring fair weather, cirrus clouds bring a change in weather and nimbus clouds bring rain or snow.

2. Explain that the children are going to work together as a group to create a weather mural of the different types of clouds and the type of weather they bring. Divide the children into four groups and ask each group to create one of the four types of clouds and the corresponding weather conditions on the mural.

3. Play a tape of weather sounds as the children work, if desired.

4. Provide cotton batting for clouds, markers, wallpaper and paint for the children to use in creating their weather scenes.

Related book

It Looked Like Spilt Milk by Charles Shaw

★ Cindy Winther, Oxford, MI

How's the Weather? . . . . .5+

Materials needed
Bar graph drawn on a piece of chart paper
Labels on each column of graph (sunny, cloudy, foggy, rainy, snowy, windy)
Small picture representing each label (umbrella for rainy)

What to do
1. Place the bar graph on a bulletin board by the calendar.

2. Tell the children that each day they will mark the graph to show the weather condition for that day.

3. Show the children how to put an X in the square above the weather label. Start at the bottom of the graph to record the weather condition and move upward each day.

4. Each day ask a child to graph the weather. Explain that if the weather changes during the day the graph should be marked appropriately.

5. As the graph progresses each day, ask the children which weather condition (column) was marked most frequently or least frequently. Introduce the concept of "equal" and ask if any of the columns are equal. Count the number of days marked for each weather condition and compare which number is bigger or smaller.

6. At the end of each month review the graph and talk about which kind of weather was most frequent, least frequent, not at all.

Note: A blank graph can be laminated, the weather markings erased and the graph reused for each month. Or each monthly graph can be saved and periodically compared to determine which month had the most rain, sun, snow.

More to do
Math: Photocopy a weather graph and ask each child to record the weather daily.

Science: Use the graph to talk about how the weather varies in the different seasons.

★ Barbara Saul, Eureka, CA

Five Little Snowmen Fat . . . . .3+

Materials needed
None needed

What to do
1. During circle time talk about all the things you can do in the snow, such as sledding, ice skating, building snowmen.

2. Talk about how to make a snowman. Ask the children if they have helped build a snowman. Talk about why snow melts.

3. Show the children the motions for the following fingerplay.

"Five Little Snowmen Fat"

> *Five little snowmen fat (hold up five fingers and then hold arms out in front as if a fat snowman)*
> *Each with a funny hat. (hold hands on top of head to represent hat)*
> *Out came the sun and melted one. (hold arms above head to represent sun)*
> *What a sad thing was that. (make a sad face)*
> *Down, down, down. (move hands down each time down is said)*
> *Four little snowmen fat.... (hold up four fingers)*
> *Three little snowmen fat.... (hold up three fingers)*
> *Two little snowmen fat.... (hold up two fingers)*
> *One little snowman fat.... (hold up one finger)*

4. Ask the children to say the words and do the motions with you.

More to do
Art and Math: Make a snowman puppet. Children cut three different sized circles from white construction paper, glue the circles together from largest to smallest (seriation). Decorate face with markers and glue a tongue depressor to the back.

Large motor: After a snowfall go outside and build a snowman or make snow angels.

Related books
Geraldine's Big Snow by Holly Keller
Our Snowman by M. B. Goffstein
Sadie and the Snowman by Allen Morgan
Snow by Kathleen Todd
The Snowman by Raymond Briggs

★ Cory McIntyre, Crystal Lake, IL

Winter

Let's Go Ice Skating! . . . . .3+

Materials needed
Small bowls, such as margarine tubs (1 per child)
1 large shallow container
Water
Small plastic people (1 per child)

What to do
1. In advance, fill containers halfway with water and freeze.

2. At circle time show the children the containers of ice and ask the children to describe the ice, such as cold, smooth, slippery.

3. Ask the children to gather around the large container and show the children how to slide the plastic people across the ice in the container. Talk about ice skating and how children would dress if they were going ice skating.

4. Give the children each a bowl and a plastic person to pretend to skate across the ice.

More to do
Dramatic play: Provide mittens for the children to wear during pretend snow play.

Field trip: Take a field trip to a skating rink.

Science: Allow the ice to melt and make periodic observations during the day and talk about the ice melting.

Related book
Ice Is...Wheee! by Carol Greene

★ Susan Rinas, Parma, OH

Matching Mittens . . . . .3+

Materials needed
Mitten pattern
Paper (wrapping paper, textured, patterned)
Scissors
Tagboard
Clear self-adhesive paper or laminating film

What to do
1. In advance, trace and cut pairs of mittens (one per child) from a variety of kinds of paper. Mount the mittens on tagboard and cover with clear self-adhesive paper or laminate (involve older children in making the mittens).

2. At circle time show the children and talk about the items of clothing you need to keep warm when it is cold outdoors, such as hats, boots, warm coats, heavy socks, mittens.

3. Show the children one paper mitten of each pair and lay them on the floor. Explain that you need to find the mate for each mitten.

4. Hold up the mate to one of the mittens and ask the children to find its mate.

5. Give each child a mitten and ask them to find a matching mitten on the floor to make a pair of mittens.

More to do

Art: Decorate paper mittens with various collage items—sequins, glitter, felt, tissue paper.

Games: With older children play a memory game by placing the pairs of mittens face down on the floor and ask the children to take turns turning the mittens over two at a time to find the matching mittens. If the mittens match, the child places the pair of mittens in front of her. If the two mittens do not match, the child turns the mittens face down again and the game moves to the next person. The game continues until all the mittens are matched. Ask the children to go on a Mitten Hunt. Hide the single mittens throughout the room and give each child one of the single mittens and ask them to find its matching mitten. Put the children's real mittens in a pile, mix up the mittens and ask the children two or three at a time to find their pair of mittens in the pile.

Original song

(Tune: "Mulberry Bush")

> *This is the way we put on our mittens,*
> *Put on our mittens, put on our mittens.*
> *This is the way we put on our mittens*
> *Before we go outside.*

For additional verses substitute boots, scarf, hat, coat, ski pants.

Related books

The Mitten by Jan Brett
The Snowy Day by Ezra Jack Keats
Thomas' Snowsuit by Robert Munsch

★ Mark Crouse, Nova Scotia, Canada

Snow Day . . . . .3+

Materials needed

Large bucket
Snow
Trays
Mittens (1 pair per child)

What to do

1. In a large bucket collect snow by simply leaving a bucket outside to catch the snowflakes or scoop up fallen snow into the bucket.

2. Show the children the bucket of snow and talk about exploring snow. Give each child a scoop of snow on a tray. Ask the children to touch the snow and describe how it feels, such as cold, icy, freezing.

3. Ask the children to put on their mittens and to form snowballs and to play in the snow on the tray (or ask several children to share the snow in a tub or at the water table). Ask the children about how they play in the snow outside, such as making snowmen, snow houses, snow angels.

4. Return the snow to the large bucket. Place the bucket where the children can observe the snow as it melts.

More to do

Outdoors: Take a walk in the snow. Ask the children to compare their footprints and make patterns in the snow.

★ Susan Rinas, Parma, OH

Snowfolks . . . . .3+

Materials needed

Construction paper
Patterns for snowfolks and the
    sun
Paper towels
Glue
Flannel board

What to do

1. In advance, cut the outlines of five snowfolks and the sun out of construction paper and glue the outlines to paper towels (to provide a surface that will adhere to the flannel board).

2. At circle time place the five snowfolks on the flannel board and tell the children a story about the snowfolks.

3. Remove the number of snowfolks according to the words of the following poem.

"Snowfolks"

> *Five people made of snow.*
> *Five snowfolks in a row.*
> *They like to feel the cold wind blow, wsh-wsh. (blow into cupped hands)*
> *Bright sun shines down one day. (hold hands over head)*
> *One snow child melts away.*
> *Now there are four left in the row.*

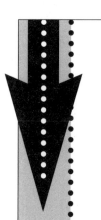
Four people made of snow.
Four snowfolks in a row.
They like to feel the cold wind blow, wsh-wsh. (blow into cupped hands)
Bright sun shines down one day. (hold hands over head)
One snow girl melts away.
Now there are three left in the row.

Three people made of snow.
Three snowfolks in a row.
They like to feel the cold wind blow, wsh-wsh. (blow into cupped hands)
Bright sun shines down one day. (hold hands over head)
One snow boy melts away.
Now there are two left in the row.

Two people made of snow.
Two snowfolks in a row.
Bright sun shines down one day
Both snowfolks melt away.
Now there are none left in the row.

Related song
"Five Green Speckled Frogs"

★ Barbara Anthony, Boston, MA

Snowman, Snowman . . . . .3+

Materials needed
Picture of a snowman

What to do

1. At circle time show the children a picture of a snowman and talk about how a snowman is made.

2. Ask the children the following questions: What shape is his body, round or square? What kind of eyes, nose, mouth, arms does he have?

3. Ask the children to pretend to make a snowman or snow woman using their hands to pack the snow.

4. Ask the children what will happen when the sun shines on the snow.

5. Tell the children to pretend to be snowmen or snow women and to follow you in acting out the words of the song.

"Snowman, Snowman" (Tune: "Twinkle, Twinkle, Little Star")

Snowman, snowman where did you go?
I built you yesterday out of snow.
I built you round, I built you fat. (make body look fat)
I love you and that is that.
But the sun melted you away. (slowly lower body to the floor)
Goodbye for now, I guess I'll play.

More to do

Art: Make a paper bag snowman or snow woman. Stuff small, medium and large paper bags with newspaper. Paint the bags white and tape the bags together. Add facial features and a hat.

Outdoors: If there is snow make a snowman as a class project.

Science: Conduct a melting experiment. Place the same number of ice cubes in the sun and the shade. Periodically observe the ice cubes and record your observations.

★ Jennifer Joy Lee, San Antonio, TX

What Can You Do in Winter Time? . . . .3+

Materials needed
Pictures of winter activities and snow

What to do
1. At circle time show the children the pictures of winter activities and snow and talk about the kinds of activities children can do in the winter.

2. Sing the following song to the children and explain that you will ask them to suggest ways to keep warm and you will add their suggestion to the song.

"What Can We Do in Winter Time?" (Tune: "Muffin Man")

What can we do in the winter time, the winter time, the winter time?
Oh, what can we do in the winter time
To keep ourselves warm?

Ask children to suggest a way, such as wear a coat.

Children put your coats on
Children put your coats on
Children put your coats on to keep yourselves warm.

3. Make up additional verses adding the children's suggestions, such as drink hot chocolate, get under the covers.

More to do
Math: Provide a basket of summer and winter clothes and ask the children to sort the clothing into a summer pile and a winter pile. Ask the children the kind of fasteners they have on their coats and make a graph comparing the number of coats that have zippers, buttons, velcro.

★ Jennifer Joy Lee, San Antonio, TX

Winter Wonderland . . . . .3+

Materials needed
Cotton batting and cotton balls
Styrofoam balls
Sowmen figures
Plastic snow

What to do
1. In advance, cover the circle time area with cotton batting, cotton balls and plastic snow to make it look snow covered.

2. Cover the styrofoam balls with cotton batting to make pretend snowballs.

3. Place the snowmen figures in the snow.

4. At circle time tell the children that you have made a pretend snow scene for them to play in. Talk about some of the activities they could do together in the pretend snow.

5. Allow time for the children to play and to talk about what they are doing in the snow.

More to do
Sensory table: Put ice and salt in the sensory table and ask children to describe how it feels as they play in it. Add ice cubes and encourage the children to make igloos.

Writing: Encourage the children to write or dictate a story about what they like to do in the snow. Compile the papers into a class book. Ask the children to illustrate the pages and select a title for the book.

Related books
The Snowy Day by Ezra Jack Keats
Snow Day by Betsy Maestro
The Snowman by Raymond Briggs
The Black Snowman by Phil Mendez
Owl Moon by Jane Nelson
The Snow Speaks by Nancy White Carlstrom
First Snow by Emily Arnold McCully

★ Janet K. Nobles, Tulsa, OK

Winter

Ice Sculptures . . . . .3+

Materials needed
Ice frozen in different sized containers
Tub or water table
Mittens or gloves
Chart paper
Marker
Camera (optional)

What to do
1. In advance, freeze water in different types of plastic containers.

2. Prior to circle time put the frozen containers in a tub or water table.

3. At circle time show pictures of children playing in the snow and ice and talk about what they are doing and what they are wearing, pointing out the mittens and gloves.

4. Ask each child to wear one mitten or glove while their other hand is uncovered. Pass several ice cubes around the circle and ask the children to describe the ice cubes (cold, wet, slippery, melting, freezing). Ask the children how their hands feel, does the hand with the covering feel different from the uncovered hand. Ask the children to hold an ice cube in each hand and compare the temperature of the ice cubes.

5. Show and talk about the pieces of ice in the tub or water table. Explain how ice sculptures can be made by stacking the ice in different shapes. Provide mittens or gloves for children to wear while they are playing with the ice. Allow a few children at a time to play with the ice.

6. Encourage the children's exploration of the ice by asking questions and record their comments and share them at group time (list the comments on chart paper). If possible, take pictures of the ice sculptures and display for children to look at to write stories about how they made their sculptures.

More to do
Math: Match mittens or mitten shapes made of wallpaper or construction paper.

Outdoors: Make ice sculptures on the playground during warm weather.

Science: Observe different shapes of ice melting. Place a plastic bottle with ice on the table for the children to observe and estimate how long it will take before all the water can be poured from the bottle. Talk about the problem solving approaches the children use, especially when they realize that the frozen water has to almost melt completely to pass through the small opening at the top of the bottle. Refreeze the water in different shaped containers and discuss how frozen water takes the shape of the container.

Related song
"The Three Little Kittens"

Related book
The Mitten by Alvin Tresselt

★ Anne M. Sullivan, Seminole, FL

Winter

Planting Paperwhites . . . . .4+

Materials needed

5 narcissus (paperwhite) bulbs
Shallow pot
Potting soil or gravel
Ruler or yard stick
Water

What to do

1. At circle time pass the bulbs around the circle so the children can observe the short roots and the shape of the bulbs.

2. Talk about the bulbs and what they will need to grow—sunlight, soil, water.

3. Plant the roots in potting soil or gravel and put the pot in a sunny window.

4. Check the pot periodically and on a daily basis when the children observe shoots.

5. Measure the growth and record on a chart and graph the growth weekly.

6. Discuss the growth of the bulbs and name the parts of the plant as they develop. This activity is an excellent study of plant growth and blooming in the winter.

★ Jan McCoy, Daingerfield, TX

Mitten Partner . . . . .4+

Materials needed

White poster board
Mitten pattern
Scissors
Markers
Clear self-adhesive paper
Chart paper

What to do

1. In advance, cut ten pairs of mittens and decorate the mittens in pairs so two are exactly alike. Cover with self-adhesive paper for durability.

2. During circle time talk about what we need to stay warm in the winter, such as boots, coats, hats, mittens.

3. Show the children the mittens and explain that each mitten has a mate that looks exactly the same.

4. Give each child a mitten and ask the children to find the child who has the mate to his mitten.

5. Use this activity when you want to pair each child with a partner.

More to do

Art: Cut mitten shapes from light colored construction paper and paint the shapes at the easel.

Math: Hang a clothesline at the children's height. Put the mittens in a pile and ask the children to match the pairs and to hang them together on the clothesline with spring clothespins.

Related books

The Jacket I Wear in the Snow by Shirley Neitzel
The Mystery of the Missing Red Mitten by Steven Kellogg
One Two One Pair by Bruce McMillan
Seasons by Brian Wildsmith

★ Cory McIntyre, Crystal Lake, IL

Painting With Snow . . . . .4+

Materials needed

White paper
Containers of snow
Smocks (1 per child)

Colored tissue paper cut into 4" x 4" squares
Spoons or small shovels (1 per child)
Old mittens (optional)

What to do

1. At circle time show the children what will happen if they put colored tissue paper on the white paper and place snow on top of the paper. (The melting snow will cause the dye to come out of the tissue paper and transfer to the white paper.)

2. Put containers of snow, tissue paper squares and white paper on tables in the work area.

3. Ask the children to put on smocks and mittens (optional) and stand around the tables.

4. Ask the children to explore the materials by putting different colors of tissue paper on the white paper and putting small piles of snow on top of the paper to melt.

5. Ask the children to experiment with the color of the tissue paper and the amount of snow to vary the design on the white paper.

6. After the snow has melted remove the tissue paper from the white paper. The longer the tissue paper is on the white paper, the brighter the colors.

More to do

Language: Ask the children to describe the snow and list the responses on chart paper. Ask the children to describe how they made their designs.

Science: Place a container of snow and encourage children to observe if the snow melts faster in their bare hands or with mittens on their hands.

Sensory table: Put snow in the sensory or water table to allow the children to explore the properties of snow.

Related books

White Snow, Bright Snow by Alvin Tresselt
Look! Snow! by Kathryn O. Galbraith
The Snowman by Raymond Briggs

★ Glenda Manchanda, Huber Heights, OH

Snowman for the Birds . . . . .4+

Materials needed

Snow
Suet
Popcorn
Cranberries

Birdseed
Carrot (for nose)
Fruit slices
2 sticks (for arms)

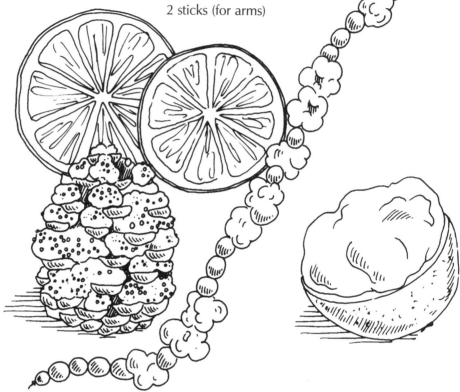

What to do

1. On a snowy day ask the children to help build a class snowman outside (preferably in front of a classroom window so children can see it from inside).

2. Make accessories for the snowman from foods that birds eat, such as fill pine cones with peanut butter rolled in birdseed, string popcorn and cranberries, fruit slices on sticks, suet filled orange cups.

3. Decorate the snowman using the accessories made from food.

4. Observe which birds eat which food (blue jays eat cranberries).

More to do

Rebuild the snowman each time it begins to melt. Save the last bit of snow in the freezer to start next year's new snowman.

Related books

Friendly Snowman by Sharon Gordon
Frosty the Snowman by Carol North
Have You Seen Birds? by Joanne Oppenheim
Sadie and the Snowman by Allan Morgan

★ Janice Bodenstedt, Jackson, MI

Winter Fun . . . . .4+

Materials needed
Snowy Day by Ezra Jack Keats
Scrap paper, preferably white
Paper plates (2 per child)

What to do
1. At circle time read *Snowy Day* and discuss the story.

2. Talk about the different things that the character did in the story.

3. Ask the children what they would like to do on a snowy day.

4. Tell them that they can practice doing those things inside.

5. Encourage the children to lie down and practice making snow angels.

6. Give each child two paper plates (one for each foot) and show them how to "ice skate" by gliding across the floor without lifting their feet.

7. Ask the children to crumble up scrap paper into balls.

8. Divide the children into two groups and ask them to stand several feet from each other.

9. Invite the children to have a snowball battle using the crumbled balls of paper.

10. Save the "skates" and "snowballs" for another snowy day.

More to do
Art: Paint with white paint on dark paper and sprinkle with glitter. Make cotton ball snowpeople or paint with cotton balls.

Related books
Geraldine's Big Snow by Holly Keller
Winter Rabbit by Patrick Yee

★ Teresa J. Nos, Baltimore, MD

Footprints in the Snow ....5+

Materials needed

Poster board displaying pictures and footprints of nine animals (bear, cat, dog, bird, rabbit, fox, deer, horse, raccoon)

Large footprint of each animal drawn on sheets of paper

What to do

1. At circle time ask the children to stand and form a circle.

2. Put a sheet of paper with a footprint in the center of the circle.

3. Ask the children to join hands and walk around the circle clockwise singing the call verse of the following song. The tune is "The Farmer in the Dell."

Call verse:

> A footprint in the snow!
> A footprint in the snow!
> Who came this way,
> One winter day?
> A footprint in the snow!

4. Ask a child to match the large footprint to the smaller footprint on the poster board, naming the animal.

5. The children walk around the circle counter clockwise and sing the response verse of the song naming the animal that matches the footprint.

Response verse:

> A (animal name) was in the snow!
> A (animal name) was in the snow!
> We know the (animal name) was in the snow
> The footprint tells us so!

6. Continue until all animal footprints have been identified.

More to do

Language: Discuss the parts of a human foot: ball, heel, arch, toes, toe nails and compare the parts to the different animal footprints.

Math: Count and compare the number of toes or claws on the different animal footprints and record and graph the number to determine which animal has the most.

Science: Children categorize animal feet as hooves, webbed feet, paws, flippers.

Related books

The Big Snow by Berta and Elmer Hader
Big Tracks, Little Tracks by Franklyn M. Branley
The Snowy Day by Ezra Jack Keats

★ Debbie A. Eikland, Palmdale, CA

Winter

Animal Sounds and Faces ....3+

Materials needed

Pictures or drawings of many different zoo animals
10" x 12" cardboard pieces
Tongue depressors or straws
Glue or paste
Staples

What to do

1. Locate pictures of many different zoo animals (preferably their heads) or draw favorite zoo animals.

2. Glue the pictures to the 10" x 12" cardboard, one per piece.

3. Staple a tongue depressor or straw to back of the cardboard. Allow 4"-5" to extend from the bottom of the picture (to be used as a handle of the mask.)

4. Use completed masks to help introduce a theme on zoo animals during circle time by talking about zoo animals and the food they eat.

5. Have all the children close their eyes while you describe the characteristics of one of the animals pictured on a mask. Ask the children to guess what animal you just described.

6. Give the mask to one child. Repeat until all the masks are distributed. Have the children open their eyes.

7. Choose one child with a mask to stand and ask him to tell everything he knows about the animal. Ask the child to make the sound that the animal makes. Continue until all children have had a chance to talk about their animals.

Note: If all the children in the circle do not have a mask, ask the children with masks to give their masks to other children who describe the animals.

More to do

Art: Encourage the children to create their own masks of their favorite animals.

Field trip: Plan a field trip to your local zoo.
social studies: Make arrangements for a local veterinarian or local zoo keeper to come and answer children's questions.

Related books

Baby Animals by John Wexo
Endangered Animals by John Wexo
Koalas by John Wexo

★ Mike Krestar, White Oak, PA

Elephant Epidemic . . . . .3+

Materials needed

Seven Blind Mice by Ed Young
Flannel board with the following cutouts—1 large gray elephant and 7 small mice (1 of each color: white, blue, red, purple, yellow, green and orange)

What to do

1. Talk with the children about elephants (shape, size) and that they live in the zoo.

2. Read *Seven Blind* Mice to the children.

3. Hand out the felt mice. Reread the story, having the children place the mice on the correct areas of the felt elephant.

4. Discuss what a "blind mouse" might think if it climbed onto a child's hair, ears, fingers.

More to do

A discussion of colors or days of the week can come from this story, too.

Game: A game of Concentration can be played with the colored mice.

Original song

"The Elephant Stomp" (Sing to tune of "Ballin' the Jack," or chant)

Use body movements to underline the actions.

> *First you put your big feet close up tight.*
> *Sway your trunk to the left, sway your trunk to the right. (use arm for trunk)*
> *Stomp around the forest, (really stomp)*
> *Nice and light. (walk on your tiptoes)*
> *Then you swing your trunk and swing your trunk with all its might.*
> *Spread your big ears way out in space. (put your hands on either side of your head)*
> *Flap your ears with style and grace. (wave hands back and forth)*
> *Pull your trunk in. Now bring it back. (using your arm for a trunk)*
> *Let's pick up a peanut sack. Yum! (rub tummy)*

Related books

But No Elephants by Jerry Smath
Seven Blind Mice by Ed Young
When the Elephant Walks by Keiko Kasza

★ Christina Chilcote, New Freedom, PA

How Animals Move . . . . .3+

Materials needed

Brown paper shopping bags
Scissors
Markers
Pictures of animals

What to do

1. Cut out several shapes (about 26) of one animal track.

2. Put them in a circle in the room. Some will be close. Some will be far apart.

3. Tell the children, "Today there is a ring of tracks going around the room. Who made these tracks? How did the animal move? Let's use our feet and see how they move."

4. Put your feet, each on a different track and move around the room.

5. Ask the children, "Did you hop, skip or jump? How do you know? What would a hop be like? What would a skip be like? What would a jump be like?"

6. Ask them, "Do all animals move the same? Let's look at some animal pictures and imagine how they move." Suggestions include an elephant, a monkey, a bird, a lion, a frog, a snake.

7. Choose an animal then walk like it.

Original song

(Tune: "This is the Way We Wash Our Clothes")

This is the way we move around, move around, move around....

★ Dorothee Goldman, Chevy Chase, MD

Peek-a-Zoo . . . . .3+

Materials needed
Manila file folders
Pictures of zoo animals

What to do
1. Make five or six small flaps in the front of the file folder.

2. After gathering children for circle time, place one picture of a zoo animal inside the file folder.

3. Lift one flap at a time to let children "peek" at the animal picture.

4. After lifting all of the flaps, ask the children to guess the animal. Open the file folder to reveal the zoo animal.

More to do
Art: Ask the children to draw a zoo animal and then paste black strips of construction paper over their drawings to create a caged look.

★ Kari Young, Niagara, ND

Stripes on the Zebra . . . . .3+

Materials needed
Pictures of zebras
Zebra shapes cut out of black and white construction paper (at least one per child)
White paint in pie pan or flat container
Black paint in pie pan or flat container
Various sizes of hair picks (1 per child)
Smocks

What to do
1. At circle time talk with the children about zebras.

2. Show pictures of the zebras.

3. Ask the children questions about the zebras. "What color are the zebras? Is the zebra white with black stripes? Is the zebra black with white stripes? What do zebras eat? Do all the zebras have the same stripe pattern?

4. Ask the children to work at the table (put on the paint smocks).

5. Give each child a black or white zebra shape (their choice).

6. Give each child a hair pick.

7. Encourage the children to put the stripes on their zebra shape.

8. Allow the children the opportunity to explore all the materials.

9. When finished, hang the zebras up to dry.

10. Ask the children to wash their hands and put away their smocks.

More to do

Bulletin board: Put the zebras that the children created on the bulletin board for all to see.

Language: At group time make a language chart of the children's ideas or comments to the zebra questions.

Math: Add a matching game of zebras to the mathematics area. (Use a number of different stripe patterns to create zebra pairs that match.)

Original song

"Zebras" (Tune: "Twinkle, Twinkle, Little Star")

> *Zebras black and zebras white,*
> *Zebras have many stripes.*
> *If they're black, or if they're white*
> *I don't know but that's all right.*
> *Zebras black and zebras white*
> *Zebras have many stripes.*

★ Glenda Manchanda, Whitewater, WI

The Animals in the Zoo . . . . .3+

Materials needed

None needed

What to do

1. Gather children together in a circle, standing up with everyone holding hands.

2. Begin to march in a circle while you sing the following song to the tune of "The Farmer in the Dell."

> *The animals are in the zoo.*
> *The animals are in the zoo.*
> *Heigh Ho the Derry Oh*
> *The animals are in the zoo.*

3. On the next verse, ask the children to drop hands and imitate a zoo animal style of walking while continuing to march in a circle. For example:

> *The elephant walks like this.*
> *The elephant walks like this.*
> *Heigh Ho the Derry Oh*
> *The elephant walks like this. (swing arms as a trunk and stomp heavily)*

4. Continue to march around in a circle. Sing the second verse again. Let each child have a turn naming a familiar zoo animal to imitate.

More to do

Art: Use 14-inch paper plates to make animal masks. Help the children cut eye holes in the plates and let them use a variety of craft materials to create their favorite zoo animal. Punch a hole in each side of the mask and thread with a piece of elastic.

Blocks: Add plastic zoo animals to your block area. Use the blocks to make a variety of enclosures in a pretend zoo. Add your animals and plastic people to create a realistic zoo environment.

Field trip: Plan a field trip to a local zoo. Go in the morning when the animals are just waking up and waiting to be fed. Before you go, have each child state which animal they are looking forward to seeing. Take a clipboard with you and make a note of each child's comments upon seeing her chosen animal. Talk about the animal's environment, looks and eating habits.

Language: After a field trip to the zoo, make a book about your adventure. Have each child draw a picture of the animal they liked the best. Write or type what the children have to say about their animals on their pictures. Have one or two children design a front cover and title page. Bind the pictures into a class book.

Related books

Annie and the Wild Animals by Jan Brett
At the Zoo by Douglas Florian
Little Elephant by Tana Hoban and Miela Ford
Over the Steamy Swamp by Paul Geraghty

★ Virginia Jean Herrod, Columbia, SC

What's at the Zoo? . . . . .3+

Materials needed

Posterboard
Large piece of paper and markers
   or a chalk board and chalk
Pictures or stickers of
zoo animals (optional)

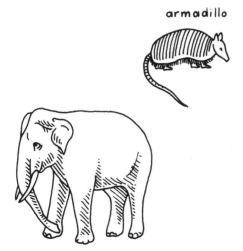

zebra

kangaroo

armadillo

giraffe

lion

elephant

monkey

What to do

1. At circle time talk about the upcoming trip to the zoo.

2. Ask children to generate a list of things they will see at the zoo. This can be done as a whole group process or in smaller groups of about five children.

3. On the list draw a picture (or rebus) next to the written word, or use stickers or pictures so that the children can "read" the chart.

4. Review the chart after the zoo trip. Check off everything that you saw. Did you see everything on your list? If not, why not? Were there any animals that should be added to the list?

More to do

Ask the children to take a copy of the list with them and check off animals as they see them. This activity can be done for any field trip or walk around the block.

Related book

1, 2, 3 to the Zoo by Eric Carle

★ Linda N. Ford, Sacramento, CA

Zoo Animal Musical Chairs . . . . .3+

Materials needed

Chairs
Pictures of zoo animals, enough to put 1 under each chair
Recorded music

What to do

1. Arrange chairs (one more than the number of children in the group) in a circle with backs toward the inside or in a double row with chair backs together.

2. Place one picture, upside down, under each chair.

3. Start the music and have the children walk in a circle around the chairs.

4. Stop the music and instruct the children to sit down quickly on the chairs. One chair will remain empty.

5. Turn over the picture under the empty chair and instruct the children to walk or move (noises are fun, too!) around the chairs like the pictured zoo animal when the music starts again.

6. Replace the picture and repeat from Step 3.

More to do

Art: Encourage the children to create the pictures used in this activity.

Language: For older children use written words instead of pictures to practice their reading skills. Repeat using pictures of farm animals.

★ Leslie Kuehn Meyer, Vermillion, SD

Zoo Animals . . . . .4+

Materials needed
Pictures of zoo animals
Chart paper
Markers

What to do
1. Following a field trip to the zoo, talk about the animals the children saw at the zoo. Write the names on chart paper.

2. Show pictures of the animals and ask the children to describe them.

3. Sort the animals into different groups, such as four legs, two legs, no legs.

4. Allow the children to choose their favorite animals. Sing the following song to the tune of "Mary Wore Her Red Dress."

"At the Zoo"

> (Child's name) saw a (animal's name), (animal's name), (animal's name)
> (Child's name) saw a (animal's name) at the Zoo.

Child answers with an animal name. Continue until all the children have had a turn.

More to do
Blocks: Place plastic zoo animals in the block area. Children can build their own zoo.

Dramatic play: Provide animal puppets for the children to use.

Language: Encourage the children to draw pictures of their favorite animals. Children can write or dictate their descriptions of their pictures. Use the pictures to make a class book. Children can write and illustrate their own books about the zoo and animals that live there.

Math: Graph the children's favorite animals. Count the different animals found at the zoo. A zoo map can be used as a reference.

Science: Discuss different animal habitats. Children can illustrate different habitats.

Water table: Provide plastic and sponge water animals to be used at this center.

Original poem
"Who Went to the Zoo?"

> (Child's name, child's name), went to the zoo.
> What did (child's name) see at the zoo?
> (Child's name) saw a (animal name).

★ Frances A. Ferguson, Tampa, FL

ZOO

Zoo in the Room . . . . .4+

Materials needed

Stuffed zoo animals
Play money
Zoo tickets
Popcorn, peanuts and juice (sell at concession stand using play money)

What to do

1. Talk with the children about how to create a zoo in the room using stuffed animals. Involve the children in planning the zoo. Make play money and tickets.

2. Ask the children to play the roles of zoo keepers, tour guides, ticket and snack vendors and tourists.

3. Set up the room as a zoo. Group stuffed animals together such as elephants, monkeys, tigers, etc.

4. Guide children through the zoo. Talk about each animal in the room and answer children's questions.

More to do

Language: Put out several books about zoos and wild animals for children to look at.

Social studies: Talk about the zoo keeper's job.

Science: Discuss what animals eat.

Related book

If I Ran the Zoo by Dr. Seuss

★ Penni Smith and Donna Karnes, Riverside, CA

Index of Children's Books

Index of Children's Books

Index of Materials

Index of Materials

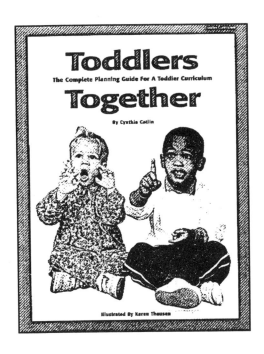

Toddlers Together

The Complete Planning Guide For A Toddler Curriculum

Cynthia Catlin

Toddlers (children 1 to 3 years old) experience the joy of learning all year long with these hands-on, seasonal activities. Cynthia Catlin, who has worked with toddlers for over ten years, brings you fun, easy-to-do activities geared toward the toddler's unique stage of development. The first chapter offers special activities to help toddlers adjust to a new environment and encourage interaction. 319 pages.

ISBN 0-87659-171-3
Gryphon House
17721
Paperback

Where is Thumbkin?

500 Activities To Use With Songs You Already Know

Pam Schiller and Thomas Moore

Sing over 200 familiar songs and learn new songs set to familiar tunes. Organized by month, with a special section just for toddlers, teachers and parents will find easy-to-do, song-related activities that span the curriculum in areas, such as math, art and language. Accompanying each song are ideas for themes and lists of children's books, records and tapes to provide learning connections. A finalist for the 1994 Benjamin Franklin Award. 256 pages.

ISBN 0-87659-164-0
Gryphon House
13156
Paperback